Revolution in Central Europe
1918–1919

Also by F. L. Carsten

THE ORIGINS OF PRUSSIA
PRINCES AND PARLIAMENTS IN GERMANY
THE REICHSWEHR AND POLITICS 1918–1933
THE RISE OF FASCISM

Revolution in Central Europe

1918-1919

F. L. CARSTEN

University of California Press
Berkeley and Los Angeles 1972

University of California Press
Berkeley and Los Angeles, California
Copyright © F. L. Carsten 1972

ISBN: 0–520–02084–7
Library of Congress Catalog Card
Number: 78–165225

Printed in Great Britain

Contents

Contents

Illustrations

(between pages 160 and 161)

Acknowledgments

The illustrations are reproduced by kind permission, as follows: Ullstein Bilderdienst, West Berlin, 1, 2, 3, 4, 5, 6, 7, 8, 9, 10, 11, 12, 13; Bildarchiv des Osterreichischer National-Bibliothek, 14, 15, 17; Photo Simonis, Vienna, 16; Maygar Munkasmozgalmi Muzeum, Budapest, 18, 19, 20, 21.

Preface

In the year 1848 central Europe was engulfed by a series of revolutions which, if they had been successful, might have transformed state and society. Seventy years later there was another series of revolutions which, although they were outwardly successful, failed in their principal objective: to bring about a 'democratization' of state and of society. How and why this happened is the subject of this book. There is no doubt in my mind that this course of events was not inevitable, that the revolutions of 1918 could have been far more successful, that 'democratization' was a real possibility. But once more the forces of conservatism and of social inertia prevailed; in the end, parliamentary institutions were destroyed and the limited gains made in 1918 wiped out. Parliamentary democracy in central Europe suffered from weaknesses which marred its birth. I have described some of them in an earlier volume, *The Reichswehr and Politics, 1918–1933*. This new book is a further contribution to the subject.

I have tried to translate as many German terms as possible into English. In doing so I have used the English word 'council' for the German *Rat*. The *Arbeiter- und Soldatenrat* thus becomes a workers' and soldiers' council, and not a Soviet—a term which has quite different connotations. The *Münchener Räterepublik* becomes the Munich Councils' Republic, and not a Soviet Republic, as it was controlled by Communists only for a very short time. But for Hungary under Béla Kun I have used the term Soviet Republic, for it was largely controlled by the Communists and in constant contact with Moscow. The German USPD (*Unabhängige Sozialdemokratische Partei Deutschlands*) I have called the Independent Social Democrats, or Independents for short, the German *Zentrum* the Centre Party, the Austrian *Christlichsoziale* the Christian Socials (and in general the word *sozial* is translated as social).

My thanks are due to the historians and archivists who have helped me with their advice during years of research in many different archives. To name them all would make a very long list, and I hope that this collective token of gratitude will be sufficient. The Council of the School of Slavonic and East European Studies has generously granted me two terms leave of absence, which have made it possible to collect some of the material and to write this book. For this I am most grateful. But my greatest debt of gratitude is due to my wife who has unfailingly helped me when I turned to her for advice as well as during the final revision of the typescript.

FLC

London, March 1971

Introduction: Before the Revolution

The First World War—that great dividing line of European society and politics—caused the collapse of four great empires some of which had shaped the history of the continent for centuries. Their internecine conflicts, their struggles for influence and supremacy, had brought about their destruction. Yet, within their own frontiers, they had also provided stability and order; their collapse caused instability and disorder, the outbreak of revolutionary movements such as Europe had not seen since the French Revolution, movements that strongly influenced each other and everywhere threatened the old social order.

It is true that of the four empires destroyed by the First World War one—the Ottoman Empire—had long ceased to play an active and expansionist part in European affairs and no longer held any major lands in Europe. But the other three—the Austrian, German and Russian empires—between them dominated most of the continent. In the nineteenth century their rulers had been linked by 'holy alliances' or 'emperors' leagues' aiming at the maintenance of the status quo and the preservation of the monarchical order. This order meant the continuation of semi-absolute government within their own territories, although the German Empire created by Bismarck had at its foundation been granted a constitution; it also meant the continued subjugation of other nationalities included within the boundaries of the three empires which were denied the right of self-determination and of national autonomy. The Poles, the Czechs and Slovaks, the Croats and Slovenes, the Lithuanians, Latvians and Estonians continued to be ruled by alien bureaucracies in the interests of alien empires. During the war, indeed, these had been anxious to ensure the loyalty of the smaller nationalities, to hold out to them promises of greater freedom in exchange for their political support of one or the other belligerent, but no progress had been made on the path towards national self-determination.

Nor was there any progress towards more constitutional or more liberal government. In Austria, the central parliament, the *Reichsrat*, was suspended during the first three years of the war and the authoritarian rule of the bureaucracy continued unchallenged; the later meetings of the *Reichsrat* only produced more and more oppositional speeches by the non-German deputies who realized that the Habsburg Monarchy was unlikely to survive the war. In Germany, the *Reichstag* continued to meet and to grant the war credits demanded by the government, but it wielded no real power. Under the arrangements of internal truce proclaimed at the outset of war, political life had come to a standstill. With the progress of the war, even the constitutional authorities—the emperor and the government appointed by him—lost their powers increasingly to the High Command of the army, the *Oberste Heeresleitung*, which established its strong rule under the twin-axis of Hindenburg and Ludendorff. The recently published war diaries of the Chief of the Imperial Naval Secretariat, Admiral von Müller, amply prove how feeble the power of William II had become. Their title significantly is: 'Did the Emperor govern?'[1] It was only when defeat was certain and when General Ludendorff had resigned his office of quartermaster-general that the new government of Prince Max of Baden in October 1918 hastily introduced political reforms. They made Germany a parliamentary constitutional monarchy, deprived the emperor of his power of command over the armed forces and transferred to parliament the decision in questions of war and peace. But these reforms came too late to save the Hohenzollern dynasty. In Austria, on account of the far more complex internal situation, there was not even this belated attempt at reform. In Russia, Tsarist autocracy continued unchanged until it was overthrown by the outbreak of the February revolution.

Yet even after the outbreak of the Russian revolution the war continued for another twenty months, and with it conditions of near-starvation, frightful misery, mounting casualties, devastation on a hitherto unknown scale. The masses remained largely apathetic, at home as well as in the armies of the central powers. There was no mass mutiny, no revolutionary movement; but there were the great strikes of the armament workers in January 1918 which spread like wildfire from Lower Austria and Vienna to Budapest and then to Berlin and most German industrial towns. The movement began on 14 January in the Daimler works at Wiener Neustadt for entirely non-political reasons: a cut in the meagre flour ration. The management

---

[1] *Regierte der Kaiser? Kriegstagebücher, Aufzeichnungen und Briefe des Chefs des Marine-Kabinetts Admiral Georg Alexander von Müller 1914–1918*, ed. Walter Görlitz, Göttingen, 1959.

tried to persuade the strikers to return to work while awaiting a reply to their complaints from the authorities; but the workmen unanimously refused to do so and decided to demonstrate in front of the town hall. Their procession was immediately joined by the workers of other factories. The leaders negotiated with the town council which then telephoned to the regional administrative authority, the *Statthalterei*, so as to obtain authority to issue, at least for the present week, the previous flour ration, but permission was not given. A similar telephone call to the Ministry of Food in Vienna equally produced no result; the minister merely promised that he would receive a deputation from Wiener Neustadt on the next day.[2]

From Wiener Neustadt the strike movement quickly spread to the small industrial towns of the area; on 16 January it reached Vienna. In Lower Austria, according to the Social Democrats' estimate, about 250,000 men downed tools. During the following days they were joined by the industrial areas of Upper Austria and Styria and by Budapest. The striking workers elected local workers' councils, the initiative for this significant move coming from the Social Democrats and the trade union leaders. In Vienna the workers' council demanded not only better food rations, but the abolition of the censorship, the reintroduction of normal civil law procedures, the eight-hour day, and the release of Friedrich Adler, imprisoned after his successful attempt on the life of the prime minister, Count Stürgkh, in 1916—a deed of protest against the war and arbitrary government. The strike movement lasted only a few days; on 21 January work was resumed without the gain of any important concessions. But the workers' councils continued in being if only in a reduced and semi-underground form.[3]

They revived at the time of the military collapse, under the guidance of the Social Democratic Party. On 26 October 1918 the party summoned the Viennese workers' councils to inform them about current political events. The principal speaker, the deputy Karl Seitz, emphasized that neither Austria nor Germany had a chance of defeating the Entente powers, hence peace must be made as soon as possible; democracy was on the march, but the political transformation—in state, provinces and communes—should if possible take

[2] *Arbeiter-Zeitung*, Vienna, 16 Jan. 1918; Ernst Winkler, *Der grosse Jänner-Streik 1918*, Vienna, 1968, pp. 3–4.

[3] Karl Heinz, 'Die Geschichte der österreichischen Arbeiterräte', MS. in Arbeiterkammer Wien, pp. 7–12; Stenographisches Protokoll der II. Reichskonferenz der Arbeiterräte Deutschösterreichs am 30. Juni 1919, pp. 20, 36. Karl Heinz later was the secretary to the executive of the Austrian workers' councils; his MS. is thus a source of primary importance.

place peacefully. The representatives of several factories from Floridsdorf then demanded an end to army control of the factories, the removal of the military managements and the release of those arrested since January for revolutionary propaganda; a woman leader declared that the time had come for women to be given equal rights and the franchise.[4] The police report did not mention any more radical or revolutionary demands voiced at the meeting.

In Germany, there had been sporadic strikes during the later years of the war, notably in Berlin and in Saxony. As the Social Democratic and trade union leaders wholeheartedly supported the war policy and the imperial government, left-wing opposition groups were formed which opposed the war effort and called for militant working-class action. Leading among these in Berlin were the so-called Revolutionary Shop Stewards, a group which originated in the turners' branch of the metal workers' union—skilled workers who occupied a key position in the armaments industry. The turners' leaders systematically extended their links to other branches of heavy industry and from Berlin to other industrial centres. On the day when the radical *Reichstag* deputy, Karl Liebknecht, the most prominent spokesman of anti-war sentiment, was tried for treason by court-martial (28 June 1916) the turners suddenly stopped their machines in several Berlin factories and 55,000 workmen came out on strike to express their solidarity with Liebknecht. A second much larger strike movement followed in April 1917; it was caused, as in Austria some months later, by the government ordering the bread ration to be cut by one quarter. The strikers' demands were mainly economic and not political. Only in Leipzig did the workers call for the introduction of the direct, general and equal franchise, the lifting of the state of siege and of the censorship, the release of all political prisoners, the right to strike and to hold political meetings, and a declaration by the government in favour of immediate peace without any annexations. These strikes were of very short duration and had no immediate result.[5]

In January 1918 the German workers were slow to follow the Austrian example although the movement caused a stir in Germany. The leader of the small anti-war Independent Social Democratic

[4] Report of 28 Oct. 1918: Polizeiarchiv, Vienna, Staats- u. sicherheitspol. Agenden 1918, box 10.
[5] Richard Müller, *Vom Kaiserreich zur Republik*, i, Vienna, 1924, pp. 56, 59, 64, 79–84. Richard Müller was the leader of the turners' branch and of the Revolutionary Shop Stewards in Berlin. His account, although written several years later, is of great importance.

group in Munich, Kurt Eisner, reported from Berlin that the workers urgently demanded action to bring about the conclusion of peace 'without annexations and indemnities and with the right of all nations to self-determination'; negotiations, he wrote, were taking place among the left-wing groups to bring about a mass strike.[6] This began on 28 January and quickly assumed mass proportions. In Berlin alone about 200,000 workers went on strike and elected an action committee consisting of eleven Revolutionary Shop Stewards and three representatives each of the pro-war Social Democratic and the anti-war Independent Social Democratic parties. The first of the strikers' demands significantly read: 'Speedy conclusion of a peace without annexations and indemnities, on the basis of the nations' right to self-determination, according to the provisions formulated by the Russian People's Commissars at Brest-Litovsk' (where the representatives of Imperial Germany and Austria were then negotiating with the Bolsheviks). This was followed by other political demands, such as the abolition of the state of siege and of military control of the factories, the release of all political prisoners, the introduction of a general and equal franchise, and a 'thorough democratization of all institutions of the state'. The strike quickly spread to Cologne, Mannheim, Brunswick, Bremen, Hamburg, Kiel, Danzig, Leipzig, Nuremberg, Munich and other towns, and everywhere led to similar demands. But only in Berlin and Munich did it last for as much as a week; it only came to an end when the Military Command put the leading Berlin armament factories under martial law.[7] In Munich Kurt Eisner attempted to call an unlimited general strike to bring about peace and the removal of the government. But his arrest on 31 January deprived the movement of its leader and enabled the moderate Social Democrats to regain control and to terminate the strike after a few days.[8]

The January movement was the only mass movement on a national scale directed against the war until the outbreak of the November revolution. In some of its demands, and equally in the formation of local workers' councils, it showed the influence which the Russian revolution exercised on the working class, or at least on its more radical elements. In Berlin the movement, like the earlier ones, was

[6] Gerhard Schmolze (ed.), *Revolution und Räterepublik in München 1918/19 in Augenzeugenberichten*, Düsseldorf, 1969, p. 45.

[7] Müller, *Vom Kaiserreich*, i, pp. 102–10, 204 (the workers' demands), 206–7 (the declaration of martial law).

[8] Willy Albrecht, *Landtag und Regierung in Bayern am Vorabend der Revolution von 1918*, Berlin, 1968, pp. 296–8; Karl Ludwig Ay, *Die Entstehung einer Revolution—Die Volksstimmung in Bayern während des Ersten Weltkrieges*, Berlin, 1968, pp. 199–200.

firmly controlled by the Revolutionary Shop Stewards who strongly
sympathized with the Russian revolution. The Austrian Ministry of
the Interior reported that, during the strike in Vienna, several
'agitators, mainly of youthful age', had been busy spreading revolutionary propaganda identical with the views held by the Bolshevik
Party and that several such agitators had been arrested. [9] In Vienna
and elsewhere leaflets were distributed in March accusing the Social
Democratic leaders of having betrayed the strikers, demanding an
immediate and general peace and calling for a social revolution. In
April more leaflets were found in Vienna and Lower Austria attacking the Social Democratic leaders as traitors to the working class and
urging the latter to elect workers' councils and to organize a general
strike in favour of immediate peace without waiting for Germany. [10]
In general, however, the revolutionary groups were much weaker in
Austria than they were in Germany; above all, there was no split as
it occurred in Germany with the foundation of the Independent
Social Democratic Party in 1917. Thus the Social Democrats remained firmly in control of the working-class movement, including
the incipient workers' councils. It was only in Vienna and the few
industrialized districts of Lower Austria, Upper Austria and Styria
that the movement possessed any real strength. This virtual isolation
in a still very largely agrarian country also explains the weakness of
the extreme left; the only signs of its activities were the few leaflets
mentioned above. The direct influence of the Russian revolution was
very small.

In Germany, which was much more industrialized and economically more developed, there was not only the split between the
moderate Social Democrats and the radical Independents—a source
of never-ending conflicts and friction—but there also existed groups
far to the left of the Independents: the Revolutionary Shop Stewards,
the Spartacus League of Karl Liebknecht and Rosa Luxemburg, the
so-called Bremen Left which had been founded under the guidance
of Karl Radek and stood closest to the Bolsheviks, and several others.
Thus the German left, although much stronger and better organized
than the Austrian left, [11] was enfeebled by internecine struggles—a

[9] The imperial and royal Ministry of the Interior to the Governor in Graz, 24
Jan. 1918: Steiermärkisches Landesarchiv, Akten der k.k. Statthalterei-Präsidium,
E. 91, 1918 (i).

[10] Letters from the same Ministry dated 11 March and 12 April 1918, ibid.

[11] Before the outbreak of the revolution the German Independent Social Democrats (USPD) were already a mass party with about 100,000 members; early in
1919 they had about 300,000: business report of Luise Zietz at the party conference
of March 1919: *Unabhängige Sozialdemokratische Partei Deutschlands—Protokoll über die*

fatal weakness which must be reckoned one of the principal causes of the defeat of the revolutionary movement. In Austria the Social Democratic Party remained united, and the Communists never gained much ground. But the Socialists remained isolated, geographically as well as politically, faced by the majority Christian Social Party with whom they would either have to combine in an uneasy coalition or to whom they would have to leave the government of the country. This party owed its strength to the support of the Church and virtually dominated rural Austria; it had a counterpart in Germany only in the Centre or Bavarian People's Party of Catholic Bavaria.

In both countries, the local Communists, the true protagonists of the Russian revolution, remained a small minority, strong enough only to attempt a *Putsch*, but never representing a serious danger to the government. Although the Bolshevik revolution evoked widespread sympathy among the working classes it found few emulators. The strong socialist parties and trade unions acted as a barrier to the spread of Bolshevism; they helped to establish order out of the disorder of the collapse, and succeeded in establishing, for the first time in the history of central Europe, democracies in the place of semi-authoritarian governments. This is the true achievement of the revolution of 1918; but all attempts to establish a new social, and not only a new political order, were defeated. The following pages will attempt to show how and why this happened.

If the Russian revolution called forth a wave of sympathy in the working-class camp, affecting much wider circles than those of the Communists, it also had the opposite effect. Outside the working class, among the middle and lower middle classes, the civil servants, white-collar workers, officers, university students, independent artisans and shopkeepers, it brought about extremely strong anti-Bolshevik feelings. Their economic existence was being undermined by the war and its effects, they feared and hated the socialists and their political aspirations, and these fears were given a new and violent impetus by the events in Russia. Under the new republics, the middle and lower middle classes thought longingly of the golden days of the Hohenzollern and Habsburg empires when their countries had been strong and respected, when there was prosperity and security. That the empires themselves were largely responsible for the disappearance of these conditions, that the war and the peace

Verhandlungen des außerordentlichen Parteitages vom 2. bis 6. März 1919 in Berlin, Berlin, 1919, p. 50. The membership of the extreme left-wing groups was very small, and they exercised no mass influence.

settlements could not be blamed on the socialists was not admitted in wide bourgeois circles. Scapegoats for the conditions of economic and political crisis, of unrest and strikes, of slow inflation of the currency, of humiliating defeat could easily be found in the 'Marxists' or the Jews.

During the war millions of men had become accustomed to systematic violence—a sacred duty when committed against the enemy. At the end of the war tens of thousands found it impossible to find employment; for the professional soldiers there was no return to normal civilian life. There were the hundreds of thousands of wounded and crippled for whom the state would only provide scanty pensions.[12] When the German government called for volunteers to fight the Bolsheviks in the Baltic lands and the Poles along the eastern frontiers or the internal enemies of the new order, thousands were eager to enlist, to prolong the life of violence to which they had become accustomed, to fight against the external and the internal enemy. In the Free Corps they could continue to defend the fatherland. In Austria, a similar part was played by the *Heimwehren* which sprang up like mushrooms all over the countryside in opposition to 'red' Vienna, although Free Corps in the German sense did not make their appearance. That the government which recruited and paid them was dominated by socialists mattered little to the *Landsknechte* of the Free Corps, for governments did not last for ever. The weapon they had forged might be turned against them.

The aftermath of war and defeat was like a blight frustrating all the efforts of the new and weak governments. The problems of bringing back the armies from the territories they had occupied, of finding employment for the demobilized, of feeding the starving populations, of converting industry to peaceful purposes, of defending the frontiers against hostile incursions, and last but not least the dangers of internal unrest and incipient revolt, loomed overlarge. The task might have seemed hopeless from the start, yet it was mastered after a fashion, and more orderly conditions slowly returned. With all the criticism which might legitimately be levelled against the new governments of central Europe these facts should also be borne in mind. The government machinery, the civil service, the police continued to function— there was no breakdown, and no chaos. One of the most important achievements of the Habsburg and Hohenzollern monarchies was the

[12] In Germany the number of wounded was officially given as 4,247,000. At the beginning of 1923 there were still 1,537,000 war wounded classified as totally unable to earn a living or able to do so to a limited extent only: Paul Frölich, *10 Jahre Krieg und Bürgerkrieg*, Berlin, 1924, p. 226.

creation of large and well-functioning bureaucracies; they outlived the disappearance of their masters, in complete contrast with Soviet Russia where revolution and civil war destroyed the government machinery totally and irrevocably. In this respect too, the situation in Russia was completely different from that which existed in central Europe. Indeed, in Russia war and civil war continued for years after the outbreak of the revolution, while in central Europe the war reached its end with the collapse of the monarchies. Opposition to the war and to the semi-autocratic régimes no longer provided the impetus of revolutionary movements; the vast armies quickly dissolved themselves; the masses above all desired the return of peaceful and orderly conditions, and not new upheavals. All this explains why the revolution petered out so quickly, why the extreme left remained so isolated, and why the Bolshevik revolution did not spread to central Europe.

1 Revolution and New Governments

On 21 October 1918, when the military collapse and the dissolution of the Habsburg Monarchy were clearly discernible, the *Reichsrat* deputies of all the German districts of Austria assembled in Vienna, constituted themselves as a 'Provisional National Assembly of the independent German-Austrian state' and elected an executive committee of twenty which assumed the power of government. A few days later three representatives, one from each of the three major political parties—Christian Socials, Social Democrats and German Nationalists (known as either *Deutschnational* or *Deutschfreiheitlich*)—were elected chairmen with equal rights, anticipating the coalition government which was to be formed. Unaminously the deputies claimed for the future German-Austrian state 'territorial power within the entire area settled by Germans, especially the Sudeten lands' (the German-speaking areas of Bohemia) and strongly rejected any possible annexation of such districts by other nations. For the Social Democrats their leader Victor Adler demanded that German Austria should constitute itself a democratic republic and set up its own government as the existing constitution had entirely collapsed. This new republic should either form a free union with its neighbours 'if the peoples so desired'; if not, German Austria, which on its own was economically not viable, would 'be forced to join the German Reich as a separate federal state.'[1] Although the emperor had not abdicated—he never did so officially—this meant in practice the end of the old régime. During the following days the Czechs, the Poles, the southern Slavs declared their independence and set up their own governments which had been preceded by national committees or provisional governments formed abroad. But the deputies' declaration also indicated the most controversial issue which the new state had to face; for the new Czech government claimed the historical frontiers of Bohemia, i.e. large German-speaking areas in the north

[1] Otto Bauer, *Die österreichische Revolution*, Vienna, 1923, pp. 77-8; Erich Zöllner, *Geschichte Österreichs*, Vienna, 1961, p. 491; Hugo Hantsch, *Die Geschichte Österreichs*, ii. 2nd ed. Graz and Vienna, 1953, pp. 570-1.

and the south; the Yugoslavs laid claim to the southern parts of Carinthia and Styria; and the Italians demanded—according to the terms of the secret treaty of London of April 1915—the Brenner frontier, i.e. the cession of the German-speaking South Tyrol.

So far only the Social Democrats had insisted that a republic be proclaimed, while many others still hoped to preserve the monarchy. Pressure on the socialist leaders came from the Viennese factories, and many sent deputations demanding that the party organize mass demonstrations in favour of a republic. On 30 October huge masses demonstrated in the capital for this goal and for the liberation from prison of Friedrich Adler, Victor Adler's son, who had become the hero of the war-weary masses, exactly as had Liebknecht in Germany. In the evening the crowds, among them many soldiers, began to tear down the imperial eagles from official buildings, and the black and yellow colours and imperial emblems from the uniforms, forcing many officers to do the same. Meanwhile the provisional National Assembly decided to assume legislative powers and to entrust executive powers to a State Council elected by it which was to exercise the rights of the emperor. The Social Democrat Karl Renner became head of its chancery and his draft of a constitution was accepted. But there were only two Social Democratic ministers: Victor Adler for foreign affairs and Ferdinand Hanusch for social welfare, while the large majority belonged to the two bourgeois parties; and there were only two Social Democratic under-secretaries of state.[2] All this mirrored the weakness of the Austrian Socialists, while the government formed in Germany ten days later was purely Socialist, consisting of three representatives of the Social Democrats and three of the Independents. Through the incorporation of the industrial areas of northern Bohemia in the Czechoslovak Republic during the following months the weight of the Austrian Social Democrats diminished further. They remained in the government until the autumn of 1920, but their influence steadily declined.

A proclamation addressed by the three elected chairmen 'to the German people' of Austria emphasized the necessity of maintaining law and order:

> the authorities of the former Austrian state do not render any resistance to the taking over of the administration by the new people's government. There is thus no reason to threaten these

[2] Bauer, *Österreich. Revolution*, pp. 82–3; Charles A. Gulick, *Austria from Habsburg to Hitler*, i, Berkeley, 1948, pp. 57–9.

authorities. . . . It is equally inadmissible to use violence against
the members of other nations. . . .[3]

Indeed, the old authorities not only did not oppose the new order,
they co-operated actively. In Vienna the chief of police, Johann
Schober, put the whole police apparatus at the disposal of the new
government.[4] The officials of the Viennese ministries and of the
governments of the *Länder*, the principal local officials, the *Bezirkshauptleute* appointed by Vienna, the officers and men of the mili-
tarized police, the *gendarmerie*, all continued to function and to carry
out the orders of the government transmitted through the customary
channels. In the central ministries, the last ministers appointed by
the emperor and the new ones elected by the deputies sat in neighbouring rooms during the transitional period, and the senior civil
servants would sometimes apply to the one, and sometimes to the
other for instructions.[5] It was, above all, due to this continuity that
law and order were largely preserved and that there was no major
breakdown in food distribution or in other essential services.

This also applied to the grave problem of the demobilization of the
army which was dissolving itself, especially on the Italian front,
under the impact of last-minute allied offensives.[6] Semi-mutinous
and disorderly troops had to be transported through Austria to reach
their garrison towns often situated in Bohemia or Hungary. There
was the danger that the soldiers marching back from the front would
plunder and loot, if only to feed themselves. With ample weapons in
their hands armed bands and brigands might appear. All discipline
was endangered. As a report to the British Foreign Office described
it a few weeks later:

> Soldiers simply left the front and their officers. . . Soldiers rushed
> the trains, broke the windows to get in, the roofs of the railway
> carriages were packed with men. In the Tirol . . . the tired out
> soldiers fell asleep on the roofs and rolled down at the curves, if not
> knocked down by their comrades, owing to lack of space. Most of
> the soldiers on the roofs, however, were knocked down and killed
> passing the tunnels, the rails being lined with dead all along. . .

But the report added:

> On the Trieste-Vienna railway line the railways are said to have

[3] *Salzburger Chronik*, 31 Oct. 1918.
[4] Julius Deutsch, *Aus Österreichs Revolution-Militärpolitische Erinnerungen*, Vienna,
1921, p. 17.
[5] Gulick, *Austria from Habsburg . . .*, i, p. 120.
[6] Ernst Fischer, *Erinnerungen und Reflexionen*, Hamburg, 1969, pp. 72ff., gives a
dramatic description of the disorderly retreat from Italy.

been organized very well for the retreat of the army, i.e. from Laibach, where all the various armies had to meet, a train left about every twenty minutes carrying off 70,000 to 100,000 men a day. . .

According to this writer, the whole demobilization, expected to last for about two years, only took three weeks. Although there was great anxiety in the capital, 'Vienna remained almost quiet, every soldier only thinking of getting home as quickly as possible. But a precaution which was taken also may have caused things to go so smoothly, i.e. all soldiers were disarmed completely at certain centres before reaching or passing Vienna. . .'[7]

The tenor of this report was confirmed by official accounts from the districts affected by the disorderly retreat. In the Tyrol the newly formed National Council decided to take over the provisioning of the returning troops 'because the military administration is no longer able to arrange for an orderly provisioning on account of the lack of discipline among the troops and the fact that officers, NCOs and other ranks are ruthlessly deserting their posts and their duties'. Thus on 7 November all food and clothing stores and depots were taken over by the National Council.[8] In Carinthia it was feared that the soldiers would form robber bands; masses of disorganized soldiers congregated at the stations; there was wild shooting, and the magazines were broken into and plundered, with the active participation of the local population; the commanding officers and the police were powerless.[9] Yet as early as 7 November it was stated officially that the passage of the troops through Carinthia was proceeding quietly and orderly, that the same applied to rail transport, in spite of all difficulties, and that on the preceding day as many as 70,000 men had been moved on by the railways.[10] As the railways continued to function the floods could be controlled. Units belonging to different nationalities could be moved back to their home territories, and the worst fears did not materialize.

There was a considerable amount of looting—and more often the

[7] Report by L. H. Faber, a British businessman interned in Austria during the war, London, 8 Jan. 1919: Public Record Office (PRO), FO 371, Austria-Hungary, vol. 3514, no. 6173.

[8] The chairman of the National Council, Schraffl, to the Ministry of War, Innsbruck, 9 Nov. 1918: Kriegsarchiv Wien, Staatsamt für Heerwesen, Org.-Gruppe 1/4.

[9] Meetings of the Carinthian 'Vollzugsausschuss', 1 and 2 Nov. 1918: Kärntner Landesarchiv, Umsturzzeit, Lt. III/5; report of 'Bezirkshauptmannschaft' Hermagor to the Klagenfurt government, 6 Nov. 1918: ibid., Präsidialakten, Fasz. V a, no. 36.

[10] Announcement of 7 Nov. 1918: ibid., Umsturzzeit, Lt. III/5.

fear of it—but it did not become general. Many small towns and even villages formed local volunteer units to cope with the danger. The Ministry of War was inundated with requests for the issue of arms to these units, requests which were often granted. The Styrian village of Wartberg formed a defence unit from members of all parties to prevent the plundering of the local factory and was allocated forty rifles with bayonets and ammunition. At Ternitz in Lower Austria the workers themselves formed a factory defence force and maintained law and order. Fifty rifles were given to the Lower Austrian village of Himberg where a *Bürgerwehr* was founded. At Brunn near Vienna, where there was a large clothing depot, not only a cyclists' company but the *Bürgerwehr* too engaged in plundering so that military assistance had to be sent. At Tulln the food depot was handed over to the *Bürgerwehr*, but the town cleared out the depots and sold their contents. From two other small communities in Lower Austria it was reported that 'for days there has been robbing, murdering and looting' in their whole area; and similar instances occurred in some suburbs of Vienna.[11] But here too order was gradually restored. On 10 November Julius Deutsch, the under-secretary of state in the Ministry of War, was able to report to the cabinet that the conditions at the railway stations were improving from day to day. The movements of the returning troops, he estimated, would be completed within another eight to ten days.[12] Already before, the government had decided to discharge immediately all soldiers except those born between 1894 and 1898, and to speed up general demobilization,[13] which indeed was completed surprisingly quickly. Even the prisoner-of-war camps which emptied themselves when their guards went home did not cause any major disturbances. The Allies saw to the speedy repatriation of their nationals; though many Russian prisoners remained, as they could not be repatriated.

As we shall see, the new German government thought that it could only carry out the demobilization of the armies—many of which stood on enemy soil when the collapse came—with the help of the officer corps and its skilled technicians. Yet the Austrian army was

[11] Reports of 4, 7 and 18 Nov. 1918: Kriegsarchiv Wien, Staatsamt für Heerwesen, Org.-Gruppe 1/1; Verwaltungsarchiv Wien, Beschlüsse des deutschösterreichischen Staatsrates, 35. Sitzung. There are many similar reports in both archives.

[12] Verwaltungsarchiv Wien, Kabinettsratsprotokolle, no. 7.

[13] ibid., Beschlüsse des Vollzugsausschusses der deutschösterreichischen Nationalversammlung, 23. Sitzung, 7 Nov. 1918. Deutsch was appointed *Unterstaatssekretär für Heerwesen* on 31 Oct. on a provisional basis and finally on 3 Nov.: ibid., 13 and 16. Sitzung. *Staatssekretär für Heerwesen* was Josef Mayer.

considerably more disorganized and in a virtual state of dissolution, partly due to its multi-national composition. Discipline had broken down to a much larger extent than in the German armies at the front. In spite of this, demobilization proceeded rapidly and without a major hitch: the soldiers, either singly or in groups, or in whole units, simply went home as fast as they could and demobilized themselves. Admittedly, a catastrophe might have occurred if the railways had broken down; that this did not happen was due to the discipline and sense of duty of the railwaymen and the railway managements, but not to any assistance by the military authorities. There can be little doubt that the German armies would have marched back safely from France and Belgium even if this move had not been directed by the military authorities. Special problems, on the other hand, existed for those forces stationed in Russia and the Baltic lands, which continued fighting against the Red Army for a considerable time; their withdrawal could in any case not take place immediately, nor did the Allies insist on such a withdrawal from the east.

Developments outside Vienna were similar to those in the capital. Indeed, if there had not been a measure of agreement between Vienna and the provinces no German-Austrian state could have come into existence. For the time being the new central ministries established in Vienna had little jurisdiction in the southern provinces, which had their own problems and were threatened by the advance of the Italians and the Yugoslavs. Some of them showed a tendency to join a neighbouring state, be that Switzerland or Germany, rather than come under Vienna. Thus for political and other reasons there was friction from the outset, but in the end common sense prevailed. As early as 25 October the provisional National Assembly decided that in all *Länder* provisional assemblies and governments (*Landesausschüsse*) should be formed by an agreement of the political parties which should all be represented in them[14] (previously the Social Democrats had hardly been represented). This directive was generally followed, but the results varied considerably.

In Linz, the capital of Upper Austria, which had a strong and active socialist movement, the workers demonstrated on 31 October under the Red flag and with shouts for the Russian revolution. On the next day the demonstration was repeated on a larger scale, preceded by the railwaymen's band and followed by soldiers and officers sporting red cockades. From the town hall they were addressed by representatives of the Social Democrats, the Christian Socials and the

[14] ibid., 7. Sitzung, 25 Oct. 1918.

German Liberals. In the afternoon a soldiers' council was formed on which each unit was to be represented by two other ranks and one officer.[15] A provisional government was created on 3 November by agreement between the three parties, with seven Christian Social, three German Liberal and only two Social Democratic members. A provisional assembly was set up by a similar agreement on the basis of the *Reichsrat* elections of 1911, with sixty-three Christian Social, twenty-three German Liberal and fifteen Social Democratic deputies. This assembly elected the *Prälat* Johann Hauser as *Landeshauptmann* (governor), or rather confirmed him in office (he had held the post since 1908); he was given three deputies, one from each of the parties. The Christian Social leader's inaugural speech strongly repudiated any idea of a centralist constitution, which would mean the supremacy of Vienna, and advocated a federal system with complete cantonal self-government on the pattern of Switzerland and the United States; in his opinion, centralism had been the blight of the old Austria, under its absolute government as well as after 1861, to the detriment of the economic and cultural development of the *Länder*, and centralism had been strongly opposed by the people of the monarchy. He equally repudiated any rule by one class, and came out in favour of a democratic and social republic. The Social Democratic spokesman emphasized the necessity of cooperation with the bourgeois sections, with burghers and peasants, 'to save the German people . . . in the hour of the most abject misery.'[16] There was party unity, but the Christian Socials had the paramount influence.

In Salzburg a People's Council (*Volksrat*) was elected on 24 October by representatives of all political parties and of various local institutions. It had eighteen members, six each from the major political parties. The Social Democratic spokesman declared that everything must be avoided which might disturb the new-found unity; on this basis his party would join the People's Council.[17] The parties also agreed some days later to form a provisional government with four German National members, two Social Democrats and one Christian Social, and a provisional assembly with a similar

[15] Notes among the Protokolle der Arbeiterräte Oberösterreichs, Parteiarchiv der SPÖ, Vienna.

[16] Anton Staudinger, 'Die Ereignisse in den Ländern Deutschösterreichs im Herbst 1918', in Ludwig Jedlicka, *Ende und Anfang Österreich 1918/19*, Salzburg, 1969, pp. 79–80; protocol of the meeting of 18 Nov. 1918: Oberösterreichisches Landesarchiv, Landtagsakten no. 28 (speeches by Dr Max Mayr and Josef Gruber).

[17] *Salzburger Chronik*, 25 Oct. 1918.

composition, half of the seats being allocated to the German Nationals. This assembly then decided to join the German-Austrian state as a separate province and to recognize the Viennese central authorities.[18]

A similar council, the *Tiroler Nationalrat* (National Council), was formed in the neighbouring Tyrol on 26 October by the political parties, trade unions, corporations and similar bodies. The Tyrolese deputies to the *Reichsrat* and the local Diet constituted themselves as a 'national assembly'. The political composition of the National Council was to be based on the results of the 1914 elections, three members each being allocated to the Christian Socials, Conservatives and Social Democrats, and four to the German Nationals. The *Landeshauptmann* Josef Schraffl was elected chairman of the National Council, indicating the same continuity as in Upper Austria. The Council demanded that, on account of the Tyrol's dangerous and exposed position—the danger being that of partition or the separation of the German or Ladin-speaking districts—it should be represented in all armistice or peace negotiations and their preliminaries, especially with regard to the future frontier with Italy. It further urged the removal of all refugees and those not domiciled in the Tyrol. It formed special committees for food and for military questions, and on 1 November it took over the 'entire civil and military power in the German Tyrol as the executive organ of the German-Austrian State Council'.[19] Vorarlberg separated itself from the Tyrol and set up its own provisional assembly and *Land* government, with three *Land* presidents chosen from the three major parties.[20]

In Graz, the Styrian capital, a 'Welfare Committee' of thirty-three members was set up by the political parties on 21 October. It sent a deputation to Vienna which insisted that it be responsible for food and raw materials, for which two economic plenipotentiaries were to be nominated. As the Welfare Committee had no executive apparatus of its own, the existing administrative machinery was put at the disposal of its plenipotentiaries, to be used 'in the interest of providing food for the population'. The imperial governor, Count Clary und Aldringen, was forced to resign. On 1 November three military plenipotentiaries—one from each party—also took over the military apparatus in the name of the Welfare Committee, removing the commanding general a few days later. A soldiers' council was

[18] ibid., 28 Oct. 1918; Staudinger, p. 77 (with different figures).

[19] *Neue Tiroler Stimmen*, Innsbruck, 28 Oct. 1918; Staudinger, pp. 70–1. Ladin is a Romance language, spoken by about 20,000 people in certain areas of the South Tyrol, akin to the Ladin spoken in the Engadine.

[20] Staudinger, p. 74; Bauer, *Österreich. Revolution*, p. 105.

formed to assist them. All German military units were to be at the disposal of the Committee. Even after the formation of the State Council in Vienna the Welfare Committee claimed complete autonomy in economic and food questions, 'until the new state authority can permanently secure the provisioning of the country'. The provisional Styrian assembly consisted of sixty members, twenty from each of the major parties, according to an agreement reached between the parties. The provisional *Land* government was also based on parity between them, four seats being allocated to each. A German Liberal was elected *Landeshauptmann*, with deputies from the two other parties. All administrative organs in Styria were subordinated to the new authorities.[21]

In Klagenfurt, the capital of Carinthia, representatives of the political parties met on 26 October and formed a 'provisional executive committee' which took over the administration. In the place of the imperial *Landespräsident* and head of the administration, Count Lodron-Laterano, who resigned when his conditions were not accepted, three *Landesverweser* were appointed and took over the administrative machinery; the senior one was a German Nationalist with two deputies from the Social Democrats and the Christian Socials. The three parties also agreed on the composition of the provisional *Land* assembly in which the Social Democrats occupied one-third of the seats. In the Tyrol the main issue was the future frontier with Italy; in Carinthia the problem was where the frontier with Yugoslavia would be fixed. On 25 October the *Land* Committee insisted that the Karawanken mountains formed the natural frontier in the south, and on the following day the *Land* assembly took up the issue and declared that Carinthia for a thousand years had been an economic entity, consisting of German-speaking and of mixed German and Slovene districts: these districts also formed a cultural entity, and any arbitrary division would cause grave damage to the whole country.[22]

While the provinces thus set up their own provisional authorities and assemblies and insisted on their rights of semi-autonomous government, the question of the future form of the state was still undecided. The largest party, the Christian Socials, might have

[21] *Tagespost*, Graz, 25, 26 Oct., 1, 4 Nov. 1918; *Stenographische Berichte über die Sitzungen der steiermärkischen provisorischen Landesversammlung vom 6. November bis 30. April 1919*, pp. 3, 6, 47–50; Staudinger, pp. 63–5.
[22] Kärntner Landesarchiv, Umsturzzeit, Lt. III/5 (meetings of 25–26 Oct. 1918); Landesausschuss, Fasz. II, no. 8 (meeting of 12 Nov.); Staudinger, pp. 67–9.

wanted to maintain the monarchy, but the Tyrolese National Council unanimously declared itself in favour of a republican order, and from other areas too there came growing support for a republic. Finally on 12 November—after the overthrow of the monarchy in Germany—the Provisional National Assembly in Vienna proclaimed the republic, declared the privileges of the Habsburgs null and void, and announced that elections to a National Assembly would be held in February 1919 on the basis of a general, equal and proportional franchise; the assembly would then adopt a new constitution. These proposals—and equally one which declared that German Austria was part of Germany—were adopted unanimously. On 11 November the Emperor Charles formally renounced 'any participation in the affairs of government' and announced his willingness to accept any decision on the form of the future state.[23] The republic of German Austria had finally come into being, although its frontiers were to be delimited by the peace negotiations.

How did the population—the man in the street—react to the political changes which swept away the dynasty that had ruled in Austria for more than six centuries? This question is difficult to answer as even the numerous Viennese police reports say little about it. In mid-November the police commissariat of the Favoriten district noted: 'The vast transformation in Austria has left no traces here. The people naturally talk about it, but without showing any sign of emotion. Yesterday we still belonged to a monarchy, and today to a republic. That is all. If only we have something to eat, that is the main thing. . .'[24] And a week later another district reported: 'The overwhelming majority of the population is in favour of the republican form of state. Dynastic sentiment has disappeared because of the war being lost. . .'[25]

The Austrian workers reacted somewhat more positively. Thus the workers' representatives of Ternitz in Lower Austria sent their fraternal greetings to the comrades of all countries, especially to Friedrich Adler—now released from prison—and to the 'Russian workers' republic which for twelve months has set a shining example to the whole international proletariat'; they expressed their satisfaction at the collapse of the old system and expected from the new one guarantees for the permanent maintenance of the rights of a free

[23] Bauer, *Österreich. Revolution*, p. 101; Gulick, *Austria from Habsburg . . .* i, p. 61; Zöllner, *Geschichte Österreichs*, p. 491. Charles did not abdicate.

[24] Stimmungsbericht of Bezirks-Polizeikommissariat Favoriten, 14 Nov. 1918: Polizeiarchiv, Vienna, Staats- u. sicherheitspol. Agenden 1918, box 9.

[25] Report of Bezirks-Polizeikommissariat Neubau, 21 Nov. 1918: ibid., box 10.

press and of free association and assembly.[26] The socialist workers looked on the Austrian republic as their creation which they would defend against any reactionary attempts if need be. Many peasants, too, welcomed the republic joyfully at first because they were looking forward to a partitioning of the large estates and the forests— expectations which were not fulfilled.[27] As to the middle and lower middle classes, they naturally feared the growing power of the socialists and the workers, especially 'red' Vienna and its socialist administration. But there was no marked tendency in favour of a monarchist restoration—the emperor was too discredited—and for a considerable time more material needs (the provision of food, cloth- ing and coal) took precedence over any political resentments.

From the outset the Social Democratic leaders realized that conditions in Austria were entirely different from those in Russia and that—however much they might dislike it—they had to cooperate with the bourgeois parties. At the party conference held at the end of October even Otto Bauer, who stood on the left of the party and had witnessed the Russian revolution as a prisoner of war, declared:

It is not the case that the German workers alone could build the German-Austrian Republic. Many people are captivated by the idea that the methods of our Russian comrades, the Bolsheviks, could without much ado be transferred to Austria, that workers', peasants' and soldiers' councils could be formed and take over the government. But thereto not only the workers and soldiers are needed but also the peasants. The great difference between our situation and that in Russia is above all that the Russian peasant— socially, culturally, economically and legally—is quite different from our peasant here. While the Russian peasant, at least yester- day, felt like a proletarian—today this is already questionable— our peasant feels like a bourgeois and a determined enemy of the working class. (Hear, hear.) For Russia one could maintain that, if workers', soldiers' and peasants' councils are formed and take over power, they are the representatives of the overwhelming majority of the population, the whole working people. . . But with us in Austria the representation we could have—the repre- sentation by workers' councils and a section of the soldiers, the section which is of working-class origin—would not be the repre- sentation of the whole German nation, but only that of a minority of the German nation. That such an order could maintain itself can be believed only by those who have never thought about it seriously. Eight days after the attempt such a government would

[26] Letter to Friedr. Adler of 7 Nov. 1918: Adlerarchiv, Arbeiterkammer Wien.
[27] Gulick, *Austria from Habsburg* . . . i, p. 171; Gerhard Botz, 'Beiträge zur Ge- schichte der politischen Gewalttaten in Österreich 1918–1933', Vienna Ph.D. thesis, 1966, MS., p. 75.

be bound to collapse through famine, because from the day such an attempt was made we would not receive any food from the peasants. The use of force against the peasants would only be possible in the neighbourhood of industrial towns; but little food could be collected that way and it would cause a bloody civil war. . . [28]

With the same argument Otto Bauer was later to refuse to rescue the Hungarian Soviet Republic by the proclamation of a Soviet republic in Vienna. There is no doubt that he was right. This attitude of the socialist party exercised a strong influence on the working class, which remained loyal to it throughout; it guaranteed that the Austrian republic was established by peaceful transformation rather than by revolutionary action.

In Germany meanwhile far more revolutionary events had taken place. Yet these were set in train not by working-class action or by left-wing radicals but by a military revolt, or rather by a naval mutiny. On 29 October, when it had become obvious that Germany had lost the war, the navy received orders to leave harbour for a last desperate attack on Britain. On board, dissatisfaction was rife on account of strict discipline, bad food and marked officer privileges. There had been an earlier oubreak in 1917 which was ruthlessly suppressed; ten of the ringleaders were condemned to death and two actually shot. Now smouldering discontent flared into open mutiny. When the fleet put to sea the crews refused to obey orders as they did not want to sacrifice their lives for a lost cause, and the fires were extinguished by the stokers. The red flag was run up on the masts of some battleships. The officers carried out mass arrests, but the mutiny quickly spread to the shore where huge demonstrations of sailors and dockworkers took place. At Kiel a violent clash occurred on 3 November between demonstrators and an officers' patrol; there were more than thirty casualties. The sailors succeeded in freeing their arrested comrades; they elected soldiers' councils, and the dockers elected workers' councils. Soon the town and the garrison were in their hands. The Kiel soldiers' council on 4 November proclaimed that it had taken over power and warned the population against any incautious action, against looting and robbing: 'quiet and iron nerves are what the hour demands'.[29]

[28] Stenographisches Protokoll des Parteitages der sozialdemokratischen Arbeiterpartei, 31 Oct.–1 Nov. 1918, pp. 110–12: Parteiarchiv der SPÖ, Vienna.

[29] The text in Frölich, *10 Jahre Krieg und Bürgerkrieg*, p. 251. In general see: Heinrich Neu, *Die revolutionäre Bewegung auf der deutschen Flotte 1917–1918*, Stuttgart, 1930; Wilhelm Deist, 'Seekriegsleitung und Flottenrebellion 1918', *Vierteljahrshefte für Zeitgeschichte*, xiv, 1966, pp. 341–68.

Many of the sailors supported the Independent Social Democratic Party, the only party in favour of immediate peace without annexations or indemnities, and they telegraphed to Berlin inviting the party leader, Hugo Haase, or one of his colleagues, to come to Kiel. The imperial government sent two *Reichstag* deputies, a liberal and the Social Democrat Gustav Noske, the spokesman of his party on military affairs; they were to persuade the sailors to return to duty, promising them an amnesty and investigation of their grievances. On 5 November Noske told another mass meeting that the movement required a firm directing hand; he had been unable to find anyone who would give orders and negotiation was impossible in mass meetings; thus the various units should send representatives with whom he would begin to work in the afternoon if they had confidence in him. This proposal was tumultuously acclaimed. The afternoon meeting was attended by about fifty to sixty soldiers to whom Noske proposed that they should elect a soldiers' council of seven or nine, with himself as chairman. As those present did not know each other he himself finally selected the members according to the impression which their faces made upon him. In this extraordinary fashion the Kiel soldiers' council—the first in Germany—came into being. On the same day it issued an order, signed by Noske, that peace and order in the town must be preserved, that arms were not to be carried without authority, and that civilians must hand in all weapons to the military offices.[30] Thus Noske, sent to Kiel to restore order, emerged as the leader of a revolutionary organ, the soldiers' council, but an organ determined to preserve law and order. The sailors, to whom the differences between Social Democrats and Independents must have seemed minor squabbles, were only too willing to accept him as leader; he himself testifies that the members of the large soldiers' council 'honestly worked to restore an orderly state of affairs', and that he formed a high opinion of several of them 'on account of their honest endeavours and their unselfishness'.[31]

From Kiel the movement spread like an avalanche through Germany, starting with the coastal towns of Hamburg, Bremen and Lübeck, without meeting any resistance. Sailors from the main naval bases of Kiel and Wilhelmshaven everywhere acted as the carriers of revolutionary slogans and the demand for an immediate armistice. At Bremen on 6 November the local Independent leader announced

[30] Text in *Die deutsche Revolution 1918–1919*, ed. Gerhard A. Ritter and Susanne Miller, Frankfurt, 1968, p. 47; in general Noske's description in *Von Kiel bis Kapp*, Berlin, 1920, pp. 17–19.
[31] Noske, *Von Kiel . . .*, p. 29.

at a mass meeting the formation of a workers' and soldiers' council
which was to exercise military command and to control the public
authorities. On the same day an agreement was reached between the
soldiers' council and the garrison commander that military power in
Bremen would be exercised jointly by him and four members of the
soldiers' council, that officers should retain their swords and epaulettes, while the soldiers' council undertook to preserve law and
order. A local newspaper described the proceedings as 'lacking any
acerbity' and showing a *gemütlich* management of affairs.[32] At Hamburg on 6 November a general strike broke out, officers were arrested
and deprived of their weapons, the stations were occupied, the
imperial eagles and emblems were torn down, and red flags hoisted.
A workers' and soldiers' council was hastily founded. It proclaimed
that it had taken over 'the largest share of political power' and published a long list of demands, such as the release of all political
prisoners, complete freedom of speech and the press, abolition of
postal censorship, amnesty for the mutineers and better treatment
of other ranks by their officers. It further announced immediate
measures for the protection of private property and welcomed all
officers who consented to the measures taken by the soldiers' council;
looting would be punished by summary execution. On the next day
the workers' council demanded control over the provision of food,
and the soldiers' council over public transport, as well as the
removal of the general in charge of the military district. The
Senate of the Hanse towns declared its willingness 'to serve the new
order and the new conditions'—and continued to exercise its former
functions.[33] Here too the movement showed very moderate traits;
remarkable above all is the absence of any demands for the
Kaiser's abdication or immediate peace from the programme of 6
November.

Also on 6 November a workers' and soldiers' council was set up at
Wilhelmshaven; this elected an inner council of twenty-one which
took over executive power. At Hanover the railway guard was disarmed by sailors during the night of 6 November; the security
companies went over to the side of the revolutionaries. On the

[32] Paul Müller, in *Bremen in der deutschen Revolution vom November 1918 bis zum
März 1919*, Bremen, 1919, pp. 12, 15; *Weser-Zeitung*, 7 Nov. 1918.
[33] The text of the proclamation of 6 Nov. in Paul Neumann, *Hamburg unter der
Regierung des Arbeiter- und Soldatenrats*, Hamburg, 1919, p. 8; in general, ibid., p. 12;
Rich. Müller, *Vom Kaiserreich . . .*, i, p. 136; R. A. Comfort, *Revolutionary Hamburg*,
Stanford, 1966, pp. 38–41. Neumann was the secretary of the local workers' and
soldiers' council.

seventh a mass meeting resolved to set up a soldiers' council, three delegates being allocated to each barracks. Here too an agreement was reached between the workers' and soldiers' council and the garrison commander: military power in Hanover was to be exercised jointly with the soldiers' council; the latter guaranteed the maintenance of law, order and security; discipline was to be maintained; the officers were permitted to retain their swords and epaulettes, and their orders while on duty were to be carried out; work in the factories was not to be interrupted. Social Democratic deputies and trade union officials were strongly represented on the local council.[34] Here too moderate influence was paramount.

At Cologne the development was somewhat more radical. Sailors from Kiel reached the town on 5 November and established contacts with the garrison and with sailors home on leave. By the seventh they were ready to take immediate action with the aim of liberating political prisoners and setting up a soldiers' council. Early on the morning of the eighth the Social Democratic and Independent leaders met; they agreed on a programme largely drafted by the Independents, and on the names of those to be elected to the workers' council, six from each party, to which the corresponding number of soldiers should be added. Then a mass meeting took place in the market square; it was addressed by members of both parties and accepted a much more political programme than in the Hanse towns: immediate peace, abolition of the dynasties, release of all political prisoners, an end of the call-up, the army to take an oath to the constitution, and the cancellation of the war loans. The party representatives suggested were duly elected to the workers' council, and joined by an equal number of soldiers. The new council immediately posted a proclamation warning the citizens against any attacks on life and honour, against looting and disturbances of any kind. All authorities were requested to carry on their duties under the council's control; the mayor, Konrad Adenauer, immediately put rooms in the town hall at the disposal of the workers' and soldiers' council. Sub-committees were formed for security, food and accommodation, demobilization and clothing, press, sanitation, finances, and transport, showing the wide range of functions the council was prepared to tackle. Indeed, two days later members of the council were appointed as supervisors of all local authorities, including the mayor, the railway administration, the posts and telegraphs, the

[34] Karl Anlauf, *Die Revolution in Niedersachsen*, Hanover, 1919, pp. 15, 17, 20-3, 33, with the names of some council members.

police headquarters, the various courts, the Reichsbank office, and the military commands.[35]

In Munich the developments were even more radical. On 7 November a vast open air meeting of the two Social Democratic parties took place in favour of peace and against any last-ditch measures of 'national defence'. At the end of the meeting the Independents, led by Kurt Eisner and the peasant leader Ludwig Gandorfer, separated from the majority of the demonstrators, forced their way into a school used as an arms depot, and thus armed marched to the military barracks; their occupants quickly hoisted the red flag and joined the march into the city. In a beer cellar near the centre a workers' and a soldiers' council were elected separately, the former presided over by Eisner. From there armed workers and soldiers were sent out to occupy the public buildings, a task accomplished by 10 pm. Then the crowd marched to the Diet where Eisner opened the constituent meeting of the workers' and soldiers' council and was elected its president. A proclamation with his signature was issued to the population notifying it of the formation of a provisional workers', soldiers' and peasants' council; Bavaria henceforth would be a free state; a constituent national assembly, elected by all men and women, would meet as soon as possible; the strictest order would be preserved; security of person and property was guaranteed; officers not opposing the demands of the new times should continue to serve without any molestation; all disturbances would be ruthlessly suppressed. Another proclamation announced that the people had overthrown the old civil and military authorities and taken over the government; the workers', soldiers' and peasants' council was functioning as the highest authority and exercising legislative power; the royal house of Wittelsbach was declared deposed and the Bavarian republic proclaimed.[36]

Shortly before 1 am on the eighth, however, it was discovered that the police headquarters had not yet been occupied by the revolutionaries, and a troop was dispatched there led by one of Eisner's collaborators. The chief of police was informed that the councils had taken over provisional power and was asked to continue in office until the security services had been reorganized. The royal police chief then agreed in writing to carry out the orders of the Munich workers' and soldiers' council; if he felt unable to do so he would

[35] Wilhelm Sollmann, *Die Revolution in Köln*, Cologne, 1918, pp. 7–12, 16.

[36] The two proclamations in Bundesarchiv Koblenz, NS. 26, vorl. 70. In general, Allan Mitchell, *Revolution in Bavaria 1918–1919*, Princeton, 1965, pp. 92–101; Schmolze (ed.), *Revolution . . .*, pp. 97, 109.

resign.[37] The take-over in Munich was completed; the king left his capital. The small Independent Social Democratic Party—in June 1918 it had about 400 members[38]—seemed to be in control. But on 8 November it formed a government together with the moderate Social Democrats—their leader Erhard Auer became Minister of the Interior—and a few non-party experts, with Eisner as prime minister of the Bavarian republic. The meeting of the provisional National Council of the Bavarian People's State which approved this list was attended by members of the workers' and soldiers' council, the Social Democratic parties, Gandorfer's small Bavarian Peasant League, and a few isolated liberals. When Auer suggested that the leaders of the much larger Christian Peasant Associations be invited to join the assembly, Gandorfer opposed this as he believed that the provisioning of Munich could be arranged without their support. But at least one observer noted that it would be practically impossible to provide the necessary food without the cooperation of the Christian peasant leaders because they alone possessed the necessary authority. Gandorfer and Eisner were close personal friends, and this guaranteed the support of at least one peasant organization for the new régime; but his Peasant League was strong only in Upper and Lower Bavaria, and even there it did not represent the majority of the rural population. On 9 November the new ministers were introduced to their offices by their predecessors.[39]

These momentous events in the north, west and south of Germany had left Berlin, the centre of left-wing radicalism, virtually untouched. As late as 7 November the military commandant issued a proclamation which prohibited the setting up of workers' and soldiers' councils 'on Russian lines' as contrary to the existing public order. The Revolutionary Shop Stewards were planning an uprising for the eleventh.[40] But events moved faster than the revolutionary planners. On 9 November the last imperial Chancellor, Prince Max of Baden, announced that William II had abdicated and then handed over the government to the leader of the Social Democrats, Friedrich Ebert. About the same time, to the indignation of Ebert, another

[37] Schmolze (ed.), *Revolution . . .*, p. 102; Franz Schade, *Kurt Eisner und die bayerische Sozialdemokratie*, Hanover, 1961, p. 60.
[38] Police report of 28 June 1918 quoted by Ay, *Entstehung einer Revolution*, p. 195. This was the only party group in Upper Bavaria.
[39] Schade, *Eisner . . .*, pp. 61, 64; Josef Hofmiller, *Revolutionstagebuch 1918/19*, Leipzig, 1938, p. 35. Gandorfer's Bayerischer Bauernbund had about 10,000 members, the Christian Bauernverein led by Dr. Heim had at least 140,000: Schade, p. 127 n. 32; Wilhelm Mattes, *Die bayerischen Bauernräte*, Stuttgart-Berlin, 1921, p. 41. Albrecht, *Landtag und Regierung . . .*, p. 428.
[40] R. Müller, *Vom Kaiserreich . . .*, i, pp. 139–41.

party leader, Philipp Scheidemann, proclaimed the German republic from a balcony of the *Reichstag* building, while from the palace Karl Liebknecht later declared Germany 'a free socialist republic'. The Berlin workers downed tools and marched to the city centre. The demonstrators were joined by many armed soldiers; there was no resistance. Special editions of *Vorwärts*, the Social Democratic organ, announced that the movement was jointly directed by the two left-wing parties; that Ebert was forming a new government from men who possessed the confidence of the working people in town and country; that public power had passed into the people's hands; a constituent assembly would meet as soon as possible; law and order would be preserved by the workers and soldiers.[41] The old authorities simply abdicated. Thus a representative of the Independent Social Democrats, Emil Eichhorn, was fetched from the party offices to negotiate the surrender at the police headquarters. There he met chaotic conditions and demanded a formal transfer of the institution and its continuation under a new director appointed by the revolutionaries. After some hesitation this was accepted, and a formal contract incorporating his demands was signed by the chief of police and by Eichhorn who took over as head of the Berlin police, an office in which he was confirmed on the eleventh by the Berlin workers' and soldiers' council.[42]

The formation of the new government took a little longer, partly because the chairman of the Independents, Haase, had gone to Kiel at the request of the mutinous sailors. In the *Reichstag* leading Social Democrats negotiated with the Independents whom they wanted to enter the government, but the latter were undecided. They were busy discussing the basic principles of the new republic when Liebknecht entered the room and demanded that 'all executive, all legislative, all judicial powers [were to be] with the workers' and soldiers' councils.' There was neither contradiction nor consent. Then Scheidemann, tired of waiting outside, came in and asked whether they had reached a decision and whether there was any proposal. Liebknecht's demand was handed to him; he looked at it and enquired tenderly: 'But, chaps, how do you envisage this?' A heated discussion ensued between Scheidemann, Liebknecht and the leaders of the Revolutionary Shop Stewards, while the Independent

[41] Extraausgaben of *Vorwärts* of 9 Nov. 1918: Friedrich-Ebert-Stiftung, Nachlass Emil Barth, nos. 339–41.
[42] Emil Eichhorn, *Über die Januar-Ereignisse*, Berlin, 1919, pp. 7–10; *Der Ledebour-Prozess*, Berlin, 1919, pp. 595–6; Friedr.-Ebert-Stiftung, Nachlass Barth, no. 58: Vollzugsrat decision of 11 Nov.

deputies remained silent.[43] It turned out that the Independent leaders were deeply disunited on this decisive issue. Finally, however, they agreed to present to the Social Democrats six demands which stipulated *inter alia* that the government should be purely socialist and that all executive, legislative and judicial powers should be exclusively wielded by elected representatives of the working people and the soldiers. These points were rejected by the Social Democrats as opposed to democratic principles 'if they implied the dictatorship of part of one class'. The reply of the Independents, handed over on the morning of 10 November, insisted that the cabinet should be composed only of Social Democrats, but this would not apply to ministerial experts who were to be considered technical aides of the cabinet; political power was to be exercised by the workers' and soldiers' councils; the issue of the constituent National Assembly—on which the Social Democrats insisted—would become 'actual only after a consolidation of the state of affairs created by the revolution' and should be discussed later. In this form the conditions were accepted by the Social Democrats.[44]

The government which thus came into being—the Council of People's Representatives—was entirely Social Democratic. It consisted of six members: the Social Democrats Ebert, Landsberg and Scheidemann, and the Independents Haase, Dittmann and Barth. They had equal rights, but in practice Ebert and Haase were the senior members; Emil Barth, the representative of the Revolutionary Shop Stewards and the only radical, was the odd man out, for Liebknecht refused to enter the government. But meanwhile the extreme left had gained an important point. In a meeting of soldiers' councils hastily summoned to the *Reichstag* on the evening of 9 November it was decided that workers' and soldiers' councils were to be elected in the Berlin factories and barracks the next morning and assemble in the afternoon in the Circus Busch 'to elect the provisional government'. It seems likely that this decision induced Ebert to accept the Independents' conditions and three Independents as members of the government, including Barth, so as not to depend on the accidents of a mass meeting over which he had no control. The meeting duly took place and 'elected', or rather confirmed, the government in the form agreed upon by the two parties.

[43] Eduard Bernstein, *Die deutsche Revolution*, Berlin, 1921, pp. 34–5; R. Müller, *Vom Kaiserreich* . . ., ii, p. 28. Both were present.
[44] R. Müller, ii, pp. 28–9; Friedrich Stampfer, *Der 9. November*, Berlin, 1919, pp. 25–6; Erich Matthias (ed.), *Die Regierung der Volksbeauftragten 1918/19*, Düsseldorf, 1969, i, no. 3, pp. 20–1, no. 6, pp. 30–1.

It also elected an Executive Committee of the Berlin workers' and soldiers' councils which was to claim a controlling right over the actions of the government. The left radicals led by Richard Müller attempted to force through a list which would have given them the decisive influence in the Executive Committee; but Ebert demanded parity between the two socialist parties as it had been established for the government. He was strongly supported by the soldiers' representatives who shouted down all opposition. Thus parity was accepted in a double sense: 14 soldiers and 14 civilians, the latter consisting of 7 Revolutionary Shop Stewards and 7 moderate Social Democrats. This mass meeting also sent its fraternal greetings to the Soviet government, expressing its 'admiration for the Russian workers and soldiers who have opened the path to revolution, and its pride that the German workers and soldiers have followed them . . . as the protagonists of the International'; Germany was proclaimed a 'socialist republic'.[45] Revolutionary events which shook the foundations of the old régime had taken place.

On the following day—11 November—a new Prussian government was formally appointed by the Berlin Executive Committee, on the same basis of parity between the two Social Democratic parties. This was carried so far that each eventually supplied an undersecretary of state for each ministry, or that two ministers presided over the affairs of one ministry. Only the Prussian Minister of War, General Scheüch, remained in office,[46] as did most senior civil servants. The situation thus created was extremely ambiguous. While Ebert considered himself the legitimate successor of the last chancellor—he was sometimes even referred to as *Reichskanzler*—and while the new government was predominantly moderate in its complexion, the Berlin workers' and soldiers' councils represented by the Executive Committee claimed a right of control over government measures and something akin to sovereign power. As the mutual spheres of influence had not been defined, and as political opinions on the left differed widely, there was plenty of material here for future conflict. Yet the old powers had vanished from the scene. It seemed as if Germany was well set on the road towards some kind of socialism, towards a state under the influence of the workers' and soldiers' councils. A highly intelligent journalist commented in a

[45] R. Müller, ii, pp. 32–40; Eberhard Kolb (ed.), *Der Zentralrat der Deutschen Sozialistischen Republik 19.12.1918–8.4.1919*, Leiden, 1968, pp. xiii–xv; Matthias (ed.), *Die Regierung . . .*, i, no. 7, p. 33.
[46] R. Müller, *Vom Kaiserreich . . .*, ii, p. 57; Matthias (ed.), *Die Regierung . . .*, p. xciv; Friedr.-Ebert-Stiftung, Nachlass Barth, no. 58.

liberal paper: 'The greatest of all revolutions has, like a sudden storm, overthrown the imperial régime, together with everything that belonged to it at the top and at the bottom. One can call it the greatest of all revolutions because a *bastille* so firmly built and surrounded by such solid walls has never been taken before in one assault; [yesterday morning the whole vast imperial apparatus still existed;] yesterday afternoon it had ceased to exist.'[47]

In the traditionally more liberal German south-west—the two states of Baden and Württemberg—developments were considerably less revolutionary. There were few industrial centres, and the Social Democrats were accustomed to cooperate with the authorities and the bourgeois parties, which they continued to do after the revolution. Most of the centres of heavy industry were situated in Prussia, hence Prussian politics were usually to the left of those in other German states, while Bavaria first swung to the extreme left, and later to the extreme right, and the south-west adhered to a more steady, middle-of-the-road course. In Karlsruhe, the Baden capital, the mayor called a meeting of party representatives on 9 November; it was agreed to set up a 'Welfare Committee' with local and political representatives which was to take all measures necessary. Those present were to inform some of their political friends and return with them in the afternoon. At that time there also took place a large soldiers' demonstration, inaugurated by sailors from Wilhelmshaven, during which the soldiers seized the officers' swords and epaulettes. They then moved to the town hall to form a soldiers' council. In the evening both the Welfare Committee and the soldiers' council met, the latter electing an Independent Social Democrat as its chairman. From the balcony it was announced that the soldiers' council had taken over power, but also that order must be preserved unconditionally and that all looters would be shot. Negotiations were opened with the commanding general to whom twelve conditions were submitted, of which the most important were: release of all political prisoners, complete freedom of speech and the press, abolition of postal censorship, amnesty for the mutineers, unlimited personal freedom for soldiers when not on duty, no military duties for members of the soldiers' council, its consent to be required for any orders issued in the future. These were very moderate conditions and after some hesitation they were accepted by the *Generalkommando* during

[47] Theodor Wolff in *Berliner Tageblatt*, 10 Nov. 1918, quoted by R. Müller, *Vom Kaiserreich . . .*, ii, p. 17.

the night of 9–10 November. It then ordered that all units were to elect soldiers' councils, two men for each unit.[48]

In Mannheim, the only important industrial town of Baden, a workers' and soldiers' council was formed on the same day. It received assurances from the military authorities 'that no difficulties would be put in the way of a take-over of power by the workers' and soldiers' council'. The officers declared that they would preserve order in collaboration with the new institution, while the latter forbade any molestation of officers and any violation of private property. On 10 November representatives of the two socialist parties and the soldiers met and agreed to propose to the other councils of Baden 'to take immediate measures for the proclamation of a socialist republic and the formation of a people's government'. The Mannheim police declared its readiness to carry out the orders of the workers' and soldiers' council, and one of its members was delegated to police headquarters. Meanwhile a new provisional government had been set up in Karlsruhe, with the Social Democratic deputy Anton Geiss as chairman and with ministers ranging from National Liberals on the right to Independent Social Democrats on the left. There were seven socialist ministers out of a total of eleven, military affairs and social welfare going to the Independents. The government ordered the soldiers to return to barracks and the civil servants to remain at their posts. An assembly elected by general franchise would decide whether Baden would remain a monarchy or become a republic. But on 13 November the Grand Duke declared that he renounced the exercise of his powers until the national assembly had reached a decision, and Baden was then proclaimed 'a free people's republic'. On the eleventh the former Minister of the Interior introduced his successor, and also the new Minister of Food—both members of bourgeois parties—to the assembled civil servants; as in Munich, the solemn transfer of functions took place in the forms customary in case of a ministerial change. The soldiers' councils of Baden met in the Ministry of the Interior and undertook to preserve law and order.[49] In Baden there was virtually no revolutionary movement, only a peaceful transfer of power to a wide coalition of political parties.

In neighbouring Württemberg things took a similar course. In the days before 9 November soldiers' councils had been elected in some

[48] W. E. Oeftering, *Der Umsturz 1918 in Baden*, Constance, 1920, pp. 69–71, 87–90, 105–9, 116–19, 157.
[49] Oeftering, *Der Umsturz . . .*, pp. 153–63, 168; R. Müller, *Vom Kaiserreich . . .*', ii, pp. 74–5; Adam Remmele, *Staatsumwälzung und Neuaufbau in Baden*, Karlsruhe, 1925, p. 23.

units in an orderly fashion, among them several officers; the soldiers' demands were approved by the officers as justified. On the ninth, representatives of the two Social Democratic parties, the trade unions and the soldiers' council met in the Diet at Stuttgart and agreed on the composition of a provisional government. The leaders of the Social Democrats and the Independents were to become chairmen with equal rights. The Independents provided two ministers— one of them the chairman of the Stuttgart soldiers' council; one seat was offered to the Spartacists but they refused to form a government together with the Social Democrats, exactly as Liebknecht refused in Berlin. The government was confirmed by the local workers' and soldiers' council and proclaimed a republic; the king left Stuttgart. The commanding general expressed his willingness to maintain military order in cooperation with the soldiers' council. On the following day, however, the Social Democrats agreed that collaboration with the bourgeois parties was essential in view of the impending demobilization and the position of the government vis-à-vis the civil servants. To bring about such a coalition the consent of the workers' and soldiers' council was required, as this exercised political control. The decisive meeting took place in the afternoon; the proposal was hotly opposed by the Spartacists but supported by the Independent spokesmen, especially by Crispien, the co-chairman of the government. It was carried with a large majority, and three bourgeois ministers entered the government, which then declared that 'the entire public power from now on rests in the hands of the provisional government' and that the revolution was over. Workers and employees, civil servants and soldiers were to return to their duties; every disturbance of the economy was to be avoided; only the government and the ministries were entitled to issue orders and decrees, while those issued by others were declared invalid.[50] After only two days the revolutionary movement had reached its end.

In industrial Saxony with its radical working-class movement things went much further to the left. In the early days of November mass demonstrations took place in Leipzig, Dresden and Chemnitz. On the eighth the Independent Social Democrats of Leipzig formed a workers' council which combined with that of the soldiers. Armed troops occupied the public buildings; officers and the police were

[50] Wilhelm Keil, *Erlebnisse eines Sozialdemokraten*, ii, Stuttgart, 1948, pp. 93, 97–9, 104–5; Wilhelm Blos, *Von der Monarchie zum Volksstaat*, Stuttgart, 1923, pp. 22–3, 29–31; Paul Hahn, *Erinnerungen aus der Revolution in Württemberg*, Stuttgart, 1923, pp. 17–18; Karl Weller, *Die Staatsumwälzung in Württemberg 1918–1920*, Stuttgart, 1930, pp. 110–15. Blos and Keil were the leading Social Democrats.

disarmed. In Chemnitz events took a similar course; there was no resistance. On the following day Dresden followed suit. There two separate workers' and soldiers' councils had been formed by the Social Democrats and the Independents which combined on the ninth, while in Chemnitz there was equal representation of the two parties. But in Leipzig the entire Small Committee of the local council consisted of members of the Independents who refused to admit any Social Democrats on the ground that they had too few members. The first proclamation of the Dresden council declared king and dynasty deposed and Saxony to be a 'social republic'; the first and second chambers were abolished, but the existing government was to carry on 'provisionally' and to organize elections on the basis of the general, equal and direct franchise. On the fourteenth, however, the workers' and soldiers' councils of Dresden, Leipzig and Chemnitz announced that the revolutionary proletariat had taken over power with the aims of establishing a socialist republic, the transformation of capitalist production into a socialist one, the expropriation of private property in land, mines, transport, banks and raw materials; all bourgeois courts were to disappear, the will of the working class was to predominate, and the revolution was to continue until the bourgeoisie had been completely defeated. On the next day the old government was dismissed and replaced by a purely socialist one, with parity between the two socialist parties, but the more important posts in the hands of the Independents.[51]

In the small state of Brunswick, too, a purely socialist government of eight People's Commissars was formed, with an Independent as the president of the local 'socialist republic'. The workers' and soldiers' council announced on 8 November that it had taken over power and would exercise it; the ducal estates were declared public property.[52] But these were isolated instances. In general the German revolution pursued a non-violent and far from radical course. The extreme left was weak and divided and quite unable to influence events. The Independent Social Democrats were comparatively strong but again far from united. Their principal leaders, men like Hugo Haase and Dittmann, were moderates who were not separated from the Social Democrats by any differences of principle; they might have wished to postpone the elections to, and the meeting of, the National Assembly so as to become stronger, but they were not opposed to it.[53] If one

[51] Bernstein, *Deutsche Revolution*, pp. 58–9; R. Müller, *Vom Kaiserreich . . .*, ii, pp. 68–70; Rudolf Lindau, *Revolutionäre Kämpfe 1918–1919*, Berlin, 1960, pp. 167, 172.   [52] Anlauf, *Revolution in Niedersachsen . . .*, pp. 98–9.
[53] This is also the opinion of Matthias, *Regierung der Volksbeauftragten . . .*, p. cxxviii.

reads through the protocols of the cabinet meetings held in November and December 1918 one realizes that the representatives of the two parties worked together reasonably well and that there was less conflict between them than has often been assumed. On 10 November one perceptive observer stated that during the past two days the attitude of the people had been characterized by discipline, sangfroid, the love of order and of justice; what he thought was missing was political sense. And some days later he noted that the palace guards were marching through the Brandenburg Gate in good military order and to the accompaniment of the '*Hohenfriedberger Marsch*' as of old: only now under a red flag, and not quite as 'Prussian' as the pre-war guards.[54] There had certainly been changes in Berlin, yet many things had not changed.

What had changed least was the bureaucratic apparatus which had governed Prussia for centuries. This machinery was created by the Hohenzollerns and served them loyally and devotedly. The large majority of the higher civil servants—the *Regierungsräte*, the *Landräte*, the *Ministerialräte* who administered the country as well as the judges, police officers and secondary school teachers (all these were state officials)—were firm conservatives and monarchists, as all dissidents had been carefully weeded out. Even after the king had released them from the obligations of their oath their emotional ties linked them to the old order, and not to the new government and republic. To the civil servants men like Ebert and Scheidemann remained parvenus with a questionable past, whom they despised and ridiculed, not to speak of the leaders of the Independents who to them were Bolsheviks and traitors. There was a famous scene at a cabinet meeting when Dr Solf, who remained as Under-Secretary in the Foreign Office, refused to shake Haase's hand because Haase had allegedly taken Russian gold for his party before the revolution.[55] Not only Solf remained in office for the time being, but equally the secretaries in the ministries of justice, finance, labour, posts and telegraphs, the Secretary for the Navy, and General Scheüch, the Prussian Minister of War (there was no Reich office for the army which had remained Prussian), although the Social Democrats had at first thought it essential to remove Scheüch.[56]

Ebert resolutely opposed any attempts to replace leading officials

[54] Harry Graf Kessler, *Tagebücher 1918–1937*, Frankfurt, 1961, pp. 26, 31 (10 and 14 Nov. 1918).

[55] Matthias (ed.), *Regierung der Volksbeauftragten* . . ., i, no. 46, p. 300, cabinet meeting of 9 Dec. 1918.

[56] ibid., p. lv; R. Müller, *Vom Kaiserreich* . . ., ii, p. 47.

by Social Democrats. At the conference of prime ministers of the German states on 25 November he declared:

> The machinery of the Reich is a somewhat more complicated apparatus than that of the states, even the largest. We were obliged, after we had taken over political power, to see to it that the machinery of the Reich did not collapse; we had to see to it that the machine continued to run so that our food supply and economy could be maintained. . . We six men could not achieve that alone; we needed the experienced cooperation of experts. If we had removed the experienced heads of the Reich offices, if we had had to fill these posts with people lacking the necessary knowledge and experience, within a few days we would have been at the end of our tether. (Hear, hear!) Therefore we did appeal urgently to all Reich offices (sic) to continue with their work until further notice. Only thus were we able to prevent the collapse and to overcome the difficulties. (Renewed approval!) . . .[57]

Even in retrospect this policy has been defended by another leading Social Democrat, the later Prussian Prime Minister Otto Braun:

> The new government had to work with this body of officials if the state machine was not to stall and the fulfilment of the most urgent tasks—provision of food for the people, setting in motion and conversion of the economy, and demobilization of an army of millions without friction—was not to be endangered. The reform of this body had to be left to the future. . . .[58]

Nor is there any evidence that the Independent members of the cabinet opposed this policy. There was an additional argument: that the Social Democrats simply did not have the qualified people available to fill even the most important posts. As the new socialist Under-Secretary of the *Reichskanzlei* allegedly told one of his underlings: 'We cannot govern because we have never wanted to and thus have never learnt it. We do not have a hundred men with whom we could fill the most senior appointments.'[59]

In the Wilhelminian empire the Social Democrats had been the opposition party *par excellence*, but they had never considered the possibility that the empire might collapse and had made no preparations whatever for such a contingency. The spontaneous outbreak of

[57] Matthias (ed.), i, no. 5a, p. 27; no. 30, pp. 180–1. There were several instances of State Secretaries submitting their resignation, but being persuaded to stay on.

[58] Otto Braun, *Von Weimar zu Hitler*, Hamburg, 1949, p. 14.

[59] Walter Oehme, *Damals in der Reichskanzlei*, Berlin, 1958, p. 344, recording a conversation with Curt Baake held in 1918, forty years before.

the revolution caught them completely unprepared, and this applied equally to the Independents, who were a party of idealists without practical experience. Even the radical Berlin Executive Committee, which in theory claimed sovereign power for the councils, issued a proclamation on 11 November enjoining all Reich, *Land* and military authorities to continue with their work, and every citizen to obey their instructions which would in future be issued on behalf of the Executive Committee. In Prussia the urban administrations were controlled by the local workers' and soldiers' councils, but according to one close observer, 'so loosely and superficially that the former mayors and town councillors could continue to rule as they pleased'. In Berlin the Executive Committee two days after the revolution declared all 'irregular' or 'provisional' councils dissolved and their administrative measures null and void.[60] In Bavaria, Auer, as Minister of the Interior, quickly confirmed all civil servants in their old rights and duties and kept the old bureaucratic apparatus intact.[61]

On the local level too, the workers' and soldiers' councils, as soon as they had come into being, reached agreements with the existing provincial governments, the police and other authorities. Even before the victory of the revolution the Kiel workers' and soldiers' council informed the population of Schleswig-Holstein that a provisional provincial government was being formed which would, in cooperation with the existing authorities, establish a new order. 'Our aim is the free and social People's Republic.' At Stendal in the Old Mark the workers' and soldiers' council reached an agreement with the mayor on 8 November according to which it would share the power of command in the town with the garrison commander and it undertook to preserve law and order.[62] At Hanover a similar understanding was reached with the chief of police on 9 November, according to which he recognized that the council exercised military control and promised to use his powers in cooperation with the council; one of its members was delegated as advisor to the chief of police. A separate agreement was drawn up with the headquarters of Tenth Army Corps, the officials of which continued their work as before.[63] At Cassel the mayor as well as the chief of police declared in writing that they were content with the new order of things and put themselves at the disposal of the workers' and soldiers' council. On 11

[60] Müller, *Vom Kaiserreich . . .*, ii, pp. 60, 235: proclamation of 11 Nov. 1918.
[61] Mattes, *Bayerische Bauernräte*, p. 70.
[62] Hermann Müller, *Die November-Revolution*, Berlin, 1931, pp. 37, 40.
[63] Anlauf, *Revolution in Niedersachsen*, pp. 38–9.

November similar declarations were obtained from the head of the provincial administration of Hessen-Nassau, *Oberpräsident* von Trott zu Solz, and the chief of staff of Eleventh Army Corps, General Freiherr von Tettau.[64]

At Münster the command of Seventh Army Corps had taken the initiative on 8 November and approached the chairman of the local trade union council: they urged him to form a soldiers' council and thus 'save the situation'. On the following morning the officers negotiated with some soldiers and the trade union secretaries. It was decided that in future the corps command would issue orders together with the elected soldiers' council, that looters would be summarily shot and all disturbances ruthlessly punished, that all offices and all ranks would continue to fulfil their functions, and that orders must be obeyed unquestioningly. This was repeated in a joint order of the corps command and the soldiers' council which threatened any culprits with severe punishment; all soldiers were ordered to wear on their caps the German and the Prussian cockades which had been removed through a 'misunderstanding'; strict discipline and obedience were expected from the members of the new 'people's army'. In practice it turned out that the trade unionists with their organizational experience and their 'art in the treatment of proletarian circles' easily prevailed against certain unruly elements, excluded them from all positions of influence and quickly got rid of them by sending them to their home towns.[65] The large majority of the soldiers willingly accepted this lead, exactly as the mutinous sailors of Kiel accepted Noske as their representative. At Augsburg the soldiers went to the local Social Democratic paper on 8 November and urged that a party spokesman should come to the barracks where the soldiers were busy electing a soldiers' council, and the journalist Ernst Niekisch went to address them. He also talked to the officer commanding the division who was anxious to avoid any disorders. At Niekisch's suggestion he issued an order for the three local regiments to parade in the afternoon; Niekisch made a political speech and encouraged them to elect soldiers' councils which was done in an orderly fashion. The cooperation between officers and men was close, and there was no conflict.[66] At Grafenwöhr, the Bavarian military training grounds, the officer corps even partici-

[64] Int. Inst. of Social History, Amsterdam, Nachlass Grzesinski, no. 422: letter of Arbeiter-Rat Cassel of 12 Jan. 1920.

[65] Eduard Schulte, *Münstersche Chronik zu Novemberrevolte und Separatismus 1918*, Münster, 1936, pp. 33–4, 53–4, 73–5.

[66] Ernst Niekisch, *Gewagtes Leben*, Cologne-Berlin, 1958, pp. 39–41.

pated in the election of the soldiers' council and several officers were elected to it.[67]

At Magdeburg the Social Democrats seized the initiative and had a workers' council elected at a meeting of the local party and trade unions; this was then joined by representatives of the National Liberal and Progressive parties and of the white collar workers' and civil servants' associations. At Breslau the council from the outset called itself a 'people's council'. It was composed of representatives of the Social Democratic, Progressive, National Liberal, Conservative and Centre parties. In Bielefeld too the bourgeois parties sent delegates to the local 'people's and soldiers' council'. At Iserlohn, another Westphalian town, bourgeois representatives were admitted to it after only one week. At Regensburg in Bavaria the mayor took the initiative and invited members of all parties and trade unions to the town hall where they agreed to set up a 'council of order' on which all shades of opinion were represented.[68] Thus the movement, although practically everywhere led by Social Democrats, was by no means confined to them. Especially in the small towns, the non-working-class element participated actively. In many large towns, too, 'councils of the intellectual workers' were founded to represent writers, artists, academics, etc. Elsewhere the civil servants aimed at representation on the councils. There can be little doubt that at the end of 1918 and the beginning of 1919, the whole council system enjoyed much popularity in Germany, not only among the working classes. The class which showed least enthusiasm for it was the peasantry, and this applied even more strongly to Austria.

The council movement contained elements of a genuine popular initiative which seemed to augur well for the future, especially in countries which had never known such an initiative from below in the past. In November 1918 nobody could foresee that within a few months the movement would lose its impetus and would soon peter out altogether.

In the last days of October a revolution of an entirely different type took place in Prague. It was preceded, on 14 October, by a short general strike in which 35,000 industrial workers participated, caused

[67] Pressebüro report of 11 Nov. 1918: Bayer. Hauptstaatsarchiv, Munich, Arbeiter- und Soldatenrat, vol. 23.

[68] Eberhard Kolb, *Die Arbeiterräte in der deutschen Innenpolitik 1918–1919*, Düsseldorf, 1962, pp. 92–3; Ernst Hesterberg, *Alle Macht den A.- und S.-Räten*, Breslau, 1932, pp. 13–14; R. Müller, *Vom Kaiserreich . . .*, ii, p. 64; information given by Mr D. M. Mühlberger from his draft London thesis, based on the issues of the *Iserlohner Anzeiger* for Nov. 1918.

by the severe food shortage. Crowds assembled in the Wenceslas Square, and the Ministry of War in Vienna was informed from Prague that 'the general strike would be continued until Vienna consented to the independence of the Czechoslovak State. . . .' Leaflets were distributed according to which independence was to be proclaimed from the balcony of the Prague town hall. The organizers of the movement were the Socialists, and in the suburbs of Prague columns of workers under red flags were organized to march to the centre, but they were prevented from doing so by strong military counter-measures. The crowds assembled in Wenceslas Square were dispersed by the military. But there had also been visible reluctance on the side of the Czech National Committee (an underground all-party body formed in the course of the war) to join the movement which they considered premature and which was not controlled by them. Its members did not aim at revolutionary action but, if possible, at a peaceful transfer of power; and owing to the military collapse, this power was now within their grasp.[69] In Prague there was to be no 'red' revolution, nor any workers' and soldiers' councils; the influence of the Bolshevik revolution remained very slight.

The aim of the National Committee was achieved: on 28 October power fell into their hands and the imperial authorities abdicated in a more or less peaceful fashion. On the previous day the Austro-Hungarian Foreign Minister, Count Andrássy, asked President Wilson for an immediate armistice and declared the monarchy's willingness to conclude a separate peace with the Allies. When this news was posted up in Wenceslas Square on the twenty-eighth large crowds quickly collected. Shouts went up that the Czechs were now independent and free, the first red and white flags were hoisted, national songs were sung; the long-awaited hour of liberation had finally come. Enthusiasm quickly grew; large processions were formed with officers and soldiers in Austrian uniforms at the head. There were shouts: 'Long live Masaryk!', 'Long live Wilson!' and 'Down with the Habsburgs!' The vast masses soon began to take more violent action: the imperial eagles and emblems, the Austrian rosettes and cockades were torn down from public buildings and soldiers' caps; those who refused to do so had them removed by force. German inscriptions and signs followed suit. Speakers addressed the crowds from the steps of the Wenceslas monument and the balcony of the town hall, demanding the proclamation of a social

[69] Richard G. Plaschka, *Cattaro-Prag*, Graz-Cologne, 1963, pp. 195–200; Z. A. B. Zeman, *The Break-up of the Habsburg Empire 1914–1918*, London, 1961, pp. 223–4.

republic, the republic of Czechoslovakia. Meanwhile around midday four members of the Czech National Committee went to see the deputy governor of Bohemia—the governor himself being absent in Vienna—and informed him that they had decided to take over the administration in the interest of public order and the continuous functioning of the authorities, so that the new state might come into being without any public disturbances. The governor's office reported to Vienna that it proposed not to do anything about the political demonstrations as long as these did not interfere with the right of property and as long as personal security was guaranteed. Within a few hours the National Committee emerged as a kind of new government which negotiated as an equal with the highest civil and military authorities.[70]

By the evening of the twenty-eighth public power had virtually been transferred to the National Committee. It took over the task of maintaining order in the streets of the capital from which the Austrian and Hungarian troops had been withdrawn. This task it was able to carry out with the help of the *Sokols*, the uniformed and well disciplined national sports organization which was mobilized and which set up a guard and patrol service. Military units were hastily formed from Czech officers and soldiers of the Austrian army, who obtained their first weapons by disarming other units. An agreement was reached with the military authorities according to which the two sides would cooperate 'to restore law and order in the interior', and exchange liaison officers; the National Committee would take over the supply of food and coal. The military authorities retained the power of command for the non-Czech units under their jurisdiction, but the National Committee replaced the office of the governor as their civilian partner. In the evening it issued a proclamation to the nation which began with the words: 'The independent Czechoslovak State has come into being.' Its constitution would be decided by a National Assembly. Until then sovereignty would be exercised by the National Committee; until further notice all existing laws would remain in force.[71]

The take-over from the military authorities proceeded equally smoothly. On the morning of the twenty-ninth several Czech officers (i.e. former Austrian officers) went to negotiate with General Kestřanek at military headquarters; he was an officer of Czech

---

[70] Plaschka, *Cattaro-Prag*, pp. 223–5, 232, 237, 249–50.
[71] Eduard Beneš, *My War Memoirs*, London, 1928, pp. 453–4 (with the full text of the proclamation); Plaschka, op. cit., pp. 239, 250, 257, 260.

extraction but absolutely loyal to the emperor. The Czech officers urged him to transfer to them an arms depot and the cadet school, the latter to be used as their central offices. The general's chief of staff, Colonel Stusche, refused his consent, but the general hesitated and asked him to telephone Vienna to obtain permission for the transfer. The Czech negotiators further demanded that officers and men of the Austrian army should not be hindered if they wanted to transfer their loyalty to the National Committee. In practice Czech soldiers in large numbers had already left their units, and the military headquarters realized that an order to the contrary could not be enforced. Vienna could do little but bow to the inevitable, and Czech officers were accepted by the Prague headquarters to introduce them to their new tasks and arrange for a peaceful transfer of military authority. The National Committee quickly took over the food and coal supply, the railways, the posts and telegraphs, and national defence. The non-Czech troops were withdrawn from the country. There was no resistance. On 14 November a National Assembly met in Prague, composed of the deputies of the existing Czech parties in proportion to their relative strength, to which forty Slovaks were co-opted. It proclaimed once more a democratic Czechoslovak Republic within the historical frontiers of Bohemia, Moravia and Slovakia and unanimously elected Thomas Masaryk as president of the new state.[72] There had been a national liberation and there was national unity; but no social revolutionary movement originated under these conditions. The question that remained unresolved was that of the large German and Hungarian minorities which were incorporated in the new state but were not represented in the National Assembly. National, and not social, issues were to dominate the history of the Czechoslovak Republic during the following twenty years.

In Hungary too a National Council was formed on 24 October from members of the opposition parties, which aimed at the reorganization of the country and the introduction of a parliamentary and democratic régime, as well as an immediate peace. Its president was Count Mihály Károlyi who had made a name for himself as an opponent of the war and an advocate of liberal reforms. His party and another radical party which supported the National Council were small; the only considerable party behind the Council was the Social Democratic Party which had a strong following among the industrial working class, especially in Budapest, but was weak in the

[72] Plaschka, *Cattaro-Plag*, pp. 274–5, 278; Beneš, *War Memoirs*, pp. 456–7, 470–1.

countryside. During the following days the government steadily lost influence, while that of the National Council grew. As the government proved incapable of acting at home and terminating the war, the people of the capital and even the authorities increasingly turned towards the National Council for guidance and instructions, and it became in practice a kind of counter-government. Many officers and soldiers took an oath to the National Council; it saw to the billeting and feeding of returning units; more and more of the authorities followed its orders; finally the officers and detectives of the Budapest police declared their adherence; so did the organizations of the postmen and railwaymen and certain municipalities outside the capital. Strikes broke out in protest against shots fired on a peaceful demonstration, and the workers of an armaments factory broke into the stores and armed themselves. During the night of 30–31 October the public buildings, the barracks, the military and police head-quarters, and the post and telegraph offices were occupied by detachments organized by a hastily formed soldiers' council. Power was passing into the hands of the National Council through the inertia and helplessness of the government.[73]

King Charles had thought of appointing Count Károlyi prime minister and had even taken him to Vienna for the purpose, but in the end had opted in favour of a less radical politician, Count Hadik. By the end of October there was no alternative but to appoint Károlyi who alone possessed the confidence of the masses. The prime minister appointed only a few days before resigned, and the Archduke Joseph, acting on behalf of the king, nominated Károlyi as his successor. No government programme and no conditions were discussed. Károlyi then formed his government from politicians of the parties which had previously joined his National Council: the two small radical parties and the Social Democrats. The latter were given only two posts of small importance, those of trade and social welfare, while the key ministries went to liberal politicians. There-after the members of the new government went to the castle of Buda to render the oath of loyalty into the hands of the Archduke Joseph. In the streets the news of the formation of the Károlyi government was hailed by enthusiastic crowds sporting white asters.[74] The war was over, a new era was beginning, and there had been no bloodshed.

[73] Michael Graf Károlyi, *Gegen eine ganze Welt*, Munich, 1924, pp. 454, 487, 489–92, 502; Wilhelm Böhm, *Im Kreuzfeuer zweier Revolutionen*, Munich, 1924, pp. 49, 53–5.
[74] Károlyi, *Gegen eine ganze Welt*, pp. 507, 510, 514; Böhm, *Im Kreuzfeuer . . .*, p. 58.

Outwardly continuity between the old régime and the new was preserved to a much larger extent than anywhere else in central Europe. For the time being even the monarchy was not abolished; a workers' council came into being only some days later. But the revolutionary troubles of Hungary were only beginning, and soon events took a much more radical turn. Upon the 'revolution' of 31 October 1918 (a term used by all contemporary writers) there was to follow a second revolution.

2 Generals and Soldiers' Councils

On 10 November, after Ebert's return from the Circus Busch, where the new government had been confirmed in office by the workers' and soldiers' councils, he received a telephone call from the High Command of the army. General Groener, Ludendorff's successor and the right-hand man of Field-Marshal von Hindenburg, informed Ebert that the High Command put itself at the disposal of the government: in his turn the Field-Marshal expected that the government would fight Bolshevism and support the officer corps in the maintenance of order and discipline in the army.[1] As Groener explained in court some years later[2] the term Bolshevism also included 'the system of councils' or Soviets which indeed had been formally established as the ruling power in Russia by the Bolsheviks. In Germany, the councils had just confirmed the composition of the government and some claimed a right of control over its actions. The German councils, especially those of the soldiers, clearly were equally obnoxious to the High Command. Thus the arrangement between Ebert and Groener—soon termed an 'alliance'—had far-reaching internal implications. And the same applied to Groener's later explanation:

> We hoped, through our actions, to secure for the army and the officer corps part of the power in the new state; if we succeeded in this, then the best and strongest elements of the old Prussia were saved for the new Germany, in spite of the revolution.[3]

The theme was repeated a few weeks later in a letter of the Field-Marshal to Ebert couched in very strong terms: as the officer corps had put itself at the disposal of the government, it was entitled to 'demand support from it against the unheard-of encroachments of the local workers' and soldiers' councils. It is obvious that we can only overcome this state of affairs if the government possesses an organ capable of ruthlessly enforcing its orders and the existing laws.

[1] Groener's diary for 11 Nov. 1918 and his *Lebenserinnerungen*, p. 467, quoted by F. L. Carsten, *Reichswehr und Politik*, Cologne, 1964, p. 20.

[2] *Der Dolchstoss-Prozess in München/Oktober-November 1925*, Munich, 1925, p. 225.

[3] Wilhelm Groener, *Lebenserinnerungen*, Göttingen, 1957, p. 468.

As things are at present this organ can only be the army, and that means an army ruled by an iron discipline.' Therefore politics must be removed from the army—a clear hint at the activities of the soldiers' councils. [4]

In the days of November, soldiers' councils sprang up spontaneously, not only in all major German towns but also in the field armies in Belgium and France as well as in Russia; this aroused strong apprehensions at army headquarters. In Brussels—a communications centre of vital importance for the retreat from occupied France and Belgium—a soldiers' council was formed on 10 November and took over the control of all military and civil authorities in the place of the *gouvernement*. It undertook to carry out the demobilization as speedily as possible and emphasized that for this purpose the 'strictest order and discipline' were essential; committees were set up for demobilization, transport, food, security, and the press. The council declared the duty to salute abolished, but equally that there was to be no war against epaulettes and cockades; officers were not to be molested. According to a report by the captain attached to the press committee, 'officers and soldiers' councils worked hand in hand.' [5]

At Malines on the same day a soldiers' council of twenty was elected for the Fourth Army, among them two lieutenants. On the following day it issued a proclamation which abolished the separate officers' messes and hospitals and the duty to salute when off-duty; in future the relations between officers and men should be 'comradely', but orders would have to be obeyed; officers should no longer be addressed in the third person, but simply by 'you' (*Sie*). When these demands were submitted to the commanding general, Sixt von Arnim, the last point was the one to which he objected: 'Thus from today any soldier can address me as *Sie* in the street!' But he agreed that on the next day all units should elect soldiers' councils which were to cooperate with the officers and were to have advisory powers. [6] When this order reached the front line at least one company reacted by electing its commanding officer who was then further elected chairman of the regimental and divisional soldiers' councils. In this capacity he was sent to address a mutinous *Landwehr* unit

[4] Letter of 8 Dec. 1918 drafted by Groener: Bundesarchiv-Militärarchiv, Nachlass Schleicher, no. 9; copy in Nachlass Groener, box 22, no. 241.

[5] Report by Hauptmann Bertkau of 18 Nov. 1918: Friedr.-Ebert-Stiftung, Nachlass Barth, V; *Die Revolution in Brüssel*, Neukölln, s.d., pp. 9–11.

[6] Ludwig Lewinsohn, *Die Revolution an der Westfront*, Charlottenburg, s.d., pp. 8–12.

where the officers' epaulettes had been torn down and the officers themselves had disappeared. In his speech he emphasized the need to maintain discipline so that everybody could get home as quickly as possible; otherwise, there would be such a muddle that the roads would get jammed, and a catastrophe might occur; if the men fetched back their officers they would thus help their own cause. His arguments prevailed. 'After ten minutes order in this unit was restored.'[7]

In occupied Poland, the soldiers' council elected at Grodno proclaimed on 12 November that it was taking over the power of command within the *gouvernement* of South Lithuania; under it, the local soldiers' councils were to take over power in their own areas; but orders given by officers and NCOs were to be carried out as before; the black-white-red cockades and officers' epaulettes were retained; officers and men were to salute each other 'simultaneously' and in a disciplined fashion.[8] A few days later the command of Tenth Army telegraphed to Berlin that the retreat was proceeding according to plan and that there was no danger of dissolution within its area, 'because the soldiers' council is supporting the efforts to maintain discipline in a selfless and most devoted fashion. . . .' The soldiers' council of Liège in Belgium informed the *gouvernement* at Cologne that the transport of the troops back to Germany was now proceeding in a very orderly fashion, that the soldiers were fed at Liège, and that all troop trains were sufficiently guarded; for these purposes the council was cooperating with the railway office at Hamm.[9] The picture thus emerges of soldiers' councils elected in an orderly fashion, anxious to maintain discipline, and fulfilling very useful functions, even in the difficult matter of an orderly retreat from enemy-occupied territory which they helped to organize. As one officer recalls, discipline improved further the closer the units got to the German frontier. When they crossed it, the red flags which some units carried disappeared, and most marched under the old black-white-red flags 'which clearly enough indicated their views'.[10]

The new government in Berlin was weak and totally unprepared for the vast tasks which confronted it. Order had to be maintained, the troops had to be brought back quickly, the harsh armistice conditions had to be fulfilled, the left bank of the Rhine was to be evacuated. Ebert abhorred mutiny and revolution; he was highly indignant

[7] Ernst Lemmer, *Manches war doch Anders*, Frankfurt, 1968, pp. 32–8. Lemmer later was a minister in the Bonn government.

[8] Oehme, *Damals in der Reichskanzlei*, pp. 13–14.

[9] Reports of 16–17 Nov. 1918: Friedr.-Ebert.-Stiftung, Nachlass Barth. V.

[10] Lemmer, *Manches . . .*, p. 40.

when Scheidemann proclaimed the republic.[11] It is thus no wonder that he accepted Groener's offer on 10 November, especially after the disorderly meeting of the workers' and soldiers' councils in the Circus Busch that afternoon. Six weeks later—when demobilization was practically complete except for the armies still in Russia—he still maintained:

> There can be no doubt that, if the High Command resigned today, an orderly return of the soldiers would no longer be possible. If the field railways break down the whole demobilization collapses. Much worse still is the question of the armistice. We need the technical officers, in particular General Winterfeldt, who has been able to obtain the best conditions for us. . . .[12]

It was the same motive which induced the government to retain the high civil servants: it needed technical experts, but many of the experts did not confine their activities to technical matters. Among these the demobilization problem ranked very high. As another minister, this time the Independent Social Democrat Dittmann, put it in mid-December:

> In the present situation we no longer need the officers as urgently as during the first days of the revolution. Then . . . above all our task was to bring back our troops from the occupied areas of France and Belgium and from the German ones west of the Rhine within the short time stipulated by the Entente in the armistice treaty. . . .[13]

In his unpublished memoirs Dittmann develops the same argument in greater detail:

> If the government of the People's Representatives had immediately removed the old army command and the leading officers of the individual armies, there would have been a complete disorganization of the retreat, and the danger existed that large parts of the western armies would have been caught by the Entente troops which followed them closely and thus would have been taken prisoner shortly before the end. This would have caused a justified storm of indignation in Germany against those responsible, and the right-wing circles behind the officers would have had a popular argument to make propaganda against [the government

[11] Thus Groener's letter of 5 Feb. 1936: Bundesarchiv-Militärarchiv, Nachlass Groener, box 8, no. 37.
[12] Ebert in a cabinet meeting on 20 Dec. 1918: Matthias (ed.), *Regierung . . .*, ii, no. 62, p. 6; E. Kolb (ed.), *Der Zentralrat der Deutschen Sozialistischen Republik*, Leiden, 1968, no. 4, p. 31.
[13] Dittmann on 16 Dec. 1918: *Allgemeiner Kongress der Arbeiter und Soldatenräte Deutschlands vom 16. bis 21. Dezember 1918*, Berlin 1919, col. 161.

of] the People's Representatives and the revolution, which they would have used liberally. . . . Therefore my consent to the leading back of the army by the old command was a foregone conclusion.[14]

Perhaps the Independents were not aware of the political implications of the deal with the army command, but they did not dissent. Nor, it seems, was there any disagreement when the High Command on 12 November requested the government to issue an order for the field army which conceded to the soldiers' councils merely an advisory role in questions of food, leave and disciplinary punishments; their principal duty should be to prevent any disorder and mutiny; 'unconditional obedience when on duty is of vital importance for the success of the return home; military discipline and order in the army must therefore be maintained at all cost.' This request was fulfilled by the government, and the order was issued without any changes over the signatures of the six people's representatives and then communicated to all units by the High Command.[15] Curiously enough, even the most radical member of the cabinet shared the apprehensions of his colleagues about a disorderly demobilization and the demoralization of the army. Although Emil Barth later asserted that he dissented from the order just mentioned, he declared in the cabinet only some days after its publication that everywhere the soldiers were the disturbing element: 'Therefore the demobilization must proceed as fast as possible. . . . If we cannot retain a firm hand on the returning, completely demoralized troops who mutiny at the slightest provocation, then everything goes to the devil. . . .'[16]

By the beginning of December the position of the High Command had been consolidated and the government had become more dependent on it owing to the growth of political radicalism. Thus a new letter addressed to Ebert, signed by Hindenburg but again composed by Groener, read like an ultimatum:

> If the army is to remain a useful means of power in the hands of the government, the authority of the officer must be restored immediately at all cost and politics must be removed from the army. For this purpose a government decree is required which stipulates clearly:

[14] Erinnerungen Wilh. Dittmann, D. 14, p. 39, Int. Inst. of Social History, Amsterdam. These were written many years later.

[15] Request of the High Command of 12 Nov. 1918: Friedr.-Ebert-Stiftung, Nachlass Barth, no. 191. The order as issued: G. A. Ritter and Susanne Miller, *Die deutsche Revolution*, p. 95; but Barth, *Aus der Werkstatt der deutschen Revolution*, Berlin, 1919, p. 65, asserts that he dissented from it.

[16] Matthias (ed.), *Regierung der Volksbeauftragten*, i, no. 13, p. 63: cabinet meeting of 16 Nov. 1918.

1 The power of military command is vested solely in the legitimate authorities.
2 The authority of the officer and the regulations connected with it must be completely restored. . . .
3 The soldiers' councils must disappear from the units; only trusties (*Vertrauensleute*) may remain who inform the commanding officers of the mood of the other ranks and transmit their wishes and complaints. A participation of the trusties in the exercise of military authority cannot be permitted. . . .

To these military demands were added several equally important political ones: the National Assembly must be summoned in the course of that month; only the government and the legitimate administrative authorities were entitled to conduct administrative business (meaning no interference by the workers' and soldiers' councils); the government's orders must be backed by a reliable police force, or—after the restoration of discipline—by the army; the maintenance of security must lie solely in the hands of the legal police forces and of the army.[17] To justify these far-reaching demands the letter alleged that the orders of the government were carried out by the workers' and soldiers' councils 'only if and as long as it suited them'. As we shall see, this was far from the truth, as the large majority of the councils were dominated by the moderate Social Democrats.

The army leaders were not content with the demands put forward in this letter. At the same time a counter-revolutionary plan was being prepared. Its author was Colonel von Haeften, but Groener was well aware of it. The intention was to select the best-disciplined divisions returning from the western front, to transport them directly to Berlin and to let them parade through the Brandenburg Gate. There they were to be welcomed by Ebert in the name of the nation as the glorious representatives of the German army. In his reply their leader was to express regret at the chaotic conditions in the country and to demand that Ebert should become president with dictatorial powers, that the workers' and soldiers' councils be dissolved and the officers' power of command be restored. Haeften discussed the plan with the leading legal advisor of the cabinet (especially of Ebert) Dr Walter Simons, 'who in all political matters was Ebert's right-hand man', and Simons submitted it to Ebert on 18 November. Ebert said neither yes nor no—a sign interpreted by the conspirators in the

[17] Groener to Ebert on 8 Dec. 1918: Bundesarchiv-Militärarchiv, Nachlass Schleicher, no. 9; copy in Nachlass Groener, box 22, no. 241; printed in O. E. Schüddekopf, *Heer und Republik*, Hanover, 1955, no. 7, pp. 34–6.

sense that he was willing to cooperate if they succeeded but would not take the initiative. Haeften also asked General Groener to come to Berlin for a discussion, and Colonel Heye was sent from army headquarters, now established at Wilhelmshöhe, near Cassel. The two colonels had further discussions with Simons, with the War Minister, General Scheüch, and one of his subordinates, Colonel Walther Reinhardt. Both approved of the plan but declined, for political reasons, to take part in its execution which should be handled by the High Command. But when Heye proposed this to Groener he declined equally and suggested that another general with a political flair be entrusted with the command.[18]

Preparations were also made elsewhere. As early as 16 November the Eleventh Army, acting on the instructions of Army Group B, issued a secret order that each army was to retain one strong front-line division beyond the date of demobilization, with a particularly strong complement of active officers and weapons for close combat; 'undesirable elements' were to be removed from the division unobtrusively through an exchange with others during days of rest on the return march.[19] When front-line regiments marched through Cologne at the end of November demonstrations took place outside the house occupied by the local workers' and soldiers' council; there were speeches against the red flags and the Social Democrats who allegedly were not Germans (a first sign of anti-semitic propaganda). In one suburb of Cologne the soldiers' council was declared dissolved, in another its members were arrested. To justify these actions the officers quoted alleged orders of the army command. The Cologne workers' and soldiers' council threatened to take countermeasures which were likely to endanger the army's march eastwards across the Rhine and might result in 'anarchic conditions'.[20] At Frankfurt on the Oder a unit returned from the front removed red flags and then demanded that the republican colours should disappear from the seat of the regional administration where the workers' and soldiers' council had its office. But the latter reacted vigorously and the red flags were restored.[21] Early in December another unit marched into Witkowo (in Posnania) allegedly to protect the Germans against the Poles, occupied public offices, tore down the

[18] Recollections of Colonel von Haeften, s.d.: Matthias (ed.), *Regierung* . . ., i, no. 51, pp. 316–18.

[19] Secret order I.-Nr. 1941 quoted by Otto Brass in *Allgemeiner Kongress der Arbeiter- und Soldatenräte Deutschlands vom 16. bis 21. Dezember 1918*, col. 68.

[20] Report of 27 Nov. 1918 by Informationsstelle der Reichsregierung: Friedr.-Ebert-Stiftung, Nachlass Barth, V.

[21] Report from Frankfurt, s.d.: ibid., I, no. 99.

red flags and replaced them by the imperial black-white-red colours.[22]

The general selected by the High Command to lead the front-line divisions into Berlin was Arnold Lequis. He received orders to 'act independently, if need be against the orders of the government or of military authorities, including the Ministry of War. . .'. A purge was to be carried out in Berlin and the workers' and soldiers' council to be deprived of its power. The units which were to participate in the enterprise were told that Berlin was ruled by the Spartacists, that anarchy and complete licence reigned, and order had to be restored, hence they would have to parade with weapons and live ammunition. The Berlin Executive Committee, on the other hand, demanded that the troops should march into the city without ammunition and accompanied by workers' columns—demands that were rejected by the cabinet after an intervention by the military.[23] Finally, a compromise was reached according to which only units from Berlin were to participate, with a limited amount of ammunition, and workers' deputations were to accompany them. In this form the march into Berlin took place on 10 December and there was no conflict. But at Wilhelmshöhe this compromise was considered 'a retreat before the street'; 'if the demands of the Executive Council remained unopposed the plan of the High Command to restore the government's power would have failed'. Or as Groener put it on 9 December: 'If the Executive Committee wins the Field-Marshal [Hindenburg] considers this a tyranny of the followers of Spartacus and Liebknecht and of the worst enemies of the German people. He considers it his duty to fight the Executive Committee with all the means at his disposal. . .'.[24] The failure of the enterprise was attributed by Colonel von Haeften to its betrayal by an officer and to the unsuitability of General Lequis for such a difficult political task.[25]

Yet only a week later a Berlin student overhead the commanding officer of a Pomeranian regiment address his men near the university on the subject of the soldiers' council in their home town, Stargard. He told them that its members were totally corrupt and were spending enormous sums, including the regimental funds which in truth

[22] Telegram from Gnesen, 9 Dec. 1918: ibid., I, no. 120.

[23] Groener's diary for 8–9 Dec. 1918: Bundesarchiv-Militärarchiv, Nachlass Groener, box 5, no. 16, i; notes by Major von Harbou, s.d.: ibid., Nachlass Schleicher, no. 9; *Der Dolchstoss-Prozess in München/Oktober-November 1925*, p. 224; Eichhorn, *Über die Januar-Ereignisse*, p. 36.

[24] *Die Wirren in der Reichshauptstadt und im nördlichen Deutschland 1918–1920*, Berlin, 1940, pp. 30–1.

[25] Matthias (ed.), *Regierung . . .*, i, p. 319.

belonged to the men. This corruption must be brought to an end, as the speaker had already arranged with his sergeant: '. . . as soon as we march in we are the masters of Stargard, and no one else'; they would remove the red flags and replace them by their own emblems. Until order had been restored the men should enlist as volunteers with the regiment, with the pay of four marks per day and food as on active service.[26] Meanwhile the government had begun to recruit troops to defend the eastern frontier against Polish encroachments, and this offered new opportunities to retain 'reliable' volunteers with the colours. As the same major explained to his men, these units would function 'according to the old régime, and with the old discipline—without any soldiers' councils; they should all join as he and his staff had already done'.[26] These new units could also be used against the 'internal enemy', and thus the aim of the High Command to provide the government with 'a useful means of power' would be achieved. For the units of the old army, even those selected for the Lequis enterprise, proved far from reliable. The front divisions assembled outside Berlin also had their soldiers' councils, and they had sent representatives into Berlin during the night of 9–10 December to complain about the counter-revolutionary propaganda made by their officers.[27]

This was proved once more when the same divisions commanded by General Lequis were ordered to evict the so-called People's Naval Division from the Berlin palace which they had occupied since the revolution. This was a 'red' unit formed by sailors from Kiel and Wilhelmshaven who regarded themselves as the protectors of the revolutionary achievements. But they were unruly and thefts of wine and linen had allegedly occurred in the palace. The government tried to remove them from the palace and to reduce their number to 600 men, and finally it stopped their pay. It was in vain. The irate sailors appeared in the *Reichskanzlei* on 23 December, carrying a box with the palace keys and demanding their pay, but Ebert could not be found. They were sent on to the *Kommandantur*, but the official in charge, Otto Wels, refused to pay them until Ebert had given his approval. They reacted by taking Wels and his adjutant along to the palace as 'hostages'. Meanwhile government troops had been mobilized to lift the 'siege' of the *Reichskanzlei* which the sailors had occupied for a time. On Christmas Eve the troops were ordered to attack the palace which was defended by the sailors. Groener was

[26] Protocol of Arthur Feige, 18 Dec. 1918: Friedr.-Ebert-Stiftung, Nachlass Barth, II.   [27] Eichhorn, *Über die Januar-Ereignisse*, p. 36.

eager to use the troops which had been brought to Berlin, and Ebert gave his agreement. But once more there was complete failure. The Berlin workers, drawn to the centre by the thunder of artillery fire, soon hemmed in the troops which were less than eager to carry out their allotted task. Negotiations started: the sailors agreed to evacuate the palace and to free Wels; but they withdrew only across the road to the royal stables and they had to be given their back pay. Their unit was reduced but not dissolved.[28]

The conclusion drawn by Groener and army headquarters from this humiliating defeat was that the units of the old army no longer had any military value and might be dispensed with. Reliance could only be placed on the new volunteer units or Free Corps which were then being recruited. 'On the twenty-ninth the volunteer units began to assemble and now battle could be joined,' as Groener testified later. In the course of 1919 these volunteer units were to eliminate the power of the workers' and soldiers' councils in one town after the other. The close daily contacts between the *Reichskanzlei* and army headquarters continued. As Groener also testified, he discussed with Ebert during these days the necessity of pushing the Independent Social Democrats out of the government, but the correctness of this statement has been doubted by some historians.[29] There can be little doubt, however, that this was Groener's intention, and if so he was successful. The attack on the palace was the occasion used by the three Independent members of the government to resign immediately after Christmas: the coalition between the two socialist parties came to an end and was never resumed. This brought to the High Command another great advantage. Among the Social Democrats appointed to fill the vacant places was Gustav Noske who was called back from Kiel and made responsible for military affairs. The government became much more united and much more willing to permit the use of the volunteer units recruited by the High Command against the extreme left. The opportunity was to come within a few days.

Previously Ebert had been in favour of creating 'new military organs on a democratic basis'; this *Volkswehr* should be composed of volunteers and its officers be elected; the men themselves should be responsible for disciplinary rules and punishments, leave and food

---

[28] There are conflicting versions of these dramatic events. That by Barth, *Aus der Werkstatt* . . ., pp. 98–107, is over-dramatized; cp. Arthur Rosenberg, *Geschichte der Deutschen Republik*, Karlsbad, 1935, pp. 52–4.

[29] Groener's testimony of 1925 in *Der Dolchstoss-Prozess in München*, p. 225; doubting this Rosenberg, *Geschichte* . . ., p. 244, and Matthias, Introduction to *Regierung der Volksbeauftragten*, p. lxxx. To me Groener's testimony seems credible.

regulations and the removal of officers, and pledge themselves to obey their elected leaders. The *Volkswehr* would offer security against any counter-revolutionary attempts and should be formed as quickly as possible. The Independent minister Dittmann agreed with Ebert's proposals but pointed out how difficult it would be to carry them out; he recommended the use of the workers' gymnastics clubs for the purpose.[30] But nothing seems to have been done to follow up his sensible suggestion. In any case, the recruitment of the volunteer units by the High Command put an end to such newfangled ideas, for they were commanded by members of the old officer corps and they naturally had no soldiers' councils or democratic structure. They did not march under the republican black-red-gold but under the imperial colours of black-white-red, and some sported in addition the swastika. It is true that a few republican Free Corps were also formed under Social Democratic guidance, most notably in Berlin the 'Regiment Reichstag'; but they did not play a prominent part and were soon dissolved. In this respect too, the 'alliance' between Ebert and Groener bore fruit, for the High Command was determined to retain control in the military field.

It has often been maintained that this course was inevitable if the government did not want to become the helpless victim of any radical *Putsch* or blackmail. But this seems open to doubt, for reliable *Volkswehr* units did come into being in several towns and states. The Social Democratic workers were apparently quite unwilling to enter the official Free Corps where they would have to serve under the old officers whom they distrusted, and they equally suspected the political complexion of these units—with much justification. But they could have been recruited for units such as those envisaged by Ebert. In Baden *Volkswehr* units were formed which eventually reached a strength of 12,000 men. Of these, about 1,500 were stationed in Karlsruhe and about 1,000 in Mannheim. In the towns the workers' and soldiers' councils claimed responsibility for the units, and the majority of the members were soldiers and workers, but the technical side came under the police, as Baden was situated in the neutral zone created by the armistice.[31] In Württemberg security companies with elected officers were created by Lieutenant Fischer who was responsible for their organization within the military command.[32]

[30] Cabinet meeting of 3 Dec. 1918: Matthias (ed.), *Regierung* . . ., i, no. 37, p. 247.

[31] Oeftering, *Umsturz in Baden* . . ., p. 273; Adam Remmele, *Staatsumwälzung und Neuaufbau in Baden*, Karlsruhe, 1925, pp. 43, 45.

[32] Paul Hahn, *Erinnerungen* . . ., pp. 24–5, mentions three companies recruited

Well-disciplined *Volkswehr* units also came into being in Gera and Erfurt in Thuringia, both controlled by the local workers' council. In Frankfurt on Main the local council created a sailors' unit of 300 men which effectively preserved order and became the mainstay of the chief of police. In March 1919 they quelled hunger riots in the town within a few hours.[33] In Hamburg there was a *Volkswehr* which was controlled by the Social Democrats but showed a marked left-wing tendency. It was disbanded on June 1919 on the recommendation of General von Lettow-Vorbeck and replaced by a police formation recruited from his Free Corps, which showed the opposite tendency.[34] Similar *Volkswehr* or security companies existed all over Germany. They often showed radical leanings, and within them soldiers' councils functioned on a democratic basis. They do not seem to have suffered from a dearth of recruits, which was unlikely in a country where the returning soldiers found it difficult to obtain employment.

From the generals' point of view, however, the *Volkswehr* units were unreliable or worse, and this applied *a fortiori* to the 'red' naval units, such as the People's Naval Division in Berlin, against which strong military action was taken once more in March 1919.[35] The Frankfurt sailors' unit—which was far more reliable—was surprised during a night in November 1919 by men of the Free Corps Neufville, and then disarmed and dissolved, together with the units of the auxiliary police for good measure.[36] The case of the *Volkswehr* in Hamburg has already been mentioned. A much more serious conflict developed in Königsberg, East Prussia, where a *Marine-Volkswehr* with strong radical tendencies had come into being. This unit refused to take orders from the military command of First Army Corps and to accept its officers but desired to be incorporated in the police service and to come under the orders of the chief of police. To this end the leaders negotiated with the Special Commissar of the government in East Prussia, August Winnig, but he was convinced by the military that a quick decision was essential, otherwise all might be lost. Hence preparations were made to surround the quarters of the *Marine-Volkswehr* with troops and to force it to surrender its arms. The action

outside Stuttgart by Christmas 1918, and three more in Stuttgart, one of sailors and two 'in process of formation'.

[33] Kolb, *Arbeiterräte* . . ., pp. 300–1; Hans Drüner, *Im Schatten des Weltkrieges— Zehn Jahre Frankfurter Geschichte*, Frankfurt, 1934, pp. 341–2.

[34] Comfort, *Revolutionary Hamburg*, pp. 68–9, 79.

[35] On this occasion thirty sailors who had come to collect their pay were shot dead out of hand.

[36] Drüner, *Im Schatten* . . ., p. 388.

was duly carried out on 3 March; the sailors were taken by surprise, imprisoned and disarmed. The army took the opportunity to arrest the members of the local and the provincial soldiers' councils and some members of the workers' councils at the same time. The majority of those arrested were Social Democrats, and hundreds more members of that party were also imprisoned, although most were soon released. A lieutenant, who had served devotedly at the railway station at a time when the administration was in a state of chaos, was arrested because he had sported a red cockade on 9 November and thus infringed the 'honour' of the officer corps. A state of siege was proclaimed for Königsberg and all soldiers' councils within the First Army Corps area were dissolved. Quite clearly the commanding general, Otto von Estorff, and his officers used the opportunity to settle old accounts and to get rid of the detested soldiers' councils at the same time; they had good reason to celebrate their 'victory'. The losers were the Social Democrats who lost thousands of members to the Independents.[37]

Similar actions, although not on the same scale, were taken by government troops in other parts of Germany. Workers' and soldiers' councils in the area of Thorn were dissolved by officers as early as December 1918. The soldiers' council of Seventh Army Corps at Münster was dissolved in February and its members were arrested by the Free Corps Lichtschlag.[38] When this unit marched into Hagen and neighbouring towns in May it arrested all Independent members of the local councils, men who were not extremists but moderates and opposed to any revolt or violent action—in a district where the workers were industrious and opposed to wild strikes.[39] In Pomerania the command of Second Army Corps in July proclaimed a state of siege for the districts of Stettin, Demmin, Stralsund and Anklam because the agricultural workers were striking; this was forbidden by the army as was any picketing of the estates. The result was widespread indignation against this interference in a labour dispute and a threat that the trade unions might proclaim a general strike if the

[37] All details are taken from the files of the *Reichskanzlei*, Bundesarchiv Koblenz: Winnig to the government, 26 Feb. 1919, and Besprechung mit Abgeordneten der Ostprovinzen, 16 Apr. 1919, both R 43 I/1844; protest of the soldiers' council of First Army Corps and the workers' and soldiers' council of Königsberg, s.d., R 43 I/1941. All the deputies present on 16 Apr. were Social Democrats who were highly critical of the action taken. Winnig's own version, *Heimkehr*, Hamburg, 1935, pp. 165ff., must be used with caution.

[38] Eduard Schulte, *Münstersche Chronik zu Spartakismus und Separatismus*, Münster, 1939, pp. 312–70; Friedr.-Ebert-Stiftung, Nachlass Barth, I, no. 123.

[39] The chairman of the Voerde workers' council, Dr Eichholtz, to the Central Council, 6 May 1919: Bundesarchiv, Reichskanzlei R 43 I/2706.

state of siege was not lifted. In negotiations held in Stettin the provincial *Oberpräsident* criticized the measures taken by the military command in the presence of workers' representatives, whereupon the officers declared that he no longer possessed their confidence. What was established in Pomerania during the summer of 1919 was a kind of military government superseding the civilian one. The officers developed many-sided political activities and recruited on a large scale, not only for the *Reichswehr* but also for the *Einwohnerwehren*, the local citizens' defence force—activities which aroused strong opposition in working-class circles.[40]

In the course of 1919, thanks to the volunteer units, the army regained its strength and was able to take up the struggle against the soldiers' councils and the working-class movement in general. To the majority of the officers, all socialists were birds of a feather; no fine distinctions could be drawn between Social Democrats and Independent Social Democrats, and within the latter between the moderates and the radicals (who in 1920 were to join the Communists). Strikes had to be opposed, if need be by military force. That such measures might only lead to greater conflicts and might drive moderate workers to the left was not realized by officers who had no political training but were now used for eminently political tasks. The revolution had carried politics into the army, especially with the soldiers' councils which had sprung up in all units. If the effects of the revolution were to be overcome, the soldiers' councils must disappear.

Yet the large majority of the soldiers' councils were moderate in their political composition and they often fulfilled useful functions. This was confirmed by the right-wing Social Democrat Landsberg in a cabinet meeting early in 1919:

> The soldiers' councils have also been very useful; it is true that the political revolution has brought a fair number of fools into the arena, but the prejudices about the workers' and soldiers' councils in general are not valid. Without their authority we would have been unable to save the ship of state.[41]

At the national congress of the councils in April 1919 a Social Democrat from Oldenburg claimed that the local soldiers' council had saved millions of marks for the army, seven millions by the sale

[40] Telegram of 14 July 1919, ibid.; the Central Council of Pomerania to the Ministry of War, 18 Aug. 1919: Int. Inst. of Social History, Amsterdam, Nachlass Grzesinski, no. 504. Cp. Carsten, *Reichswehr und Politik*, p. 43.

[41] Cabinet meeting of 21 Jan. 1919: Matthias (ed.), *Regierung . . .*, ii, no. 114, p. 293.

of horses alone, otherwise a source of private enrichment; and soldier delegates shouted that the same was the case everywhere.[42] The soldiers' council of Donaueschingen took over the military organization in the southern Black Forest and saved enormous sums, retrieving quantities of army supplies which had been appropriated privately.[43] As has already been mentioned, many soldiers' councils passed stringent measures against looting and pilfering which were enforced by military patrols. At Hanover a soldier and a sergeant were actually sentenced to death by the council and executed by a firing squad, the one for looting, the other for shooting people without justification.[44] But this case seems to have been exceptional. At Münster the soldiers' council for the area of Seventh Army Corps issued a circular ordering all local councils exercising functions formerly carried out by military or civilian authorities to restore these functions to them immediately; 'only if this is done by all soldiers' councils without any exception will we be able to avoid the threatening collapse'; the removal of officers or officials by local councils was unjustified, the circular continued, and the cooperation of the officers was absolutely essential, hence their authority must be supported and discipline be maintained. Even the concluding report of the officer entrusted with drawing it up admitted that the soldiers' councils of the Corps area were to a large extent responsible for the fact that order had been restored quickly and that officers, military offices and staffs were able to continue their work, although he denied that this was the sole merit of the soldiers' councils, as had been claimed by others.[45]

In this area and elsewhere the soldiers' councils quickly established their own hierarchy and their own channels of communication and rules of procedure—to the displeasure of the military authorities. There was a larger and a smaller General Soldiers' Council at Münster as well as a Garrison Soldiers' Council and councils for the several districts and units.[46] If German military bureaucracy was cumbersome and multifarious, the same was true of this latest bureaucracy to which it had given birth. In Baden and Württemberg State committees of the soldiers' councils were founded in the course of November which demanded a say in military affairs. The Baden

[42] *II. Kongress der Arbeiter-, Bauern- und Soldatenräte Deutschlands am 8. bis 14. April 1919*, Berlin, s.d., p. 109.   [43] Oeftering, *Umsturz in Baden*, p. 249.
[44] Tagesbericht 15, 19 Nov. 1918: Friedr.-Ebert-Stiftung, Nachlass Barth, V.
[45] Circular of 18 Nov. and final report of Captain Klose of 31 Dec. 1918: Schulte, *Münstersche Chronik zu Novemberrevolte und Separatismus*, pp. 124. 324.
[46] ibid., pp. 98–9.

committee delegated two members into the Ministry for Military Affairs. The soldiers' councils undertook not to interfere directly in the administration but, if they had any complaints or considered any measures necessary, to inform the Ministry in question which would then take action as required. The local soldiers' councils would receive their instructions from the committee installed in the Ministry at Karlsruhe.[47] The Württemberg committee decided that local soldiers' councils were not entitled to issue any orders interfering with an orderly administration and had only a right of supervision. The delegates to the first Württemberg State conference were largely NCOs or soldiers employed in military offices who often knew the routine better than the officers. All important issues were discussed in meetings with the Minister of War.[48]

In Bavaria too a State soldiers' council, composed of fifty members, was elected, with an executive committee of eleven acting in the Bavarian Ministry of War. The Bavarian soldiers' councils had the right of supervision of all service and social welfare matters, of receiving and handing on decisions and complaints and of imposing disciplinary punishments—the same regulations applying to officers and other ranks. The officers had at first contested these rights but had later given way. Commanding officers of units were only recognized if elected by a three-quarter majority. Technical matters were outside the soldiers' councils' sphere of competence, but in the Ministry of War they were informed of anything of importance.[49]

As to the politics of the soldiers' councils, the large majority inclined far more towards the Social Democrats and their line than towards the Independents, not to speak of the Spartacists. In the Circus Busch on 10 November it was the soldiers' intervention which enforced 'parity' and saved Ebert from a humiliating defeat at the hands of the Revolutionary Shop Stewards.[50] Two conferences of the soldiers' councils of the north-west at Oldenburg in November declared their support for the government and demanded the early summoning of the National Assembly, in spite of the intervention of the ultra-left leader Knief from Bremen.[51] A meeting of the soldiers' councils of the Fourth Army demanded that the elections to the National Assembly be held as stipulated; they would fight any

[47] Oeftering, *Umsturz in Baden*, pp. 251–2; Remmele, *Staatsumwälzung . . .*, p. 29.
[48] Hahn, *Erinnerungen . . .*, pp. 45, 54–5.
[49] Kolb (ed.), *Der Zentralrat . . .*, no. 78, pp. 563–4.
[50] See Richard Müller, *Vom Kaiserreich . . .*, ii, pp. 32ff.
[51] Report to the SPD leaders, 3 Dec. 1918: Bundesarchiv Koblenz, NS. 26, vorl. 68.

attempt at postponement and at establishing a dictatorship; all offices and authorities should support the government of *Reichskanzler* (*sic*) Ebert until the meeting of the National Assembly.[52] In January 1919 the Münster soldiers' council strongly condemned all Bolshevik activities and declared its continued support of the Ebert government, repudiating any dictatorship, either of the right or of the left.[53] The Württemberg soldiers' councils at their first State conference rejected any cooperation with the Spartacists and any dictatorship and demanded that a National Assembly should meet as soon as possible. A similar resolution was adopted by the Stuttgart soldiers' council on the preceding day. One active participant affirms that the Württemberg soldiers' councils were acting 'in the interest of the young, new state which they supported, protected and helped to preserve, rejecting any attempt of radical groups towards establishing a Soviet republic after the Russian example. . . .'[54]

There were, of course, some more radical or 'wild' soldiers' councils, especially in the early days of the revolution. At Glogau in Silesia a soldiers' council constituted itself on 9 November, deposed the officers of the local command and created 'vast disorder'. On the other hand, after much looting in the fortress, it restored there 'absolute quiet and order' and the whole military administration continued to work. On the fourteenth this council was in its turn deposed by a meeting, a new council was elected and the former district commandant, Colonel Bode, was unanimously elected commandant of Glogau.[55] In a Bavarian unit those officers who did not enjoy the confidence of the soldiers' council were deposed and new ones elected in their place; compulsory saluting and the officers' mess were abolished and all decorations removed; the council's orders were declared valid for all officers and men.[56] In Berlin the soldiers' councils of six regiments of the guards declared on 16 December that they would continue to lend their support to the Ebert-Haase government for the maintenance of law and order, but protested against any attempt to remove the People's Naval Division from the capital. The Berlin soldiers' councils desired that the government should issue a definite declaration about the election of officers and

---

[52] Lewinsohn, *Revolution an der Westfront*, p. 49.

[53] Schulte, *Münstersche Chronik zu Spartakismus und Separatismus*, p. 111.

[54] Hahn, *Erinnerungen . . .*, p. 45; Blos, *Von der Monarchie . . .*, p. 43; Keil, *Erlebnisse . . .*, ii, p. 116; Weller, *Staatsumwälzung . . .*, p. 132.

[55] Tagesbericht Nr. 20, 22 Nov. 1918: Friedr.-Ebert-Stiftung, Nachlass Barth, V.

[56] Regulations of 13 Nov. 1918: Bayer. Hauptstaatsarchiv München, Sammlung Rehse.

should take immediate steps to grant to the soldiers' councils the power of command which was to be denied to the officers; officers who had become Social Democrats after 9 November should be removed.[57] Even the radical soldiers' councils of Munich on 1 March 1919 refused to cooperate with Spartacists and Communists and declared that they would oppose 'with all the means at their disposal the terror of the street and of a clique without any conscience'; they desired a coalition government of Social Democrats, Independents and the Bavarian Peasant League and promised it their support, so that work could be resumed immediately.[58]

Another radical soldiers' council was that established at Wilhelmshaven by the sailor Kuhnt who in peacetime had been Social Democratic Party secretary at Chemnitz—the Council of Twenty-one. It proclaimed a republic of Oldenburg and East Frisia and was determined to exercise more than purely advisory powers. In December 1918 it went so far as to refuse to accept the decrees issued by the Council of People's Representatives and clearly aimed at complete regional autonomy. But significantly it did so only 'until the National Assembly will have met'. In other words, it showed no tendency to dispute the authority of a freely elected democratic parliament, only that of the—non-elected—government in Berlin, and in doing so earned the wrath of Noske. His intense dislike of the Wilhelmshaven council was shared by Admiral Beatty who refused to negotiate with three of its members accompanying the German Admiral Meurer in November 1918: the three had no choice but to leave the negotiations to the two admirals.[59]

The demand for the election of officers by the units which occurred so frequently was certainly anathema to the High Command. But its wrath was aroused even more strongly in December 1918 when the first all-German congress of the workers' and soldiers' councils adopted by an overwhelming majority the so-called Hamburg points (proposed by a Hamburg Social Democrat). These not only stipulated that officers were to be elected by the soldiers, but also that the local workers' and soldiers' councils were to exercise the power of

[57] Anton Fischer, *Die Revolutions-Kommandantur in Berlin*, Berlin, s.d., pp. 37–8.
[58] Leaflet in Stadtarchiv München.
[59] Noske, *Von Kiel bis Kapp*, p. 34, calls Kuhnt 'ein Phrasendrescher übelster Art, unwahrhaftig, dabei eitel und eingebildet'. As late as 1922 Noske composed in long-hand a MS. of twenty pages, 'Kuhnt as the leader of the revolution in Wilhelmshaven', which is bitterly hostile to Kuhnt: Friedr.-Ebert-Stiftung, Nachlass Noske, no. 62. A contemporary Social Democratic report describes Kuhnt as 'a clear thinker . . . animated by burning idealism': Bundesarchiv Koblenz, NS 26, vorl. 68, report of 3 Dec. 1918.

command over the garrisons in constant cooperation with those exercising the highest power of command, i.e. the People's Representatives; that the soldiers' councils were to be responsible for the reliability of the units and the maintenance of discipline; that all insignia of rank and the standing army were to be abolished and a *Volkswehr* was to be formed as soon as possible to take its place.[60] Although most of these points were vague and a great deal depended on their interpretation, there is no doubt that their acceptance would have meant the end of the old military system, and indeed this was clearly their purpose. Hindenburg immediately sent out an order to the army commands that he refused to recognize this resolution:

> I am of the opinion that such a change, vitally affecting the life of the nation and of the army, cannot be made by the representatives of one social group only, but can only be decided by the National Assembly summoned by the entire people.

The army would continue to support the Ebert government but would expect from it that it would honour the promises made to the army and the directives on the rights and powers of the trusties (*Vertrauensmänner*) in the army, so that officers and NCOs would be able to serve in the army.[61] Obviously, only if these conditions were met could the 'alliance' of 10 November be preserved. It was a kind of ultimatum addressed to a weak government which depended on the support of the officer corps.

The government, however, did not assess the situation in this light. On the contrary, when Groener informed Ebert over the telephone that the High Command would resign immediately if the government accepted the Hamburg points,[62] this was interpreted by one minister as proof that 'the tendencies emanating from the High Command to interfere in political matters' were 'not particularly dangerous': for the High Command had not reacted to the decision of the congress of the workers' and soldiers' councils by mobilizing the army and marching on Berlin; any potential danger coming from that quarter could thus be met by accepting the offer of resignation.[63] No member of the government seems to have dissented from this view, not even the Independents. The tactics of the High Command

---

[60] *Allgemeiner Kongress der Arbeiter- und Soldatenräte Deutschlands vom 16. bis 21. Dezember 1918*, p. 181, with the different amendments.

[61] R. Müller, *Vom Kaiserreich* . . ., ii, p. 222; Schüddekopf, *Heer und Republik*, p. 38.

[62] Groener, *Lebenserinnerungen*, p. 475.

[63] Matthias (ed.), *Regierung* . . ., ii, no. 78, p. 115: Minister Landsberg in a cabinet meeting on 28 Dec. 1918.

were entirely successful, and the Hamburg points never passed into law.

When the decree regulating 'the power of command and the position of the soldiers' councils' was published four weeks later, on 19 January, it re-established in practice the military hierarchy. The power of command remained vested in the government, but it transferred the exercise of this power to the Prussian Minister of War to whom all military authorities were subordinated. Lower down the scale, the power of issuing military orders was restored to the officers. The competence of the soldiers' councils was limited to 'orders relating to the welfare of the troops, to social and economic questions, to leave and disciplinary matters' in which they could participate, but purely military affairs were excluded from their sphere; they were not entitled to remove officers, though they could put forward requests for a removal to the authorities; nor were they entitled to interfere with the business of other authorities or to issue any regulations or orders.[64] This decree meant another victory for the High Command, although at the time it aroused the indignation of many officers because it seemed to preserve the institution of the soldiers' councils, if only in a much reduced form.

Groener, in any case, remained determined to destroy what remained of the soldiers' councils, and he found a willing collaborator in Noske who at the end of 1918 became the minister responsible for military affairs. When the soldiers' council attached to the High Command at Wilhelmshöhe approached Groener with the demand that any decrees of a political character or touching on the activities of the soldiers' councils or the structure of the army should be countersigned by them, Groener brusquely refused. Then the council members went to see Noske and enquired of him whether the government was determined to maintain Groener in his position. Noske asked whether this was a demand. The council's spokesman replied that he was not empowered to put forward such a demand, but that in his opinion Groener's resignation was the only solution of the conflict, otherwise the soldiers' council might have to arrest the whole staff. Thereupon Noske exclaimed: 'Do you realize that such a step would be condemned by the whole country?' They should do everything to avoid an open conflict with the High Command.[65] Some weeks later Groener, in a letter to Ebert, reiterated that he

[64] For the text see: Carsten, *Reichswehr und Politik*, pp. 33–4.
[65] Reports of 24 and 31 Dec. 1918: Friedr.-Ebert-Stiftung, Nachlass Barth, I, nos. 80 and 82.

considered the sanctioning of the institution of the soldiers' councils by the decree of 19 January 'a grave mistake', for 'the whole army is permeated by such a rage against the institution of the soldiers' councils that, but for the recognition they have now gained, they would soon have died an inglorious death. . . '.[66] About the same time Noske told a deputation of the general soldiers' council of Seventh Army Corps which had tried to prevent recruiting for the Free Corps: 'You are badly informed about your competences as a soldiers' council; we will show you in the next few days. Then everything will change! The government will not suffer your activities and will intervene, as it has intervened elsewhere.' During the following month, indeed, this soldiers' council was dissolved by government troops and its members put under arrest.[67]

In March a conference of the local workers' and soldiers' council took place at Cassel with the commanding officers of Eleventh Army Corps. During the conference the question was raised whether the combined workers' *and soldiers'* councils still had a *raison d'être* (*Daseinsberechtigung*), or whether the soldiers' representatives would have to leave the councils which were fulfilling political tasks. The officers were of the opinion that workers' *and soldiers'* councils no longer existed as corporations because the troops of General Maercker acting on behalf of the government were everywhere dissolving the soldiers' councils which cooperated with local workers' councils as illegal organizations; their place had been taken by the councils created by the decree of 19 January. One staff officer was then sent to the Ministry of War in Berlin where he was informed orally that, in the opinion of the Ministry, workers' *and soldiers'* councils no longer existed.[68] During the months of May and June the soldiers' councils were also dissolved in the areas of the Third, Eighth and Tenth Army Corps. All that the dissolved councils were able to do was to send strongly worded protests to the Central Council elected by the all-German congress of December 1918. But these were in vain as the Central Council could only pass on the complaints to the government.[69] In any case by that time the demobilization of the old army was completed; the new *Reichswehr* units had no soldiers' councils,

---

[66] Groener to Ebert, 27 Jan. 1919: Bundesarchiv-Militärarchiv, Nachlass Schleicher, no. 9.

[67] Kolb, *Arbeiterräte* . . ., p. 242 n. 4; Schulte, *Münstersche Chronik zu Spartakismus und Separtismus* . . ., pp. 312–70.

[68] Generalkommando XI.A.K. to Ministry of War, 12 Mar. 1919: Int. Inst. of Social History, Amsterdam, Nachlass Grzesinski, no. 456.

[69] Letters and telegrams of 24 May, 23 and 27 June 1919: Int. Inst. of Social History, Amsterdam, Zentralrat B-36, vol. i.

only *Vertrauensräte* (trusties' councils), which were responsible for giving advice on certain food and welfare issues but had no political influence.

In an internal officers' conference held in March 1919 Groener declared:

> The soldiers' councils must be classified as entirely evil; they are the worst enemies of a quick recovery because they aim at political power and undermine all discipline. In the form of *Vertrauensräte* we may consent to their cooperation, but only within the social and economic sphere; all further demands, especially those touching on politics and discipline, must be refuted most emphatically. . . .[70]

During a recent visit to the High Command Noske had indicated his attitude to the soldiers' councils in the words 'Chuck the scoundrels out!'[70] His advice was followed. It was to a large extent due to Groener that—as the title of a popular novel proclaimed—'the Emperor went, the Generals remained'. But the latter had found willing collaborators among the Social Democratic leaders. In a long manuscript written a few years later Noske summed up his opinion of the soldiers' councils:

> Most of them indulged in more or less stilted highfaluting phrases, in hollow gabbling about the liberty gained. To no one did the idea occur that freedom from the officers' power of command might bring with it the servitude of the entire nation vis-à-vis the victorious powers which Germany faced defenceless, since the mutiny of the fleet was followed by the collapse of the front in the east and in the west because the rear units ran away. . . .[71]

This was not only much over-simplified history it was also faulty logic, for the soldiers' councils were formed after, and not before, the military collapse.

Above all, it must be open to doubt whether the High Command and the General Staff were really essential to bring back the troops and to carry out their demobilization. In Germany, as in Austria, the army largely demobilized itself as soon as the units reached their garrison towns. What was essential for their return was the continued running of the railways, rather than the services of the staff officers. Many a soldiers' council proved that it could organize the retreat smoothly and efficiently. In many a military office the NCOs were

[70] Besprechung bei der OHL am 22.3.19: Bundesarchiv-Militärarchiv, Nachlass Seeckt, box 17, no. 125.
[71] Friedr.-Ebert-Stiftung, Nachlass Noske, no. 62, p. 3: Noske's MS. dated 25 Aug. 1922.

fully competent to take over the duties of their superiors. And many individual officers would have been willing to serve, exactly as many professional officers continued to serve in the Russian Red Army and in the Austrian *Volkswehr*. If the People's Representatives thought that the High Command and the old officer corps were indispensable, this judgment would be understandable in the circumstances of the time, but it was a misjudgment, as the Austrian example proved. This, moreover, did not mean that the officer corps had to be kept in being even after the end of demobilization, and it seems possible that the Independent members of the government thought along these lines.[72] Later, however, the political situation changed: there was the formidable threat from Poland, there was the alleged need to fight the Red Army in the Baltic provinces, and there was, above all, the Spartacist danger in Berlin. To ward off these dangers the Social Democratic government all too readily accepted the support of the High Command and of the officer corps. This was just another example of their lack of self-confidence, of their reliance on so-called experts, of their total inexperience in matters of government, of their inability to assess issues of power, and of the way they underrated the strength of the working-class movement. Hence the alliance of 10 November became permanent—an alliance in which a weak government depended upon the leaders of the Kaiser's army.

[72] See Dittmann's remarks at the congress of the German workers' and soldiers' councils on 16 Dec. 1918, quoted above, p. 58.

3 The Austrian Volkswehr

In November 1918 Austria had to face the same problems as Germany: to carry out the speedy demobilization of a vast army, many units of which stood on enemy territory when the armistice was signed, to preserve law and order, and to provide adequate military protection for the new state and the government. Although the problems were the same their solution was entirely different. As we have seen, the first issue solved itself within a very short time: the soldiers, either in orderly units commanded by their officers or individually in a more disorderly fashion, went home. The railways continued to run; although the Austrian army disintegrated there was no chaos and no complete break-down of law and order. As the army disintegrated quickly it was in practice impossible to retain divisions, or certain years, with the colours for a time, as was attempted in Germany. A new solution to the problem of internal security had to be found. This solution emerged in the form of the *Volkswehr*, promoted in Germany by left-wing circles but spurned by the generals, and under their influence by the government.

During the last year of the war Captain Julius Deutsch was recalled to Vienna from active service with the task of acting as a liaison officer with the trade unions and giving advice on questions of labour and the war economy. From an office in the Ministry of War he established contacts with the Viennese barracks, above all with trusted Social Democrats, and thus created a network of reliable men throughout the garrison. After the collapse this network was used to good purpose. It was due to Deutsch—now appointed Under-Secretary of State in the War Ministry—that, at least in Vienna, the cadres of the imperial army were not used as the base for the new one but that an entirely new force was created. On 3 November the government agreed to the formation of the *Volkswehr* for which volunteers were to be recruited; they were promised the comparatively high pay of six crowns per day as well as adequate food, or alternatively five crowns instead. Deutsch instructed his contacts in the local barracks and some newly won officers to act as recruiting agents for the *Volkswehr* as soon as volunteers were enlisted. The party apparatus in Vienna was mobilized to provide reliable Social Democrats. In Deutsch's eyes it was particularly important to exclude the officer corps of the old army from this operation. Professional officers had to be found to command the units and for all higher positions, but their political influence was to be closely circumscribed. Outside Vienna, however, the developments were very different. Even in Vienna only two thousand suitable soldiers enlisted during the first three days. As there was for a while a shortage of skilled workmen it was relatively easy to find jobs, often with higher pay, and after the end of the long war most workers had had enough of soldiering.[1]

What came into being in Vienna was a socialist force, almost entirely working-class in character, carrying red flags and marching to the strains of the Workers' *Marseillaise*. The pride of the organized workers in having overthrown the monarchy and having won a bloodless revolution expressed itself above all in the battalions of the *Volkswehr*. Indeed, there was a marked tendency to exclude non-socialists from its ranks. Men were rejected by *Volkswehr* recruiting bureaux because they were not organized workers, and complained about this to the military authorities. Early in December the *Volkswehr* command reported this to the Ministry of War, and Deutsch had to reply that only moral, and no political yardsticks were to be applied to the recruits: if the opposite had been done this was due to the 'excessive zeal of individual centres' which must be curbed.[2] Such zeal certainly existed, at least in certain units. When elections were held to the National Assembly at the beginning of 1919 the soldiers of some units pressed their officers to vote socialist. In one company the commanding officer was asked to contribute to the party funds but he refused. Thereupon the corporal who acted as the company's spokesman complained to the battalion's soldiers' council which asked the officer to attend. They explained to him that the *Volkswehr* supported the cause of the proletariat and was fighting for its rule; whoever disagreed with this would have to accept the consequences. They also asked him whether he would obey any orders of the Executive Committee of the Viennese soldiers'

[1] Bauer, *Österreich. Revolution*, pp. 98–9; Deutsch, *Aus Österreichs Revolution*, pp. 22–3, 27; Karl Haas, 'Studien zur Wehrpolitik der österreichischen Sozialdemokratie 1918–1926', Vienna Ph.D. thesis, 1967, MS., pp. 17–19; *Salzburger Chronik*, 11 Nov. 1918 (Landesrat proclamation to the Salzburg soldiers to enlist).

[2] Bauer, *Österreich. Revolution*, p. 99; report to Volkswehrkommando Wien, 5 Dec., and Deutsch to Volkswehrkommando Wien, 13 Dec. 1918: Kriegsarchiv Wien, Volkswehrkommando Wien 1918, Fasz. 9.

councils, and he replied only if this committee had the legal right to issue orders. To the question whether he would carry out the search of a monastery he answered only if he were ordered to do so by his superior officers, but if the order came from any other place he would not obey it because this would mean anarchy. He also protested against the view that the *Volkswehr* was fighting for the rule of the proletariat.[3] The soldiers' council of Baden near Vienna allegedly demanded from its officers their word of honour that they would vote for the Social Democrats, otherwise they would forfeit the confidence of their units. But when the higher authorities investigated the case the result was entirely negative. The reply to the complainants stated interestingly enough that only in Vienna had some such cases occurred and that there the soldiers' councils had been used to 'enlighten' the men.[4]

As in Germany, soldiers' councils sprang up spontaneously at the time of the collapse, the first one in Vienna without any election on 30 October. Proper free and secret elections were held in all Viennese barracks on 3 November by order of the State Council; the latter had been convinced by Deutsch that, as the officers had lost their authority, it was essential to replace it by a new authority in which the soldiers had confidence. In these elections the organization of trusties created by Deutsch in the course of the year functioned efficiently and was supported by the party apparatus where all details had been worked out. The result was that Social Democrats were elected by most units, 'not always old and tried comrades . . . but often the more radical youngsters who had joined us but very recently', as Deutsch wrote. The Social Democratic Party appointed a special defence committee to act as liaison with the soldiers' councils.[5] Soldiers' councils were also elected by the departments of the War Ministry and in the provinces, often by the assembled officers and men; but socialist influence on these elections was much less marked. At Linz and Salzburg the soldiers' councils deposed the local garrison commanders, and new ones had to be appointed in their place by the National Council of the province in question. In Klagenfurt the provisional assembly had to accept the council's demand that officers should be elected. In Villach the council's leader

[3] Captain Leopold Preiss to Landesbefehlshaber Wien, 23 Jan. 1919: ibid., Landesbefehlshaber Wien 1919, Fasz. 21.

[4] Letters of 23 and 31 Jan. and 4 Feb. 1919, ibid. The original complaint came from the Wirtschaftsverband der Berufsmilitärgagisten Deutschösterreichs, i.e. from the side of the officers.

[5] Deutsch, *Aus Österreichs* . . ., pp. 14–15; Parteiarchiv der SPÖ, Sitzungsprotokoll des Parteivorstandes, 20 Nov. 1918.

was a lieutenant of the reserve, a left-wing socialist; there officers were forced to remove their badges of rank. In many smaller places of Carinthia the soldiers' councils were led by prisoners of war returned from Russia. Above all, however, the Carinthian soldiers insisted on the election of officers which was conceded to them; they elected many officers of the reserve while refusing entry to barracks and offices to the professional officers and military officials whom they had not elected. They also abolished the separate officers' messes. The Klagenfurt council demanded that all orders of the provincial command must be countersigned by one of its members. At Linz executive power was exercised jointly by the soldiers' council and the *Land* government. At Salzburg officers were to be appointed by a committee of twelve, half of them elected by the officers and the other half nominated by the soldiers' council.[6]

The Viennese soldiers' councils soon created their own Executive Committee which stood entirely under left-wing influence. Its chairman was a left socialist, Captain Dr Josef Frey, the commandant of a *Volkswehr* battalion, who aimed at making it into 'a valiant, proletarian, revolutionary army' and considered it the primary task of the soldiers' councils to watch 'that this valiant army can never be used for reactionary but only for revolutionary ends'.[7] At the committee's constituent meeting on 6 December six subcommittees were set up, one for pay, food, equipment and weapons, the others for social welfare, organization, discipline, the provinces, and propaganda, indicating a very wide range of activities. They also nominated two representatives to the Viennese command of the *Volkswehr*. At the end of 1918 the Executive Committee considered the suggestion of the plenary assembly of the Viennese soldiers' councils that the general staff should be abolished altogether, but considered itself not strong enough to achieve this demand, which would cause a rupture. With regard to the Ministry of War, now headed by Deutsch, they accused it of being 'soft' and over-cautious in all political and material matters and of shelving all their demands, so that the committee was unwilling to cooperate any longer but would rather resign; the ministry should also take much more energetic measures

[6] Kärntner Landesarchiv, Umsturzzeit, Lt. V/15, 15 Jan. 1919; Kriegsarchiv Wien, Staatsamt für Heerwesen 1919, Abt. 5, Fasz. 197, reports of 6, 16 and 23 Nov. 1918; ibid., 1918, Fasz. 6, report of 24 Nov. 1918 by Landesgendarmerie-kommando Kärnten; Staudinger, 'Die Ereignisse . . .', pp. 78–9; Parteiarchiv der SPÖ, Protokolle der Arbeiterräte Oberösterreichs, 1 Nov. 1918. Many examples of the election of soldiers' councils in the files of the Kriegsarchiv Wien.

[7] Haas, 'Studien zur Wehrpolitik . . .', p. 33, quoting *Arbeiter-Zeitung* of 3 Dec. 1918.

against 'the reaction', probably meaning the conservative and right-wing circles from which most officers came.[8]

The main concern of the Viennese soldiers' councils was the restoration of discipline. Many *Volkswehr* soldiers, after four years of fighting, were not amenable to any discipline, many left the posts assigned to them; there was much petty thieving and insubordination; many doubtful elements were recruited in the early days, and had to be eliminated slowly. One company of Battalion 16 simply threw the verminous straw on which they had to sleep out of the windows into the courtyard and refused to clear it away; whereupon the soldiers' council decided that those refusing to obey orders would be discharged. The same council offered to inspect by day and night the guards posted in the barracks to stop the continuing thieving. One of its members insisted on stricter discipline and more martial behaviour of the guards posted outside because only thus would they be able to impress people and to show their power.[9] The soldiers' councils of several Viennese districts repeatedly put forward the request that, to help them in carrying out their duties, a special badge should be issued to them as well as sidearms for their personal security. The request was supported by the *Volkswehr* command of *Kreis* B because the soldiers' councils were ruthlessly eliminating all obnoxious characters some of whom might easily seek vengeance on them. The Viennese *Volkswehr* command then accepted the argument with the significant comment: 'Hitherto the soldiers' councils have worked for the purification of the *Volkswehr*. The necessary continuation of this process is only possible with their cooperation. Together with the officers they are the "supervisors" (*Ordner*) of the *Volkswehr*.'[10] In January 1919 an internal note of the *Volkswehr* command stated that the soldiers' councils and their Executive Committee consisted of serious, efficient men who in general exercised a very salutary influence with regard to obedience and discipline in their units; the Viennese command was to cooperate in all important matters with the Executive Committee which had its offices in the ministry.[11] The government of Lower Austria, too, admitted that the

[8] Verwaltungsarchiv Wien, Protokolle über die Sitzungen des Vollzugsausschusses der Soldatenräte der Volkswehr Wiens, under 6, 9, 27 Dec. 1918, 2 Jan. 1919, pp. 2, 9, 24, 28–9.

[9] ibid., Beschlüsse des Soldatenrates des XVI. Volkswehrbataillons Wien, 19 and 31 Dec. 1918, 28 Feb. 1919.

[10] Correspondence between Volkswehrkommando *Kreis* B and Volkswehrkommando Wien, 19 and 28 Dec. 1918: Kriegsarchiv Wien, Volkswehrkommando Wien 1918, Fasz. 11.

[11] Aktennotiz, 22 Jan. 1919: ibid., Landesbefehlshaber Wien 1919, Fasz. 21.

soldiers' councils in general were working to eliminate unreliable and turbulent men from the ranks, to prevent any excesses on the part of individual soldiers and to maintain law and order, especially in cases when false alarms or rumours were causing unrest in the ranks.[12]

Equally important were the relations between the soldiers' councils and the officers taken over from the imperial army. On 15 November the Ministry of War issued a decree that all officers of the Viennese command and units would be appointed from above with the consent of the Secretary of State; but they must enjoy the full confidence of their men, hence they would have to serve on probation for four weeks. Then the soldiers' council of the unit would report whether the officer in question had gained the men's confidence: if so he would be definitely confirmed in his post. A few days later the soldiers' councils were instructed to put forward the name of one man from each battalion to be commissioned as a lieutenant; the first were elected almost immediately; the majority were sergeants and other NCOs.[13] During the following weeks there were several cases of soldiers' councils withdrawing their confidence from certain officers because they had not been properly elected or because they did not take into account 'the spirit of the times', but also revoking their vote when informed of the incorrectness of their information by the authorities.[14] When the colonel commanding *Kreis* D was pensioned, the soldiers' councils put forward the name of a major to take his place because he enjoyed not only the fullest confidence of his men but was generally known 'as a just and energetic man who fully took the spirit of the times into account, who is not only a soldier but also a human being,' a front officer, four times wounded, two years a prisoner of war and then exchanged as an invalid, but nevertheless returning to the front: if another officer were appointed to the vacancy, as the Viennese command intended, they could not guarantee that the men would obey the orders of a leader appointed against their will.[15]

[12] Präsidium der niederösterreichischen Landesregierung to the Ministry of the Interior, 28 Jan. 1919: Landesregierungsarchiv Tirol, Präsidialakten 1919, xii. 76.c.I.

[13] 'Verordnungsblatt des deutschösterreichischen Staatsamtes für Heerwesen', no. 1, 16 Nov. 1918; Wahlprotokolle of 18 Nov.: Kriegsarchiv Wien, Staatsamt für Heerwesen 1918, Fasz. 4.

[14] ibid., Oberbefehlshaber 1919 (report of soldiers' council of 23rd battalion, 31 Dec. 1918); Volkswehrkommando Provinz 1918, Fasz. 2 (report from Waidhofen, 1 Dec. 1918).

[15] The soldiers' councils of *Kreis* D to the Viennese command, 21 Dec. 1918: ibid., Volkswehrkommando Wien 1918, Fasz. 11.

In one case, the soldiers' council of a battalion refused to accept a new commanding officer because the present one enjoyed the full confidence of the whole unit and he accordingly remained. When an enquiry was opened against another commanding officer on account of thefts and looting which had occurred in a unit he had commanded previously, the soldiers' council vigorously objected to his suspension. They insisted on first seeing the incriminating evidence on the basis of which they would decide; they emphasized that he could not be held responsible for the deeds of his underlings, and had always acted ruthlessly against corruption and inefficiency; 'we will protect the freedom of the republic, but above all we will protect our own freedom, and this entails that we elect our commanding officers and stand by them and do not allow them to be simply removed and replaced. . . .'[16] It is perhaps not surprising that many professional officers showed little inclination to serve in the *Volkswehr* under such conditions, and that disagreeable differences appeared between them and those who were serving. The result was a serious lack of junior officers in certain districts by the end of 1918.[17] By that time the Viennese *Volkswehr* had become a fairly efficient and disciplined force of about 16,000 or 17,000 men divided into eighty-eight infantry and eight machine gun companies and five batteries with twenty pieces of artillery; the officer corps had more than 400 members, among whom only a very small number were the recently commissioned *Volkswehr* lieutenants.[18] It certainly was a force capable of dealing with any internal unrest or attempted *Putsch*.

For the time being there was no such threat from the right, against which the entire *Volkswehr* would have been united, but there was a serious threat from the extreme left, curiously enough from its own ranks. During the early days of the revolution one unit was formed which became commonly known as the 'Red Guard', commanded by the journalist Egon Erwin Kisch who had emerged from the war as a first lieutenant. Its headquarters were in the *Stiftskaserne*, close

[16] Letters of soldiers' council of Siebenbrunnenkaserne to the Ministry of War, 4 Dec. 1918, and of battalion Wien-Sterneck to Landesbefehlshaber, 30 Jan. 1919: ibid., Staatsamt für Heerwesen 1919, Abt. 5, Fasz. 201; Landesbefehlshaber Wien 1919, Fasz. 21.

[17] Volkswehrkommando *Kreis* B to Volkswehrkommando Wien, 12 Dec. 1918: ibid., Volkswehrkommando Wien 1918, Fasz. 10.

[18] The 'Standesevidenz' of 4 Dec. 1918 gives 17,101 men and 469 officers, an 'Aktennotiz' of 8 Dec. 16,026 men and 412 officers, plus 1,510 men and 42 officers as 'Volkswehr-Hilfsdienstler': ibid., Staatsamt für Heerwesen 1918, Fasz. 7. Haas, 'Studien zur Wehrpolitik . . .', p. 24 n.3, has 31,000 men and 1,000 officers for the whole of Lower Austria in Dec. 1918, and for the whole state about 56,000 men and 1,700 officers.

to the centre of Vienna and all public buildings, a highly sensitive
location. The soldiers frequently demonstrated, usually for political
ends; many of them were anarchists or communists. On one such
occasion, when the usual fiery speeches were made, they were
addressed by a civilian at the *Schottentor*: pointing to the house of the
Vienna *Bankverein*, he exclaimed that, when they were strong
enough, they would crush down like an avalanche on those who now
exploited them; then the workers would become the masters of these
finance palaces. The ever-efficient Viennese police soon established
the name of the speaker: it was the writer Franz Werfel, a Bohemian
like Kisch, who when interrogated declared himself a follower of
primitive Christianity, hence opposed to any violence; his whole
speech, he explained, had been designed to prevent acts of violence
by the excited crowd, especially a march to the Rossauer barracks.[19]
A few days later a delegation of the Red Guard invaded Deutsch's
office in the War Ministry to demand permission for the occupation
of the Schönbrunn palace where the former emperor still resided.
Deutsch declined and instead suggested the 'seizure' of the military
command building which was only occupied by a few elderly officers.
This operation was successfully carried out by Kisch, and Deutsch
went to inspect the battalion drawn up in front of the building.
Solemn speeches were made by both, the band twice played the
Marseillaise, and then the battalion returned to barracks.[20]

On the next day, however, there was a far more serious incident.
On 12 November the Austrian Republic was officially proclaimed
from the ramp in front of the parliament house outside of which a
huge crowd had assembled. Deutsch intended to remove the Red
Guard from the scene, but its soldiers' council gave assurances of
absolute loyalty and promised that the men would parade with rifles
but without ammunition. On the previous day a new commanding
officer was appointed in the person of a veteran socialist journalist,
Captain Dr Josef Frey, who had just returned to Vienna; but he met
with the open hostility of the men. To him too the men promised to
preserve order and not to let themselves be provoked by anything.
But at their request Lieutenant Kisch was left in charge of the unit.[21]
In front of the building the new Austrian colours of red-white-red

[19] Report of Polizeikommissär Johann Presser, 21 Nov. 1918: Verwaltungsarchiv Wien, Staatsamt des Innern, 22/Nö, box 5066.
[20] Julius Deutsch, *Ein weiter Weg*, Vienna, 1960, pp. 118–19.
[21] Julius Braunthal, *Auf der Suche nach dem Millennium*, Vienna, 1964, p. 218
(Braunthal was Deutsch's adjutant); protocol about 'Die Vorfälle am 12.XI.1918
vor dem Parlament': Kriegsarchiv Wien, Staatsamt für Heerwesen 1918, Fasz. 5.

were hoisted on tall masts, and nationalist student corporations attended with their black-red-gold banners. The latter were torn up and trampled upon by left-wingers and soldiers who also removed the white from the Austrian banners—an emergency conversion to red. As the crowd grew more restless the heavy shutters were let down by anxious servants of the parliament house—a noise which seems to have been interpreted as machine gun fire or shooting by excited people. Soon shots were fired in earnest. From the parliament building shouts were heard 'Red Guards, forward!' The whole unit except a few men rushed towards the gates, which were hastily closed. There was more wild shooting; two people were killed and many more injured. The soldiers were convinced that they had been shot at, while most people put the blame on the Red Guards who had allegedly planned to overthrow the government. This version was disproved by a committee of enquiry appointed by the government. Order was quickly restored by the determined action of the soldiers' council, which also expelled those who had led the storm on the parliament building.[22] The whole episode once more demonstrated the dangers caused by the presence of the Red Guard in the centre of Vienna.

In December leaflets were posted up in the *Stiftskaserne*, signed by 'the revolutionary soldiers' councils of Vienna' and calling for open disobedience to the oath of loyalty demanded by the government from the *Volkswehr* units. The leaflets declared that the provisional National Assembly did not enjoy the confidence of the people, for it and the government consisted 'for the largest part' of capitalists, agrarians, warmongers and war-profiteers; the oath, they claimed, demanded obedience even if the soldiers were ordered to shoot on their brothers or allegedly hostile nations, the Czechs, Yugoslavs and Magyars; but they were determined to be loyal only to the working class and to obey only their elected leaders, and that only after mature consideration.[23] A week later Captain Frey announced to a meeting of the Viennese Executive Committee that it had been necessary to split the Red Guard, meanwhile converted into Battalion 40: he had moved to a different barracks with the more reasonable part, and about 600 men who remained in the *Stiftskaserne* would be transferred to a barracks on the outskirts of Vienna. At the end of

[22] 'Die Vorfälle am 12.XI.1918 vor dem Parlament', ibid.; police reports of 12 and 14 Nov. 1918: Archiv der Bundes-Polizeidirektion Wien, Staats- u. sicherheitspol. Agenden 1918, box 9; Verwaltungsarchiv, Staatsamt des Innern, 22/Nö, box 5066.
[23] Kriegsarchiv Wien, Staatsamt für Heerwesen 1919, Abt. 5, Fasz. 202.

1918 the new Battalion 41 formed by the latter had 489 men and one (!) officer.[24] The Viennese *Volkswehr* command aimed at the dissolution of the battalion which in its opinion was 'an unsoldierlike unit without any discipline and order', but had to admit that recently the commanding officer had discharged many of the worst elements. General Werz, however, added that more recently the strength of the battalion had increased by more than a hundred men and that there was the danger that it might attract many of those removed from other units.[25] Therefore the *Volkswehr* command on 24 December limited the maximum strength of the battalion to 401, while Battalion 40 commanded by Frey had a limit of 526 men. This uneven treatment caused vigorous protests by the soldiers' council of Battalion 41 which repudiated any events that had occurred in the *Stiftskaserne* and stated that since the split there had been no single case of a serious breach of discipline within its ranks. But the protest was of no avail: the loss of about 140 men by the battalion since the split was adduced as an argument by the Viennese command to prove 'how many morally unsuitable elements had belonged to this battalion'.[26]

In January Lieutenant Kisch once more attracted the attention of the police which reported that he had told a visiting American writer that he had 4,000 followers among the soldiers, returned prisoners and unemployed, and received considerable amounts of money from Russia. He had intended, the report alleged, if Liebknecht's action in Berlin had been successful, to do the same in Austria, but the failure of the Spartacus Rising had forced him to postpone his plans; if the impending elections resulted in a majority for the Christian Social Party that would be the signal to carry out his plan of establishing a socialist republic. But in reality Kisch's following had shrunk. In February a soldiers' meeting attended by about 2,500 men was addressed by Social Democratic leaders on military questions; when Kisch in the discussion sharply attacked the Social Democrats he was interrupted by loud shouts, 'We do not want any Spartacism', and prevented by the meeting from continuing his speech.[27] The strong trend in favour of the maintenance

[24] Verwaltungsarchiv Wien, Protokolle über die Sitzungen des Vollzugsausschusses der Soldatenräte Wiens, 17 Dec. 1918; 'Standesevidenz' of 21 Dec. 1918: Kriegsarchiv, Staatsamt für Heerwesen 1918, Fasz. 9.

[25] Statements of 19 and 29 Dec. 1918: ibid., Volkswehrkommando Wien 1918, Fasz. 11.

[26] Protest of soldiers' council, 7 Jan. 1919, with comment of the Landesbefehlshaber: ibid., Fasz. 10.

[27] Police reports of 25 Jan. and 24 Feb. 1919: Verwaltungsarchiv Wien, Staatsamt des Innern, 22/Nö, box 5066.

of order and against any violence induced the soldiers' council of Battalion 41 to assure the Viennese chief of police that they were only 'a guard for the protection of the republic, for the protection of the revolutionary achievements, for the defence against all reactionary endeavours'; as long as they functioned as trusties 'no Red Guard will let himself be carried away to any rash action,' for they would themselves determine when the time for action had come.[28] In fact, the few hundred men of Battalion 41—soon to be decimated by the departure of volunteers for the Hungarian Red Army—no longer presented a serious threat to law and order.

If the Viennese *Volkswehr* was almost entirely socialist and working-class in its composition, the same applied outside Vienna only to some industrial towns, especially in Lower and Upper Austria. The *Volkswehr* of Ternitz, to the south of Vienna, was joined by workers from the whole district and had strong radical leanings. From the nationalist side its members were accused of looting transports and robbing individual travellers; but an official enquiry established in November that only public property had been seized and deposited in local magazines which were kept in good order. The investigators were also impressed by the good bearing and organization of the unit. In spite of this, the *Volkswehr* command suggested that a unit from outside should be sent to Ternitz to disarm the 'red guard'. But the Viennese command turned this down: even if it were possible to find such a unit this would only lead to an armed conflict; a change of the conditions at Ternitz could hardly be achieved by such measures but rather by the personal influence of Social Democratic leaders who should be sent there.[29] As there were no further complaints about Ternitz, a gradual change seems to have been brought about.

From neighbouring Wiener Neustadt, where radicalism was equally strong, it was reported in January 1919 that discipline in the *Volkswehr* was slowly improving and that unreliable elements were being ruthlessly eliminated; numerous thefts had been prevented by a well-functioning patrol service; but the men were increasingly affected by lice as there was no coal to run the delousing establishment. In March a police report from Wiener Neustadt admitted that the local *Volkswehr* allowed the Communists to voice their opinions in meetings, but that the men—according to assurances of the com-

[28] Copy of letter of 7 Jan. 1919 in Kriegsarchiv Wien, Landesbefehlshaber Wien 1919, Fasz. 20.
[29] Documents of 16 Nov., 27 Nov. and 3 Dec. 1918: ibid., Volkswehrkommando Provinz 1918, Fasz. 1; Oberbefehlshaber 1919.

manding officer and the soldiers' councils—would do their duty if it came to looting or public disturbances.[30] The leader of the *Kreis* soldiers' council indeed emphasized in a speech to its members that they must always remember not to arouse any objections by their behaviour, even when off duty: they were authorized officials and must show themselves worthy of respect. Later in the year another local leader declared that the soldiers' councils' principal task was to maintain law and order, and this could best be achieved through a reasonable education; the appearance of a unit proved to what extent the soldiers' councils had been able to introduce discipline. Any infringements of discipline were punished by the soldiers' council, in mild cases by forfeit of pay, in others by discharge.[31] At the end of March the soldiers' council of Wiener Neustadt issued an ultimatum that they could not guarantee the maintenance of order unless the demand of the men for extra pay when they were on duty at the station to prevent food smuggling by passengers was fulfilled within twenty-four hours; but the Ministry of War declared this unjustified as service at the stations was rendered voluntarily.[32]

In the small non-industrial towns of Lower Austria the *Volkswehr* units from the outset showed no such radical tendencies. The company at Melk at the end of November had 120 men. As the inspecting colonel reported, 'it has a good spirit and makes a reliable impression' and showed 'the smartest discipline'. Its soldiers' council objected to the many 'Czechs' among the NCOs drawn from the local sappers' battalion; but on investigation these turned out to be Sudeten Germans married to local girls. Early in December the commanding officer curtly told the soldiers' council that he would not suffer any interference with his power of command; they should limit their activities to reporting the men's reasonable wishes or complaints which he would try to meet. They immediately reported three soldiers to him for rude behaviour at mealtimes and another who had used a falsified food ticket. The companies at St Leonhard and Mauk, he further reported, were in even better condition, very smart, and the inhabitants very satisfied with them.[33] At Raabs an engine driver was shot by a soldier in December because he refused to have his

[30] Reports of 14 Jan. and 18 Mar. 1919: ibid., Staatsamt für Heerwesen 1919, Fasz. 197; Verwaltungsarchiv, Staatsamt des Innern, 22/Nö, box 5066.

[31] ibid., protocols of soldiers' council of Wiener Neustadt, meetings of 27 Feb., 24 and 29 Nov. 1919.

[32] ibid., Staatsamt des Innern, 22/Nö, box 5066 (report of 1 Apr. 1919).

[33] Reports by Colonel Haas and Lieutenant-Colonel Schuster: Kriegsarchiv Wien, Staatsamt für Heerwesen 1919, Fasz. 200; Volkswehrkommando Provinz 1918, Fasz. 2.

engine searched for smuggled food. The soldier was arrested, but his unit demanded his release so that it had to be disarmed by orders of the commanding officer. A few weeks later, however, conditions had considerably improved and harmonious relations with the population were restored thanks to the energetic measures taken by a new commanding officer.[34]

At Baden near Vienna the soldiers' council demanded the right of participation when the houses of military personnel were searched for hidden food stores and when soldiers were arrested as a result of such searches. In general they complained that searches were carried out by the *gendarmerie* in a petty fashion and in the houses of the poor and of common soldiers, while those of the rich were usually left alone, all this reminding them of the times of the old régime. But these demands were strongly opposed by the Ministry of the Interior as illegal—an unwarranted interference with the powers of the police which would be opposed with all the means at their disposal.[35] The demands were apparently dropped. In the unit at St Pölten the men objected when their commanding officer, together with the soldiers' council, ordered a departure from the routine hitherto in force that a man was on duty for twenty-four hours, and then off duty for the next twenty-four hours. One company even passed a vote of no-confidence against their soldiers' council; the commanding officer considered the *Volkswehr* 'in most cases nothing but an asylum for the unemployed', while the officers had no power left.[36] At Waidhofen on the Ybbs the soldiers' council indeed informed their commanding officer that they had dismissed a lieutenant and appointed a sergeant in his place, and the commanding officer further complained about the opposition of the soldiers' council.[37]

In Upper Austria in 1919 there was considerable unrest among the lower classes, especially on account of severe food shortages, but there was no major trouble with any *Volkswehr* unit. Indeed, at Linz as well as at Steyr, the main industrial centres, the *Volkswehr* was used to quell such riots; there were no complaints about ill-discipline or independent actions by the soldiers' councils. The provisional *Land* government, which had come into being in early November, ap-

[34] Reports of 14 Dec. 1918 and 15 Jan. 1919: ibid., Staatsamt für Heerwesen 1919, Fasz. 201.

[35] Staatsamt des Innern to Staatsamt für Heerwesen, 26 Jan. 1919: Verwaltungsarchiv, Staatsamt des Innern, 22/gen., box 4860.

[36] Lt.-Col. Bussche to Oberbefehlshaber, 26 Nov. 1918: Kriegsarchiv Wien, Oberbefehlshaber 1919.

[37] Capt. Schoiber to Volkswehrkommando, 1 Dec. 1918: ibid., Volkswehrkommando Provinz 1918, Fasz. 2.

pointed an elderly local officer, Colonel von Pöschmann, as commanding officer for Upper Austria, and the Linz soldiers' council expressed its confidence in him although the colonel strongly opposed the council's power. When the Ministry of War attempted to replace him by an officer sent from Vienna, Colonel Redlich, there was such an outburst of opposition against this 'outsider' that the Ministry had to beat an ignominious retreat. As the *Land* government emphasized, even when Pöschmann would have to retire enough suitable officers were available locally so that the 'pushing in of foreigners' could not be justified.[38] In December a *Land* conference of the soldiers' councils, attended by 72 delegates, solemnly affirmed its willingness to fight Bolshevism as well as 'reaction', to protect the young republic and to preserve law and order; the *Volkswehr* was not the army of one party and they would see to it that it was not used as the helper of any one party in the forthcoming elections.[39]

In January a large socialist demonstration took place at Steyr which quickly degenerated into violence. The crowd would have stormed the local Christian Social newspaper and destroyed the machines if this had not been prevented by a *Volkswehr* detachment. The *Volkswehr* equally restored order when the crowd started to loot the vicarage. On the following day the action was continued against a monastic estate near Steyr. The mayor enquired from members of the soldiers' council whether the *Volkswehr* was reliable and was assured that it was and that order would be maintained. The council chairman, a lance-corporal, gave orders for reinforcements to be sent to the threatened estate, but they proved unequal to the task and the estate was looted. Order was only restored when further reinforcements arrived. But the returning looters were stopped near the town by gendarmes who confiscated their spoils. A *Volkswehr* detachment marching back into Steyr seems to have taken sides against the *gendarmerie*, mutual hostility quickly flared up, and shooting started. One gendarme and one civilian were killed and several more wounded. The bourgeois parties enthusiastically hailed the action of the gendarmes, while the Social Democrats defended the *Volkswehr* and named witnesses who could prove the responsibility of the *gendarmerie* for the clash. The *Volkswehr* remained bitterly hostile to the gendarmes, whom they considered 'white guards', and demanded that

[38] Col. von Pöschmann to Oberbefehlshaber, 16 Nov. 1918, Landesregierung to Staatsamt für Heerwesen, 6 Dec.: ibid., Oberbefehlshaber 1919; Oberösterreichisches Landesarchiv, k.k. Statthalterei, Präsidium, no. 398.

[39] Delegiertentag, 29 Dec. 1918: Parteiarchiv der SPÖ, Protokolle der Arbeiterräte Oberösterreichs, i.

they should not intervene in future and that the *gendarmerie* school be removed from Steyr to prevent any further conflict. The local soldiers' council guaranteed that order would be maintained and that the events of January would not recur, a guarantee which was repeated by the assembled soldiers. Friction also existed between the two forces because the *gendarmerie* was being increased at a time when the ranks of the *Volkswehr* were reduced, which was interpreted by the latter as an attempt to restore the power of the bourgeois parties. [40]

In the following month there were severe food riots in Linz. They started with workers' demonstrations against the shortages and the submission of their complaints to the *Land* government. Soon, however, a hotel was looted and the booty distributed; attacks on food shops along the main shopping street of Linz followed. The local police were helpless, and when the *gendarmerie* was called in the enraged crowd broke their ranks, and disarmed and maltreated them. Only when *Volkswehr* units in full strength appeared on the scene in the evening was order slowly restored. On the next day, however, the unrest continued. The owner of a bakery who made remarks arousing the indignation of the crowd and the soldiers, was arrested and taken away; but the crowd could not be quieted until his wares were distributed by *Volkswehr* men, and then peace was restored. On 6 February, when the worst was over, martial law was proclaimed which threatened rioters and looters with the death penalty, the verdicts to be proclaimed by courts-martial and to be carried out within two hours. The Linz workers' and soldiers' council agreed to the measures taken. [41] Although individual soldiers had apparently taken part in looting, the restoration of order was due to the prompt action of the *Volkswehr*.

During the early months of 1919 the *Volkswehr* was also employed increasingly to requisition food and cattle from a peasantry which grew more and more reluctant to fulfil its delivery quotas. For this purpose more men had to be recruited in several towns, but the requests for additional soldiers clashed with those for a reduction of the *Volkswehr* on which the Italian Armistice Commission, in particular, insisted with growing urgency. The Austrian government

[40] Reports of 11, 12, 14, 18 and 25 Jan. 1919: Kriegsarchiv Wien, Staatsamt für Heerwesen 1919, Fasz. 197; Oberösterreichisches Landesarchiv, k.k. Statthalterei, Präsidium, no. 114. According to these, the Steyr soldiers' council actually issued orders to the local units—a very exceptional case.

[41] *Tages-Post*, Linz, 4 to 6 Feb. 1919; Staatsamt des Innern, Abt. 5, to Staatsamt für Heerwesen, s.d.: Kriegsarchiv Wien, Staatsamt für Heerwesen 1919, Fasz. 197; poster of Militäranwalt, 6 Feb. 1919: Oberösterreichisches Landesarchiv, k.k. Statthalterei, Präsidium, no. 114.

tried as best it could to fulfil the demands for a reduction—which would have brought with it welcome economies—but the *Volkswehr* almost everywhere sharply opposed it. The Linz soldiers' council declared in March it could not guarantee security in the larger towns if the ranks were further reduced and Colonel Pöschmann informed the War Ministry that the dismissals ordered by Vienna could not be carried out without the soldiers' council's consent. A delegates' conference for the whole of Upper Austria, on the other hand, rejected with a very small majority a motion that discharged soldiers should receive a gratuity of a thousand crowns and accepted another that they be given three hundred crowns and a suit. A motion to elect five delegates of the soldiers' council to control the *Land* government was also rejected because the Social Democratic Party was already represented in the government, but at least one speaker sharply attacked the party 'bosses' because they stood too far on the right.[42] Two members of the soldiers' council—and two of the workers' council—were, however, delegated to a committee set up by the *Land* government to investigate whether any citizens of Linz inhabited houses or flats too large for their needs: if so, the surplus was to be put at the disposal of the local *Wohnungsamt* which would then allocate it to the homeless. At Enns the *Volkswehr* demonstrated peacefully for similar demands: confiscation of all living space above three rooms per family, price reductions, a distribution of rice as in Linz, a more orderly distribution of sugar. Colonel Pöschmann considered it necessary to discharge the unreliable elements from this unit and to send a more energetic commanding officer there.[43]

In June there were new difficulties at Linz about the drastic reductions demanded by the Italians, as the dismissals ordered in February had not been carried out. The Linz *Volkswehr* threatened to go on strike if its demands were not granted: there should be no reduction and the soldiers' food allowances should be increased by four crowns. The *Land* government had no alternative but to grant the latter demand, whereupon the strike committee agreed to the reduction 'without pressure' and guaranteed the maintenance of order in Upper Austria.[44] Sharp protests against the proposed reductions also came

[42] Col. Pöschmann and Staatsamt des Innern to Staatsamt für Heerwesen, both 18 Mar. 1919: Kriegsarchiv Wien, Staatsamt für Heerwesen 1919, Fasz. 197 and 203.

[43] *Landesgesetz- und Verordnungsblatt für Oberösterreich*, 3 Apr. 1919; reports of 30 Mar., 1 and 7 Apr. 1919: Oberösterreichisches Landesarchiv, k.k. Statthalterei, Präsidium, no. 398; Kriegsarchiv, Staatsamt für Heerwesen 1919, Fasz. 199.

[44] Reports of 3, 7 and 11 June 1919: ibid., Fasz. 202; Parteiarchiv der SPÖ, Protokolle der Arbeiterräte Oberösterreichs, ii.

from Braunau and Schärding, in the first case supported by the local authorities. They emphasized that food requisitioning in the district would collapse if the reduction was carried out suddenly; in addition it would cause grave dangers to order and property as the men threatened with dismissal might resort to violence and looting.[45] But the threats did not materialize and the reductions were eventually carried out, while the food control and requisitioning was taken over by the *gendarmerie*. To prevent the smuggling of weapons and the secret arming of 'reactionary' formations, the soldiers' council of Steyr exercised control over the consignments of weapons dispatched by the local armaments factory which had to inform the council of any such dispatch. The latter then informed the Austrian Executive Committee of the soldiers' councils in Vienna which took over the control of the consignments, together with the soldiers' council of the place of destination.[46]

A *Volkswehr* also came into being in Salzburg. It was controlled by the local *Landesrat* which appointed a military committee. Responsible to this was the commanding officer of the *Volkswehr*, Lieutenant-Colonel Burger, an officer of the local infantry regiment *Erzherzog Rainer*, or as it became known in more republican times, number 59. The local *Volkswehr* indeed was at first identical with the replacement battalion of this regiment. But there were also signs of the new times: in November two NCOs were promoted lieutenants, and soldiers' councils were elected, as were the local officers. As the soldiers' councils also demanded the right to dismiss officers, few of them were inclined to serve and a shortage of officers resulted. At the end of 1918 the Salzburg soldiers' councils elected as the new commanding officer for the *Land* a Colonel Peter, who previously had commanded the infantry regiment 107, and signed a contract with him; but Colonel Burger continued to serve with the *Volkswehr*. The main endeavour of the local authorities was to sever military ties with Innsbruck, the military command of which had exercised authority over Salzburg under the monarchy, and to establish their own military command responsible to the local authorities. As the same happened in the Tyrol, the Innsbruck commander, Colonel Dr von Eccher, had to acquiesce. The authority of the officers was slowly restored and the influence of the soldiers' councils declined.[47]

[45] Letters etc. of 19, 20, 22 and 23 May 1919: Kriegsarchiv, Staatsamt für Heerwesen 1919, Fasz. 200, A I Fasz. 25.

[46] Report of 8 Apr. 1919: ibid., Fasz. 201.

[47] *Salzburger Chronik*, 11, 26 and 30 Nov. 1918; Col. von Eccher to Staatsamt für Heerwesen, 7 Dec. 1918; Landeshauptmann and Militärausschuss Salzburg to

The tendency towards independence from Vienna in military affairs was even more marked in the Tyrol. The Tyrolese National Council also appointed a military committee which claimed jurisdiction in all military affairs and requested the commanding officer to communicate to it all orders and decrees issued by Vienna *before* they were carried out in the Tyrol. From Vienna a special emissary, Captain von Tschurtschenthaler, was sent in mid-November and reported back that it was not known in Innsbruck that the *Volkswehr* came exclusively under the orders of the Ministry of War, that the Tyrolese National Council issued orders to it without any reference to the military command, that the *Volkswehr* was functioning well, that soldiers' councils were being elected by units, garrisons, and personnel of the military command, at all three levels consisting of two thirds of other ranks and one third of officers, and that the Innsbruck soldiers' council was working satisfactorily. On 21 November Colonel Dr von Eccher reported to Vienna that he had taken over as military commander; owing to the conditions at the time of the collapse an orderly transfer of command had been impossible and the military administration ceased to function, so that the civilian authorities frequently intervened in military matters; now there was absolute quiet, and the *Volkswehr* was everywhere in the process of formation. He considered an exclusion of the National Council from military affairs a very delicate matter because it would create even stronger distrust of the military and their activities. Tschurtschenthaler wrote that in the opinion of the local authorities Vienna was too far away and independence from Vienna was very popular.[48]

The soldiers' councils, however, did not show many signs of activity. Early in 1919 they protested against the three varieties of cockades—different for officers, NCOs and men—which Colonel von Eccher was introducing and requested the same cockade for all ranks.[49] When the *Allgemeine Tiroler Anzeiger* published a sharp attack on the *Volkswehr* the soldiers' council was only with difficulty prevented by Colonel von Eccher from taking violent measures against the paper, while outside the conference room other soldiers uttered threats and curses against him; three of these were immediately

Staatsamt, 5 and 31 Dec. 1918, 13 Jan. and 12 Apr. 1919: Kriegsarchiv, Staatsamt für Heerwesen 1919, Fasz. 200 and 201, all with many details.

[48] Reports of Capt. Tschurtschenthaler to Vienna, 15 and 16 Nov., Tiroler Nationalrat to Militärkommando, 20 Nov., Col. von Eccher to Staatsamt für Heerwesen, 21 Nov. 1918: Kriegsarchiv Wien, Staatsamt für Heerwesen 1918, Fasz. 2, 5, and 7, Landesbefehlshaber Innsbruck 1919, Fasz. 2.

[49] ibid., Landesbefehlshaber Innsbruck, Fasz. 1.

discharged.[50] The soldiers' council of the company at Lienz consisted entirely of NCOs who were accused by the men of cooperating too closely with the commanding officer. They thus elected a new soldiers' council which was entirely Social Democrat—a step that met with the strong disapproval of the captain in charge, who attributed it to 'the very pernicious influence of local people which was undermining all morale and discipline'. He considered it hopeless 'to make soldiers out of men who take the obligations of their oath and the service rules less than half-seriously. That I belong to one of the first regiments of the old glorious army and have inherited my pure and unblemished name from my father of blessed memory make it impossible for me in the long run to stay under the same roof as these men without the radical elimination of such elements and to remain their leader. . .'. Some weeks later he requested, on account of continuing friction between him and the soldiers' council, that a commission of the Tyrolese soldiers' council consisting of officers and men be sent to Lienz as soon as possible. After its report the captain was removed from his post and a new commanding officer appointed. Some months later another commanding officer reported that his company was two thirds Social Democrat and one third liberal and Christian Social in composition, that he had dismissed the bad elements in cooperation with the efficient soldiers' council which favoured strict discipline, that his men had full confidence in him, and that he could vouch for their reliability.[51]

At Innsbruck, too, discipline rapidly improved. In July 1919 a professional NCO was reported because he stared at an officer, kept a cigar in his mouth and did not salute; 'his attitude was unmilitary and sloppy.' In August several lieutenants were similarly reported for not saluting and for improper dress.[52]

Meanwhile the Tyrolese government had worked out a scheme for a militia similar to the Swiss system: it was to consist in the first instance of local recruits and to be commanded by a *Landesbefehls-haber* who was to be responsible to the *Land* government; the latter's consent was to be required for all officer appointments; the soldiers' councils were to disappear and to be replaced, as in Germany, by trusties whose activities were to be limited to economic issues and the handing on of requests and complaints from the men; the new army

[50] Aktennotiz by Col. von Eccher, 11 Mar. 1919: ibid., Fasz. 2.

[51] Reports of Capt. von Wellean and Lt. Vogl-Fernheim, 16 and 28 Feb., 27 Aug. 1919: ibid., Fasz. 4. The decision to remove Capt. Wellean was taken by Col. von Eccher on 29 Mar. and in his place Capt. von Hafner was appointed.

[52] Reports of 27 July, 7, 10, and 23 Aug. 1919: ibid., Fasz. 1.

would have to be rebuilt from the bottom as a transformation of the existing *Volkswehren* was out of the question.[53] The result of these plans was new friction between the officers headed by Colonel von Eccher and the soldiers' council. The officers cooperated closely with the association of professional officers which demanded that the officers of the future Austrian army should be selected by it. Eccher in his turn declared that he was responsible to the Tyrolese government and did not care much about Vienna. He was much irritated by an earlier report that he cooperated too much with the soldiers' councils and that therefore the Tyrolese government had asked for his removal.[54] He clearly realized which way the wind was blowing and made his peace with the local powers; but among these the soldiers' councils no longer ranked. Their power evaporated in the course of 1919.

In Styria, as at Salzburg, the local regiments—in particular the infantry regiments numbers 27 and 47 and riflemen's regiments numbers 3 and 26—were used as the nuclei of the *Volkswehr* units. All soldiers of these regiments were urged to enlist. At Graz a soldiers' council was formed which demanded a reduction of the exorbitant food prices and the punishment of the guilty as well as the admission of its representatives to the provisional Diet. The soldiers' council further repudiated all rumours about a local 'red guard'. A 'Workers' Auxiliary Corps' had been formed in Graz, but this was entirely loyal to the Social Democratic Party and strongly opposed to Bolshevism; its officers were elected. Early in 1919 the Graz *Volkswehr* submitted further demands to the local government. They were again of a social, not a political character: strong measures against illicit food trading and smuggling and against the scarcity of accommodation in the towns; provision of work for the unemployed; if the *Volkswehr* ranks were reduced those discharged should receive a gratuity of three hundred crowns; those continuing to serve should be paid family allowances as before. The soldiers' council also demanded that all weapons in the possession of unauthorized persons be collected by the police, if need be by a search of houses.[55]

[53] Tiroler Landesrat to Oberösterreich. Landtag, 23 Aug. 1919: Oberösterreichisches Landesarchiv, Landtagsakten no. 66.

[54] Notes by Col. von Eccher, 23 June: Kriegsarchiv Wien, Landesbefehlshaber Innsbruck 1919, Fasz. 2; Landeshauptmann-Stellvertreter Dr Gruener to Deutsch, 2 Oct. 1919: Archiv der Bundes-Polizeidirektion Wien, Staats- u. sicherheitspol. Agenden 1919, box 2.

[55] *Tagespost*, Graz, 5, 7, 12, 28 Nov., 5 and 12 Dec. 1918, 21 Feb. 1919; Graz soldiers' council to government, 6 Mar. 1919: Steiermärkisches Landesarchiv, Akten der k.k. Statthalterei 1918, E.91 (ii).

As in Upper Austria, so in Styria *Volkswehr* units were used to requisition cattle and corn from recalcitrant peasants. While this was carried out with success in certain districts, an armed clash occurred at Pöllau in eastern Styria, where the commission was attacked and disarmed by armed peasants. Thereupon two hundred men of the Workers' Auxiliary Corps were sent there from Graz. Men of this unit were also used elsewhere and succeeded, together with *Volkswehr* units, in collecting five hundred and five head of cattle.[56] According to a police report all Communists were excluded from this formation and from the *Volkswehr*; and another affirmed that the general spirit was good and anti-communist. Only two *Volkswehr* companies were classified as 'unreliable'; but the Workers' Auxiliary Corps which consisted of older men was particularly praised. So was the *Volkswehr* Battalion 5 from Leibnitz which distinguished itself by smartness, discipline and stern organization as the men had served in the former infantry regiments 26 and 47.[57] In general, the history of the Styrian *Volkswehr* was almost entirely peaceful and there were not even any conflicts with the police. When there was unrest in Graz in February 1919 the soldiers' council insisted that the security service be entrusted solely to the *Volkswehr* and the Workers' Auxiliary Corps and vouched for the maintenance of order, while the *gendarmerie* should only guard the public buildings and military stores; the council put the blame for the riots squarely on the Communists from whom it dissociated itself sharply.[58] As in Vienna and other industrial towns, the *Volkswehr* of Graz, Bruck and Leoben was strongly Social Democrat, and this applied even more to the Workers' Auxiliary Corps of Graz; but the more radical tendencies which existed in some Viennese units were absent.

In Carinthia, finally, although there were radical influences at the outset, these did not last; for soon the national struggle against the Yugoslavs overshadowed all other issues. Even the first soldiers' council of Klagenfurt demanded—apart from the usual requests for the election of officers and the abolition of the officers' messes—the immediate expulsion of all non-German officers and military officials. It further urged that any order of the provincial command be countersigned by a member of the soldiers' council. The council at Villach even forbade the wearing of any badges of rank; unpopular

[56] Reports of Landesbefehlshaber Graz, 8 Mar., 25 Apr. 1919: Kriegsarchiv Wien, Staatsamt für Heerwesen 1919, Fasz. 196.
[57] Gendarmerie reports of 15 June and 9 July 1919: Steiermärk. Landesarchiv, Akten der k.k. Statthalterei 1918, E. 91 (iv); *Tagespost*, Graz, 28 and 30 Apr. 1919.
[58] *Tagespost*, Graz, 23 and 24 Feb. 1919.

officers were deposed. The recruiting of *Volkswehr* units proceeded very slowly. The recruits were mainly from the unemployed or from those earning less than the six crowns of the *Volkswehr* soldiers. As elsewhere, the reserve companies of the local regiments were used for recruiting purposes, but the local government considered that these companies were 'only usable to a very limited degree': in its view the only reliable elements were officers and peasants, 'but these only in case of a dire emergency'.[59] While the soldiers elected their company commanders and junior officers, the officers elected Lieutenant-Colonel Hülgert as their leader, and he was later confirmed in the office of commanding officer for Carinthia. In December he informed the Ministry of War that feeling against the officers was still running high and was further fanned by the fact that some of those wearing officers' uniforms did not conduct themselves like officers.[60] In spite of all difficulties, however, by mid-December the Carinthian *Volkswehr* units numbered 3,222 men and 101 officers.[61]

Originally the soldiers' councils of Klagenfurt and Villach had their representatives attached to important administrative offices, such as the food and housing departments, but at Klagenfurt this influence was soon lost. At Klagenfurt a *Bürgerwehr* (citizens' guard) was founded as a counterweight to the *Volkswehr* with its left-wing tendencies. But the soldiers' council vigorously opposed this formation and demanded that it be disarmed. This 'ultimatum' was sharply criticized by the bourgeois representatives in the local defence committee, who considered that to accept it would be a sign of weakness. Weapons continued to be distributed not only to this unit, but above all to the many *Heimwehren* which sprang up in Carinthia in connection with the fight against the Yugoslavs.[62] This issue now dominated local politics and strongly influenced the soldiers' councils. 'Fraternal greetings' were sent by other soldiers' councils to their comrades 'who are protecting the area settled by our nation in a defensive struggle'; 'the soil of Carinthia will be and must remain German'.[63] Even the hostile critics of the soldiers' councils had to admit that 'during the fight against the Yugoslavs

[59] Reports of 10, 16, 23 and 24 Nov. 1918: Kärntner Landesarchiv, Umsturzzeit, Lt. IV/2; Kriegsarchiv Wien, Staatsamt für Heerwesen 1919, Fasz. 197; Staatsamt für Heerwesen 1918, Fasz. 6.

[60] Kärntner Landesarchiv, Präsidialakten, Fasz. vi, no. 39; Kriegsarchiv, Staatsamt für Heerwesen 1919, Fasz. 203.

[61] Erwin Steinböck, *Die Volkswehr in Kärnten . . .*, Vienna and Graz, 1963, p. 18.

[62] Protocol of Carinthian Wehrausschuss, 12 Feb. 1919: Kärntner Landesarchiv, Präsidialakten, Fasz. vi, no. 39.

[63] Telegrams of 10 and 12 Jan. 1919: ibid., Umsturzzeit, Lt. V/14; Ludwig Jedlicka, *Ein Heer im Schatten der Parteien*, Graz and Cologne, 1955, p. 16.

most of the soldiers' councils fulfilled their duty completely and well.'
Volkswehr units from Vienna, Klosterneuburg and the Tyrol actively
participated in the fight. In May even the radical workers' and
soldiers' council of Villach unanimously expressed its agreement with
the mobilization ordered to counter the Yugoslav offensive, but
would not agree to an Austrian offensive against Yugoslavia. 'Therefore the workers' and soldiers' council of Villach will exercise control
over the strategic positions which must be occupied to guarantee our
security, in cooperation with the provincial soldiers' council of
Klagenfurt. . . .'[64]

After the fighting had come to an end strong friction continued
between the senior officers and the soldiers' councils. But according
to the former, the troops were now on their side while the roots of
the trouble must be sought in Vienna:

> The spirit of the majority of the Carinthian troops today is that
> they do not wish to have much to do with the provincial soldiers'
> council. The obstacle to its substitution by a system of *Vertrauens-
> männer* (trusties) comes solely from Vienna. . . .
>
> So long as the Social Democratic Party stands behind the
> soldiers' councils, the struggle with the latter becomes equivalent
> to a struggle with the whole of the Social Democratic Party. Only
> when the Party, as in Germany, abandons the soldiers' councils . . .
> will it be possible to direct the influence of the soldiers' councils on
> proper and profitable lines. Whosoever wishes to root out the
> disease which is hindering the recovery of German Austria must
> grasp it at its root—in Vienna.[65]

That the soldiers' councils had lost their influence in Carinthia was
equally recognized by the Social Democrats. When Deutsch reported
in September to the party executive on the position in the army, he
stated that it was good only in Lower Austria and Salzburg, bad in
Styria and the Tyrol—with the single exception of Innsbruck—and
worse still in Carinthia: there the party had lost its strong position on
account of the comrades' lack of interest and the war against Yugoslavia, and the soldiers' council had no longer any say.[66] At that time
only the Villach soldiers' council still exercised influence and enjoyed

---

[64] Kärntner Landesarchiv, Präsidialakten, Fasz. v; memorandum by an
Austrian officer, 3 Aug. 1919: PRO, FO 371, Austria-Hungary file 123, vol. 3510.
[65] Quotations from a lengthy memorandum 'The Carinthian Soldier's Council'
of 3 Aug. 1919, which was handed to Brigadier Delme Radcliffe by the Carinthian
command and which strongly influenced his attitude to the *Volkswehr*: PRO, FO
371, Austria-Hungary, vol. 3510, no. 135177.
[66] Meeting of 7 Sept. 1919: Parteiarchiv der SPÖ, Parteivorstandsprotokolle
1913–25.

the confidence of the population because it took effective measures against the illicit trading and smuggling of food, in cooperation with the military police, while the civil authorities remained passive and neglected the people's interests.[67] But the position in Villach, which also had an armed workers' battalion, was clearly exceptional in a province which was almost entirely rural and in which national passions had been stirred by the war against the Yugoslavs. In general, Deutsch's report clearly showed to what extent his party had lost influence outside Vienna during the past ten months.

In Vienna, however, Social Democratic influence within the *Volkswehr* was if anything consolidated in the course of 1919. That of the Communists increased for a while owing to the proclamation first of the Hungarian, and later of the Munich Soviet republics; but their defeat and the failure of the Communist *Putsch* in June brought about a sharp decline. When Battalion 41 was finally dissolved in August by a decision of the Executive Committee of the soldiers' councils, Communist influence within the *Volkswehr* virtually came to an end. As the moderate and right-wing parties had in practice been excluded from it, this left the Social Democrats and the Executive Committee in sole control. At the beginning of the year the position of the Executive Committee was further strengthened by an agreement with the Viennese command of the *Volkswehr* according to which all sensitive and particularly important orders had to be communicated to it; the movement of units into or out of Vienna and any use of them for political purposes required the counter-signature of the Executive Committee; officer appointments to all higher posts —from battalion commander upwards—were to be submitted to it: its decision would be reached after consultation with the unit in question, while removals of officers should only take place 'if there really is well-founded distrust'. Yet it was also stipulated that—outside purely political contingencies—the Executive Committee was not to exercise the power of command.[68] These far-reaching concessions may only have codified a state of affairs which already

[67] Landesausschuss meeting of 1 Aug. 1919: Kärntner Landesarchiv, Landesausschuss, Fasz. ii, no. 8. Cp. also meeting of 2 Dec., ibid.

[68] Report of Capt. Frey about negotiations with the Landesbefehlschaber, 27 Jan. 1919: Verwaltungsarchiv Wien, Protokolle über die Sitzungen des Vollzugsausschusses der Soldatenräte der Volkswehr Wiens, pp. 49–51. For the dissolution of Battalion 41, see ibid., Protokolle von Sitzungen des Kreisausschusses der Soldatenräte des *Kreises* D., under 5 Sept. 1919. Deutsch, *Aus Österreichs Revolution*, p. 93, states that in fact the Executive Committee exercised the power of command 'for a long time'.

existed in practice, but they indicate clearly the extraordinary powers wielded by the Executive Committee at the time.

The issue which assumed great importance in Vienna as well as in the provinces was that of the reduction of the *Volkswehr*. In January the Italian Armistice Commission enquired in Vienna how strong the *Volkswehr* was; the reply of the Ministry of War gave its strength as about 56,000 men who would be reduced to 27,000 by the beginning of February—an undertaking that was clearly impossible to carry out. A new Italian note in April demanded a quick reduction, and it was then agreed that the strength would be limited to 20,000 men by the end of June. But the attempts met with determined opposition. All that the Executive Committee would concede was the discharge of 'unreliable elements', i.e. those who neglected their duties, refused to carry out orders, were absent without leave, or left voluntarily. In February the commanding officer of Vienna reported that there was active and passive resistance by the soldiers' councils and the units to the reduction and even that new recruitment was taking place. He therefore suggested that the maximum strength for Vienna should be fixed at 17,000 and that men who were leaving or being dismissed could be replaced. The strongest opponents of any reduction were the soldiers' councils of Battalion 41 who argued that it would bring about a 'danger for the proletariat'.[69] In general the Communists found that their propaganda against any reduction was readily supported by many *Volkswehr* soldiers, anxious not to lose their livelihood; while the bourgeois parties were strongly in favour, as they considered the Viennese *Volkswehr* a party guard of the Social Democrats.

Radicalism within the units increased markedly after the proclamation of the Hungarian Soviet Republic in March. The Executive Committee sent representatives to Budapest to obtain first-hand information, and was itself addressed by several Hungarian emissaries, who pressed for similar action in Austria. When Dr Frey enquired from the Hungarian ambassador, Dr Bolgár, how far the formation of the Red Army had progressed, he was informed that it had enough men but not enough war material. When he asked what the international situation of Hungary was, this was pictured in more

[69] Resolutions of 20 and 21 Dec. 1918, report of 8 Feb. 1919: ibid., Protokolle über die Sitzungen des Vollzugsausschusses der Soldatenräte der Volkswehr Wiens, p. 19; Kriegsarchiv, Staatsamt für Heerwesen 1918, Fasz. 9; Landesbefehlshaber Wien 1919, Fasz. 21; in general, Ursula Freise, 'Die Tätigkeit der alliierten Kommissionen in Wien nach dem ersten Weltkreig', Ph.D. thesis, Vienna 1963, MS. pp. 6–7.

than rosy light, as the Slovaks were revolting against the Czechs and the outbreak of the revolution in Rumania was 'a question of days, perhaps of hours'. Bolgár also doubted whether the Entente had any reliable troops at its disposal to suppress the revolution. In April Frey himself headed another delegation sent to Budapest which enquired there whether Hungary could guarantee to supply Austria with the same quantity of food as the Entente countries if the Austrian working class joined the Hungarian Soviet Republic, but the answer was negative.[70] Communist influence within the *Volkswehr* actually diminished when hundreds of volunteers left for Hungary, where two Austrian regiments were formed. On 2 April alone, 1,300 volunteers crossed the frontier into Hungary; eighty soldiers left from Battalion 41, ninety from the five battalions of *Kreis* B. But the total number is almost impossible to determine. In the barracks of Battalion 41 a recruiting office for Hungary was opened, and those leaving the battalion were immediately replaced by new men.[71] When the volunteers returned they were interned and interrogated. It then turned out that the majority had not gone to Hungary 'out of enthusiasm for the Communist principles, but rather in the hope of ample food and pay', which consisted of seventy crowns per day. As the police further reported, many of the volunteers were disillusioned and 'did not conceal their aversion to the Hungarian Soviet government'. There had actually been a mutiny in an Austrian unit fighting against the Rumanians and many had been shot.[72]

It may be that Frey too returned disillusioned from his mission to Budapest. In any case he declared in the Executive Committee in April that he could not work with the Communists, that all their promises were entirely false, and that he must resign because he could not bear the responsibility for things staged by the Communists without any prior consultation. On the following day Deutsch summoned a plenary meeting of the soldiers' councils and asked them for a vote of confidence, which he was given. A few days later Frey was re-elected chairman of the Executive Committee by nine votes to three.[73] During the interval there had been violent Communist

[70] Verwaltungsarchiv, Protokolle über die Sitzungen des Vollzugsausschusses der Soldatenräte der Volkswehr Wiens, 27–28 Mar. 1919; Böhm, *Im Kreuzfeuer zweier Revolutionen*, pp. 386–7.

[71] Reports of 2, 4 and 6 Apr., 7 July 1919: Verwaltungsarchiv, Staatsamt des Innern, 22/Nö, box 5066; Kriegsarchiv, Staatsamt für Heerwesen 1919, Fasz. 200; Landesbefehlshaber Wien 1919, Fasz. 26.

[72] Police report of 12 July 1919: Archiv der Bundespolizeidirektion Wien, Nachlass Schober, Polit. Informationen 1919.

[73] Protocols of 15 and 24 Apr. 1919: Verwaltungsarchiv, Protokolle über die

demonstrations. On 17 April the demonstrators attacked the police, and according to the police report about fifty men of Battalion 41 then came to their aid. *Volkswehr* units were called in when the demonstrators broke into the parliament building and tried to set it on fire. These units quickly and efficiently restored order. The men of Battalion 6, many of whom served although they were off duty, distinguished themselves in the process; but a company of Battalion 13 had to be dissolved by order of the Viennese command; all those suspected of participating in the events of 17 April were dismissed from the *Volkswehr*.[74] The vice-president of the International Red Cross who visited Vienna during these days allegedly reported on his return that the government 'was unable to control troops which had practically become Red Guards', that the '*Volkswehr* had broken into Reichsrath, had ejected the deputies and had carried out scandalous orgy which had lasted throughout night. . . '.[75] Although there is no certainty what the vice-president reported, this was the form in which the scandalous news of a *Volkswehr* orgy reached the Foreign Office. If it were believed there, Austria must have seemed well on its way towards joining the Hungarian Soviet Republic.

In reality, however, the Viennese *Volkswehr* continued to be strongly Social Democratic in its politics and in general to be more concerned with pay and conditions of service than with political issues, as was only natural in a city where the severe shortage of food and coal took precedence over everything else. When their ire was aroused the men would take militant action, either against the left or against the right. At a Communist meeting in the Prater a member of a soldiers' council interrupted the speaker but was set upon by Communists; bleeding heavily he escaped and went to a nearby barracks to seek help. He reappeared accompanied by a detachment armed with loaded rifles and bayonets. A policeman went inside to inform the chairman that the *Volkswehr* had arrived in strength and asked him to apologize and to let the maltreated soldier address the meeting. This was accordingly done, the allegations of the Com-

Sitzungen des Vollzugsausschusses der Soldatenräte der Volkswehr Wiens; Haas, 'Studien zur Wehrpolitik . . .', p. 71.

[74] Reports of 11, 18 and 19 Apr. 1919: Verwaltungsarchiv, Staatsamt des Innern, 22/Nö, box 5066; Kriegsarchiv, Landesbefehlshaber Wien 1919, Fasz. 24; Staatsamt für Heerwesen 1919, Fasz. 201.

[75] Lord Acton to Foreign Office, Berne, 27 Apr. 1919, referring to information received from Prof. Lammasch who had also drawn the parallel between conditions in Austria and in Hungary: PRO, FO 371, Austria-Hungary, vol. 3530, no. 65363. It is possible that Prof. Lammasch deliberately misinformed Lord Acton for political reasons, as seems indicated by his remark that the conditions at Salzburg(!) 'were similar to those prevailing at Budapesth'.

munist speaker were 'refuted', and the detachment withdrew. When the *Staatswehr*, a right-wing paper, published an article on 28 February headed 'A Decoration for Burglary' which sharply attacked allegedly criminal elements in the *Volkswehr* and suggested that they be awarded a special medal, this was heatedly debated in a meeting of Battalion 1. The Communists moved that the editorial offices of the paper be demolished, but this did not find substantial support. A few days later, however, about a hundred soldiers led by a sergeant assembled with the intention of making the editor account for the article. Most of them belonged to the third company and its officers were invited to join the expedition; one readily agreed and another went to inform the superior authorities. The commanding officer and all available members of the soldiers' council hastily went along so as to prevent any excess. But they were unable to stop the work of systematic demolition in the editorial offices which proceeded calmly and orderly, according to plan. Not even the police could find any reason to intervene. The Executive Committee condemned the action for political reasons but considered that it was entirely understandable. In the eyes of the *Volkswehr* command, it was inaugurated and led by the sergeant 'who on previous occasions too had emerged as a particularly radical proponent of Communist ideas': his extremism was doing more damage than good to the cause of the *Volkswehr*.[76]

In May Julius Deutsch, the Defence Minister, informed the cabinet that for months there had been demands for an increase in pay, fixed at six to seven crowns a day when the *Volkswehr* was formed and since increased to seven crowns for those receiving less, and that these demands were now being pressed most forcefully on account of rapidly rising prices and the recently increased salaries of railway and state servants. After a debate the cabinet agreed to grant four crowns a day to each man for an improvement of their food. At that time the Viennese *Volkswehr* still numbered 14,000 men and 1,170 officers.[77] The issue of a reduction continued to figure prominently in the debates, the Italians demanding a reduction to 12,000 by 1 June. Members of the Executive Committee urged the units to comply because non-compliance would cause the Entente to stop food shipments to Vienna and thus provoke the hatred of the whole population against the *Volkswehr*. But in spite of these pleas *Kreis* D,

[76] Reports of 6 March and 11 Apr. 1919: Kriegsarchiv, Landesbefehlshaber Wien 1919, Fasz. 26; Verwaltungsarchiv, Staatsamt des Innern, 22/Nö, box 5066.
[77] Cabinet meeting of 13 May 1919: Verwaltungsarchiv, Kabinettsratsprotokolle, box 5.

which comprised seven battalions, decided, on the motion of a captain, to disregard the order for a reduction. Other Viennese *Kreise*, however, were more pliant; *Kreis* A reported a reduction by 26.5 per cent, and *Kreis* B by as much as 39.5. But the representatives of Battalion 41 declined to carry out any reduction, and the other battalions of *Kreis* D followed suit. All they would agree to was not to replace the men discharged or leaving voluntarily.[78]

In Vienna complaints continued to be raised about the *Volkswehr*, especially its activities in searching passengers suspected of carrying illicit food obtained in the country, or the flats of suspected food hoarders and traders, many of the complaints emanating from the police. Other complaints concerned smoking while on guard duty, soldiers playing football in the street and impeding traffic, and the molesting of passing girls by soldiers guarding the military court:[79] in general minor matters, and proof of continuing friction between soldiers and police. A letter written by a military official lamented the fact that the government had no power to cope with Czech encroachments, for no one would seriously compare the *Volkswehr* with an army—except that the former was much more expensive: the causes of this misery are 'the accursed destruction of the army and the fact that nothing useful has been put in its place, and exactly as in Germany the nebulous international socialist bustle'.[80] But the Viennese *Volkswehr* was far from nebulous and had become a well-disciplined, efficient force. When Colonel Haas inspected the different battalions his reports about at least six of them were almost entirely favourable. Battalions 14 and 17 were 'excellent in every respect'; the soldiers' council of battalion 14 assured him that they had the men entirely in their hands and that they were completely reliable. Battalion 15 also 'made a good impression' on the inspecting officer, but its soldiers' council admitted that they had the men only 'fifty-fifty' in their hands. Battalions 7, 13 and 24, on the other hand, 'with regard to discipline and training stand . . . on such a high level as I have not yet observed in any *Volkswehr* formation. The whole bearing of the men was military in the best sense of the term'. The soldiers' councils of these three battalions, he continued his report, supported the officers, exercised the best influence on the men and furthered their material welfare. The men made a satisfied impression

[78] Protocols of 21 May and 12 June 1919: ibid., Protokolle von Sitzungen der Soldatenräte des Kreises D der Volkswehr.
[79] Polizeidirektion Wien to Staatsamt für Heerwesen, 8 June 1919: Kriegsarchiv, Staatsamt für Heerwesen 1919, Fasz. 197.
[80] Letter of 3 Dec. 1918, ibid., Fasz. 198.

and had no complaints—a circumstance he attributed above all to the food which 'in quality and quantity represents a maximum achievement'.[81]

The solution found in Vienna to the problem of raising a new army and providing military security differed radically from the solution adopted in Germany. It proved that there was a viable alternative to the course followed by Ebert and Noske, that close cooperation with the old officer corps was not inevitable. But it has to be borne in mind too that the Austrian Socialists were not hopelessly split, that the Social Democratic leaders did not have to look continuously over their shoulder at what the left-wing extremists might be attempting, and that the Austrian army had disintegrated so quickly and completely that its resurrection would have been a hopeless task. When Deutsch sent his adjutant to Berlin to express the Austrians' apprehensions about the counter-revolutionary Free Corps there was a heated discussion and Noske suggested that the Austrians had better look after their own affairs. When the emissary remarked that the Free Corps would destroy the republic, Noske replied: 'That is my worry. The Free Corps leaders are better Germans than the Spartacists'.[82]

[81] Landesbefehlshaber Wien to Staatsamt für Heerwesen, 1 Apr. and 5 July 1919: ibid., Fasz. 200. It should be noted that the Battalions 14, 15 and 17 visited in March belonged to the politically radical *Kreis* D which declined to carry out a reduction. These two inspection reports are the only ones I have been able to find in the files of the Kriegsarchiv, although the other battalions too must have been inspected by the Landesbefehlshaber or his representatives.

[82] Braunthal, *Auf der Suche nach dem Millennium*, pp. 232–4, reporting his conversation with Noske in March 1919.

4 The Austrian Workers' Councils

In both Germany and Austria some workers' councils came into being during the strikes of January 1918, but during the following months they were dormant and only revived at the time of the military collapse. In November 1918 workers' councils spontaneously sprang up everywhere, the workers in the factories electing representatives who then constituted the local workers' council. In Germany, they usually formed, together with the soldiers' delegates, a local workers' and soldiers' council; but in Austria this occurred less frequently. The two branches usually remained separate for the time being, and the workers' councils only acquired strong influence locally, above all in Upper Austria and some towns of Lower Austria, such as Wiener Neustadt. There the workers' councils were active in administrative matters and were represented on local administrative organs. At Wiener Neustadt a radical workers' council even made the carrying out of Social Democratic Party decisions dependent on its consent.[1] In Vienna, on the other hand, the party was very much the senior partner and throughout maintained its dominant influence within the workers' council, to which at the outset only party members were admitted. In contrast with Germany, the Austrian workers' councils acquired a national organization comparatively late, in the spring of 1919, when the revolutionary impetus had subsided. While in Germany a national congress of the workers' and soldiers' councils met five weeks after the outbreak of the revolution and elected a 'Central Council of the German Socialist Republic', the first all-Austrian conference of the workers' councils was only held in March 1919, and without any soldiers' representatives; it then regulated the election of workers' councils on the local, district and provincial levels—a process that had taken place in Germany many months before.

It may well have been the reluctance of the Social Democratic leaders which caused this slow development. Not that the German

[1] Oskar Helmer, *50 Jahre erlebte Geschichte*, Vienna, 1957, p. 84; Staudinger, 'Die Ereignisse in den Ländern . . .', p. 82.

Social Democrats were enthusiastically for the councils, but their hand was forced by a spontaneous mass movement and by their left-wing rivals—factors which hardly existed in Austria. There the party throughout was the dominant factor in the left-wing movement and in addition possessed its own apparatus in the factories in the form of trusties (*Vertrauensmänner*). From its point of view, there was no need for another organization which might be a rival and less amenable to control. Indeed, in the summer of 1919 'grave dissatisfaction' arose among these factory trusties 'that the party organization was pushed aside' by the workers' councils: a change must be brought about 'if the party organization is not to collapse'. But characteristically no decision was taken by the party executive to which this was reported. Five weeks before, Karl Seitz had declared at another meeting of the executive that the party must define its attitude towards the workers' councils and must be informed of what happened there.[2] In spite of this no decision was reached, probably on account of differences of opinion between the left and right wings of the party. As to the latter, the State Chancellor Dr Renner later in 1919 expressed to the British High Commissioner in Vienna his dislike of the councils in no un-certain terms: 'He had always known that the Councils would soon discredit themselves and he hoped the time would come to suppress them entirely before long. . .'.[3] His attitude does not seem to have differed from that adopted by Ebert and Scheidemann. If Renner at the same time informed the High Commissioner 'that many Bolshe-viks had been elected to the Workmens' Councils', this was only correct in a very limited sense: the Communists had just gained 10 per cent of the seats in the Viennese district workers' councils, 499 out of a total of 4,921—not a very impressive performance at a time of severe economic difficulties—while the Social Democrats still mustered over 88 per cent.[4]

If the right-wing Social Democrats were hostile to the workers' councils, these found ardent champions among the left-wingers, mainly Jewish intellectuals, such as Dr Max Adler and Dr Josef Frey. Outstanding among them was Dr Friedrich Adler, the hero of the anti-war movement, who was freed from prison on 1 November and enjoyed such prestige that he was immediately offered the leadership

[2] Parteiarchiv der SPÖ, Sitzungsprotokolle des Parteivorstandes, 23 June and 1 Aug. 1919.

[3] F.O. Lindley to Lord Curzon, s.d.: PRO, FO 371, Austria-Hungary, vol. 3532, no. 157465 (Nov. 1919).

[4] Figures given in *Protokoll der Verhandlungen der Parteitages der sozialdemokratischen Arbeiterpartei Deutschösterreichs . . . vom 5. bis zum 7. November 1920*, Vienna, 1920, p. 30.

of the nascent Communist Party. This he declined, for he was determined to work 'for the international revolutionary programme of
Social Democracy' within the party, as he explained at a meeting of
the Viennese workers' council on 6 November.[5] He thus showed far
more political realism than the corresponding figure in Germany,
Karl Liebknecht, who by his courageous action had become the
spokesman of anti-war longing and political protest, and who—like
Adler—was the son of the party's founding father. While Liebknecht
was to die in the aftermath of a disastrous political venture, Adler
determinedly set his face against any political adventurism. It was
on his initiative that the Viennese workers' council in June 1919,
when the Communists were preparing a *Putsch*, adopted this resolution with an enormous majority:

> Only the Viennese Workers' Council can decide on the tactics of
> the Viennese working class and therewith on the question whether
> the rule of the proletariat in Vienna is appropriate. The Workers'
> Council is the place where the differences of opinion within the
> Viennese working class must and will be discussed. Therefore the
> Workers' Council in advance refutes any attempt of certain small
> groups to use violence against the working class. The recent de-
> velopments within the Communist Party provide ample ground
> for the fear that this is being planned. . . . The Viennese working
> class is conscious of the duty of international solidarity. . . . But it
> protests in the strongest possible manner that its political fate
> should be decided upon by the dictation of men who do not know
> the conditions existing in German Austria and know very little
> about socialism. The Workers' Council declares that it alone is
> the body responsible for the decisions of the Viennese working
> class. It expects that the Communists will uphold their cause
> within, and not against the Workers' Council. . . .[6]

Apart from Vienna and the Wiener Neustadt area, the workers'
councils were particularly strong in Linz; but even here they were
preceded by a soldiers' council formed on 1 November. On 26
November the two councils had their first joint meeting which
elected two separate chairmen and a small committee with seven
representatives each of the trade unions and the Social Democratic
Party. At a meeting held in January one of them remarked that the
party had moved too far to the right so that the Communists were

[5] Karl Heinz, 'Geschichte der österreichischen Arbeiterräte', MS, p. 38, Arbeiterkammer Wien; Gulick, *Austria from Habsburg* . . . , i, p. 72.
[6] Resolution of 13 June 1919, quoted by Julius Braunthal, *Die Arbeiterräte in
Deutschösterreich*, Vienna, 1919, p. 50; Botz, 'Beiträge zur Geschichte . . .', iii, pp.
45–6. The resolution was adopted by 235 against 27 Communist votes.

gaining ground in the larger factories: a turn towards the left was therefore necessary. Soon after, the chairman of the workers' council emphasized that they would only protect what was in their own interest, hence neither the exploiters nor the present form of state; but they would support the *Volkswehr* in its fight against looting and anarchy, and cooperate with it in maintaining law and order.[7] The Communist danger was also taken seriously by the *Land* government. In February there were rumours of a Spartacus revolt inspired from Germany, and the government got in touch with the workers' council, which had heard the same reports. It therefore summoned the workers' trusties and the local Communist leaders and soon found out that there were no such plans. They even agreed not to undertake anything without prior consultation with the workers' and soldiers' council. The mayor thought the food situation so desperate that a few determined men might be able to separate the workers from their elected leaders; the worst might happen because of the general misery. The representative of the workers' council considered the local Communists harmless; their Communism consisted entirely of attacks on the Social Democrats.[8] In fact, only 4 per cent (13 out of 310 members) of the Linz workers' council were Communists. In new elections to the council held in October 1919 the Communists obtained 11, and the Social Democrats 89 per cent of the votes,[9] virtually the same as in Vienna a few weeks later.

From Linz, too, came an initiative for a meeting of all the Austrian workers' councils. In February 1919 a conference was held there which, characteristically enough, requested the Social Democratic Party Executive to summon an all-Austrian conference of the councils.[10] When it met on 1 March only the industrial areas—Upper and Lower Austria, parts of Styria—were in fact strongly represented, and all delegates were Social Democrats, as membership of the party and a trade union was a pre-condition of election. On the initiative of Friedrich Adler who emerged as the leading personality on the left, this rule was now changed to permit Communist representation: in future all those could be elected 'who recognized that the elimination of the capitalist mode of production was the goal and the class struggle the means of emancipation of the working people, who were

---

[7] Meetings of 26 Nov. 1918, 14 Jan. and 10 Feb. 1919: Parteiarchiv der SPÖ, Protokolle der Arbeiterräte Oberösterreichs, i.

[8] Meeting of 19 Feb. 1919: Oberösterreich. Landesarchiv, k.k. Statthalterei, Präsidium, no. 114.

[9] Report of 14 Oct. 1919: Protokolle der Arbeiterräte Oberöstereichs, ii; Braunthal, *Arbeiterräte* . . . , p. 7.

[10] Bauer, *Österreich. Revolution*, p. 139; Braunthal, *Arbeiterräte* . . . , p. 5.

members of a trade union and over twenty years old. . . .' On the basis of this decision new elections were to be held so that another national conference could take place. In Adler's view the councils were to provide the common ground where Social Democrats and Communists could meet; in the councils, the majority decision could be imposed on the minority, thus avoiding the fratricidal struggle which engulfed the German working-class movement. More important from the Austrian point of view were the questions of the army and of the peasantry. Deutsch emphasized strongly that workers and soldiers belonged together: 'only when the soldiers do not make their own policy, but a workers' policy, only then will the revolution be secure. . . .' He did not indicate how this was to be achieved in a country which was so partially industrialized. A speaker from Linz and another from Leoben pointed out that most peasants were 'reactionary', that it would be impossible to win them to socialism, that peasant councils would only 'dilute' the workers' councils. At Linz requisitioning committees had been founded as direct links to the peasants; but clearly on this vital issue workers and peasants had interests diametrically opposed to each other, and there was little hope of splitting the peasantry along social lines, as the smallholders would see eye to eye with their wealthier neighbours. The conference also protested against 'the violation of the German workers of Bohemia and the Sudetenland' who 'by force of arms have been prevented from participation', and for whom six seats were reserved on the provisional national committee elected at the end.[11]

Between this meeting and the second national conference at the end of June two events of vital importance to the workers' councils occurred in neighbouring countries: the proclamation first of the Hungarian, and then of the Munich Soviet republic. On 22 March the proclamation of the Béla Kun government 'To All' reached Vienna, and the provisional national committee under Adler's guidance took it upon itself to declare that the establishment of a proletarian dictatorship was impossible in an Austria which entirely depended on food deliveries by the Entente countries. On the twenty-third the *Arbeiter-Zeitung* published on its front page Adler's reply to the Hungarian proletariat:

> You have issued the call to us to follow your example. We would joyfully do so but unfortunately cannot at the moment. In our country there is no food. Even our meagre bread ration depends

[11] Karl Heinz, 'Geschichte . . .', MS. pp. 48, 51, 66, 70–2, Arbeiterkammer Wien; Rolf Reventlow, *Zwischen Alliierten und Bolschewiken*, Vienna, 1969, pp. 51–6.

upon the food trains sent to us by the Entente. Thus we are entirely the slaves of the Entente. . . . We are convinced that the Russian Soviet Republic would do everything in its power to help us. But before that help could reach us we would have starved. Thus we are in a much more difficult position than you. Our dependence upon the Entente is a total one. . . . All our wishes are with you. With burning hearts we follow events and hope that the cause of socialism will triumph. . . .

In April telegram after telegram arrived from Munich, Passau and other Bavarian towns that Vienna should follow suit and proclaim a Soviet republic, but the national committee did not waver. Like the soldiers' councils of Vienna it established personal links with Budapest to find out whether the propaganda slogan that Hungary would supply a Soviet Austria with food was justified. The reports of those returning made clear that for some weeks Hungary would be able to provide Vienna with food for one day per week. On another occasion Vilmos Böhm, responsible for the military administration of the Hungarian Red Army, gave to the provisional national committee a detailed report on the military situation which seems to have been equally realistic. In any case, the committee did not change its attitude.[12]

This line was strongly endorsed by the second national conference of the workers' councils which met in Vienna at the end of June, this time with Communist representation. On the second day a Communist resolution was presented which demanded, in the name of 'the revolutionary proletariat assembled in front of the town hall', that the Social Democrats immediately leave the coalition government, that the workers' councils seize power and establish a Soviet dictatorship. Adler replied that the 4,000 assembled at the town hall were not the Viennese working class:

And we see that in different parts of German Austria, in Upper Austria, Salzburg, Tyrol, Styria, everywhere the bourgoisie and peasantry are constantly active with the aim of separating from the state. If we here proclaimed today a Soviet republic, as the Communists desire, the result would be that it could be proclaimed in fact in Vienna and in some industrial districts of Lower Austria, but that not a socialist proletarian German Austria would emerge but an enlarged Commune of Vienna. . . .

In general much of the conference's time was spent on heated

[12] *Arbeiter-Zeitung*, 23 Mar. 1919; Adler's report to the second conference of the workers' councils: Arbeiterkammer Wien, Stenographisches Protokoll der II. Reichskonferenz der Arbeiterräte Deutschösterreichs, pp. 28–32.

discussions between Social Democrats and Communists. One delegate was entirely justified when he complained bitterly that there had been no time to discuss the tasks of the workers' councils or to adopt a working programme for them because the conference constantly had to oppose tactics 'which under the appearance of revolutionary slogans and revolutionary aims prevented it from taking the most simple step on the road to revolutionary action'. The conference expected from the Communists that they would defend their case within the councils, but not against them. But the Communists even declined to be represented on the new National Executive Committee, although some seats were offered to them by Adler. As on the provisional national committee, the majority of its members came from Vienna and Lower Austria.[13]

The conference did provide a clear picture of the activities of the workers' councils in the different parts of Austria. The progress recorded was extremely uneven. The Tyrol was not represented at all: as Adler stated, it presented 'in general a chapter of its own'. The representative of Styria gave a lengthy report on the local situation and the activities of the Workers' Auxiliary Corps of Graz, but at the end admitted that workers' councils had only been elected in the large industrial centres and 'as such had not yet developed any activity'. The Carinthian representative complained that their activities were vastly hampered by the state of war which still existed there. Twenty local councils had been elected, and close links with the soldiers' council established at Villach. As the local authorities' attitude was still partly or totally 'imperial and royal', the workers' councils had sent delegates to supervise the local authorities, and this caused bitter enmity between them and the councils. The workers' councils also strenuously opposed schemes to make Carinthia independent and to separate from Vienna and maintained the closest links with the Social Democratic Party: without the party they would not undertake anything. In small Vorarlberg, on the other hand, there were twenty-three local councils which had separated from the peasant councils. When the Munich Councils' Republic was proclaimed there was a marked tendency to combine with Bavaria, but this called forth a strong counter-movement, and a common demonstration with the Bavarians at Bregenz on 1 May was prohibited by the government. The executive of the workers' council had to use all its influence to prove that in this small rural *Land* the pre-

[13] ibid., 2. Sitzung, 1 July 1919, pp. 1, 115; 3. Sitzung, p. 130; 4. Sitzung, pp. 47–8, 70, 78, 80.

conditions for the establishment of a proletarian dictatorship were entirely lacking.[14]

Similar tendencies existed in Salzburg. The local workers' council had sent a representative to Munich at the time of the Councils' Republic where he talked to Social Democrats and members of the Peasant League; he found the large mass of the Munich workers completely indifferent to the idea of the councils, and conditions there chaotic. The Salzburg council was active in questions of food distribution, housing and welfare matters, and had prevented evictions; its representatives were supervising the various local authorities, even military affairs. A representative also mentioned strong feelings against Vienna and the Viennese Jews, not only on the side of the bourgeois parties. The most active workers' councils existed in Upper Austria. But their sphere of activity was largely social welfare, unemployment benefits, housing, price control, and food provisioning. In negotiations with the *Land* government during the same month the Linz council had achieved an increase in unemployment benefits; and its chairman boasted that the town council would not dare to decide anything of vital importance to the workers without the consent of the workers' council. This council also played an active part in preventing the shedding of blood during the food riots of February and in restoring order. It had 310 members, 295 of whom belonged to the Social Democratic Party; 70 of the members were intellectuals. Outside Linz there were 84 local workers' councils grouped under district councils. As might be expected, there was a good deal of friction with the local peasant councils which demanded recognition of their rights. Milk deliveries were a particularly sore point. In the opinion of the Linz council, deliveries were sabotaged by the wealthy peasants, while the smallholders were more accommodating; the workers' councils in rural areas were too weak and only looked after the interests of their own communities. The peasants demanded a doubling of the milk price as a pre-condition of increased deliveries, but after lengthy negotiations with the Linz council they were satisfied with an increase of 50 per cent. In exchange the workers' council expected that the peasants too would combat the illicit food trade, but it is not recorded whether this was actually achieved.[15]

[14] ibid., 1. Sitzung, pp. 5, 41–55, 69–70; report of Landesvollzugsausschuss der Arbeiterräte Vorarlberg, s.d., Parteiarchiv der SPÖ; Braunthal, *Arbeiterräte . . .*, pp. 7–8.
[15] Arbeiterkammer Wien, Stenographisches Protokoll der II. Reichskonferenz . . . , 1. Sitzung, pp. 36–9, 63–5; 3. Sitzung, pp. 4–7; Parteiarchiv der SPÖ, Protokolle der Arbeiterräte Oberösterreichs, under 6 May, 7, 8, 29 July 1919.

The Linz workers' council in any case proved that it did fulfil very useful functions, especially at a time of great economic stress and a more or less passive attitude on the side of the local authorities. That the *Land* government resented this 'interference' is shown by the fact that at least one *Bezirkshauptmann* was instructed by telephone not to tolerate it any longer.[16]

With regard to the vital issues of food and the peasantry, Adler had to admit that socialist peasant councils did not really exist anywhere; where there were peasant councils they had usually been created for reactionary purposes. Another report delivered at the national conference stated that if the workers' councils had achieved recognition and were active in food questions, this was only the case because the bureaucracy had capitulated and was only too glad to receive help from them. The peasant councils were as strongly opposed to the bureaucracy as the workers' councils, and on this basis there existed the possibility of cooperation with them. The best means to increase food deliveries might be the Agrarian Commissions set up in Upper and Lower Austria to supervise food transports and the distribution of delivery quotas. In these commissions the representatives of the workers', the soldiers' and the peasant councils not only had a vote but they also had to take part in the practical work. This met with the opposition of the *Bezirkshauptleute* 'who still considered themselves the dictators of the old Austria' and were disregarding all demands for self-government. On the local level similar commissions were planned for each commune, and a start had been made with them in Upper and Lower Austria. In general, there was a tendency for each district to look after its own interests and to starve Vienna. But the Communists were opposed to any cooperation and any coming to terms with the bureaucracy which in their eyes amounted to a recognition of the existing social order. They put forward a motion that no one elected to a representative institution on the local, provincial or national level could be elected to a workers' council, and that any member who became a candidate or was elected to such an institution would automatically lose his seat on the workers' council. If adopted this motion would have barred the majority of the Social Democratic leaders, but it was defeated by 89 to 28 votes.[17]

[16] Bezirkshauptmannschaft Eferding to Land government, 11 Mar. 1919: Oberösterreich. Landesarchiv, k.k. Statthalterei, Präsidium, no. 401.

[17] Arbeiterkammer Wien, Stenographisches Protokoll der II. Reichskonferenz . . . , 1. Sitzung, pp. 85–6, 122, 129; 2. Sitzung, pp. 66–7; 4. Sitzung, pp. 1–7, 12; the government of Lower Austria to the Vienna workers' council, 16 Mar. 1919: Parteiarchiv der SPÖ, Anträge an den Kreisarbeiterrat Wien.

In general the conference showed that the workers' councils played an active and useful part in certain areas of Austria, that the Communists had some influence within them only in Vienna and some parts of Lower Austria, and that the left-wing Social Democrats led by Adler remained firmly in control. Indeed, in contrast with the first national conference, there had been no prominent speaker from the party's right wing.

In July another clash between Social Democrats and Communists occurred in the Vienna workers' council. From Moscow and from Budapest the idea of an international sympathy strike for the Russian and Hungarian proletariat was propagated; the Communists moved that this strike take place in Austria on 21 July, and were supported by some Viennese Social Democrats. On 12 July, however, the motion was lost by 105 to 76 votes in the Vienna district council; instead it decided to hold mass demonstrations on Sunday, 20 July. But some days later the vote was reversed and it was resolved by 142 to 104 votes to strike on Monday. This decision was carried out and many towns of Upper and Lower Austria followed suit, but elsewhere the local workers' councils voted against.[18] In October the same Vienna district council passed a strongly worded resolution against any attempt to bring about the rule of one class which would lead to civil war and the victory of the counter-revolution; hence it was unfortunately necessary to continue the coalition government as long as the vital interests of the working class were protected; in the present historical situation neither the rule of the working class nor that of the bourgeoisie was possible in German Austria.[19] At the end of 1919 Adler stated to a German audience at Leipzig that in Austria the system of the workers' councils was functioning well and that it provided an opportunity to unite the different proletarian forces for common action, to create a united front with the Communists against the danger of counter-revolution and to reach agreements with them.[20] It may indeed have been the German experience of open civil war which induced Adler and others like him to cooperate with the Communists in the councils and even to make certain concessions to them. But such an attitude would only have increased the suspicions of the right-wing Social Democrats and their disinclination to support the workers' councils.

In March 1919 a workers', peasants' and soldiers' council was also

[18] Botz, 'Beiträge zur Geschichte . . .', MS., pp. 135–7.
[19] Karl Heinz, 'Geschichte . . .', MS., p. 256, Arbeiterkammer Wien.
[20] *Unabhängige Sozialdemokratische Partei Deutschlands: Protokoll über die Verhandlungen des ausserordentlichen Parteitages vom 30. Nov. bis 6. Dez. 1919*, Berlin, s.d., p. 75.

founded at Innsbruck. The decision to do so was taken by the assembled trusties of the Social Democratic Party; the workers' council was to consist of two representatives each of every local workers' organization, and every local branch of officials was offered the same right. The new organization considered that its primary task was to prevent, if possible, any disturbance of law and order such as had occurred elsewhere; and, in view of the grave economic difficulties, it invited the authorities to cooperate with it. The 'action programme' of the council aimed, above all, at food control: all food stocks in shops, inns and depots should be listed; all larger stocks of non-rationed food should be taken over and offered to the general public at fixed and reasonable prices; all food, except only some luxury items, should be rationed and all food prices reduced; all public offices concerned with food collection and distribution should be controlled by delegates of the council who were to be paid from public funds and be entitled to inspect food shops. Apart from the Social Democratic organizations, however, only the German Liberals were willing to participate in the council's work, while the majority party, the Christian Social or Tyrolese People's Party, declined to do so. The speakers of the council, on the other hand, always emphasized that it was not the institution of one party and that it did not attempt to follow the examples of Russia, Hungary or Bavaria. As the deputy mayor of Innsbruck put it: 'In the Tyrol too the new time would dawn, not according to the Russian-Bolshevik pattern, but as the Social Democrats were envisaging it, with all the means at their disposal. . .'. It is not surprising, then, that the *Land* government took a decidedly cool view of the new institution. It declared that it would welcome any cooperation but 'only on its instructions and within the framework of the law. . . . The delegation of power must emanate from the *Land* government and any activity take place within the framework of its orders. . . '.[21]

In Vienna too, the activities of the councils were to a large extent connected with the severe food shortage and the never-ending attempts of the population to obtain some food from the countryside. Thousands and thousands went by train or any other means in search of food, but at the stations there were constant searches and confiscations, usually by *Volkswehr* detachments which at times appropriated some of the goods confiscated. Naturally, complaints never ceased, and it took several months before some order was brought into these

[21] *Innsbrucker Nachrichten*, 14 Mar., 1 and 4 Apr. 1919; letters of 12 and 14 Apr. 1919: Landesregierungsarchiv Tirol, Präsidialakten 1919, XII. 76.c.2.

procedures. The same applied to the searches for food in shops and houses which were undertaken by the *Volkswehr*, often together with members of a workers' council, but often without notifying the police in advance, or at least informing the authorities afterwards about the measures taken. In several cases where horses had been slaughtered illicitly the *Volkswehr* appeared and confiscated the meat, presumably using it for its own purposes. The municipal authorities bitterly complained that they were not notified and hence were unable to take procedures against the culprits. But a police report had to admit in March 1919 that the searches and checks by the *Volkswehr* aroused enormous interest, that they caused a lot of disquiet among the well-to-do, but were acclaimed by the mass of the people. The same, however, did not necessarily apply to the checking of the rucksacks of people reaching Vienna, as the victims of these searches often belonged to the lower classes or were unemployed men who tried in this way to augment their meagre income.[22]

The government equally tried to regulate the procedure in searches for food. In March a meeting took place in the Ministry of Food with representatives of the *Volkswehr* and of the Executive Committee of the soldiers' councils; a mixed commission was to be established in the *Kriegswucheramt* of the Vienna police on which the soldiers' councils were to be strongly represented, but the councils turned down this proposal. A few days later, however, the representatives of the *Volkswehr* in principle recognized that the *Kriegswucheramt* was competent to undertake official searches. Police President Schober strongly complained that most of the searches served no purpose and that the position of the police was made untenable by the *Volkswehr* whose activities proceeded without any plan and prevented the police from attending to their proper duties. Chancellor Renner considered that the action of the *Volkswehr* was an act of self-help because the population attributed the disastrous state of affairs to the inability of the authorities to organize the even distribution of food and to prevent illicit trading. He suggested the appointment of a commission for each district of Vienna, on which not only the police and the rationing authority but the workers and perhaps the *Volkswehr* should be represented, a suggestion which was supported by several members of the cabinet. At the same time the Executive Committee of the soldiers' councils took action to curtail the spon-

[22] 'Stimmungsbericht' of 19 Mar. and report of Bezirksamt für den III. Bezirk of 1 Apr. 1919: Botz, 'Beiträge zur Geschichte . . .', iii, p. 22; Archiv der Bundespolizeidirektion Wien, Verwaltung 1919, Präsidial-Akte, box 10; Reventlow, *Zwischen Alliierten . . .*, p. 104.

taneous activities which aroused the authorities' opposition. The
soldiers' council of each battalion was to nominate three men, who
could, but need not, be from its own members; in future those three
alone would be entitled to carry out searches for food; but searches
of houses and confiscations were only permitted with the cooperation
of the police and only with written authority.[23] Later Deutsch
claimed the credit for the adoption of this procedure, according to
which the police were to act but were to be accompanied by soldiers.
In June the Minister of the Interior suggested that the workers'
councils should be used to combat the exorbitant food prices; but
according to another minister the representatives of the Social
Democratic Party had been reluctant to accept this idea. Finally
representatives of the workers' and the soldiers' councils were delegated into a commission established within the *Kriegswucheramt* which
followed up any complaint received and ordered searches where it
seemed necessary.[24]

This, however, was not the end of the matter. The police continued
to complain about arbitrary actions of the workers' councils, and
their searches and confiscations without asking for police assistance.
In August the shop and flat of a trader were searched by the local
workers' council and 49 kilograms of sugar and quantities of soap,
cigarettes and cigars were confiscated; the goods were deposited in
the office of the workers' council. But when the police officer gave a
permit to the trader's brother to take away a small amount of the
sugar and soap, the council refused to hand over this part to him,
accusing the police of bias. Another workers' council confiscated a
consignment of 5,000 kilograms of prunes and sold them at four
crowns a kilo without informing the police. According to the police,
these were just a few examples out of a very large number of similar
'excesses' committed by workers' councils, especially that of the 11th
district of Vienna. At about the same time several small consignments
of milk destined for the archiepiscopal administration were confiscated at a Viennese station and sent to a local hospital. At another
station one night about four hundred people noisily demonstrated
against the rigorous practices of the workers' councils and the
Volkswehr checking their rucksacks—just one example of many

[23] Verwaltungsarchiv Wien, Kabinettsratsprotokolle, box 5, no. 51 (19 Mar.);
Protokolle über die Sitzungen des Vollzugsausschusses der Soldatenräte der
Volkswehr Wiens (15 Mar. 1919).
[24] ibid., Kabinettsratsprotokolle, box 7, no. 82 (24 June 1919); police report of
1 Sept. 1919: ibid., Pol. Dir. Wien Berichte 1919; Deutsch, *Aus Österreichs Revolution*,
p. 85.

turbulent scenes at the stations, as the police reported. Vociferous protests against the workers' and soldiers' councils 'which are usurping executive power in the state in an entirely unconstitutional and extra-legal fashion and are developing into an irresponsible condominium', also came from a new middle-class organization, the Vienna Burghers' Council. Its leaders urged the middle classes to adopt the council idea and to use it to achieve their own purposes, while they accused the authorities of suffering and even condoning illegal encroachments.[25]

At a time of growing coal and wood shortage the workers' councils also seized large quantities of firewood and sold some of it to the suffering population. In August 1919 alone the police reported the seizure of 151,000 kilograms of fuel, some of which had been sent immediately to the gas and electricity works and some sold for 0.4 crowns a kilo, as well as the seizure of 32,000 kilograms and 21 truckloads of wood which had been similarly distributed.[26] In the *Kriegswucheramt* the delegates of the workers' council urged that the large coal stocks of the black marketeers and war profiteers be seized and sent to the hospitals whose patients were suffering from the intense cold; they submitted lists of large coal deliveries to private households which were to be confiscated. After one month of activity in the local and central offices of the *Kriegswucheramt* the delegates proudly announced that the following quantities of goods had been confiscated: 10,200 kilograms of flour, 15,800 of potatoes, 3,000 of meat and sausages, 2,000 of butter and fat, 230,000 cigarettes and 6,070 cigars, 12,300 pairs of shoes, large quantities of eggs, cheese, soap, coal, wood, petrol, leather and textiles. A similar announcement, again stating the precise quantities seized, was published after the third month. They added that, on account of the extreme shortage of milk, the children and the sick were deprived of tens of thousands of litres which found their way into the black market, that one named trader alone had sold 70 per cent of his milk illicitly, but that this had been stopped by the workers' council.[27]

Another field of activity was the prevention of evictions—one more cause of frequent police complaints. In one instance the district

[25] Police reports of 6 and 29 Aug., 5, 11 and 12 Sept. 1919: Verwaltungsarchiv Wien, Pol. Dir. Wien Berichte 1919; Staatsamt des Innern, 22/Nö, box 5067; Kriegsarchiv, Staatsamt für Heerwesen 1919, Fasz. 196.

[26] Police reports of 29 Aug. and 1 Sept. 1919: Verwaltungsarchiv Wien, Pol. Dir. Wien Berichte 1919.

[27] *Arbeiter-Zeitung*, 3 Dec. 1919, 17 Feb. 1920: reports of the Approvisionierungsausschuss des Kreisarbeiterrates, with many details.

workers' council simply forbade the removal of the furniture of a party to be evicted. In another, where the party had been evicted, a workers' and a soldiers' councillor appeared accompanied by four armed soldiers and ordered the door to be opened and the furniture to be put back. A list compiled in the Ministry of Justice listed twenty-four similar cases for Vienna, and one for Wiener Neustadt. When a flat in the Nobilegasse became vacant two members of the local workers' council accompanied by ten soldiers appeared and, against the owner's wish, allocated it to a war invalid. The district workers' council of Hietzing protested that parts of the palace of Schönbrunn were to be let to middle-class tenants and demanded that the palace must be preserved for 'the children of the proletariat' and not become the object of private letting. Another palace which had been inhabited by Archduke Rainer was claimed by the local workers' council to house invalids.[28] At Graz the workers' council desired that confectioners' shops should be closed so that more sugar could be distributed, but the bourgeois parties vetoed the proposal. Two members of the local council went on a tour of inspection of night clubs and bars and found that they served pastries 'exactly as in time of peace'; everywhere they also found party comrades sitting, and the greeting of 'Servus, comrade' in constant use. But again the proposal of the workers' council that something be done to control places of amusement had no success.[29] In Innsbruck *Volkswehr* men were used to assist the searches carried out by the *Kriegswucheramt*, but as early as June 1919 these services were terminated by the authorities.[30] In practice it was only in Vienna that these activities reached considerable proportions; there even the police finally reached a *modus vivendi* with the representatives of the workers' councils.

Many local workers' councils—like the National Executive—had sub-committees for questions of food, public health, housing, and workers' education. Another committee was formed for the *Ordner-ausschüsse* or *Ordnergruppen*, organized groups of workers responsible for preserving order during demonstrations and protecting meetings against political enemies, especially against attacks of the *Heim-wehren* which sprang up in the countryside. Indeed, the arming of the

[28] Police reports of 17 Aug., 1 Sept., 3 and 25 Oct. 1919, 6 July, 20 Aug. 1920: Verwaltungsarchiv, Pol. Dir. Wien Berichte 1919, Pol. Dir. Wien Berichte 1920; report Staatsamt für Justiz, 19 Apr. 1920: ibid., Staatsamt des Innern, 22/Nö, box 5068; decision of Bezirksarbeiterrat Hietzing, 14 July 1919: Parteiarchiv der SPÖ, Anträge an den Kreisarbeiterrat Wien.
[29] Police report of 27 Feb. 1920: Steiermärk. Landesarchiv, Akten der k.k. Statthalterei, Präsidium, E. 91, 1918 (iv).
[30] Landesregierungsarchiv Tirol, Präsidialakten 1920, XII 76 c (16 June 1919).

peasantry, especially in Carinthia, Styria and the Tyrol, partly as an aftermath of the war but also for internal purposes, dominated the proceedings of the National Workers' Council which met in Vienna in the spring of 1920. Added to this was the controversial issue of armament shipments to 'reactionary' countries, such as Poland or Hungary after the collapse of the Soviet republic, which occupied the workers' councils. Adler reported that in this field the Executive had continuously done practical work, and the meeting demanded that all deliveries of war material to Poland and Hungary be stopped as the Hungarian counter-revolution might combine with its sympathizers in Austria. The representative of Styria reported that there every village was crammed with arms, that machine guns were posted when the Social Democrats held a meeting. The Carinthian representative said that 20,000 rifles destined for the war against Yugoslavia had been distributed among the peasants of villages far removed from the Yugoslav frontier, and that only very recently the Klagenfurt workers' council had confiscated a consignment of 3,000 rifles sent under the seal of the War Ministry; while Dr Frey reported on the armaments of the *Heimatwehr* and the *Standschützen* of the Tyrol. Demands that in view of all this the workers should be armed were received with prolonged applause. Otto Bauer admitted that the power of the left to counteract such tendencies had shrunk and was 'already very small'; but he still hoped that the hour might come when the left could take another step forwards.[31]

Clearly, after Horthy's victory in Hungary and after the Kapp *Putsch* in Berlin, there was a widespread fear that similar attempts would be made in Austria, while other issues receded into the background. Later the workers' councils reported that altogether they had seized 456 railway trucks with war material and 2,000 aeroplane engines which were to be shipped to 'reactionary' countries.[32] Hence the principal activity of the workers' councils came to concentrate on the *Ordnergruppen* which began to receive some kind of military training. But this policy was essentially defensive.

In Austria as well as in Germany, in spite of all political differences, the political pendulum swung to the right in the course of 1919. Thus the workers' councils whose activities in the economic and social fields had been so important, virtually disappeared from the scene or became factory councils without any political influence. It

[31] Parteiarchiv der SPÖ, Stenographisches Protokoll der Tagung des Reichsarbeiterrates, 31 May–2 June 1920, pp. 90, 105, 118, 150, 196, 200, 205, 282, 305, 308.
[32] Reventlow, *Zwischen Alliierten* . . . , pp. 113–14, 130, 139.

was a complete misreading of the situation when the Communist International in the summer of 1920 pronounced that, because of the strength of the workers' councils, the situation in Austria was similar to 'the situation in Russia between February and October 1917. The workers' councils of German Austria represent an important political factor and form the nucleus of the new power'.[33] Even Bauer's hope that the time would come when the left would be able to advance again was not to be fulfilled.

The peasant councils which came into being in certain parts of Austria in 1919 did not give rise to any great activity, and where they did it was above all in opposing the demands of the workers' councils. The representation of the peasants on the Innsbruck workers', peasants' and soldiers' council mentioned above seems to have been purely nominal. The *Land* peasant council of Carinthia only appeared in the files of the authorities when it complained because the military police at Villach came under the orders of the soldiers' council, and not under those of the military command; but even the government had to admit that the military police was working 'very well'.[34] In eastern Styria peasant councils were organized in thirty-nine communes under the direction of the owner of a castle near Graz.[35] But there is no record of what they did.

In Upper Austria, on the other hand, the workers' councils negotiated with the peasant councils, mainly about agricultural prices and deliveries. And the *Landtag* too appealed to the councils of peasants and agricultural workers as well as to the workers' councils to support the authorities when 'irresponsible elements' encouraged the peasants not to fulfil their delivery quotas and to pursue demands which simply could not be granted: the *Landtag* urged the authorities to use force if need be and break all resistance to the carrying out of the food regulations. But fifteen months later there were renewed threats on the side of the peasantry to stop deliveries altogether so as to obtain the abolition of the regulations governing the trade in cattle.[36] The Linz workers' council realized that cooperation with

[33] 'Leitsätze über die Bedingungen, unter welchen Arbeitersowjets geschaffen werden dürfen': *Der zweite Kongress der Kommunist. Internationale—Protokoll der Verhandlungen . . .*, Hamburg, 1921, p. 745. But in the version published in Vienna this sentence is missing: *Der zweite Kongress der Kommunistischen Internationale*, Vienna, 1920, p. 137.

[34] Meeting of the Landesrat, 2 Dec. 1919: Kärntner Landesarchiv, Landesausschuss, Fasz. ii, no. 8.

[35] *Tagespost*, Graz, 12 Nov. 1918.

[36] Meetings of the Upper Austrian Landtag, 11 Sept. 1919 and 14 Dec. 1920: Oberösterreich. Landesarchiv, Landtagsakten no. 28.

the peasant councils was essential if the rural surplus was to be brought into the towns; it accused the peasant councils of passivity in view of the refusals, especially of the well-to-do peasants, to deliver milk.[37] But it seems likely that on this issue rich and poor peasant were united, and that any attempt to play off the one against the other was bound to fail.

One district peasant council of Upper Austria, in any case, had found the solution to all political and economic ills. In its journal, *Der Bauernrat*, it published in large type an appeal to all people's representatives calling upon them, if they were 'German men, honest and loyal, without falsehood and stealth', to drive out the Jews; only thus would the people be liberated 'from the claws of the hyenas desecrating the corpses': therefore 'out with the Jews!'[38] This appeal was published at a time when several members of the Viennese government were Jews, striving as best they could to alleviate Austria's economic plight. But resentment against the towns, especially against 'red' Vienna, was rife in the countryside, and anti-semitism a slogan always popular among a people hit by the war and its aftermath. Politically, the large majority of the peasants were, and remained, loyal to the Christian Social Party, a party hostile to the councils and their political and social aspirations—another cause of the hesitant and very partial development of peasant councils.

In general, the Austrian workers' councils developed too late and their geographical distribution over the country was too uneven. Their political support came from the left wing of the Social Democrats, while the attitude of the party as such remained cool to say the least, and the other political parties were openly hostile. In such circumstances, the councils in the course of 1919 could develop useful activities in food and social welfare matters, especially in Vienna. But they were unable to acquire any strong political influence, and their activities were short-lived. Any cooperation with the nascent peasant councils was impeded by antagonistic interests, in particular in the crucial field of food control. With the return of more normal conditions from the year 1920 onwards, the usefulness of the councils' work in the social sphere was bound to diminish, so that the workers' councils in the early 1920s died a slow death. Meanwhile their development in Germany was a very different one, and

[37] Meeting of the Linz workers' council, 29 July 1919: Parteiarchiv der SPÖ, Protokolle der Arbeiterräte Oberösterreichs, ii.

[38] *Der Bauernrat*, no. 12, 20 Sept. 1919, ed. by the Unparteiischer (*sic*) Bezirks-Bauernrat Vöcklabruck: copy in Oberösterreich. Landesarchiv, k.k. Statthalterei, Präsidium, no. 114.

the original strength of the workers' councils on a national scale was far greater; but in both countries the year 1919 marked the high-water mark of their influence, which then declined sharply. In contrast with Germany, political power had never been within the grasp of any Austrian workers' councils.

5 The German Workers' and Soldiers' Councils: Berlin

In Austria the soldiers' councils and the workers' councils did not come into being simultaneously and did not coalesce, nor did they exercise any influence on the formation of the central and local governments: these facts indicate the councils' weakness even at the beginning of the revolution. In Germany, on the other hand, they sprang up all over the country in the days of November as workers' *and* soldiers' councils, and exercised a strong influence on the composition of the new governments, not only in Berlin but equally in the capitals of the German states. This influence was stronger in Berlin and Munich than it was in Karlsruhe and Stuttgart. It was even less marked in the smaller states, although Brunswick and Oldenburg constituted notable exceptions, not to mention the Hanseatic cities of Hamburg and Bremen.

In Berlin, as has been mentioned, the same meeting of the workers' and soldiers' councils on 10 November confirmed the composition of the new government and elected an Executive Committee which claimed to be the 'supreme organ of the revolution' as well as to possess legislative and executive rights. On 11 and 12 November it arrogated to itself 'dictatorial powers' and the sole right to issue 'valid regulations' which alone would possess 'legal power'.[1] These claims were bound to clash with those of the government, which might be willing to acknowledge the Executive Committee's right of supervision and even control but which itself claimed executive and legislative powers—powers it could not easily cede to another authority without ceasing to be a government. Matters were not eased by the fact that both the government and the Executive Committee owed their authority to the same 'sovereign' power, the workers' and soldiers' councils of Berlin, which felt entitled to wield power until a national meeting of the councils could be convoked. Until then the Executive Committee could only try to strengthen its hand by adding to its

[1] R. Müller, *Vom Kaiserreich* . . . , ii, p. 55; Matthias, introduction to *Regierung* . . . , i, pp. xciv-xcv; Friedr.-Ebert-Stiftung, Nachlass Barth, I, no. 58: decision of the Executive Committee of 11 Nov. 1918.

ranks more members from important towns or army units outside the capital. This was not the 'dualism' which in 1917 had developed between the Russian Provisional Government and the Soviets, but it contained the germs of such a dualism. As a leading German Communist formulated it some years after, 'in November 1918 state power became a "no man's land"; it had slipped out of the hands of the bourgeoisie' but the working class had not picked it up'.[2] The ambivalence of the whole situation proved clearly that a revolution had taken place, and not a mere transfer of power. None of the different authorities striving for power was any more legitimate than the other. But the outcome of their struggle would decide the fate of the revolution.

The same decision of the Executive Committee which claimed 'dictatorial power' also confirmed Eichhorn in his office of chief of the Berlin police and agreed to the composition of the government of Prussia, with parity between Social Democrats and Independents. Indeed, all those appointed at that time to any office only required a confirmation by the Executive Committee 'as those appointed were nominated by the two parties concerned'.[3] (This was affirmed by the Social Democrat Brutus Molkenbuhr, a moderate leader of the Executive Committee, as a witness in the Ledebour trial some months later.) When a new German ambassador was to be sent to Warsaw the cabinet approved the name of Count Kessler; but it had to be confirmed by the Executive Committee 'which at present fulfils the role of the sovereign', as Kessler noted in his diary.[4] If the powers of the Executive Committee were indeed analogous to those previously wielded by the emperor they would have been very far-reaching, but they were from the outset contested by Ebert and his party friends.

Only a few days after the outbreak of the revolution, fundamental differences appeared between the government and the majority of the Executive Committee because the former claimed a monopoly of executive power. On the eighteenth Ebert declared in a cabinet meeting that he feared a conflict with the Executive Committee because this claimed all authority and was constantly interfering; but the people's representatives could not be puppets in its hands; 'the

[2] Paul Levi, *Unser Weg wider den Putschismus*, 2nd ed., Berlin, 1921, p. 14.
[3] *Der Ledebour-Prozess*, Berlin, 1919, p. 270.
[4] Kessler, *Tagebücher 1918–1937*, p. 34 (16 Nov. 1918). Although K. was not a socialist, there was no note of irony or resentment in this purely factual statement, however surprising it may seem. It is, however, indicative of the readiness with which certain liberal circles accepted the new state of affairs.

workers' and soldiers' council had delegated to them its factual executive power' and they therefore were 'the executive committee for the Reich'. On the same day he repeated in a joint meeting of the cabinet and the Executive Committee that it was 'impossible' if the latter, without getting in touch with the government, interfered with the work of the central authorities, issued orders, and even removed certain officials; 'then naturally a machine as large and as complicated as the Reich cannot work. If we continue this, within a week all will be ruined, all will be idle, all will collapse'. Ebert was seconded by his colleague Landsberg who emphasized that it would lead to anarchy if the workers' and soldiers' councils removed officials from their posts; no one denied them a right of control, they could initiate enquiries or bring to light defects, but they were not entitled to usurp the executive. The Independent leader Haase pointed out that all power came from the workers' and soldiers' councils, from whom the government's power too was derived; but as long as they had confidence in the government they had no right to interfere with its administrative measures, 'otherwise the whole organism comes to a standstill'. If the councils no longer wanted the government it would resign, and they could put other people in its place.[5] There was no disagreement between him and the moderate Social Democrats. A new source of conflict appeared on the same day when the Executive Committee handed to the government guiding principles for the tasks of the soldiers' councils; in these it claimed that it represented the highest military power in Germany and controlled the Ministry of War to which all other military authorities, including the High Command, were subordinate. In addition the Committee claimed that it exercised political and military executive powers, while it regarded the government only as its mandatory.[6]

After negotiations lasting several days the government and the Executive Committee reached an agreement on 22 November. In this the government recognized that political power rested in the hands of the workers' and soldiers' councils of the German Socialist Republic and that their functions were exercised by the Executive Committee 'in cooperation with the workers' and soldiers' councils of Greater Berlin . . . until an assembly of delegates of the workers' and soldiers' councils has elected an Executive Committee of the German Republic'. The government also confirmed that the

[5] Matthias (ed.), *Regierung* . . . , i, nos. 15b and 16, pp. 75–6, 93, 95, 103.
[6] 'Richtlinien über Wesen und Aufgaben der Soldatenräte', 18 Nov. 1918: Friedr.-Ebert-Stiftung, Nachlass Barth, I, no. 59.

Executive Committee was entitled to appoint and dismiss the members of the cabinet and the Prussian government and to control their actions; its opinions were to be heard before the appointment of ministerial experts (*Fachminister*) by the cabinet. But the fact that the Berlin workers' and soldiers' councils had appointed the government meant that they had transferred executive power to it.[7] This presumably indicated that the Executive Committee had no right of interference with the executive—as Ebert and Haase had declared some days before. The agreement did not mention the legislative power which apparently thus remained with the government exercising it at the time. It was a compromise solution, but it conceded to the government the powers without which it would have been unable to function. The government had gained the essential points.

This was confirmed on the following day, 23 November, in a proclamation of the Executive Committee to the German workers' and soldiers' councils. This affirmed that the executive power was transferred to the People's Representatives of the Reich and of Prussia, who could only fulfil their administrative tasks if their measures were not crossed by interventions of local workers' and soldiers' councils. These—like the Executive Committee—had a right of control within their spheres of activity but must abstain from any direct interference with the administration; they were not to take any independent decisions in matters of food or allocation of raw materials which could only be settled for Germany as a whole. The Executive Committee therefore requested the local councils to leave the conduct of administrative business to the authorities which had accepted service under the new régime; but they were to be continuously and watchfully controlled by the councils; only where this seemed insufficient were new appointments to be made to the most important posts 'in agreement with the revolutionary government', but any disturbing interference must cease. As examples of such interference, the committee specifically listed arrests, confiscations of stores or public funds, meddling with public transport or postal services, and the seizure of bank deposits. Important duties were allocated to the local councils 'for the time of the demobilization . . . in cooperation with the competent authorities', but these functions were obviously of a transitory nature. Except their ill-defined right of control, the principal duty of the local councils was to see to it 'that the revolutionary achievements are secured and consolidated', but

[7] Printed in Matthias (ed.), *Regierung* . . . , i, no. 22d, pp. 127–30; Kolb (ed.), *Zentralrat* . . . , p. xx; R. Müller, *Vom Kaiserreich* . . . , ii, p. 253.

no hint was given how this was to be done.[8] In its essential points the proclamation was vague—and so were the duties and rights allocated to the workers' and soldiers' councils. Only a week before, the Executive Committee had insisted that all *Landräte* and other officials who continued their work 'according to the old system or showed and supported counter-revolutionary tendencies' were to be removed by the competent workers' and soldiers' council, while open resistance was to be broken by force if need be.[9] Compared with this encouragement to drastic intervention the proclamation of 23 November marked a clear retreat and a victory for the moderates and the government.

What was established during the weeks of November and December in the Prussian provinces was a system of supervision of the administrative authorities, in particular of the *Oberpräsidenten*, the *Regierungspräsidenten* and the *Landräte*, by the local councils, which aimed at opposing any counter-revolutionary tendencies and anti-republican influences during the elections. This system began to function reasonably well in many places, but it naturally met with widespread passive—and sometimes more than passive—resistance by the old authorities. The delegates of the councils participated in meetings, supervised the correspondence, countersigned orders and decrees, and made themselves responsible for the maintenance of law and order, for measures necessary in connection with the demobilization, the distribution of food and social matters. They were usually given offices and other facilities in public buildings and clearly obtained official status. They often demanded the replacement of officials who had made themselves obnoxious in the past; but they were hardly ever successful as the officials in question were backed by the Prussian government.[10] Very few qualified Social Democrats were available to fill the administrative posts, and the large majority of the civil servants were willing to serve under the new régime. At the Social Democratic party conference held in June 1919 it was stated, without contradiction, that only one party member had been appointed *Regierungspräsident*, and only one *Landrat* (out of a total of 36 and 470 respectively for the whole of Prussia).[11] The picture was very similar on the local level. When certain workers' councils

[8] R. Müller, *Vom Kaiserreich . . .* , ii, pp. 255–7; Oehme, *Damals in der Reichskanzlei*, p. 127.
[9] R. Müller, *Vom Kaiserreich . . .* , ii, p. 252; Walter Tormin, *Zwischen Rätediktatur und sozialer Demokratie*, Düsseldorf, 1954, p. 91 n.1.
[10] ibid., p. 90; Kolb, *Arbeiterräte . . .* , pp. 108–12.
[11] *Protokoll über die Verhandlungen des Parteitages der S.P.D., abgehalten in Weimar vom 10. bis 15. Juni 1919*, Berlin, 1919, p. 270: quoted by Kolb, p. 280.

attempted to replace the town councils and urban deputations, elected on the basis of a very limited franchise, the Prussian prime minister strongly objected: 'Such measures run counter to the basic decrees of the new central organs and endanger in the highest degree the continuing provision of food for the people, the support of needy families, the care of the sick, and all other functions of the local authorities'.[12] Thus even in fields where the workers' councils were better qualified to act, their endeavours were stultified by the higher authorities.

The agreement of 22 November did not lead to a clear delimitation of responsibilities, nor—from the point of view of the central government—did it sufficiently curtail the interventions of the workers' and soldiers' councils in the administration. Hence there were immediate complaints about unwarranted interference by local councils. On the twenty-third, Scheidemann complained in the cabinet about infringements of the freedom of the press by the Düsseldorf workers' and soldiers' council, and Dittmann reported that the Salzwedel council was threatening to impose the death penalty for illicit trading in food; the cabinet voted that such special courts were 'impossible'.[13] On the following day Dr Solf, the Undersecretary in the Foreign Office, submitted a memorandum to the government in which he stated unequivocally: 'The central authority of the Reich is not subject to any control of a workers' and soldiers' council not recognized by the member states; in its decisions and their execution it is not circumscribed by any local orders and influences'[14]—a clear hint at the control claimed by the Executive Committee. Solf further demanded, like the High Command, the immediate announcement of early elections to a Constituent National Assembly at a specified date—thus anticipating any decision on this controversial issue by a national congress of the workers' and soldiers' councils. The decision on this and other vital issues was not to be left to them, but was to be taken by a conference of the governments of the German states scheduled to meet on 25 November: otherwise a curse would fall on the government which suffered the destruction of the unity of the Reich, a curse which Solf wanted to ward off from himself and his office.[14]

On 13 December—only a few days before the meeting of the national congress of the councils—Ebert declared in a cabinet meet-

---

[12] Telegram of 13 Nov. 1918, quoted ibid., p. 263.
[13] Matthias (ed.), *Regierung* . . . , i, no. 26, pp. 140–1.
[14] Memorandum of 24 Nov. 1918: Bundesarchiv Koblenz, Nachlass Solf, no. 59.

ing that things could not continue in this fashion: 'we make ourselves ridiculous in the face of history and before the whole world. . . . A sharp delimitation is necessary, we carry the responsibility. The workers' and soldiers' councils must stop their arbitrary interventions in the country. They are advisory authorities and nothing else. If this cannot be achieved we must leave the cabinet. We cannot accept the responsibility for buffooneries (*Narrenhausstreiche*)'.[15] The Independent leader Haase agreed that neither the Executive Committee nor any local soldiers' council must interfere with the work of any branch of the administration; but if 'excesses' were mentioned those committed by officers should not be forgotten. His argument was immediately countered by Landsberg who claimed that the officers in question were 'a few misguided chaps' (*verrannte Kerle*) but that the workers' and soldiers' councils were responsible for 'the organization of disorder'. In his opinion numerous unsuitable people were members of the Executive Committee; it seemed doubtful to him whether this would change in the Central Council, which was to be elected by the national congress of the workers' and soldiers' councils, for there too 'the desire for power may ruin much'.[16]

When the national congress met on 16 December it turned out that these fears were unjustified. Of the 490 delegates, only 84 represented soldiers' councils—a sign of how far the demobilization of the army had progressed—and more than 400 workers' councils. Even among these less than one hundred—a fifth of the total—belonged to the Independents, including about ten Spartacists; and another ten or so were members of the United Revolutionaries, an ultra-left group from Bremen and Hamburg. The majority—something like 60 per cent of the total—were members of the Social Democratic Party, and another thirty or so left-wing liberals (the remaining 75 did not declare their membership of a political party).[17] This meant that the Social Democrats were firmly in control of the proceedings, and that all important decisions went their way. At the beginning a motion to admit the Spartacist leaders Liebknecht and Luxemburg with an advisory voice was rejected with an overwhelming majority. There was only one exception from this general rule. On the military issue, the radical Hamburg points, which allocated decisive powers to the soldiers' councils and provided for the election of officers, were

---

[15] Matthias (ed.), *Regierung* . . . , i, no. 55, p. 374.   [16] ibid., pp. 374–5.
[17] The figures are given with slight variations by the different authorities: see R. Müller, *Vom Kaiserreich* . . . , ii, p. 203; *Illustrierte Geschichte der Deutschen Revolution*, p. 250; Kolb, introduction to *Der Zentralrat* . . . , p. xxvii; but they do not change the picture. There was only one woman delegate, a Social Democrat from Dresden.

accepted with a large majority.[18] On this issue right and left saw eye to eye: the old army and its officer corps must disappear.

The most important issue before the congress was that of the election of the National Assembly, but this was never in doubt, and no vote was taken on whether elections should take place or not. What was in doubt was only the date, which the Independents wanted to postpone to allow for a consolidation of the 'revolutionary achievements', and the Social Democrats wanted to be as soon as possible. A large majority first rejected the date of 16 March, then of 16 February 1919, and then voted in favour of 19 January—only four weeks after the closure of the congress.[19] This meant in effect that the future of Germany would be decided upon not by the workers' and soldiers' councils but by a freely elected parliament which might or might not have a socialist majority, and in which there certainly would be a strong bourgeois representation. Connected with this was the question of the respective powers of the councils and their Central Council and of the government. Leading Social Democrats put forward a motion that the congress, representing the entire political power in the country, should transfer the legislative and executive powers to the government, and that the congress should further appoint a Central Council of the workers' and soldiers' councils which was to exercise 'the parliamentary supervision of the German and Prussian governments' and was to be entitled to appoint and to dismiss their members. The decisive term of this motion was 'parliamentary supervision': Haase, speaking in the name of the government, declared 'that all legislative drafts would be communicated to the Central Council, and all important ones would be discussed with it'. This was considered insufficient by the Independents who moved that the Central Council should be entitled to accept or reject bills before their publication. The motion was strongly opposed by the Social Democratic leaders and rejected by 344 to 83 votes. Another Independent motion, which declared that the council system formed the basis of the constitution and that the decision on the future constitution of Germany was to be left to a national congress of workers and soldiers, met with the same fate: it was rejected by 344 to 98 votes.[20]

Having suffered defeat on the issues which were vital to them, the

[18] See above, p. 72–3.
[19] *Allgemeiner Kongress der Arbeiter- und Soldatenräte Deutschlands Vom 16. bis 21. Dezember 1918*, col. 282.
[20] ibid., col. 176, 252, 283, 288, 300; Friedrich Stampfer, *Der. 9. November*, Berlin, 1919, p. 30.

Independents then committed a tactical mistake of primary importance. They declared that they would not participate in the election
of the Central Council. There was thus only one list, that of the Social
Democrats, which contained 27 names and was approved by a
majority. The announcement of the result was accompanied on the
side of the Independents by laughter and wild curses; the noise lasted
several minutes; some sailors shouted: 'We will talk again! We will
go on to the streets again!'[21] But the net result was that the Independents had deprived themselves of any influence in the—in their
opinion—supreme organ of the 'German Socialist Republic', and
had at the same time deprived the Independent members of the
government of their backing—an act of political ineptitude which
was to bear fruit during the government crisis a week later. All
members of the new Central Council were staunch Social Democrats
who believed that their own functions would be terminated with the
election and meeting of the National Assembly early in 1919; they
intended to ensure a smooth transition to a democratic republic and
to prevent any revolutionary 'experiments', in close cooperation with
Ebert, their party leader. In any conflict they would side with him
and against the local workers' and soldiers' councils.

Only after the important political decisions had been taken did the
congress turn its attention to the issue of socialization. On this the
major speech was made by Dr Hilferding, an Independent and a
leading Marxist theoretician. He advocated the socialization not only
of the major industries but also of the large estates and the forests; in
this way it would be possible to fulfil the promise of settling the
returning soldiers. Not all large estates were to be divided for this
purpose, however, because they were technically superior to small
farms. Hilferding's argument in favour of peasant settlement was
opposed by another prominent Independent who spoke for preserving the large and more efficient estates so that production could be
stepped up, and for the creation of agricultural cooperatives so that
the smallholders could be won for socialism. Only a democratic
delegate from Silesia pleaded for the partitioning of the large estates
to the benefit of the peasantry.[22] No single Social Democrat spoke on
this issue, vital for the development of German society. In general,
there were only three delegates with agrarian occupations, two of
them representing the Bavarian peasant council, and the other farming a large estate in Silesia. Among the delegates there was a sprink-
ling of academics, but the majority were apparently leaders and

[21] *Allgemeiner Kongress* . . . , col. 300–1.   [22] ibid., col. 318, 327, 339–40.

functionaries of the two Social Democratic parties who dominated the proceedings. Very little was said by either side on what should have been the central question: the future tasks and functions of the workers' and soldiers' councils. Everything was overshadowed by the clash between Social Democrats and Independents; the principal debates quickly degenerated into a slanging match between the speakers of the two parties—a bad omen for the future of the government, and equally for that of the workers' and soldiers' councils. In his opening speech Richard Müller had apostrophized them as 'the only achievement of the revolution': if they fell, nothing would remain of it.[23] The congress had done nothing to ensure their future or to define their rights. The large majority of the delegates believed that they had to choose between the councils and the National Assembly, and they chose the latter.

The chairman of the new Central Council of the German Socialist Republic (as it was called officially) was Robert Leinert, who had presided over the meetings of the national congress; he was the Social Democratic party secretary for the province of Hanover and since November mayor of the city. The vice-chairman was Hermann Müller who had represented his party on the Executive Committee; in 1919 he was to succeed Ebert as party chairman and to become Foreign Minister, and in the following year (for the first time) Chancellor of Germany.[24] In such hands firm Social Democratic control of the Central Council was a foregone conclusion. Many of its other members, too, were to rise to high office during the years of the Weimar Republic.[25] Yet on certain issues the Central Council took a fairly independent line and would not simply approve the actions of the Social Democratic leaders. During the government crisis at the end of December caused by the attack of government troops on the palace in Berlin,[26] the Central Council declared that it strongly disapproved of this military action. Within it a strong minority aimed at preventing the break-up of the coalition between the two socialist parties and was willing to sacrifice Scheidemann and Landsberg—but apparently not Ebert—if this could be achieved, and to replace them by other Social Democrats. It now became clear that the Independents had committed a fundamental mistake when

---

[23] ibid., col. 16.   [24] Kolb, introduction to *Der Zentralrat* . . . , pp. xliii-xlv.
[25] Notably Albert Grzesinski who later became police president of Berlin and Prussian Minister of the Interior, Karl Zörgiebel, who succeeded Grzesinski as police president of Berlin when the latter became Minister of the Interior, and Heinrich Kürbis, who in 1919 became *Oberpräsident* of the province of Schleswig-Holstein.   [26] See above, pp. 63-4.

they declined to enter the Central Council, where their influence might have been decisive at this juncture. This was pointed out by Haase only a few months later; in his opinion, the Independents alone could have formed the government because Ebert, Scheidemann and Landsberg 'were completely broken' after the failure of the attack, but this was impossible because the Central Council consisted entirely of moderate Social Democrats.[27] As it was the Independents were forced out of the government which now became purely Social Democratic in composition.

Some friction with the government also continued because the Central Council—like the Executive Committee—issued directives to certain offices and interfered in administrative matters. On 31 December Ebert strongly complained about new disturbances of this kind; senior civil servants who were indispensable had declared they would resign if their work continued to be interfered with; Germany was faced with enormous difficulties on account of the return of the troops from eastern Europe; coal production in the Ruhr and Upper Silesia was endangered by radical agitation, and food production was in ruins. If these difficulties were not surmounted collapse was inevitable; it was uncertain whether the United States would be able to send food in time; the situation was terribly serious, and it would become impossible if several authorities intervened in the administration; the country would be ruined and the government would stand disgraced. In the same meeting Noske, now a member of the government, objected to the claims of the seven 'controllers' of the War Ministry and the Demobilization Office, who had been elected by a conference of the workers' and soldiers' councils and considered themselves entitled to countersign any orders issued by these offices: if such claims were recognized this would mean the end of the government's executive powers, for any conference could appoint numbers of people to control the central offices. Grzesinski replied that the question had already been decided. The Central Council would be guilty of a dereliction of duty if it consented to these claims; the national congress had transferred the executive to the government and the Central Council was entitled to control it, hence the claims must be refuted.[28]

On 19 January, as the national congress had decided, the elections

[27] Kolb (ed.), *Der Zentralrat . . .* , no. 12, p. 91; Unabhängige Sozialdemokratische Partei Deutschlands, *Protokoll über die Verhandlungen des ausserordentlichen Parteitages vom 2. bis 6. März 1919*, Berlin, s.d., pp. 75, 84, 176.

[28] Matthias (ed.), *Regierung . . .* , ii, no. 89, pp. 163–4; Kolb (ed.), *Der Zentralrat . . .* , no. 19, pp. 127–8.

took place to the National Assembly which was to decide on the political future of Germany and adopt its constitution. In the elections the two socialist parties remained in the minority, polling together only 45.5 per cent of the total and gaining 185 out of 421 seats. The question was now what would be the future of the Central Council and of the workers' and soldiers' councils in general in a country which clearly would not be socialist. A few days before the elections Grzesinski had stated in a meeting of the Central Council that they considered 'the introduction of a bourgeois republic as a counter-revolutionary intention'.[29] After the election it was clear that Germany would be a bourgeois republic, and there was a change of opinion. Grzesinski now declared that on the day of the meeting of the National Assembly the government would resign its power and functions to it; the National Assembly would then take the place of the Central Council which would lose its controlling function over the government and would have fulfilled its task as a parliament of the revolutionary era when no proper parliament existed. Another member of the Central Council argued, however, that it would continue to be the highest authority of the workers' and soldiers' councils as long as these existed; the best thing would be for them to be dissolved as quickly as possible, for their many excesses had caused such ill-feeling that the National Assembly would have to tackle the problem very soon. The functions of the Central Council would be terminated as soon as the government was confirmed by the National Assembly and the constitution was passed; then they would dissolve themselves.[30]

Once the National Assembly had met at Weimar neither the government nor the assembly itself took much notice of the Central Council, and all complaints by the latter that it was being ignored had little effect. At the end of January one member said he was not surprised about this, for the ministers had always considered the Council as a necessary evil and had done everything to reduce it to insignificance. Another member complained that the workers' and soldiers' councils were being underestimated in a way which would be 'detrimental to our later movement'. And a third bleakly said that they had not made the revolution in order to combine with the old bureaucracy.[31] At about the same time Ebert informed the Central Council that he doubted whether the workers' councils would be

---

[29] Kolb (ed.), *Zentralrat*, no. 48, p. 353 (14 Jan. 1919).
[30] ibid., no. 64, pp. 476–8: meeting of 25 Jan. 1919.
[31] ibid., no. 74, pp. 533–5: meeting of 30 Jan. 1919.

mentioned in the new constitution; but in any case their political activities must cease after the meeting of the National Assembly and of the parliaments of the federal states. As a possible further development he could only envisage the extension of a system of workers' chambers.[32] In this unpropitious climate the work of the Central Council with regard to the central government reached its end, but it continued somewhat longer with regard to the Prussian government. The Central Council supervised the latter much more energetically until March 1919 and repeatedly asked its members to report on their work and on their legislative plans. Its principal aim was to achieve a democratization of the Prussian administration and of the laws governing the composition of local councils and the local administration, and these aims were at least partially achieved.[33]

On 4 February 1919 the Central Council officially transferred the power granted to it by the national congress of the workers' and soldiers' councils into the hands of the National Assembly. It declared at the same time that it would continue to exercise its remaining functions until the National Assembly had allocated them to another organization.[34] The Council never received a reply to this message: the National Assembly clearly had no wish to be reminded of its revolutionary origin and to acknowledge this act of self-denial emanating from the highest organ created by the revolution. But some months later even the Under-Secretary of State in the Ministry of Justice had to admit that the Central Council had in fact wielded the highest authority in the Reich and had exercised the political supervision of the government of the Reich as the central organ of the workers' and soldiers' councils. Coming from this quarter it was an official acknowledgement that a revolution had taken place, but also that meanwhile the revolutionary organs had been deprived of their power, for 'the Central Council no longer exercises such powers. Its remaining rights of control it uses outside the framework of the official organization of the Reich into which it has not been fitted by any legal directives.'[35] By the spring of 1919 the old bureaucracy was once more firmly in control and able to deny any official position to the workers' and soldiers' councils, to the moderation of which it owed its survival.

In February Prime Minister Scheidemann, denying a newspaper

[32] ibid., no. 68, p. 496: meeting of 28 Jan. 1919.
[33] Kolb, ibid., pp. liii, lix.
[34] ibid., no. 77, p. 546.
[35] The Minister of Justice to the president of the Reich Ministry, 23 May 1919: Bundesarchiv Koblenz, Reichskanzlei, R 43 I/1940.

report that the government intended to combine the system of councils in some form with the administration, declared officially that no member of the cabinet had any intention of doing so, for Social Democracy had always been a bitter opponent of any dictatorship which was of necessity linked to the system of political councils.[36] But in reality at least one member of the cabinet, the Foreign Secretary Count Brockdorff-Rantzau, favoured the council system as the basis of economic reconstruction, although he was not a socialist. In his opinion, the workers' councils should be made responsible for increasing production, for the care of the unemployed and for the maintenance of law and order, and they should be granted the necessary powers; Scheidemann and the Centre Party should leave the government and the Independents re-enter it and guarantee work and order.[37] Clearly Brockdorff-Rantzau believed it possible to combine the council system with democracy and did not think that it would 'of necessity' lead to dictatorship.

The second, and last, national congress of the workers' and soldiers' councils which met in April 1919 saw a repetition of the clashes between Social Democrats and Independents which had virtually wrecked the first congress. Again the Social Democrats had a safe majority, 146 out of 257 German delegates (there were also nine Austrians); the Independents had only 56, and the Communists only one.[38] The Independent speakers sharply attacked the government, and in particular Noske and the Free Corps which had meanwhile started their victorious march through Germany, destroying the power of the left-wing councils. The Social Democrats now favoured the creation of 'chambers of labour' which should be elected by all working Germans organized according to their occupations. These chambers should be formed at local, provincial, state and national levels and should be second chambers at each level, with powers similar to those elected by general franchise. Although this motion was passed it produced no result and was not incorporated in the Weimar Constitution. When it came to the election of a new Central Council the Independents demanded parity with the Social Democrats, while the latter were only willing to give them ten out of twenty-eight seats. This was rejected by the Independents who thus continued their tactics of abstention or boycott—recognized by their leaders as a fundamental mistake. On the new Central Council

---

[36] Official announcement of 25 Feb. 1919: *II. Kongress der Arbeiter-, Bauern- und Soldatenräte Deutschlands am 8. bis 14. April 1919*, Berlin, s.d., p. 190.

[37] Kessler, *Tagebücher 1918–1937*, p. 144: conversation of 4 March 1919.

[38] *II. Kongress der Arbeiter-, Bauern- und Soldatenräte . . .*, pp. 260–4.

the Social Democrats occupied sixteen out of twenty-one seats, the remainder going to splinter groups and soldiers' representatives.[39] Seven seats were kept open for the Independents who never occupied them.

By this time the split between Social Democrats and Independents was much deeper on account of the incipient civil war in Germany. The left wing of the Independents had become more radical and was beginning to move towards the Communists. Its principal speaker, Ernst Däumig, demanded that the workers' and soldiers' councils should exercise the highest power in the country and that the government should receive its directives from their national congress. Such ideas naturally were anathema to the Social Democrats. Their speaker, the Minister Wissell, declared on the contrary that any large-scale socialization was out of the question on account of Germany's desperate economic plight: a reply which the liberal Count Kessler considered 'pathetic'.[40] One speaker at the congress, Luise Kautsky, rightly said that the split between Social Democrats and Independents was 'the root of all evil'; in her opinion, it had caused a government created by the revolution to become 'dependent upon the old bureaucrats, generals, capitalists. . . . If the proletariat had been united from the beginning of the revolution, it would have obtained an undivided government which would have accomplished much in the field of socialization. The result of the general election too would have been different in that case. . .'.[41] The split and the developments flowing from it were the tragedy of the German working-class movement. To both sides their differences were much more important than what they had in common. As the right wing of the Independents slowly approximated to the position of the moderate Social Democrats, the split between them became more and more unreal, while the real division of opinion now ran right through the Independent Party. Yet both sides continued to malign each other and to hold each other responsible for the defeat of the revolution.

At the outbreak of the revolution the Independent leadership had simply adopted the attitude that power rested with the workers' and soldiers' councils and that the government depended on their confidence, at least as long as there was no parliament to express it:

[39] ibid., pp. 256–7, 267.
[40] Kessler, *Tagebücher 1918–1937*, p. 172 (9 April 1919).
[41] *II. Kongress der Arbeiter-, Bauern- und Soldatenräte . . .* , p. 230. Luise Kautsky spoke on behalf of her absent husband; both belonged to the right wing of the Independent Social Democrats.

'Political power is vested in the workers' and soldiers' councils on the basis of the law of revolution. The government exercises power because and as long as it possesses the confidence of the workers' and soldiers' councils. . . '.[42] By the time that a full party conference met in March 1919 the attitude of the party had become more specific:

> The class-conscious proletariat has recognized that its struggle for liberation can only be carried out by its own forces; the existing organizations are not enough, a new proletarian fighting organization is needed.
>
> In the *council system* the proletarian revolution has created this fighting organization. It welds together the working masses in the factories for revolutionary action. It gives to the proletariat the right to self-government in the factories, in the communes and in the state. It carries out the transformation of the capitalist system into a socialist one.
>
> The council system develops in all capitalist countries out of the same economic conditions and becomes the carrier of the proletarian world revolution. . . .
>
> The Independent Social Democratic Party takes its stand on the basis of the council system. It supports the councils in their struggle for economic and political power. It fights for the dictatorship of the proletariat, the representative of the great majority of the people, as a necessary precondition for the attainment of socialism. Only socialism brings the elimination of class rule, the elimination of any dictatorship, true democracy.[43]

In the conditions prevailing in Germany in the spring of 1919 such a declaration was completely unrealistic. In the national elections of January the Independents had polled 7.6 per cent of the total vote. They represented a small minority of the working class although their following was increasing. To proclaim in such conditions—with the Free Corps victoriously advancing through Germany and destroying the power of the workers' and soldiers' councils—a fight for the dictatorship of the proletariat, a struggle for power and revolutionary action was playing into the hands of the enemy. But there was not one word in the whole proclamation about the workers' councils' administrative functions, the right of control exercised by them, their daily struggles with the Prussian bureaucracy, the work of the Central Council in Berlin and its role after the meeting of the National Assembly: it had very little connection with any practical politics.

[42] Proclamation of Nov. 1918, quoted by Eugen Prager, *Geschichte der USPD*, Berlin, 1921, p. 184.
[43] 'Programmatische Kundgebung', quoted ibid., p. 193.

Many years later a leading Independent Social Democrat, the former Minister Dittmann, wrote about the differences separating the two socialist parties on the issue of the workers' and soldiers' councils:

We Independents saw in them transitional forms, but also the carriers and guarantors of the revolution whose activities must continue until a consolidation had taken place. We too were in favour of a delimitation of their rights and were opposed to the excesses committed by some councils; but we resisted the opinion held by our Social Democratic colleagues that they must disappear again as quickly as possible. From the bourgeois side an infamous campaign was waged against the workers' and soldiers' councils which made an impression on Ebert, Scheidemann and Landsberg. It occurred quite often that Scheidemann at the beginning of a cabinet meeting moaned how in that and that place the workers' and soldiers' council had forced a bourgeois newspaper into its service or had seized a passing food train. He then added full of indignation which had a comic effect: 'I am ashamed in front of the bourgeois and do not want to be seen by them any more. I cannot stand this any longer!' . . . With Ebert the animosity against the workers' and soldiers' councils took the form of annoyance with their arbitrary interferences which he saw as disturbances of the economic or state machinery.[44]

Even in these notes written so much later there is no awareness of the real issues at stake in Germany in 1918: only of the animosity which characterized the relations between the leaders of the two socialist parties. But the outcome of the real issues depended only partly on the decisions taken in Berlin, for in November a spontaneous revolutionary movement had broken out all over Germany: a movement which had no central direction and on which the central government exercised but little influence.

[44] *Erinnerungen Wilhelm Dittmann*, D 15, pp. 7–8: Int. Inst. of Social History, Amsterdam. They were written while Dittmann was an exile.

6 The Council Movement outside Berlin

In Berlin the course of events was dominated by conflicts between the government and the Executive Committee which was backed by the radical local organizations. Outside the capital, developments differed widely. Although the large majority of the local councils were controlled by moderate Social Democrats, there were areas—in Saxony, central Germany, the Ruhr and elsewhere—in which the Independents were leading, and others where even more radical influences were paramount, at least for a short time. It is thus essential to look at the main industrial centres and the different regions of Germany to see how the power of the workers' and soldiers' councils developed in the months following upon the revolution, and why it declined so quickly in most areas. This was not primarily a question of military power—which hardly existed until the formation of the volunteer units—but of local factors and leaders, on neither of which the central authorities could exercise much influence at the beginning.

In the Hanseatic city of Hamburg the provisional workers' council consisted entirely of Independents who had taken the first initiative in its formation. Proper elections in the factories and enterprises were held on 8 November and about six hundred delegates were elected. They assembled on the following day and appointed an executive council of thirty members: eighteen from their own ranks and three each chosen by the two socialist parties, the trade unions and the extreme left. At its first meeting it elected a Presidium which was dominated by the Independents. Its chairman was Dr Heinrich Laufenberg, a journalist and the leader of the Independents' left wing. Thirty soldiers' representatives were added to the executive council. On 12 November Laufenberg proposed at its meeting that the Senate and town council (*Bürgerschaft*) be dissolved and replaced by the organs of the workers' and soldiers' councils; and the motion was carried against the opposition of the Social Democrats. It was then announced that the workers' and soldiers' council had taken over the exercise of political power and that the Senate and town council had ceased to exist; law and order were guaranteed, as was the protection of private property; all officials should remain at their posts; looters would be sentenced by courts martial. The workers' and soldiers' council took up quarters in the town hall on which the red flag was hoisted. Negotiations were carried on with the Senate; its members were encouraged to cooperate with the new régime and elected a committee of five Senators to collaborate with a committee elected by the executive council, so that the city's administrative machinery should continue to function and orderly conditions could be restored. The courts, too, were to function as before, all taxes were to be paid, and all contracts to remain valid.[1]

To cope with its manifold tasks the executive council formed twelve committees for political affairs, military matters, transport, food, law and prisons, security and police, health, education and art, trade, shipping and industry, finance and taxes, and social policy. But these committees were only able to function in cooperation with the officially dissolved Senate and the urban administration. On 16 November a Senator, Dr Petersen (later the lord mayor of Hamburg for many years) informed the executive council that the leading banks of Hamburg, Berlin and Frankfurt were trying to obtain from the United States a large credit for imports; their negotiations—as he had been told by the banker Max Warburg— would be endangered if the name of the Senate was changed as all financiers were notoriously suspicious, and the same applied to the name of the town council (*Bürgerschaft*). In his reply Dr Laufenberg gratefully acknowledged the cooperation with the gentlemen of the Senate and expressed the expectation that it would continue. Two days later Warburg himself took part in the negotiations and the workers' and soldiers' council had taken over the political and executive power, but if a council and communal representation appeared instead of Senate and *Bürgerschaft*, people would believe that Hamburg was no longer a city state but a town like Hanover or Altona. He advocated not only a retention of the names Senate and *Bürgerschaft*, but a division of power in which political power would be vested in the workers' and soldiers' council, and communal tasks and financial matters in Senate and *Bürgerschaft* as of old, with a right of veto given to the workers' and soldiers' council:

[1] Neumann, *Hamburg unter der Regierung* . . . , pp. 14, 17, 24, 27, 132; Walther Lamp'l, *Die Revolution in Gross-Hamburg*, Hamburg, 1921, pp. 14–16; Comfort, *Revolutionary Hamburg*, pp. 42–8. Neumann and Lamp'l were active participants in the events described by them.

only in this way would it be possible to preserve Hamburg's credit.[2]

His arguments had the desired result. On 18 November the executive council accepted a proposal of the Senate according to which both Senate and *Bürgerschaft* resumed their activities so as to safeguard the city's administration and finances. The workers' and soldiers' council nominated four members who were to attend the Senate meetings with an advisory voice and could object to its decisions, which in that case were to be referred to the workers' and soldiers' council for its opinion. A new *Bürgerschaft* was to be elected before 1 April 1919 by general franchise. Laufenberg advocated acceptance of the proposal on the grounds that months would pass before the elections could take place: meanwhile administrative affairs could not remain at a standstill, otherwise there would be enormous confusion and the whole food supply might be endangered. The population was notified of the agreement on the same day. In this proclamation the workers' and soldiers' council asserted that it 'retained complete political power' and emphasized that it would use its right of veto against any decisions 'contrary to the new socialist order'. But there can be no doubt that in reality the old authorities resumed their functions after an interval of a few days, under a loose supervision by the workers' and soldiers' council, in spite of the large radical majority on its executive council.[3] Radical influence was also strong in the *Volkswehr* unit founded in November; but the more general arming of the workers demanded by the left radicals was not carried out. The attitude of the Social Democrats to the councils was remarkably cool—not surprisingly so as they were in a minority on the executives of the workers' as well as of the soldiers' council.[4]

In January 1919, however, the Social Democrats were able to increase their strength on the executive of the soldiers' council, and to obtain a majority in February after new elections. In March new, almost general elections were also held to the workers' council which gave to the Social Democrats an absolute majority with 239 out of 400 seats, while their left-wing opponents only gained 62 seats between them, the remainder going to the trade unions and various bourgeois parties. A new *Bürgerschaft* had been elected a few days before; the Social Democrats gained just over 50 per cent of the total

[2] Neumann, *Hamburg unter der Regierung* . . . , pp. 28–9; Lamp'l, *Die Revolution* . . . , pp. 98, 102–3, 128–9, with the protocols of the negotiations with the Senate.

[3] Lamp'l, *Die Revolution* . . . , pp. 18, 116–17, 129; Neumann, *Hamburg* . . . , pp. 30–2. According to Lamp'l the radical majority on the executive council was about two-thirds.

[4] Comfort, *Revolutionary Hamburg*, pp. 68, 98; Lamp'l, *Die Revolution* . . . , p. 129; Neumann, *Hamburg* . . . , p. 69.

vote, and the Independents a mere 8 per cent. Laufenberg resigned as chairman of the Presidium in January because the soldiers' council and the police did not consult him about security measures and the workers had not been armed: this situation made it impossible for him to accept responsibility any longer. After the March elections the Social Democratic chairman of the Presidium declared in a session of the new *Bürgerschaft*: 'The workers' and soldiers' council herewith resigns its political power, which it has exercised on account of the revolution, into the hands of the *Bürgerschaft*.' And its chairman announced that it had now taken over political power in the state of Hamburg.[5] The revolution was over. The secretary of the workers' and soldiers' council at the end of his report listed its achievements: the dismissal of reactionary chairmen of local councils and of *Landräte*, the commutation of one death sentence to life-long imprisonment, the election of headmasters, the granting of permission to female teachers to get married, the limitation of working hours, and legal help rendered to the sailors.[6] These were changes principally in the field of social services and labour conditions in which the council was best qualified to act. This list is not very impressive, but then truly revolutionary changes could hardly be expected in a single German city. Perhaps it was the merit of the Hamburg socialists that they realized this and confined their efforts to what was possible and practicable.

In Hamburg's sister city, Bremen, things took a different course. Here the so-called 'Bremen Left' which maintained close relations with the Bolsheviks had been influential since the war years.[7] On 8 November the large workers' council, which consisted of about 180 factory delegates, appointed an action committee of 15 on which the radicals were in a majority. On the fourteenth its chairman, the Independent Alfred Henke, declared that it was necessary to follow the Hamburg example and to dissolve the Senate and *Bürgerschaft* which no longer had any legal basis; but he hoped that the Senate would continue its work in cooperation with the workers' and soldiers' council so that administrative activity would not stop and no danger to law and order would ensue. Henke's motion was accepted and those assembled took possession of the town hall on which the red flag was run up. A proclamation was issued that the workers' and soldiers' council had taken over political power, closely following in

---

[5] Neumann, *Hamburg* . . . , pp. 69, 83, 126–9; Comfort, *Revolutionary Hamburg*, pp. 58, 62, 179; Lindau, *Revolutionäre Kämpfe* . . . , p. 123.

[6] Neumann, *Hamburg* . . . , p. 131.　　　　　　　　[7] See above, p. 16.

its wording the proclamation issued in Hamburg two days before. To achieve a smooth transition to the new conditions, a committee was set up with representatives of the workers' and soldiers' council and of the city administration in even numbers; all administrative authorities and deputations were confirmed in their functions and powers; taxes were to be paid and contracts to be fulfilled. The Senate undertook to see to it that public and local administration would continue without any disturbance and that no danger would befall the city. The workers' council created sub-committees for industrial affairs, demobilization etc., and separate councils for the intellectual workers, the white-collar workers, and the officials.[8]

Although the administrative machinery continued to work under the control of the workers' and soldiers' council, developments soon took a more radical turn. On 19 November the council, in a plenary meeting, accepted a motion proposed by Henke against the summoning of a National Assembly, by 116 against 23 votes. But a few days later the garrison declared its support for the central government and its opposition to the formation of red guards and to a dictatorship of the workers' and soldiers' councils. The soldiers were also opposed to the arming of the workers, but the workers' and soldiers' council by a large majority decided in favour. Even under pressure of a large communist demonstration, however, it declined by 97 to 56 votes to proclaim the dictatorship of the proletariat, thus implicitly reversing its previous decision against the summoning of a National Assembly. In December, after the vote of the national congress of the workers' and soldiers' councils in favour of elections to such an assembly, the workers' council of Bremen resolved not to recognize this decision and declared its determination to work for the realization of a socialist republic.[9] Clearly there was much confusion; it is not known how the majority hoped to steer a middle course between the Scylla of the National Assembly and the Charybdis of the proletarian dictatorship.

No clear decision emerged from new elections to the workers' council at the beginning of 1919, for the two left-wing parties—the Independents and the Communists—obtained only a few hundred votes more than the Social Democrats, and together gained 117 seats

[8] Peter Kuckuk (ed,), *Revolution und Räterepublik in Bremen*, Frankfurt, 1969, no. 6–8, pp. 39–40, no. 33, pp. 71–2; *Bremen in der deutschen Revolution . . .*, pp. 18–25; Kolb, *Arbeiterräte . . .*, p. 94.

[9] Kuckuk (ed.), *Revolution und Räterepublik . . .*, nos. 10–11, pp. 42–3, nos. 15–16, pp. 46–7; *Bremen in der deutschen Revolution . . .*, pp. 29–30; Lindau, *Revolutionäre Kämpfe*, p. 94.

to their rivals' 113. But then the radical parties decided not to admit the Social Democrats to sessions of the council and to conduct its business on their own in accordance with the demands of a Communist mass demonstration. Inspired by the Spartacist Rising in Berlin, the purged workers' and soldiers' council decided on 10 January to proclaim a socialist republic and to establish a council of people's representatives or people's commissars as the new city government. The Senate was once more deposed, and any counter-revolutionary attempt was threatened with the death penalty, as was any theft, robbery or looting. But three days later the proletarian dictatorship was declared abolished: apparently it had not aroused much enthusiasm among the population. The council of people's representatives then decided to hold elections to a city parliament on the basis of an equal and general franchise; this assembly was to exercise legislative power and to appoint the executive. In these elections, which eventually took place on 9 March, the two left-wing parties only gained 53 out of 200 seats, the Social Democrats 67, and bourgeois groups the remaining 80. The council of people's representatives would have had to resign or once more try and impose its will on the majority of Bremen's population. But it was relieved of making this agonizing choice by a decision of the central government to intervene with military force 'to restore orderly conditions in Bremen'. The decision was announced at the end of January, all attempts at negotiation proved in vain, and Bremen was conquered in fierce fighting by government troops in early February—the first such intervention on any scale outside Berlin. The council of people's representatives was deposed and the workers' council and its organs were dissolved; the Bremen socialist republic had reached its end.[10]

In north-west Germany there was only one other city where events took a similar turn, and that was Brunswick. With the outbreak of the revolution, the local workers' and soldiers' council took over the state apparatus of the duchy; the property and estates of the ducal family were declared state property. A government of people's commissars was formed, with the Communist tailor August Merges as president of the local socialist republic. At the meeting of representatives of the German states in Berlin on 25 November he accused the Ebert-Haase government of following the line of Kerensky: if it continued to do so a second revolution would follow upon the first;

[10] Kuckuk (ed.), *Revolution und Räterepublik* . . . , nos. 19–20, 25, 27a, 28–9, pp. 52–66; *Bremen in der deutschen Revolution* . . . , pp. 59–60, 66–7, 239–41; Richard Müller, *Der Bürgerkrieg in Deutschland*, Berlin, 1925, pp. 116–17.

the results of the revolution must be secured before the National Assembly could be summoned.[11] Later the Brunswick government declared its opposition to the date of 19 January for the elections, agreed on by the national congress of the workers' and soldiers' councils. In a mass meeting in January 1919 the people's commissar for the interior, Sepp Oerter, exhorted the revolutionary workers and soldiers to chase away a National Assembly of which they disapproved. But in reply the Brunswick workers' and soldiers' council decided to take the elections under its protection and to arraign any disturber before a people's court, and the elections were duly held. In December 1918 a new Brunswick Diet had also been elected; the two socialist parties gained a slight majority, with 31 seats to the 29 of the different bourgeois parties.[12]

In February 1919 the Brunswick government was transformed into a coalition between the two socialist parties, with Oerter as prime minister and four Social Democratic members to the three of the Independents. The two parties also agreed on constitutional principles according to which political power was to be exercised by the Diet, the workers' and soldiers' council and the council of people's representatives. The Brunswick workers' council was to be elected by a democratic franchise; it was to prepare measures of socialization, and have the right to reject decisions taken by the Diet. The latter was to elect the council of people's representatives which was to be responsible to it. Only the Communists were opposed to this agreement, and did not join the government. It thus seemed as if Brunswick would follow an evolutionary course similar to that prevailing in Hamburg. But in April, when mass strikes broke out all over Germany, a revolutionary action committee proclaimed a general strike, and the workers' council submitted far-reaching political demands to the Diet which adjourned itself. The strike committee in fact exercised power, regulated the food supply and ordered the banks to make payments only if the order was countersigned by the strike committee. These events were used by the central government as a pretext to order General Maercker to occupy Brunswick with military force. Representatives of the local government tried to negotiate with him, but he demanded its resignation and the dissolution of the workers' council. When his forces marched into Brunswick on 17 April there was no resistance: the Brunswick govern-

[11] Matthias (ed.), *Regierung* . . . , i, no. 30, p. 175.
[12] Anlauf, *Revolution in Niedersachsen*, pp. 98–100; Matthias (ed.), *Regierung* . . . , ii, p. 218, n. 35.

ment had called on the citizens to surrender all weapons and not to oppose Maercker's forces. A state of siege was proclaimed and the government reformed in accordance with the general's wishes.[13] For these strong measures, there was much less justification than for the intervention against Bremen. In Brunswick, there was no disorder, general elections had been held and the government was supported by a majority of the deputies; even the general strike had been called off before Maercker's troops marched into Brunswick, allegedly to 'restore law and order'.

In the other principal towns of the area the moderate Social Democrats were firmly in control. This applied in particular to Hanover where Leinert, the chairman of the Central Council elected in December 1918, was not only the mayor but also the chairman of the workers' and soldiers' council. For the province of Hanover a workers' and soldiers' council for the area of Tenth Army Corps exercised control over the military command, the police headquarters, the Prussian administrative authorities, etc. As early as 23 November a conference of the workers' and soldiers' councils of this area appointed the Hanover council as a central council acting on their behalf and adopted, with 140 to only 4 votes, a resolution against any dictatorial tendencies and in favour of the National Assembly. In January 1919 the Hanover workers' and soldiers' council complained to the Central Council in Berlin that recent decrees of the Reich and Prussian governments in effect curtailed the activities of the councils and prevented their representatives from doing useful work; these decrees also encouraged the authorities to dispute the councils' rights of control and of counter-signature; all this applied even more strongly to the small towns and rural communes; but, so the letter continued, the workers' and soldiers' councils, even after the meeting of the National Assembly, must safeguard the achievements of the revolution and their work should not be impeded or curtailed. When the Hanover workers' council was re-elected in March the Social Democrats easily secured an absolute majority, with 83 delegates to 11 of the Independents and 45 of bourgeois groups.[14]

The moderate influence was equally strong at Cassel where Grzesinski became the chairman of the local workers' and soldiers'

[13] Anlauf, *Revolution in Niedersachsen*, pp. 105–6; *Illustrierte Geschichte der Deutschen Revolution*, Berlin, 1929, pp. 379–81.

[14] Anlauf, *Revolution in Niedersachsen*, pp. 55–6, 151; Kolb, *Arbeiterräte . . .* , pp. 110, 265. Letter of 21 Jan. 1919: Int. Inst. of Social History, Amsterdam, Zentralrat, B-22, III.

council. This controlled the military and administrative authorities in the area of Eleventh Army Corps, and its authority was recognized by its chief of staff, by the Prussian administrative authorities, the mayor and the chief of police of Cassel. As the local workers' council pointed out later, it had not only exercised rights of control over the different authorities, but had issued orders and fulfilled important administrative functions. Two of its members were coopted as aldermen by the town council, and another was responsible, jointly with a military representative, for military affairs. The local workers' and soldiers' council had above all to cope with the scarcity of food and of living accommodation, the illicit food trade and exorbitant prices, duties undertaken in close cooperation with the police. But it also paid attention to the problems of a land reform, especially where large estates and domains provided an opportunity to meet the strong demands for peasant settlement.[15] In 1918, before the High Command moved to Wilhelmshöhe near Cassel, the workers' and soldiers' council even issued a proclamation assuring Hindenburg and the High Command of its protection 'in the name of the German people': 'Hindenburg, carrying out his duties superbly, has never been closer to us than today'.[16] Cassel provides an interesting example of a strong and influential council which at the same time was very moderate in its politics.

In the small and agrarian state of Oldenburg the paramount influence was at first exercised by radical sailors from Wilhelmshaven who were entirely unwilling to limit the power of the workers' and soldiers' councils to advisory functions and who proclaimed a Republic of Oldenburg and East Frisia. Their leading spirit was the sailor Bernhard Kuhnt who in peace-time had been Social Democratic Party secretary at Chemnitz. He now became president of the Free State of Oldenburg, presiding over a government of 9 members, 5 of whom were Social Democrats and 2 taken over from the old grand-ducal government. But when elections took place in February 1919 the Social Democrats only gained 12 seats, and the bourgeois parties 27.[17] All radical influence disappeared very quickly, and the

[15] The Nachlass Grzesinski, Int. Inst. of Social History, Amsterdam, contains many pieces relating to the Cassel workers' and soldiers' council; the nos. quoted here are 422, 424, 452, 474.
[16] Quoted by Hermann Müller, *Die November-Revolution*, Berlin, 1931, p. 182.
[17] Detailed unsigned report to the *Parteivorstand* of the SPD of 3 Dec. 1918: Bundesarchiv Koblenz, NS 26, vorl. 68; Anlauf, *Revolution in Niedersachsen*, pp. 92, 66. The new prime minister of Oldenburg was Theodor Tantzen, a member of the Democratic Party. For Kuhnt cp. above, p. 72.

same applied to the small towns and rural districts of north-western Germany in general.

Things were very different in the Ruhr with its strong and radical working-class movement. Most of the workers' councils formed in November were dominated by the Social Democrats, but at Essen they agreed with the Independents on parity. At Duisburg, Reckling-hausen, Oberhausen, Bottrop and Buer representatives of the Christian trade unions and the Centre Party were immediately admitted to the workers' councils.[18] Particularly radical was the workers' council of Düsseldorf which was dominated by the Independents and had two Spartacist members. It controlled the local authorities and in practice exercised power as the authorities had no force at their disposal and depended on the support of the workers' council. The police were assisted by a unit of about 1,500 men which was recruited by the council and consisted almost entirely of organized left-wingers. The bourgeois groups were completely passive, and the police showed signs of demoralization.[19] At the end of November the workers' and soldiers' council issued a proclamation that its organs were vested with public authority, hence any resistance against its decrees and against persons entrusted by it with police duties was punishable as if it were resistance to the authority of the state; such actions as well as breaches of the peace, looting, robberies, arson, illicit food trading, etc., would be tried by special courts appointed by the workers' and soldiers' council. Against this decree the local lawyers' associations immediately protested; but the public prose-cutor and the president of the court of appeal (*Oberlandesgericht*) declined to join because they feared that if they did so the workers' council would prevent them from exercising their official functions. As the proclamation ran counter to various decrees of the Prussian government, which prohibited any interference with the courts, it proved impossible to establish the special courts desired by the workers' council. But the proclamation and especially the fears expressed by the highest legal officials indicated to what extent power was exercised by the council, and how impotent the authorities had become.[20]

In the Ruhr the miners in November gained the eight-hour day and higher wages, but these concessions did not satisfy them as the prices of coal and food increased rapidly. Many strikes ensued, and

[18] Kolb, *Arbeiterräte* . . . , p. 91.

[19] *Tagesbericht* 42, 12 Dec. 1918: Friedr.-Ebert-Stiftung, Nachlass Barth, V.

[20] Telegram and letter of 26 Nov. 1918 to the Ministry of Justice: Geh. Staats-archiv Berlin-Dahlem, Rep. 84a 22473.

further concessions were gained, but there were violent clashes with the security guards and troops. Soon demands were raised for changes in the composition of the workers' councils where these were dominated by moderate Social Democrats. In December the national congress of the workers' and soldiers' councils pronounced in favour of immediate steps of socialization, especially of the mines, which caused the strikes to spread and to become more political in character. On 9 January 1919 the Essen workers' and soldiers' council, which consisted of representatives of Social Democrats, Independents and Communists, decided to proclaim the socialization of the mines. On the eleventh the offices of the Coal Syndicate and the Mining Corporation were occupied. All wages and prices were to be controlled by the workers' council and all workers, employees and managers to continue to work as before. These steps the council considered necessary to calm the miners, in preparation for public control of the mining industry and socialization of the mines. A Social Democratic judge, Ruben, was elected 'people's commissar' to prepare this measure, with assistants from the three left-wing parties, which called on all miners to stop their strikes. A conference of the workers' and soldiers' councils and trade unions of the Rhenish-Westphalian industrial area was called to Essen.[21]

The conference, which met on 13 January, confirmed Ruben in his office and decided on the immediate socialization of the coal mines 'which more than anything else belong as of right to the whole people and not to any privileged individuals'. The work of socialization was to be based on the council system; workers' trusties were to be elected by the miners at the coal face who were to be responsible for supervising working conditions and the observation of safety rules. These trusties were to elect the pit council on which the technical and other employees were also to be represented and which was to be responsible for all matters concerning the pit in question. From the pit councils an area council was to be elected in each of the twenty mining districts of the Ruhr. The twenty area councils in their turn were to elect the central mining council, and this was to supervise the work of Ruben and his nine assistants, the Committee of Nine—three representatives of each of the left-wing parties. One of their first tasks would be the introduction of uniform wage settlements for all Ruhr miners, for which purpose they were to cooperate with

[21] R. Müller, *Der Bürgerkrieg . . .* , p. 130; *Illustrierte Geschichte der Deutschen Revolution*, pp. 313–16; Peter von Oertzen, *Betriebsräte in der Novemberrevolution*, Düsseldorf, 1963, p. 113.

the miners' unions; another task would be to achieve a reduction of food prices.[22] The ideas permeating the conference and the whole council movement in the Ruhr were to combine all those working in the mining industry, whether workmen or managerial and technical staff, to whatever party or trade union they belonged, and to create at each level from the pithead upwards organs of democratic control to supervise the bureaucratic machinery of the Coal Syndicate.[23] These ideas were not promoted by any particular party or trade union but developed spontaneously under the influence of the council movement.

But the Prussian state authorities—the mines were state property—strongly opposed any such schemes, the central government rejected the demands of the Committee of Nine, and its work never prospered. The trade unions mainly used it to settle differences over wages and labour conditions, and after a few days it gave up its attempt to control the Coal Syndicate; it was never officially recognized. Large strikes by miners in support of their demands failed to achieve them. Soon Free Corps and other units were brought into the Ruhr 'to restore law and order'; thereupon a general strike was proclaimed in April, and the government imposed a state of siege. The members of the Committee of Nine and many others were arrested by soldiers, there were violent clashes, and finally the strike movement collapsed. By the end of April it had petered out; the only practical gain was the further reduction of the mining day to seven hours.[24] There was to be no socialization, and the structure of miners' councils soon disappeared as the old authorities resumed their control.

There could hardly be a stronger contrast than that between the Ruhr district with its radical and activist working-class movement and the largely agrarian south-west where the revolution had assumed constitutional forms and the state governments from the outset included bourgeois ministers.[25] Yet in spite of the liberal local traditions and the absence of sharp class conflicts which made the social climate so different from that prevailing in Prussia, the council movement of the south-west was for a time strong and spontaneous, affecting not only the few large towns but the country as a whole—proof that it really was a movement on a national scale, carried by

---

[22] Text of the proclamation in R. Müller, *Der Bürgerkrieg* . . . , pp. 242–3.
[23] Oertzen, *Betriebsräte* . . . , p. 130.
[24] *Illustrierte Geschichte* . . . , pp. 316–33; Carl Severing, *1919/1920 im Wetter- und Watterwinkel*, Bielefeld, 1927, pp. 13–46.
[25] See above, pp. 42–3.

a genuine popular impetus. In Baden alone as many as 240 local workers' councils registered with that of the state—we do not know how many failed to do so. In their political complexion the large majority were entirely moderate. In the capital, Karlsruhe, the trades-council assembled on the evening of 11 November to elect a workers' council, and after a discussion it decided to appoint itself as the local workers' council. On the thirteenth it reached an agreement with the mayor not to interfere with the urban administration but to address its demands and wishes to the town council; the latter undertook to acquiesce in measures taken by the workers' council in the interest of law and order. One member of the workers' and one of the soldiers' council were attached to police headquarters to coordinate measures taken to that end and to ensure cooperation between the old and the new authorities. On the eighteenth the provisional government issued a decree: it had received information that in some places the workers' and soldiers' councils demanded that the local authorities, the *gendarmerie* and police should carry out their instructions and submit to them; the government requested the councils to abstain from any such interference, especially in the economic field and with regard to food supply; the councils should limit their activities on the local level to suggestions, and if they had any complaints about local authorities, should address them to the competent ministry in Karlsruhe which would investigate them.[26]

The Baden workers' and soldiers' councils were not entirely satisfied with this very modest role. When a state conference of the councils met at Mannheim on 21 November it was attended by representatives of seventy local councils. The assembly declared itself 'the pre-parliament of the free people's republic' and elected a committee of eleven as its executive. In its turn this elected a smaller committee of three members to control the provisional government; without their consent it was not to take any action of principal importance, and they attended its meetings. The assembly agreed that the elections to the Baden National Assembly were to take place on 5 January 1919—earlier than those to the German National Assembly—on condition that the government could guarantee 'an orderly and really democratic mode of election'. The assembly further assured the governments in Karlsruhe and in Berlin of its confidence in them and of its active support; it also expressed the expectation

[26] Oeftering, *Umsturz in Baden*, pp. 180–1, 268–71, 275–6; the figure of 240 workers' councils according to a report of the *Landeszentrale* of Baden to the Central Council of 3 Oct. 1919: Int. Inst. of Social History, Amsterdam, Zentralrat, B-12, VI.

that they would continue to promote with determination the interests of the social groups which hitherto had been suppressed and exploited. The last passage was adopted against six dissentient votes of the left, the rest of the resolution unanimously. The three members of the small committee not only supervised the government but attended its meetings as participants with equal rights. On the local level, representatives of the workers' councils were admitted to the organs of local government with an advisory voice, especially where the workers so far had not been represented at all. They cooperated with the police to control the trade in food and attended searches to discover illicit food stores. In the towns the councils controlled the local *Volkswehren*, while the police were responsible for the technical side and the conditions of service. 'Guiding principles for the workers', peasants' and people's councils of Baden', published at the end of November, enumerated among their tasks not only the defence of the achievements of the revolution against any reactionary movements, but also the 'maintenance of order and public security, protection of life and property', as well as 'control of the government and the public executive authorities and of the communes'; similar powers were allocated to the local councils, but these were again warned against any direct interference with the process of administration.[27]

The elections to the Baden National Assembly duly took place on 5 January and brought—as might have been expected—a severe defeat of the left. The Independents polled only 14,500 votes and did not gain a single seat. The Social Democrats polled over 300,000 votes and obtained 36 seats, but they were confronted by 40 Catholic, 25 Democratic and 6 Nationalist deputies: the bourgeois parties polled twice as many votes as the socialists. In consequence the two Independent ministers resigned from the government which remained a coalition of the Social Democrats and the bourgeois parties. A few days later another state conference of the councils met at Durlach. It declared that the workers', peasants', people's and soldiers' councils would continue to exist until the success of the revolution was guaranteed by the National Assembly: especially until local elections had taken place, the democratic republic and the eight-hour day were securely established, a people's army had been created on a democratic basis, and the process of socialization of those industries where the required pre-conditions existed, had started. These pre-conditions were not defined, but as Baden hardly had any

[27] Oeftering, *Umsturz* . . . , pp. 279–84, 288–90 (with the text of the documents quoted); Remmele, *Staatsumwälzung und Neuaufbau* . . . , pp. 31–6, 42–3.

heavy or mining industry considerable socialization was clearly not envisaged. As soon as these aims had been achieved the workers' councils would consider their activities to be terminated and would dissolve themselves. This was more closely defined by a further conference in May 1919 which declared that the work of the councils would be concluded when elections to the different organs of local government had been held. In July the Baden government informed the workers' councils that in future it would not be able to grant state funds to them or to the *Volkswehren*. The sixth and final state conference of the councils in August was only attended by representatives of 63 local councils. The majority accepted a resolution submitted by the committee of eleven that the workers' councils be dissolved, and the government then suspended all payments to them.[28]

By the autumn of 1919 the Baden workers' councils had in practice died a peaceful death. Even before that time many of them were no longer politically active but had become little more than citizens' advice bureaux, busy with questions of food and housing and with answering enquiries in social matters. On the local level their functions were taken over by the elected organs of the communes to which many workers' representatives were elected. The overwhelming majority of the workers' councils thought that the economic and social functions should be fulfilled by these elected representatives and by the trade unions and considered it unnecessary to create between them new organs in the form of permanent communal workers' councils; indeed they believed that such councils were as unnecessary 'as a goitre'. By the end of September about 140 workers' councils had dissolved themselves, leaving barely a hundred in the field; but out of these hundred, 21 councils no longer reacted to any communications. Even the council of Mannheim, the main industrial centre of Baden, met only very rarely, and its committee only in case of need. The council of Karlsruhe had dissolved itself. Within less than twelve months what had begun as a strong popular movement, forcefully voicing its demands and wielding considerable powers, came to an end, and all local initiative petered out.[29]

The development was very similar in neighbouring Württemberg, although this was more industrialized and in Stuttgart there was a

[28] Remmele, *Staatsumwälzung* . . . , pp. 54, 89–90; Oeftering, *Umsturz* . . . , p. 302; *Mitteilungsblatt für die Arbeiter-, Bauern- und Volksräte Badens*, Karlsruhe, 16 Jan. 1919, with the text of the resolution of 10 January.
[29] All details from a 15-page letter of the *Landeszentrale* to the Central Council, Karlsruhe, 3 Oct. 1919: Int. Inst. of Soc. Hist., Amsterdam, Zentralrat, B-12, VI.

comparatively strong group of the extreme left. On 25 November the enlarged workers' council of Stuttgart accepted by an overwhelming majority a Social Democratic resolution obliging the councils to support the provisional government 'in the interest of the common weal', rejecting red guards and dictatorship as means to obtain 'the socialist people's state', and demanding the immediate holding of elections to a National Assembly as well as a *Land* parliament. The resolution allocated to the workers' councils functions of control over measures taken by the government and the communes, but significantly declared that they would only exercise their rights until the *Land* parliament had met and formed a government. There was only one dissentient voice. On the same day the constituent assembly of the workers' councils met for the whole of Württemberg. There too the radicals were defeated after long discussions. A resolution in support of the provisional government and against dictatorship was accepted by 200 to 75 votes. On the executive committee elected by the conference the Social Democrats occupied eleven seats and the Independents four. The soldiers' councils which had met some days before were even more moderate and voted a similar resolution by 128 to 2 votes. A state committee of the workers' and soldiers' councils was formed. On 14 December the provisional government issued statutes for the workers', peasants' and soldiers' councils in which it undertook to consult the state committee 'in important cases'; the local councils were to control the carrying out of the measures decided upon by the government and the local authorities; but executive power was to rest solely in the hands of the government, and the local councils were to abstain from any interference with the administration; if they were hindered in their activities by any public authorities they should complain to the state committee which would settle the question together with the government.[30]

In spite of these legal provisions, however, the Württemberg councils did not develop any great activity in public affairs, perhaps because of the internal conflicts between Social Democrats, Independents and Communists.[31] This applied even more strongly after the elections of the constituent *Land* parliament which took place on 12 January 1919—a week before those to the German National Assembly. As in Baden—and in Germany as a whole—the socialists were defeated: of 150 seats, the Social Democrats gained 52 and the Independents 4. Among the bourgeois parties, the Democrats were

[30] Blos, *Von der Monarchie* . . . , pp. 44–5, 49–51; Weller, *Staatsumwälzung* . . . , pp. 132–3; Keil, *Erlebnisse* . . . , ii, p. 121.　　[31] Thus Keil, *Erlebnisse*, ii, p. 122.

the strongest with 38, followed by the Catholic Centre with 31 and several smaller parties with together 25 deputies, a total of 94. Here too the Independent ministers resigned; the government now consisted of five Social Democrats and three bourgeois ministers; its composition was approved by the executive of the workers' and soldiers' councils.[32] The bourgeois parties soon used their majority in the Diet to declare that the workers' councils no longer had a *raison d'être* because parliament had taken over and the local assemblies too had been elected on the basis of a very liberal franchise. In June the Diet majority decided to limit the authority of the councils to 15 July so that from that date onwards they would lose their legal basis.[33] In this way the life of the councils was terminated at a comparatively early date—before it came to an end in the other major states of Germany.

In the whole of the south-west it was only in the city of Frankfurt that developments were somewhat more radical. The first workers' councils in the factories were elected on 8 November on the initiative of the local Independents. A meeting called by them also elected a city workers' council; this caused a conflict with the Social Democrats which lasted throughout the ninth. Then a compromise was enforced by a soldiers' council formed meanwhile by a student serving in the army as a sergeant, and seven members each of the two parties became members of the workers' council. The soldiers' council occupied the public buildings; the military and civil authorities declared their readiness to cooperate with it; the lord mayor appeared and had himself confirmed in office; but the chief of police refused to bow to the new order and was deposed and replaced by a Social Democratic town councillor, the lawyer Dr Sinzheimer. In nearby Offenbach the Social Democrats took the initiative, formed an action committee and took over power on 9 November. On the same day a few Independents and Democrats were added to their ranks.[34] The Frankfurt workers' and soldiers' council was careful not to interfere with the internal administration of the city and did not set up committees to supervise the different branches of it, as the councils did in Bremen and Hamburg. It only insisted on recognition as 'the highest authority of the town'; and this was duly conceded by the aldermen on 12 November, whereupon the council consented to let aldermen and town council continue as the representation of the

---

[32] Blos, *Von der Monarchie* . . . , pp. 102–3; Weller, *Staatsumwälzung* . . . , pp. 169–72.
[33] The Bavarian envoy in Stuttgart to the Bavarian Foreign Office, Stuttgart, 21 June 1919: Bayer. Hauptstaatsarchiv, Staatsministerium des Innern, 54190 (copy).   [34] Kolb, *Arbeiterräte* . . . , p. 93.

1   Street scene, Berlin, 9 November 1918

2   Crowd assembled in front of the palace in Berlin awaiting
the cortège of those killed on 9 November 1918

3 General Wilhelm Groener, 1918

4 Kurt Eisner, 1918

5 Friedrich Ebert welcoming the returning troops in front
of the Brandenburg Gate, Berlin, 1918

6 Gustav Noske, 1919

7 and 8   Street scenes in Berlin during the Spartacus Rising, January 1919
(In 7 above negotiators are trying to reach the Chancery under a
white flag.)

9 and 10 Free Corps units in Munich, May 1919

11 Karl Liebknecht
(photograph taken in 1912)

12 Hugo Haase

13 Rosa Luxemburg
(photograph taken about
1914)

14   Otto Bauer   15   Friedrich Adler

16   Karl Renner   17   Julius Deutsch

18 (*above left*)   Béla Kun

19   Vilmos Böhm

20   Ernö Bettelheim

21   József Pogány, Military Commissar, Inspecting a Red army unit, 1919

burghers. But four members of the workers' council were added to the aldermen, and its representatives also joined the town's offices for food, housing and labour. For the offices of the police, the railways, and posts and telegraphs, which came under the Prussian state, special committees were formed which acquired comparatively strong influence there. The workers' council was given offices in the town hall on which the red flag was hoisted.[35]

The workers' council which installed itself at the regional railway directorate claimed not only a right of control but of real participation which was in vain disputed by some railway officials; its members were allowed to take part in all important meetings and decisions. The council slowly extended its sphere of influence with the aim of 'a complete transfer of the state railways into the hands of the workers and works' councils'. It initiated the setting up of a central council for the railways which successfully carried the propaganda for the council system and the right of workers' control into all railway districts: a system of socialism would guarantee the fulfilment of the workers' wishes. During a great strike in the summer of 1919 the workers' council entirely took over the direction of the administration and the whole enterprise, but it retained all officials working under its control while cutting all communication between them and the Ministry in Berlin—a move classified by the latter as threatening the very existence of the state and aiming at the establishment of the dictatorship of the proletariat.[36] The city workers' council, too, came under more radical influence and there was growing friction with the municipal authorities, which were no longer willing to concede powers of control to the council. When, on the other hand, severe food riots broke out at the end of March 1919 the town council decided to employ 'workers' supervisors' to register and distribute stores of food and to set up a committee at the food office whose members were entitled to conduct searches and to confiscate illicit stores. This committee of trusties of the workers' council continued to function and to supervise the food office during the following months and to render extremely useful services at a time of severe shortages and black market conditions.[37]

The industrial areas of central Germany—the states of Saxony and

[35] Hans Drüner, *Im Schatten des Weltkrieges—Zehn Jahre Frankfurter Geschichte*, Frankfurt, 1934, pp. 332–4, 340–1; Toni Sender, *The Autobiography of a German Rebel*, London, 1940, pp. 105–6, 341.

[36] Report of Minister der öffentlichen Arbeiten, Berlin, 4 July 1919: Bundesarchiv Koblenz, Reichskanzlei, R 43 I/2118.

[37] Drüner, *Im Schatten . . .* , pp. 369, 378; the soldiers' council had to be dissolved at the orders of the French Commander in Chief.

Thuringia and the Prussian province of Saxony—were centres of a radical and militant working-class movement, and later of strong Communist influence. In 1921 the Halle-Merseburg district was to become the scene of a notorious Communist *Putsch*, and in 1923 Saxony and Thuringia were to have short-lived Socialist-Communist coalition governments. In 1919 large parts of the area were dominated by the Independent Social Democrats, especially their left wing. On 14 November 1918 the workers' and soldiers' councils of Leipzig, Dresden and Chemnitz proclaimed somewhat prematurely that the capitalist system had collapsed and the revolutionary proletariat had seized power; the realization of the republic, they declared, was identical with the absolute rule of the will of the working class and the elimination of servitude in any form; the special task of the new republican government was the liquidation of the Saxon state which was to be absorbed in the unified German socialist republic; the revolution must be continued and its momentum increased until the ruling bourgeoisie was totally defeated. Yet the new socialist government of Saxony, in which the Independents held the most important posts, only two days later curtailed the functions of the workers' and soldiers' councils to those exercised by them throughout Germany, functions of control of the existing local authorities and attendance of their representatives at meetings of the district councils (*Bezirksausschüsse*); but in the eyes of the government even the control functions were only 'desirable', and attendance at meetings of the *Kreisausschüsse* was not considered necessary; any disturbance of law and order must be avoided. This decree, published only one week after the outbreak of the revolution, gave no real power to the workers' and soldiers' councils and left the old administrative authorities virtually undisturbed in exercising their functions. On the eighteenth the Saxon government issued a proclamation to the people which envisaged important social reforms and local self-government but no changes in the social structure. The workers' and soldiers' councils were only mentioned once: their task was the protection and control of 'the socialist people's government', but it was not said how this was to be achieved.[38]

While the Independents dominated the workers' and soldiers' council of Leipzig, the moderate Social Democrats gained control of those of Dresden and Chemnitz. In Dresden elections took place by districts on 24 November, in which the Social Democrats gained

---

[38] R. Müller, *Vom Kaiserreich . . .*, ii, pp. 69–70, 244–6, with the text of the proclamations of 14–18 Nov. 1918. Cp. above, p. 44.

fifteen times as many votes as the Independents and obtained the large majority of the seats. At Chemnitz, all inhabitants above the age of 18 were entitled to vote and the Social Democrats polled twelve times as many votes as the Independents in elections held on 9 December.[39] In Saxony there was, according to a confidential report, a strong movement to replace leading civil servants by Social Democrats, but the plan to remove all mayors and heads of communes was given up. Yet at Leipzig and Chemnitz the town councils were dissolved by the workers' and soldiers' councils. These also demanded that their officials should be paid from public funds, otherwise they threatened to take over the Reichsbank offices. In general the report noticed marked centrifugal tendencies which the moderate Social Democrats were trying to counter by the demand for the summoning of a Saxon National Assembly which should then proclaim that Saxony was joining the Reich.[40] In January 1919 the Independent ministers resigned—as they had done some weeks before in Berlin—and the Social Democrats alone formed the state government. In parliamentary elections held at the beginning of February they obtained 42 seats and the Independents only 15, while several bourgeois parties gained 40. Conflicts between the government in Dresden and the radical workers' and soldiers' council of Leipzig continued, especially when a general strike movement engulfed most of central Germany in the early months of 1919. In April there was severe rioting in Dresden during which the War Minister of Saxony, a Social Democrat, was lynched and other casualties occurred. In April the Saxon government proclaimed a state of siege; treason, murder, looting, rioting, breaches of the peace, resistance to the authorities, mutiny, arson and a whole host of other crimes were to be dealt with by military courts; armed force would be used if necessary to enforce these stringent orders, which were backed by the Reich government. In May the troops of General Maercker, in execution of its orders, occupied Leipzig without meeting any resistance. The protest of the workers' and soldiers' council was disregarded.[41]

In some towns of Thuringia too the local workers' councils consisted entirely of Independent Social Democrats. At Gera and Gotha

---

[39] Kolb, *Arbeiterräte* . . . , p. 96; Matthias (ed.), *Regierung* . . . , i, p. 193, n. 93; Lindau, *Revolutionäre Kämpfe* . . . , p. 173.

[40] *Persönliche Information*, Berlin, 2 Dec. 1918, signed von Olberg: Friedr.-Ebert-Stiftung, Nachlass Barth, III.

[41] *Illustrierte Geschichte der Deutschen Revolution*, pp. 381–2; Ernst Rudolf Huber, *Dokumente zur Deutschen Verfassungsgeschichte*, iii, Stuttgart, 1966, nos. 123–8, pp. 108–11.

they dissolved the town councils and replaced them by their own commissions. The fact that Thuringia consisted of several little states enabled the local workers' councils to function as the governments of the free states of Reuss and of Coburg-Gotha. All protests were unsuccessful. As late as February 1919 the workers' and soldiers' council of Gotha declared that the town council would remain dissolved. Elections held in the same month gave to the Independents a slight absolute majority, with 10 out of 19 seats. In Gera and Erfurt the workers' council created well-disciplined *Volkswehr* units which successfully maintained law and order. In Gera the workers' and soldiers' council legislated on working hours and introduced minimum wages against the protests of the local industrialists. At Erfurt, which belonged to Prussia, three members of the workers' council established control over the machinery of administration. When General Maercker in February 1919 issued an ultimatum and demanded that all weapons be handed over, the workers' council organized their collection and thus prevented the occupation of the town by Maercker's forces.[42] When the seven free states of Thuringia combined at the beginning of 1920 to form the state of Thuringia, the left-wing governments which had existed in some of them lost their power; even this was accompanied by new protests and government intervention, especially after the defeat of the Kapp *Putsch* in March 1920.

The council movement in the district of Merseburg, a part of the Prussian province of Saxony, noted for its mining and chemical industries, was particularly determined and well organized. The movement was led by two energetic Independent deputies, Wilhelm Koenen and Bernhard Düwell, both members of the National Assembly. At Halle the workers' and soldiers' council on its own initiative tried to introduce the Hamburg points adopted by the national congress of the councils in December, but it met with the vigorous counter-action of the medical officers who refused to look after the thousands of wounded in the military hospitals.[43] At Halle, too, police duties were undertaken by a unit which consisted almost entirely of Independents and their sympathizers. But the principal attention of the workers' councils was directed towards economic issues, especially socialization and workers' control, exactly as in the

[42] Kolb, *Arbeiterräte* . . . , pp. 109, 300–1, 326; protest of 17 industrialists of Schleiz of 7 Dec. 1918: Friedr.-Ebert-Stiftung, Nachlass Barth, V.

[43] The matter was discussed on 10 Jan. 1919 by the cabinet which decided that such attempts must lead to catastrophe: Matthias (ed.), *Regierung* . . . , ii, no. 99, p. 205. See above pp. 72–3.

other mining region, the Ruhr. In January 1919 the workers' and soldiers' council of Merseburg decided to assume control over the Prussian *Oberbergamt* (Mining Office) at Halle which supervised all mines in central Germany: a control to be exercised jointly by representatives of the council and of the miners. At the end of January a conference of the workers' and soldiers' councils of the area declared that the councils—this was ten days after the election of the National Assembly—still claimed the highest political authority; in all enterprises employing more than twenty workmen works' councils were to be appointed to maintain production and to bring about a speedy socialization; their representatives were to be entitled to participate with equal rights in all questions concerning the management and to be given seats on the directorial boards.[44]

The movement quickly grew. In February another miners' conference was held at Halle which had a strong radical composition. It demanded immediate democratization in all public enterprises, immediate recognition of the elected works' councils and of the area miners' council which was based upon them. It also decided to call a general strike for these demands and warned against any acts of violence. Koenen opposed any measure of socialization from above which would deprive the workers of their right to participate in decisions: 'Hence socialization must come from below, and this required a democratic extension and erection of the council system in which the works' councils, above all, would have to secure the workers' right to participate throughout the process of production'. The government was forced to make concessions. It proclaimed that it would create a unified socialist labour law: 'the organs of economic democracy, the works' councils' would become the legitimate spokesmen of all workers; the government's aim was 'the constitutional factory on a democratic basis'; the branches of the economy, such as mines and electricity, which were suitable to be transferred to public or common ownership, would be socialized. The general strike petered out. At the end of April the Prussian Ministry of Trade and Industry asked the *Oberbergamt* at Halle to take energetic measures against the election of works' councils in the mines and the re-election of the area miners' council. Thereupon the *Oberbergamt* in May refused to admit any further control by the miners' council and excluded its representatives from all participation: the period when the council had been permitted a semi-official position came to an end. The control of the Prussian regional administration at

[44] Oertzen, *Betriebsräte* . . . , pp. 134–7; *Illustrierte Geschichte* . . . , p. 375.

Merseburg by the local workers' and soldiers' council continued for another few months. As late as September 1919 the *Regierungspräsident* acknowledged that it was taking place in a suitably objective form and that the district workers' council was conscientiously observing the agreements reached.[45] The council movement in the Halle-Merseburg area was one of the most vigorous in the whole of Germany. It had more clear-sighted leaders than those in other parts and was much less vague in its aims; it also had strangely modern connotations in the issue of workers' control and participation; these were absent in most other districts, where the struggle often became a party conflict between Social Democrats and Independents (and later Communists) and exhausted itself in mutual recriminations.

In contrast with central Germany, the north-east—the Prussian provinces of Brandenburg, Pomerania, Silesia, East and West Prussia—was largely agrarian, with few large towns (notably Berlin) and only one important industrial area: Upper Silesia. In spite of this, workers' and soldiers' councils sprang up everywhere in the days of November and usually assumed controlling functions similar to those they exercised elsewhere. In the province of Brandenburg a central office was established at the *Oberpräsidium* and a strong organization for the province was created: there was a *Kreis* workers' council for each of the 31 *Kreise* and about 700 local workers' councils, which controlled the *Landräte* and town councils respectively. In the small town of Salzwedel the council threatened to impose the death penalty on traders in and purchasers of illicit food. In the province of Pomerania the workers' councils met at the end of November, voted guide-lines for the conduct of their affairs and entrusted the Stettin council with the control of the *Oberpräsidium* in Stettin. At the beginning of 1919 a provincial council of four members was appointed. In East Prussia a similar provincial council decreed that in each commune a workers' council, and in each garrison town a workers' and soldiers' council, was to be set up; the local councils were to control all local authorities, as the provincial council controlled the *Oberpräsidium* and the provincial administration in Königsberg. Any official decrees and communications were only valid if countersigned by the council in question. On the local

[45] Oertzen, *Betriebsräte* . . . , pp. 143, 151 and n. 4; *Illustrierte Geschichte* . . . , pp. 373–4, with the proclamations of the general strike and of the government, the latter announcing: 'Socialization is on the march!'

level the control exercised varied from a superficial acknowledgement of official actions and correspondence to a detailed supervision of all important matters, participation in all important meetings and countersignature of the entire correspondence. On 13 November the Prussian prime minister especially warned the councils not to dissolve the town councils and urban deputations—actions which were contrary to government policy and impeded the work of the local authorities in matters of food, health and support of needy families. At the beginning of 1919 a Prussian decree again warned the workers' councils not to interfere with the financial or legal administration: all they were entitled to do was to register an objection to measures taken by the local authorities, but not to take part in their meetings, nor to be informed of confidential affairs.[46]

The issue which became prominent in the eastern provinces was that of the conservative Prussian civil servants who resented any control by a workers' council as an unwarranted interference by men who came from the lower classes and were totally unqualified for such duties. The workers' councils in vain attempted to get such officials removed and replaced by men with a more democratic outlook. Any compromise between such diametrically opposed views seemed out of the question, and the Prussian government only too often took the side of the civil servants who had made themselves very unpopular by their autocratic methods, and naturally were unable to change these overnight; the government was thus often siding with their political enemies against their own party comrades. At the end of November the workers' council of Gleiwitz in Silesia decreed the immediate introduction of the six-hour day and the payment of overtime. This was considered 'illegal' by the royal (*sic*) regional administration at Oppeln which protested in no uncertain terms to Berlin and instructed the local authority to reject the request.[47]

The *Regierungspräsident* at Oppeln was von Miquel who in the past had made himself highly unpopular with the Polish population and many Germans by his chauvinism and his personal behaviour; the local Social Democrats strongly demanded that he be replaced. But although the name suggested was that of a Breslau Catholic lawyer, a prominent member of the Centre Party, this was not done. The Independent minister Breitscheid simply took the view that no

[46] Kolb, *Arbeiterräte* . . . , pp. 111–12, 262–3, 265; Matthias (ed.), *Regierung* . . . , i, no. 26, p. 140; Int. Inst. of Soc. Hist., Amsterdam, Nachlass Grzesinski, no. 407 (council organisation in East Prussia).

[47] The Oppeln government to the Ministry of Finance, 3 Dec. 1918: Friedr.-Ebert-Stiftung, Nachlass Barth, V.

complaint from the workers' and soldiers' council of Oppeln had reached the government and that von Miquel seemed to cooperate well with the local trade union secretaries who were willing to submit to him. But the Social Democrat who represented Silesia on the Central Council declared that the local party officials and trade unionists simply could not stand up to Miquel and were unable to make their will felt; they nevertheless favoured an immediate change. Even more glaring was the case of the *Regierungspräsident* of Breslau, Dr Traugott von Jagow, who had made himself notorious before the war as the 'strong' chief of police of Berlin. From Breslau it was suggested as early as November that he should be removed and replaced by a former *Landrat*, Freiherr von Reibnitz, who was strongly recommended. But the government turned him down because he had joined the Social Democrats a few days after the revolution, as Breitscheid told the complainants. But they countered this by the argument that Reibnitz for years had sympathized with the socialists and for this reason had been victimized under the old régime; he was moreover well known for the useful work he had done, especially in the social sphere, contrary to the ruling conservative tendencies. Thus von Jagow was kept in office until the end of 1918, and then granted three months' leave of absence.[48] But the whole affair showed the extraordinary ineptitude of the new Prussian government even in a province vital on account of its industries and the incipient clash between Germans and Poles, its extraordinary reluctance to replace senior civil servants even when well qualified successors were available.

Similar conflicts occurred when local workers' councils attempted to get the *Landrat* removed on account of his reactionary policy or his refusal to cooperate with the workers' council. As the *Landrat*, even more than the *Regierungspräsident*, had been the representative of the *ancien régime* in the countryside, and as the large majority of the *Landräte* came from a socially exclusive group, the landed nobility, it was more than natural that the groups hitherto excluded from participation in local government used the opportunity of the revolution to bring about a change. In this, however, they were only rarely successful. At Stallupönen in East Prussia there was a state of war between the workers' council, the majority of whose members belonged to bourgeois groups, and the *Landrat* who openly sided with the big landowners. When the workers' council initiated checks on

[48] Matthias (ed.), *Regierung* . . . , ii, no. 76, pp. 57–8, 61–2, 68–70: cabinet meeting of 28 Dec. 1918.

food deliveries and stores the *Landrat* in advance informed the land-owners; important correspondence was not shown to the workers' council; its representative charged with the supervision of the *Landrat* office was shouted down. In February 1919 the council decided to request the *Landrat*'s removal and to impede him in the carrying out of his duties; but the Minister of the Interior decreed that he should continue in office until the official enquiry was con-cluded. The East Prussian provincial council, however, refused to accept this and ordered the Stallupönen council to prevent the *Landrat* from exercising his office, but the *Regierungspräsident* in-structed him to continue. Thereupon the workers' council renewed its decision to impede the *Landrat* in his work because he continuously rendered passive resistance to the policy of the new government. All protests to Berlin were unsuccessful as the *Landrat* was backed by the Prussian Ministry of the Interior. At the end of March the workers' council requested the Central Council in Berlin to take the case up with the new Minister of the Interior, and to get him to send new *Landräte* to the three neighbouring *Kreise* also; but the Central Council considered the case hopeless. In May the *Landrat* refused to admit representatives of the workers' council to *Kreis* committee meetings and gave notice to one of his employees who was elected deputy chairman of the local Social Democratic group: only then was he finally moved to another post.[49]

At Greifswald in Pomerania the Social Democrats desired that the police director and chairman of the local workers' and soldiers' council, Burmann, be appointed *Landrat* for the surrounding country district. From this post the former *Landrat*, Count Behr-Behrenhof, had been removed on account of his reactionary views and former activities as a parliamentary deputy, and Burmann was then pro-visionally appointed to his post. The local conservative circles protested strongly to the Ministry of the Interior against his definitive appointment, for which the Social Democrats were agitating, as an unwarranted interference by the town population in the affairs of the countryside; they had no desire to see a Social Democratic agitator installed as their *Landrat* and instead demanded the re-appointment of Count Behr-Behrenhof whose dismissal had been entirely unjustified.[50] At Deutsch-Krone in the east of Pomerania the workers' and soldiers' council removed the mayor as well as the *Landrat* from their offices, but after a re-election of the council both

[49] Kolb, *Arbeiterräte . . .*, pp. 375–8.
[50] Letter to Ministry of Interior, s.d.: Bundesarchiv Koblenz, NS 26, vorl. 71.

resumed their posts. But the *Landrat* refused to make any payments to the workers' council and to let its committee countersign correspondence in matters of taxation and forestry; there were constant complaints about his administrative method, and his views, which were unchanged. In this extremely conservative *Kreis* the workers' council found it impossible to induce the landowners, who were also the local authorities, to submit to the new government, and counter-revolutionary activities were rife. Pathetically the council's chairman enquired: 'Are these the achievements of the revolution?'[51]

At Crossen on the Oder a conflict arose at the beginning of 1919 because the *Regierungspräsident* at Frankfurt declined to pay the costs of secretarial assistance and an office for the workers' and soldiers' council: its activity was to be limited to the control of local authorities, and for this purpose two people were sufficient for the *Landrat* office and another two for the municipality. But the executive committee declared that in these conditions it was unable to fulfil its duties: its members not only controlled the *Landrat* and the municipality, but also the local garrison and prisoner-of-war camp and thus had no time for other work; in addition it had to support and advise the peasant councils of 86 local communes, and therefore they needed an office and a typist, apart from the chairman and the treasurer: where should these do their work? Did the *Regierungspräsident* do his without an office? Their patience was at an end, and they would resign if the Central Council did not intervene. In February a new conflict occurred, this time with the Crossen *Landrat*, von Gottberg, because he refused to instruct the local authorities to hold elections for representatives of the communes, but instead announced that the peasant councils were to be re-elected. He claimed that the latter came under his authority, while the executive committee claimed that this was its responsibility. Several local authorities (usually identical with the big landowners) refused to hold the communal elections decreed by the government, and the *Landrat* did nothing to remind them of their duty. For these reasons the executive committee complained to the *Regierungspräsident* at Frankfurt who promised to instruct the *Landrat* that the elections must be held on 2 March. Meanwhile part of the Crossen population, without the knowledge of the executive committee, put an ultimatum to the *Landrat* either to instruct the local authorities in this sense and to cancel the order about the re-election of peasant councils, or to

[51] Letters from Deutsch-Krone to the Central Council of 28 April, 8 and 13 May 1919: Int. Inst. of Social History, Amsterdam, Zentralrat, B-12, III.

resign. All attempts of the *Regierungspräsidium* and the citizens of Crossen to bring about a settlement of the conflict were in vain.[52]

In January 1919 the municipality of Tempelburg in Pomerania informed the local workers' and soldiers' council that in future, instead of three, only one of its members would be paid by the town —a decision which received the approval of the *Landrat*. In this case the local council was backed by the provincial council for Pomerania in Stettin which sent a strong letter to Tempelburg: in 'the socialist republic in which we now live' the old authorities no longer had a monopoly of political power; any of their decisions must be counter-signed by the local workers' and peasants' council, otherwise it was invalid; the Stettin council was the highest authority in Pomerania and therefore instructed the municipality to pay 7.50 marks a day to three members of the workers' and peasants' council, half of this expenditure to be met from the *Kreis* funds; if they refused to do so counter-measures would be taken.[53] In Greifswald the workers' and soldiers' council occupied an office in the town hall where its meetings were held, its correspondence was dealt with and applicants seeking advice were received; it exercised the usual supervisory functions but did not interfere with the running of the administration. But it experienced strong difficulties with the railway directorate and the regional post office which both refused to admit the controllers appointed by the council and to recognize any right of control over their functions, so that the Central Council in Berlin had to intervene.[54]

From the extreme west of Prussia, the workers' council of Aschendorf, near the Dutch frontier, also complained to the Central Council in May 1919: they had been involved from December 1918 in continuous conflicts with the local *Landrat* and had petitioned the government many months ago for his removal, but without result. Therefore a mass meeting in the market square took up the demand and gave the government two weeks to decide on it, otherwise they would hold a plebiscite in the *Kreis* to determine the *Landrat* question.[55] In March 1919 even the chairman of the Central Council (Leinert, the mayor of Hanover) asked the Prussian government whether it was not possible to inculcate a new spirit in the Ministry

[52] The Crossen council to the Central Council, 23 Jan. and 19 Feb. 1919: ibid., B–22, III.

[53] The Stettin workers' and soldiers' council to the Magistrat of Tempelburg, s.d.: ibid., B-19, I.

[54] Letters of 2 and 8 Jan. and 4 Feb. 1919: ibid., B-22, III.

[55] Letter to the Central Council of 23 May 1919: ibid., B-12, VI.

of the Interior: so much that had been decided was being ruined by its *Geheimräte*. The *Oberpräsident* of the province of Hanover, von Richter, had not been dismissed although he had sent a telegram in January to the former Emperor on the occasion of his sixtieth birthday; nor had anything happened to the *Landrat* of *Kreis* Soltau, von Rappard, who had expressed 'the deepest sorrow to His Majesty' as well as his 'gratitude and reverence' in the name of the whole *Kreis*. In reply the Prussian Minister of the Interior, Heine, only referred to the difficulty of finding suitable people; as quite unsuitable comrades were often proposed, a state had been reached when local wishes were simply disregarded. The Minister of Education, Haenisch, another Social Democrat, confirmed the lack of suitable candidates which had forced him to give posts to liberals; there were younger people, but they could not be given senior posts.[56]

From the island of Rügen in the Baltic the workers' and soldiers' council in February 1919 complained in strong terms that very little had changed in the countryside and that things were rapidly reverting to their former state: originally, the workers' and soldiers' councils had really possessed power—a remarkable statement from such a remote corner of the agrarian east—'and here in the East Albian lands the Junkers and agrarians were full of fear what would come next'; the workers' and soldiers' councils, not hindered by the bureaucratic ways of the old régime, were feared and were able to intervene much more forcefully than the authorities; it would have been a thankful task to take truly revolutionary measures without spilling any blood. But in these rural districts no fundamental legal changes were noticeable; the *Gutsbezirke* (on which the landlords exercised police powers) had not been abolished; the landowner was still the pasha on his estate, most agricultural labourers were still living under the same oppression as previously, and there was still corporal punishment on the estates. To give some examples: the landowner Kroos at Güttin had beaten a girl employed by him without reason until she bled and then refused to pay her and to give her her papers. At Heidhof a domestic servant who demanded higher wages was beaten on her head and face and then thrown out. According to the local Catholic priest, the harvesters were treated so abominably that they had no wish but to disappear from this 'Eldorado' even without their back pay; and the Russian prisoners were treated even worse. Eighteen labourers were dismissed at Güttin in January and, when they demanded what was due to them,

[56] Kolb (ed.), *Der Zentralrat . . .* , no. 99, pp. 779–81: meeting of 8 March 1919.

threatened by the landowner with a revolver. German refugees from the Ukraine were in practice sold to the estate owners by the office responsible for their settlement. They received miserable terms and only signed their contracts with three crosses. In all these matters the workers' and soldiers' council had helped and earned the blessings of the labourers: the moment the council finally disappeared the land-lords would be jubilant and the old state of affairs would be restored in the 'new Germany'. Owing to the dissolution of the soldiers' councils the workers' councils were now more or less enfeebled be-cause they could no longer back their demands with a show of strength; if they ceased to control the *Landrat* offices it would soon be clear which way things would go.[57]

Much of the local power of the workers' and soldiers' councils had indeed rested on their combined organization which had come into being practically everywhere during November. This was confirmed from another area of the agrarian east of Germany by a witness who can hardly be suspected of bias, the Social Democratic party secretary of Königsberg, Friedrich Seemann. He stated in April 1919 that in East Prussia workers' *and* soldiers' councils hardly existed any longer because the Special Commissar of the Reich government, August Winnig, took the view that the soldiers' councils were not entitled to occupy themselves with civilian matters and therefore had to leave the joint councils: their only functions were those allocated to them by the decree of 19 January 1919;[58] but these were more than limited because most of the units in East Prussia belonged to the 'mobile formations', to which the decree did not apply and which came exclusively under the orders of the military hierarchy. Significantly, Seemann added that from the day which had brought the separation of the soldiers' councils from the workers' councils the Junkers in the East had begun to raise their heads again and to show their old impudence.[59] With the collapse of one pillar the other was also seriously weakened. In fact the local power of the workers' councils survived that of the soldiers' councils by only a few months.

This, however, was not the only reason for the speedy collapse of the councils' power. In November 1918 there existed for a short time a vacuum: the old authorities, although they did not disappear, were passive and unable to cope with the revolutionary wave which engulfed the country. It took them a little time to re-emerge and to

[57] The workers' and soldiers' council of *Kreis* Rügen to the government, Bergen, 25 Feb. 1919: Bundesarchiv Koblenz, R 43 I/1941.
[58] For this decree, see above, p. 74; for Winnig, see above, pp. 66–7.
[59] *II. Kongress der Arbeiter-, Bauern- und Soldatenräte . . .*, pp. 89–90.

resume their former functions. As another leading Social Democrat noticed in November, the same applied to the political parties, including the Social Democrats who 'for some days simply ceased to exist'. Later, however, the parties resumed their former functions, and 'the tried forces of the trade unions' became more and more strongly represented in the workers' and soldiers' councils.[60] But the trade unions were even more opposed to the rival power of the councils than were the Social Democratic party officials who, locally, were often identical with the chairmen of the councils. Hence the councils were unable to retain the power so suddenly acquired against the combined and old-established forces of the government, the bureaucracy, the political parties and the trade unions. They were soon limited to a supervisory function which was never clearly defined; after a few months even this function ceased to be of any importance.

Politically, the large majority of the councils were dominated and led by moderate Social Democrats and trade unionists, not by the Independents. The latter exercised strong influence only in the mining districts of the Ruhr and of central Germany and in a few large towns, especially in Berlin, Bremen, Leipzig, Brunswick and Düsseldorf. This very limited influence was mirrored in the results of the elections to the two national congresses of the workers' and soldiers' councils in December 1918 and April 1919. A Social Democratic majority was never in question, and the Independents reacted to that by condemning themselves to political impotence. But it is, of course, possible to argue that the super-radicalism of certain councils, their ill-considered attempts to establish a 'dictatorship', the anarchic tendencies especially at work in Munich, created a reaction not only in bourgeois circles, but also among the moderate Social Democrats; the latter thus tended to reject the whole council 'system' and grossly overestimated the radicalism of all councils in general. The fear of 'Bolshevism' certainly was a powerful force in Germany, not only in 1918. In particular the government of the people's representatives 'saw in the councils a confirmation of their own fear that the revolution would deteriorate into Bolshevism'.[61]

The spring of 1919 saw the dissolution of the large majority of the workers' and soldiers' councils. Once town councils were elected on the basis of a democratic franchise and the same was done on the level of the rural communes, the supervisory functions became un-

[60] Thus Dr Gradnauer, later prime minister of Saxony, on 25 Nov. 1918: Matthias (ed.), *Regierung . . .* , i, no. 30, p. 192.   [61] ibid., p. cxxix.

necessary in the eyes of the local authorities, nor were they any longer willing to pay for activities of which most of them wholeheartedly disapproved. Without funds and without offices the local workers' councils were unable to carry on, and many of them very willingly handed over to the new elected assemblies. In Prussia, the creation of such democratically elected local councils was certainly one of the achievements of the revolution, and there was no need to 'safeguard' it any longer if it was considered that the establishment of political democracy was the primary aim. The dilemma was recognized as early as February 1919 by the workers' and soldiers' council of Hameln on the Weser:

> ... It would be superfluous to let the workers' and soldiers' council continue as a separate organ of control, unless one adopts the point of view that a workers' and soldiers' council must be forced upon the workers and soldiers even where they are politically opposed to the council organization, . . . a council that would have to supervise the management of the local authorities even where the population rejects the council system, or where the large majority of the population has shown in the elections that it does not agree with the Social Democrats. In places, on the other hand, which have a largely Social Democratic population and the corresponding local council and local administration, in our opinion no workers' and soldiers' council would be required. In places of a different political complexion its existence would only be justified if the administrative organs rendered active or passive resistance to the execution of government orders. But in such cases it would suffice if the government appointed a special commissar to these local authorities. . . .[62]

During the following months many local authorities terminated the functions of the workers' and soldiers' councils by dissolving them or, more simply, depriving them of the necessary funds. In March the mayor of Pritzerbe—a small Brandenburg town—dissolved the workers' and soldiers' council which originally had been elected by all citizens, and demanded that the chairman's wife hand over the council's official stamp, although all its members were working in an honorary capacity without receiving any wages.[63] In the same month the important workers' council of Gelsenkirchen pointed out to the Central Council that, after the local elections, the functions of the workers' councils were very ill-defined because the towns would no longer recognize their right of control, and this would result in a general loss of prestige; their mayor also refused to pay any longer

[62] The Hameln council to the Central Council, 5 Feb. 1919: Int. Inst. of Soc. Hist., Amsterdam, Zentralrat, B-22, IV.
[63] The Pritzerbe council to the Central Council, 17 March 1919: ibid., B-12, I.

the costs of the workers' council.[64] In April the workers' councils of Hückeswagen and Lüttringhausen in Westphalia reported that the bourgeois majorities of the local councils had decided to refuse all funds to the workers' councils and that one mayor insisted on a new election which had been boycotted by the workers.[65] At Düsseldorf too the bourgeois majority declined to pay the costs of the office and the employees of the workers' council so that the latter had to borrow money to the tune of 30,000 marks and declared it would have to dissolve itself by 1 May if its finances were not secured.[66] In the course of May more and more workers' councils in the Ruhr area were dissolved by decisions of the town councils where the majority favoured such a policy. All the local workers' councils could do was to protest to the Central Council that it should exercise pressure on the Reich government.[67]

The policy of the Prussian government was to leave the decision whether the supervisory functions of the workers' councils should continue or not to the local councils and, on the level of the *Kreis*, to the elected *Kreistage*. But in most cases the decision was a foregone conclusion as the Social Democrats were unable to muster a majority in the rural communes and *Kreise* and were in a minority even in many of the larger towns. In July 1919 a bourgeois newspaper welcomed this policy 'with satisfaction' because it meant 'without doubt the casting off of an irksome fetter which hitherto has hindered the development of a healthy self-government'.[68] In August the town council of Insterburg in East Prussia decided to terminate the work of the workers' council and all payments to it, while the latter thought it essential to continue its activities, especially in the distribution of food, the fight against the black market (which was still flourishing) and the control of housing: a sudden cessation in these fields would be 'positively dangerous'.[69] For the whole province of East Prussia, the provisional *Oberpräsident*, 'comrade' August Winnig, decreed that the *Kreistage* should decide whether the supervision of the *Landrat* by the workers' council should continue or not; in the opinion of the East Prussian provincial council such a circular 'enormously encourages the reaction from the right which in any case is more than active here and is destroying the achievements of the

[64] The Gelsenkirchen council to the same, 11 March 1919: ibid.
[65] Letters of 23 and 29 Apr. to the same: ibid, B-12, II.
[66] The Düsseldorf council to the same, 24 Apr. 1919: ibid., B-12, III.
[67] Letters of 16, 17, 19 and 20 May to the same: ibid., B-12, II.
[68] *Hannoversche Landeszeitung*, 5 July 1919.
[69] The Insterburg council to the Central Council, 9 Aug. 1919: Int. Inst. of Soc. Hist., Amsterdam, Zentralrat, B-12, IV.

revolution'.[70] In October Winnig went further and declared that any control of the local authorities by the workers' councils was super-fluous as the former were subject to his supervision; he instructed the *Landräte* to inform the workers' councils accordingly and to stop any payments from public funds to them. By this time, in Winnig's opinion, the control had in any case become a mere formality without any content.[71]

The prime minister of the state of Oldenburg, Tantzen, decreed in August 1919 that the political cooperation of the workers' councils with any public authority was to cease forthwith: as all representative bodies and local councils had been elected on the basis of a democratic franchise, there was no room any longer for the workers' councils to share in political life; all financial contributions to them were to end within a fortnight, and the local authorities were left free to adopt the same principles.[72] Many local workers' councils quietly stopped all activities in the summer of 1919, often without a formal dissolution. The council at Iserlohn dissolved itself as early as February by 15 votes to 3. In Marburg and its neighbourhood the councils simply ceased to function without any formal resolution, as the chairman explained in September; any new elections, such as the Central Council desired, were simply out of the question.[73]

Deprived of funds and without a proper field of activity, faced with the hostility of the bureaucratic authorities, those councils which took no formal decision of dissolution simply died a slow death. By the end of 1919 the movement reached its end. It had been much more broadly based than it was in Austria and much more evenly distributed over the country as a whole. There can be no doubt that it was a genuine and spontaneous popular movement which initially possessed great strength. But, except for a few intellectuals and a minority of the peasantry, it did not attract other social classes; on the contrary it alienated them and called forth a reaction. The same social classes, however, remained alienated from the Weimar Republic: the defeat of the council movement and of any tendency towards 'Bolshevism' did not reconcile the middle and lower middle classes to political democracy, to the loss of their old positions of social and political prestige.

[70] The East Prussian provincial council to the Central Council, 25 Aug. 1919: Bundesarchiv Koblenz, R 43 I/1940.
[71] Winnig to the Reichskanzlei, 3 Nov. 1919, with copy of his decree: ibid., R 43 I/1942.
[72] Decree of 1 Aug. 1919: Int. Inst. of Soc. Hist., Zentralrat, B-12, IV.
[73] ibid., Nachlass Grzesinski, no. 475; information on Iserlohn given by Mr D. M. Mühlberger. For the end of the councils in Baden and Württemberg, see above, pp. 158–60.

7 The Councils in Bavaria — the Peasant Councils

On the local level, the council movement was particularly strong and active in Bavaria—surprisingly enough considering the rural and strongly Catholic character of most of the country and the weakness of the left wing. But Munich was one of the first towns in Germany to be engulfed by the revolutionary movement, and it possessed in the person of Kurt Eisner—the new prime minister—an energetic and idealistic socialist leader who enjoyed tremendous popularity. His personal friendship with the peasant leader Ludwig Gandorfer, moreover, provided the new régime with at least one very valuable asset lacking in other parts of Germany: the support of the Bavarian Peasant League (*Bauernbund*) which had a strong organization in Upper and Lower Bavaria (but not in Franconia, Swabia and the Upper Palatinate). Unfortunately, Gandorfer was killed in a car accident on 10 November; and the leadership of the Peasant League passed into the hands of his younger brother Karl who continued the close cooperation with the Eisner government and supported the creation of peasant councils. When a Central Peasant Council was hastily formed, Eisner appointed Gandorfer its chairman, and the latter then nominated its fifty members, very largely from the leaders of the Bavarian Peasant League. This naturally aroused the hostility of the other much larger peasant organizations of Bavaria, which were strongly Catholic and more conservative than Gandorfer's Peasant League. Apparently the leaders of the Peasant League aimed at excluding from all influence the Catholic Centre Party and the large peasant organizations associated with it, but this policy was fraught with danger. As at least one observer noted as early as 9 November, it made the food supply of Munich 'as good as impossible', for only the Catholic leaders 'have authority vis-à-vis the peasants'.[1]

Five days later the same observer noted: 'The enemies are collect-

---

[1] Hofmiller, *Revolutionstagebuch 1918/19*, p. 35. In general see Mitchell, *Revolution in Bavaria . . .* , p. 156, and Mattes, *Bayerische Bauernräte*, p. 117.

ing quietly. The Centre Party seems to be active and will sooner or later put an end to the affair. And the centre of the resistance and of the organization to oppose the revolt is not in Munich but in Regensburg: Heim, Held, Schlittenbauer. . . .' He also mentioned that the middle class was beginning to recover and to find its self-confidence after the first shock. At Regensburg there was the central office of the Bavarian Peasant Associations (*Bauernvereine*) and from there Dr Georg Heim wrote to Eisner at the end of November in no uncertain terms: 'You have created a Peasant Council which has fifty members. If it is meant to represent the Bavarian peasantry, this representation has to be undertaken by the peasant organizations. . . . Dr Schlittenbauer and I must refuse to sit together with another forty-eight men appointed arbitrarily and collected from all over the country. . . '.[2] On the side of the Bavarian Catholics, antagonism to the left-wing leaders in Munich and to the Peasant League which cooperated with them was extremely strong. It was similar to the hostility which existed in Austria against 'red' Vienna and the Social Democrats, exacerbated by the fact that in both cases the left-wing leaders were often Jews.

On the local and district levels, too, the initiative for the formation of peasant councils usually came from the Peasant League. Its members were much more strongly represented in the councils than was warranted by its strength; together with the Social Democrats they dominated the majority of the district peasant councils in Upper and Lower Bavaria and in Swabia. Many hundreds of local peasant councils came into being, often with the aim of balancing the influence of the workers' council or of making it impossible for the latter to create a peasant council. The large majority of the members were peasants; contrary to the wishes of the Reich government, which desired parity of peasants and agricultural labourers, the latter were only very weakly represented, with a few per cent of the total membership. In Upper Bavaria there were as many as 708 registered peasant councils, in Lower Bavaria 512, in Swabia 599, in the three parts of Franconia 1,511, in the Upper Palatinate 225, a total of 3,555.[3] Although most of them were only active on the local level these figures show how general and widely spread the peasant councils were in Bavaria compared with the other parts of Germany. The elections were often held in public, by acclamation or a show of

[2] ibid., p. 56 (14 Nov. 1918); Heim to Eisner, 29 Nov. 1918: Bayer. Hauptstaatsarchiv, Geh. Staatsarchiv, MA. I. 986.
[3] Mattes, *Bayer. Bauernräte*, pp. 75, 89, 96–7, 103, 113.

hands. The majority of those present decided either on individuals or on a list proposed by the mayor or another local dignitary. Usually the mayor was a member, and sometimes the only member, of the peasant council. A significant report from the Upper Palatinate ran: 'The local peasant councils in this area were elected so that they should be elected.' And another from Upper Franconia said: 'Our local peasant council was founded in the critical days of November to prevent a foundation by the Social Democrats so that radical elements would not pester us. No real activity was intended and until today virtually nothing has been done.'[4]

From the point of view of the Bavarian government, it was the purpose of the peasant councils 'to promote more than hitherto the direct political and economic cooperation of the rural population and thereby to further its interest in the state and in the common weal. . . . The peasant councils are the place where all wishes, suggestions and complaints of the population should be expressed continuously. The peasant councils, together with the workers' and soldiers' councils, with whom the closest cooperation is desirable, form the basis of the new system of government until the final decision of the National Assembly. Through their work . . . they should get the new popular spirit (*Volksgeist*) to strike root in the state so firmly and deeply that the coming elections confirm and strengthen the provisional order of things. The public authorities and offices have to give information about all public affairs to the legitimate representatives of the peasant councils and hear their proposals and suggestions in all important matters. . . . But the peasant councils possess no executive powers. . . '.[5] Apart from these vaguely defined functions and pious hopes, however, there was one very practical reason for the promotion of peasant councils: the hope that they would speed up food deliveries to the starving towns. Thus the district workers' council of Stadtamhof (Upper Palatinate) simply reported to Munich at the end of 1918 that one of their most difficult tasks was to obtain milk and that many families had to go without. 'We have become active in this matter in so far as we have founded peasant councils in individual places so as to achieve better deliveries of milk.'[6]

Yet these hopes were not fulfilled. Early in 1919 the *Bezirksamt* (District Office) of Zusmarshausen informed the government of

---

[4] ibid., pp. 100–1, 112, 135, with quotations from two undated reports.
[5] 'Vorläufige Richtlinien für die Bauernräte', Munich, 26 Nov. 1918: Bayer. Hauptstaatsarchiv, Staatsministerium des Innern, 54190–91.
[6] Report to the *Landesarbeiterrat*, s.d.: ibid., Arbeiter- u. Soldatenrat, vol. 35.

Swabia bluntly: the hopes which official quarters attached to the cooperation of the peasant councils in the fight against food hoarding and smuggling—hopes which the *Bezirksamt* had never shared—'have not been fulfilled to the slightest degree. The peasant councils are also peasants and as the saying goes, dog won't eat dog. In spite of all exhortations it has not been possible to induce the rural population to cooperate in combating the black market.'[7] A few months later the district government of Lower Bavaria confirmed this gloomy view:

> The peasant councils by and large only represent the agricultural interests. Their activity in the interest of the common weal is hindered by the regrettable lack of public spirit, the conflict between their own private interests and the duty to promote deliveries of the full food quotas and to fight the black market. In addition, the members of the peasant councils anxiously try to avoid any friction with members of their own villages. Only in a few communes was it possible to use the peasant councils to advantage to obtain deliveries of cattle. But in other communes we have found that their members even participated in food smuggling. In general, however, they have remained completely passive. . . .[8]

Somewhat less gloomy was the official report of the district government of Upper Bavaria:

> They have done much useful work with regard to deliveries of food and inventories and have supplied the offices with much valuable material to improve food conditions; in this respect too the moral support which their activities have lent to the authorities . . . must be mentioned. . . . With great energy they started combating the black market and food hoarding, but in this field, according to all reports, their efforts have been in vain. They could not bring themselves to take measures against co-citizens, good friends, relatives and neighbours; they backed away from the friction which would have resulted, and some peasant councils perhaps did not dare to take strong measures because their own members were not very painstaking in the fulfilment of their delivery quotas. . . .

Interestingly enough, the same report also mentions that in the district of Garmisch the councils occupied themselves with forest and grazing rights and had obtained far-reaching concessions in this respect as well as the removal of the two foresters of Garmisch and Partenkirchen.[9]

[7] Report of 15 Feb. 1919: ibid., Staatsministerium des Innern, 54208.
[8] Report to Staatsministerium des Innern, 6 Sept. 1919: ibid., 54190.
[9] Detailed report by Regierungsassessor von Welser to the Staatsministerium des Innern, 24 June 1919: ibid., 54190.

The inability or unwillingness of the peasant councils to deal with the black market naturally aroused great indignation among the workers' councils which—exactly as in Austria—retaliated by conducting searches for hidden food. In March 1919 the district peasant council of Altötting complained to Munich that they daily received complaints from local councils about such measures, that the workers' council of Burghausen had on the occasion of a wedding celebration not only searched the inn in question but also the farms of the groom and his brother, that the workers' council of Neuötting daily conducted such searches on the basis of slight information given from any quarter.

> The manner in which the workers' councils proceed here cannot continue if the gulf between town and country is not to become unbridgeable. . . . The guilt is not always that of the peasant. The smuggling of food and exorbitant prices are not alone responsible for many peasants being unable to fulfil their delivery quotas. The main reasons are:
> pity for the small food hoarders,
> fear of threats,
> and above all the decline of production. . . .
> The bitterness among the peasants is now worse than in the most difficult period of the war: this should not be overlooked. . . .

To this complaint Gandorfer added that such differences served to bring discredit to the whole council system in the countryside.[10]

Apart from assistance with food deliveries, the local peasant councils helped in the work of demobilization, finding accommodation for returning troops, guarding and maintaining supplies and army property, minor duties which soon petered out. The functions of the district peasant councils were similar; they were usually represented on the committees responsible for cattle delivery but only seldom interfered with the allocation of milk and fats; they often rendered help in confiscating corn or cattle where delivery quotas had not been met. There was hardly any cooperation between them and the district workers' councils. The Central Peasant Council in Munich carried out an important task in the sale of army horses after demobilization—a favour secured by Gandorfer through his close connections with Eisner. This sale was carried out with the help of the peasant councils by a special organization which employed many

---

[10] *Bezirksbauernrat* Altötting to *Zentralbauernrat*, 9 Mar. 1919, with note by Gandorfer, 11 Mar.: Bayer. Hauptstaatsarchiv, Arbeiter- u. Soldatenrat, vol. 31. Burghausen, Altötting and Neuötting are situated due east of Munich on the right bank of the Inn.

officers. Otherwise the Central Council advocated measures against entail and non-peasants who derived benefits from land: the land should belong to those who farmed it; returning soldiers and people who had lost their livelihood should be given land; ground rents should be abolished, and the large estates be expropriated against compensation. But it was opposed to any socialization of land and firmly upheld the principle of peasant ownership. There was considerable opposition to the Central Council on local and district levels because its members had not been elected but selected in Munich in an arbitrary fashion. Its membership and following coincided to a large extent with that of the Bavarian Peasant League and was strong only where the latter had influence, above all in Upper and Lower Bavaria. Like Eisner, Gandorfer and his friends aimed at preserving the councils with rights of control and initiative vis-à-vis the Diet; they wanted to curtail its power and that of the old political parties, so as to secure to the people a direct influence in political affairs.[11]

Eisner himself was not a wild radical nor a revolutionary opponent of parliament, but he aimed at a combination of the parliamentary system with that of the councils. At the meeting of the representatives of the German states in Berlin in November, he explained his political ideas:

> The workers' and soldiers' councils must remain the basis of the whole movement, and in the south the peasant councils too, which in the east would be agricultural labourers' councils. The more the workers' and soldiers' councils were given an opportunity to do fruitful work the less we would have to fear the bogy of chaos.
>
> With regard to the question of the National Assembly it was entirely obvious that it must be summoned. This applied to the Reich as well as to the individual Diets. The revolution was not the same as democracy, the revolution would have to create democracy. (Hear, hear!)
>
> It must thus be our task to use the time to lead the whole mass of the people towards democracy. There were people who maintained that democracy consisted of elections every five years and then remaining at home for five years. That was the bourgeois parliamentarianism of the past. Now all productive forces must be employed in the work of democratic consolidation. . . .
>
> The revolution was only two weeks old, and if there was much discussion about the excesses of the workers' and soldiers' councils, one thing was certain: they had not yet ignited a world war; such small matters should not be taken too seriously. . . .

[11] Mattes, *Bayerische Bauernräte*, pp. 124, 128–9, 140–1, 144–5, 149, 154–5, 168; Mitchell, *Revolution . . .* , p. 157, n. 24.

Eisner used the same occasion to protest in strong words against the employment of compromised politicians such as Erzberger and Solf in the negotiations with the Entente powers, as they would only aim at saving the guilty of the old régime from the wrath of the people.[12] After his return to Munich Eisner reported to the workers', soldiers' and peasant councils on this point: 'In Berlin the counter-revolution governs quite happily as if nothing had happened. . . . We know that our friend Karl Kautsky sits in the Foreign Office, but Herr Solf conducts his own policy, and Karl Kautsky is not even told what occurs in the Foreign Office. . . '.[13]

Characteristically Eisner also used the opportunity of his stay in Berlin to address the Executive Committee of the Berlin workers' and soldiers' councils and to make the same points:

> The revolution is not democracy but will have to create it. Everywhere workers' and soldiers' councils must form the basis of the new development. The National Assembly can and must only be summoned when the workers', soldiers' and peasant councils have developed to such an extent that the new spirit permeates everything. . . . The workers' councils are destined to form the district and local councils. Nowadays we hear a lot about the Bolsheviks. I am not one. My convictions are against Bolshevism, and I dislike its methods. I believe in the spirit and the power of ideas. . . .
>
> Should we take over production when it is close to the abyss? At the moment this is pointless as our economic strength is exhausted. The whole capitalist society is collapsing; as long as this collapse is imminent, there is no point in carrying out socialization. The revolution can only be secured through a strengthening and democratization of the workers', soldiers' and peasants' councils. . . .[14]

All this was far removed from the super-radicalism of the extreme left which strenuously opposed parliamentary democracy and the summoning of the National Assembly. Eisner, by contrast, wanted to underpin its strength—which certainly was not considerable in Germany—by the force of a genuine popular movement as it had spontaneously developed in the councils. Even retrospectively, there is much force in his arguments compared with the pusillanimity of the Social Democratic leaders and their constant fear of Bolshevism and 'chaos'. At the heart of Eisner's ideas there was a strong belief 'in the people'—reminiscent of the liberals of 1848 and going back to the

---

[12] Matthias (ed.), *Regierung* . . . , i, no. 30, pp. 164, 178–9: Reichskonferenz, 25 Nov. 1918.

[13] Schmolze (ed.), *Revolution und Räterepublik* . . . , pp. 165–6.

[14] Speech quoted in *Berliner Tageblatt*, 27 Nov. 1918.

ideals of the French Revolution—an idealism not based on fact but on Eisner's philosophy of life:

> We do not want a parliament any longer without the representatives of the people, in which only men sit who every five years solicit the confidence of their electors, but we desire a parliament backed by the whole people. I have an unshakeable confidence in the people. I was the first to demand the union of the two brotherly parties. I was the first to say: Auer must be a member of the government. As I was the symbol of the revolution, so he was the symbol of the new unity of Social Democracy. . . .[15]

In reality, however, there was no unity but only the bitter fight between moderate and Independent Social Democrats. Like the other leaders of his party, Auer, the Minister of the Interior, had no intention of supporting Eisner on the issue of the councils nor was he in favour of any political experiments.

In the Bavarian cabinet, too, Eisner's views were sharply criticized. In December the Minister Frauendorfer declared that parliament and the councils could not possibly exist side by side as constitutional organs: 'Sovereignty lies with parliament. It may recognize them as advisory organs. The Peasant Council is more than ridiculous. It represents only 10,000 peasants. . . . I cannot allow any expansion of the councils, otherwise I must resign. That leads to the ruin of the fatherland'. In reply Eisner had to concede that the workers' councils had only advisory and controlling rights, but no legislative ones. 'That would be Bolshevism. . . . I am against the dictatorship of the councils and for the sovereignty of parliament'.[16] But some days later, when addressing a conference of the Bavarian workers' councils, the emphasis was different:

> The workers' councils shall be the parliaments of those doing physical and also intellectual work, and if this is countered by the view that the National Assembly, the Diet, will make these workers' councils redundant, then I maintain: on the contrary, we may do without the National Assembly rather than without the workers' councils. (Tumultuous applause.)
>
> For, if the National Assembly is not to lead again into empty parliamentarianism, then the living force of the workers' councils must unfold itself. The workers' and the other councils are as it were the organization of the electors. The electors must watch and be active and must not leave it to the deputies to do whatever

[15] Speech to the Bavarian soldiers' councils: *Bayerische Staatszeitung*, 3 Dec. 1918.
[16] Ministerratsprotokolle, 5 Dec. 1918: Bayer. Hauptstaatsarchiv, Geh. Staatsarchiv, GN 2/1–2/2, quoted by Schmolze (ed.), *Revolution und Räterepublik . . .*, pp. 175–6.

clever or stupid things they see fit to undertake. The function of these councils in my opinion is the direct politicization and democratization of the masses. . . .[17]

In another speech, at the beginning of 1919, Eisner allocated to the councils the tasks of supervising measures of nationalization and the execution of the laws: he would oppose any curtailment of their rights which on the contrary must be extended; they should, for example, organize plebiscites and politicize the masses; they should show their mettle, and then they would have 'rights and competences'.[18]

All this was fairly vague—but no vaguer than the public pronouncements of the other protagonists of the German councils. In reality the large majority of Germans—and this included the extreme left—saw the issue as a straight alternative of National Assembly *or* the council system, and hardly anyone considered that the two might be combined in a democratic form. For Bavaria, this was proved by the general election held on 12 January 1919—two days before the last-quoted speech by Eisner. In the elections his party, the Independent Social Democrats, received a mere 86,000 votes or 2.5 per cent of the total, and the Bavarian Peasant League which co-operated with him 310,000 votes or 9.1 per cent. The Social Democrats, on the other hand, gained 1,125,000 votes or 33 per cent, and even they were outdistanced by the Catholic or Bavarian People's Party with 1,193,000 votes or 35 per cent. The left-wing parties which supported the government remained in a minority, as they did in the whole of Germany a week later, polling together only 44.6 per cent of the total vote.[19] It was a severe defeat for Eisner and his policy based on the councils, and it seemed only a question of time until he would be forced to resign and make way for a moderate coalition government.

This, in any case, was the general opinion in Munich, as the Austrian ambassador in Berlin, the historian Ludo Moritz Hartmann, reported to his government. But Eisner still hoped for a majority, together with the Peasant League, while the ambassador's other informants considered the League 'not much more than a radicalized Centre Party and entirely unreliable'. Eisner explained to the ambassador that he would submit to the Diet a draft constitution which would preserve the workers', soldiers' and peasants' councils;

[17] *Stenographischer Bericht über die Verhandlungen der bayerischen Arbeiterräte am 9. und 10. Dezember 1918*, p. 132.
[18] Speech of 14 Jan. 1918, quoted by Mattes, *Bayerische Bauernräte*, p. 167.
[19] Figures given by Huber, *Dokumente zur Deutschen Verfassungsgeschichte*, iii, p. 610. The Independents had only three deputies out of 180, the Social Democrats 61.

if it were rejected there would be a plebiscite; in concrete matters such as these 'the people would stand on his side. If not he would resign'. Eisner also developed to Hartmann another scheme which the latter considered really dangerous:

> His principal idea is that he, as he puts it, intends to reverse the scheme of Bismarck, who achieved German unity through the unification of the north and its hegemony. The north must now be deposed. The north is also the centre of the counter-revolution. The Junkers have not abdicated. The ruling socialists have (what is partly true) changed nothing in the administration and its personnel. . . . The 'reverse' of Bismarck naturally is that Eisner intends first to ally with the south (perhaps including the Rhineland) and to impose its predominance—a word he of course did not use—on the north, especially on Berlin which he wholeheartedly despises and considers decadent. . . . This rebuilding, starting from the separate states to the Reich (the unity of which he really desires) seems to be his pet idea apart from the continuation of the workers' and soldiers' councils—the latter because thus the people can continuously asserts its sovereignty and would not be sovereign only at the election once every four or five years. The dangers he does not see, or he denies them when they are pointed out to him. . . .

Hartmann's general opinion was that Eisner's edifice was built on sand and that he did not see things as they really were. Hartmann thought that Eisner envisaged a South German government with the participation of Austria, but Austria could only join a united Germany and should oppose any separatist ventures.[20]

In practice things took a very different turn. However unreal Eisner's goals may have been, he was forced to acknowledge the reality created by the elections of 12 January. In a speech to the delegates of the workers', soldiers' and peasants' councils on 20 February he stated clearly: 'The bourgeois majority will now implement bourgeois policies. We will see whether they are capable of ruling. In the meantime the councils should do their job: to build the new democracy. Then perhaps the new spirit will arrive in Bavaria. . . '. It was a very large 'perhaps'. On the same day the cabinet passed a provisional basic law which recognized unequivocally the responsibility of ministers to the Diet, and Eisner was persuaded to offer the resignation of his government on the following day at its opening session. On the morning of that day, 21 February, on his way to the Diet, Eisner was murdered by the young Count

[20] Hartmann to Otto Bauer (?), Romanshorn, 17 Jan. 1919: Haus-, Hof- u. Staatsarchiv, Vienna, 5860/68, carton 261.

Anton Arco-Valley; in the victim's pocket was found his speech of
resignation—the final proof that he was prepared to accept the
verdict of the general election.[21] It was one of the many tragedies by
which the German socialist movement was deprived of its most
important leaders. Eisner's adversary Auer was shot an hour later in
the Diet by a revolutionary worker, and was severely wounded.

In Bavaria, thanks to the support of the Eisner government and that
of the Bavarian Peasant League, the council movement was more
active than in almost any other part of Germany. Yet the powers
conceded officially to the local councils were if anything more
restricted than in Prussia. Above all, they did not include any right
of control as it was exercised in Prussia over the administrative
authorities, and in Berlin over the central government. As the right
of control more often than not soon became a loose right of supervision, this is perhaps not a very important difference. In any case,
when the provisional regulations for the councils were published on
26 November 1918, they declared that the councils together formed
the 'legal basis of the new system of government' but—what was more
important—expressly excluded them from the exercise of executive
power, and warned them not to interfere with the work of any
administrative authority. The old administrative authorities were
left to carry out the orders of the government. Auer, the leader of the
moderate Social Democrats and new Minister of the Interior, kept
intact the old bureaucratic apparatus and confirmed the civil
servants in their rights and duties. No attempt was made to assign
to the councils any function within that apparatus: they received
their own separate structure, parallel with that of the general
administration, but never became part of it. When more definitive
regulations about the 'organization and rights of the workers'
councils' were published in December, it was once more stipulated:
'The workers' and peasants' councils and their committees possess
no executive power.'[22] These regulations too owed their publication
to the initiative of Auer. There can be little doubt that his motives
were the same as those of the central government in Berlin which
above all wanted to avoid administrative disorder and 'chaos' at a

[21] Mitchell, *Revolution* . . . , pp. 269–72, with the quotation of the speech of 20
Feb. 1919.
[22] Mattes, *Bayerische Bauernräte*, pp. 67, 70; Mitchell, *Revolution* . . . , pp. 155–60,
emphasizing that the sentence just quoted was the only one italicized in the entire
regulations. The text of the provisional regulations in Bayer. Hauptstaatsarchiv,
Staatsministerium des Innern, 54190. Those of 17 Dec. 1918 were published in the
Bayerische Staatszeitung of 19 Dec. 1918.

time of severe economic and political difficulties. Between Auer and Eisner there was a strong personal and political antagonism, going back to the split between moderates and radicals in the years of the war.

In the larger towns of Bavaria workers' councils were formed on or about 9 November 1918—if it was a garrison town, as a workers' and soldiers' council. The smaller towns followed suit later. Eventually, the large majority of the towns and villages had a council, either a workers' council, or a workers' and peasants' council, or a workers', peasants' and burghers' council (sometimes also called a people's council). The members were usually elected in a public meeting, by acclamation or a show of hands, hardly ever by a ballot. The chairman was often a local dignitary, a teacher, local official or intellectual; sometimes it was the chairman of the Social Democratic organization, where this had sufficient influence. At Würzburg the chairman of the party organization and of the trades council was also elected chairman of the workers' and soldiers' council. At Augsburg it was a socialist journalist who had taken the initiative in the formation of a soldiers' council when the party leaders were hesitating.[23] Workers' and soldiers' councils were hastily formed at Schweinfurt and Sulzbach, took over power and occupied the public buildings. At Grafenwöhr the local officer corps joined the movement and several officers were elected to the soldiers' council.[24] At Sonthofen the workers' and soldiers' council was elected in a large open-air meeting in front of the barracks. It saw to the maintenance of law and order, the introduction of the eight-hour day, unemployment relief and public works; and it cooperated with the local peasant council to promote better milk deliveries, as well as with the Social Democratic Party in the holding of public meetings.[25] At Neustadt on the Saale it was the municipal administration which took the initiative; as a precautionary measure it instructed one of its members, a lawyer, to summon a public meeting; but its move was forestalled by workers and soldiers who formed a provisional workers' and soldiers' council, and this then called a meeting where a definitive council was elected. It declared that it had taken over power and ordered all authorities to carry out its instructions. With the help of a guard consisting of twenty men it confiscated black market stocks of food and other

[23] Fritz Endres to Eisner, 18 Nov. 1918: Bayer. Hauptstaatsarchiv, Geh. Staatsarchiv, MA. I. 983; Niekisch, *Gewagtes Leben*, p. 40.

[24] Pressebüro report, 11 Nov. 1918: Bayer. Hauptstaatsarchiv, Arbeiter- u. Soldatenrat, vol. 23.

[25] Report from Sonthofen, 28 Dec. 1918: ibid., vol. 14.

items and sold them. A red flag was forcibly hoisted on the town hall.[26]

Conflicts about the composition of the workers' councils also arose elsewhere. At Freilassing in Upper Bavaria the Social Democrats founded a workers' council on 18 November, while the *Bezirksamt* of Laufen sponsored another with members of the Catholic Centre but did not succeed. In December there existed a workers' council, which was purely Social Democratic and included representatives of the local officials and teachers, a peasant council, which contained one Social Democrat and had a Catholic chairman, a soldiers' council which had only one member, a Social Democrat, and finally a trades' council (*Gewerberat*) with a mixed composition. Together they formed the local *Volksrat*, but within it the workers and soldiers had 'of course' retained the majority and the leadership.[27] At Mittenwald, on the other hand, the Social Democrats only occupied about one third of the seats in the workers' and peasants' council; all the rest were 'black', and the local authorities tried everything to make 'black' predominate entirely and disregarded all requests and suggestions of the Social Democrats.[28] At Herrsching near Munich the Social Democrats in their turn dissolved the workers' council, because it did not represent working-class interests but only those of the burghers who had elected it, and then elected a new workers' council of their own.[29] At nearby Starnberg the mayor summoned a meeting which was attended by all groups of the population to elect a workers' council. For this, it was suggested, six representatives of the workers, three of the burghers and two of the intellectuals should be chosen. The Social Democrats put forward six names in the first category, but the 'Christian' workers suggested another, while the five remaining workers' representatives were elected unopposed. Yet the majority of the 'workers' council' members were middle-class in origin, such as a publisher, an art historian, a steamboat captain, an industrialist and two civil servants.[30]

At Lichtenfels in the north of Bavaria the Social Democrats appointed a workers' and peasants' council, but ten days later the town council summoned a public meeting to the town hall by publishing an advertisement in the local paper on the same day. It was attended by '50 to 60 black gentlemen from the Centre'. The chairman of the

---

[26] Report from Neustadt, 3 Jan. 1919: ibid., vol. 36.
[27] Report from Freilassing, 26 Dec. 1918: ibid., vol. 7.
[28] Report from Mittenwald, 4 Feb. 1919: ibid., vol. 7.
[29] Report from Herrsching, 2 Jan. 1919: ibid., vol. 8.
[30] Protocol, Starnberg, s.d.: ibid., vol. 32.

workers' and peasants' council in vain protested against the procedure and declared it was a counter-revolutionary meeting, but he was shouted down. The meeting then elected another peasants' council consisting of nine employers and one single 'Christian' workman. The matter was referred to the Ministry of the Interior for decision, but weeks later it had not yet replied, in spite of protests sent by telegram and express letter.[31] In the village of Mering near Augsburg 'a section' of the inhabitants deposed the workers' and peasants' council as well as the mayor; they proceeded to form a new council and appoint a new mayor, and they also demanded that the local administration be transferred to the new council and that the old local authorities resign.[32]

There were many other instances where the working-class element was in a definite minority on the local workers' or workers' and peasants' council, and even two small communities in Lower Bavaria where it was non-existent.[33] Nor were the peasants the preponderant element in these cases, but rather the middle and lower middle class: independent craftsmen, innkeepers, lower officials, school teachers, small businessmen, a miscellaneous assortment of salaried employees and independent people which is almost impossible to classify. Preponderant among them were those who had qualified as a *meister*, master craftsmen typical of a small town or rural commune more than fifty years ago, and proof of the widely spread social roots of the Bavarian council movement. Of the twelve members of the workers' council of Landsberg on the Lech one was a lawyer, others a police official, a prison inspector, an innkeeper, a merchant, a brewer, a storekeeper.[34] At Hausham, also in Upper Bavaria, the chairman was the manager of the local cooperative, and among the members were a doctor and the owner of a sawmill.[35] At Tegernsee there was a lawyer, a shopkeeper and an engineer.[36] At Neumarkt the chairman was the local vet; other members were a master baker and a master plumber.[37] At Weilheim there was a lawyer, an official and five independent business people as against five workers.[38] At Wolfrats-

[31] *Stenographischer Bericht über die Verhandlungen der bayerischen Arbeiterräte am 9. und 10. Dezember 1918*, p. 190.
[32] Reports from Mering, 24 Feb. 1919, and of the Ministry of the Interior, 10 Mar. 1919: Bayer. Hauptstaatsarchiv, Arbeiter- u. Soldatenrat, vols. 7, 37.
[33] Kirchberg im Wald and Jandelsbrunn: ibid., vol. 33.
[34] Report from Landsberg, 10 Feb. 1919: ibid., vol. 8.
[35] Report from Hausham, 3 Jan. 1919: ibid.
[36] Report from Tegernsee, 14 Dec. 1918: ibid.
[37] Report from Neumarkt, 26 Dec. 1918: ibid.
[38] Reports from Weilheim, 2 and 4 Mar. 1919: ibid.

hausen near Munich the chairman was the local bailiff (*Gerichts-vollzieher*) and among the members were an architect, a millowner, a local government official and three master craftsmen.[39] At Vilshofen even the mayor was a member, apart from a lawyer, two merchants, two local officials and a baker.[40]

These are just a few examples, mainly from Upper and Lower Bavaria where the council movement seems to have had stronger popular roots than in the other parts of Bavaria. In the voluminous files of the Central Workers' Council there is, strangely enough, only one case where it objected to the composition of a workers' council on the grounds that 'only real workers' representatives can form a workers' council'. At Neuötting a new workers' council had been elected in February 1919 at a general meeting; its chairman was a manager, and its secretary the town clerk; only two workers were members, out of a total of nine. But the objection of the Central Council was unanimously overruled by the local workers' council because it was elected legally, was recognized by the town council and the *Bezirksamt* and had a composition similar to that of the neighbouring Altötting: 'what is valid for Altötting must also be valid for Neuötting'. The Central Workers' Council did not insist.[41] Apparently it found it very difficult to establish its authority over the whole country. At the end of November 1918 the workers' councils of Swabia decided not to recognize it as the central authority because it was not composed of representatives of the whole of Bavaria: 'we are not willing to accept in Swabia dictatorship of the workers' council of Munich. . . '.[42] As we have seen the same also applied to the Central Peasant Council of Karl Gandorfer on account of its one-sided composition, drawn almost exclusively from the Bavarian Peasant League. The Central Workers' Council was much more radical than many of the local councils, hence their disinclination to recognize its authority. Their principal interests were local affairs, and this went often hand in hand with a lack of interest in what was happening in Munich.

Even the district workers' councils and their executive committees in many instances had few or no workers as members. At Landau on the Isar there was a united peasants', burghers' and workers' district

[39] Report from Wolfratshausen, 29 Dec. 1918: ibid.

[40] Report from Vilshofen, 28 Dec. 1918: ibid., vol. 10.

[41] *Arbeiterrat* Neuötting to *Zentralarbeiterrat*, 27 Feb. and 7 Mar. 1919, reply of the latter, 3 Mar. 1919: ibid., vol. 32.

[42] *Arbeiter- u. Soldatenrat* Augsburg to *Arbeiterrat* München, 30 Nov. 1918: ibid., vol. 14.

council of seven which had no working-class member; and at Rottenburg near Landshut a district workers' council of four which was
entirely middle-class.[43] The district workers' and peasants' council of
Dillingen on the Danube had a chairman who was a managing
director, a second chairman who was a carpenter, a third who was a
mayor, a secretary who was an elementary school teacher and a
treasurer who owned a brewery; among its seven assessors there were
two peasants but no worker, the rest were middle-class.[44] The district
workers' council of Wolfratshausen was presided over by a bailiff,
with a teacher as vice-chairman and a bookkeeper as secretary; there
were also two workers.[45] The chairman of the district workers' and
peasants' council of Ingolstadt was a mayor and architect who also
represented the district on the Central Peasant Council in Munich;
among the members were the owner of a brewery, a master lock-
smith, a farmer and two peasants; in three cases the occupation was
not given.[46] At Sulzbach in the Upper Palatinate a district executive
committee was elected by the local trusties of the workers and
peasants; of its nine members four were working-class, and the others
were a police sergeant, a local official, a master mason, a technician,
and a farmer.[47] It is almost impossible to say to what party the
members of all these councils belonged. Very often the local initiative
came from the Social Democrats, and in certain cases their chairman
was also the chairman of the local workers' council. But this was by
no means always the case, and in general the party was very weakly
represented in the small towns and the villages which made up most
of Bavaria.[48] But there can be no doubt that in Bavaria the council
movement also attracted many men who were not Social Democrats.
There is virtually no evidence of any social conflict between these two
groups in the official files, such as undoubtedly existed between
workers and peasants.

The local workers' councils were mainly busy with social matters,
such as protection of workers, settlement of labour disputes, unemployment benefits, public works, housing, milk and fat deliveries, coal

[43] Report from Landau, 16 Jan. 1919, protocol, Rottenburg, 14 Dec. 1918:
ibid., vol. 10.

[44] Report from Dillingen (Swabia), 20 Jan. 1919: ibid., vol. 14.

[45] Report from Wolfratshausen, 10 Feb. 1919: ibid., vol. 8.

[46] *Bezirksamt* Ingolstadt to the government of Upper Bavaria, 17 Jan. 1919:
ibid., vol. 7.

[47] Report from Sulzbach, 17 Feb. 1919: ibid., vol. 34.

[48] In 1918 Bavaria had something like 8,000 communes, but Social Democratic
party organizations can only have existed in a small number of these, and far fewer
still of the Independent Social Democrats. But most communes, whether large or
small, had a council.

and wood supplies, rent control matters, and above all the never-ending fight against black marketeering and the illicit trade in food. These services were extremely valuable at a time of severe shortages and great difficulties in the work of the public authorities, but they were entirely non-political. The workers' council of Münnerstadt near Kissingen reported briefly that their principal task was to fight the black market which was flourishing in the district; they saw to a fair distribution of food and had, as in all other places, to cope with the passive resistance of the peasants.[49] The workers' and peasants' council of Marienweiher near Stadtsteinach stated at the end of 1918 that for the past six weeks the peasants had not delivered any milk or butter although there were 170 cows and butter could be bought illicitly for 10 to 12 marks; therefore they had decided to take over the control of milk and butter, but the *Bezirksamt* of Stadtsteinach had forbidden them to interfere with the control of milk so that any peasant was now entitled to shut his door in their faces.[50] The workers' council of Tettau near Teuschnitz, on the other hand, reported that it had established a milk collection centre because even infants and patients had been unable to get milk in spite of medical certificates; they had at least managed to see that children under two years now received some milk, but many of the older ones and many sick people still had to go without; they also inspected the butchers once a week to establish the weight of killed animals.[51] From another place in Franconia, the small town of Forchheim, the workers' and peasants' council confirmed that its main work was concerned with the milk question, as some communes delivered almost none; they had now appointed a committee and were taking determined measures; they had stopped a black market in flour in the local mills and had seen to it that barley was added to the flour to make it go further; 320 army horses had been auctioned, and the whole demobilization had proceeded in a smooth and orderly way.[52] The *Bezirksamt* of Höchstadt on the Aisch reported to Munich that the workers' council of Adelsdorf supervised the allocation of food and that it was supporting the justified demands of the council.[53]

From the Upper Palatinate several workers' councils referred to their activities on behalf of the unemployed. The district workers' council of Stadtamhof had induced the *Bezirksamt* to start public

[49] Report from Münnerstadt, 11 Mar. 1919: ibid., vol. 13.
[50] Report from Marienweiher, 28 Dec. 1918: ibid., vol. 11.
[51] Report from Tettau, 14 Jan. 1919: ibid.
[52] Report from Forchheim, 7 Jan. 1919: ibid.
[53] Report from Höchstadt, 17 Jan. 1919: ibid.

works, such as road-building and water supply; they had also seen to it that food stores were used for the benefit of the community from which they had been unjustly withheld.[54] The workers' and peasants' council of Floss took special pride in providing jobs for the unemployed and preventing dismissals in factories; it claimed that within a week the number of unemployed was reduced by 90 per cent, while the local authority was completely passive.[55] The workers' council of Windischeschenbach confiscated 900 cwt of potatoes from the peasants because many workers' families had none, but the commune refused to cooperate with the council and to pay its members.[56] The workers' and peasants' council of Runding reported in March 1919 that, although it had been elected in December in a public meeting, it had no functions because the local authority refused to allocate any to it, in spite of all admonitions.[57] A similar note of frustration is noticeable in the complaint of the people's council of Rosenheim on Inn that the authorities were deaf and blind when the shopkeepers charged more than the permitted maximum prices and exploited the consumers. They proposed to act independently in future, to let people buy things in various shops and, if exorbitant prices were charged, to confiscate the stocks: 'The government is taking things easy, but this cannot possibly continue any longer'.[58] Equally significant is the complaint of a member of the workers' council of Hartkirchen near Landau on Isar that they should be informed more accurately about their rights and duties; at the time of their election they were told that this was done only because it was ordered from above and that it served no purpose.[59]

While some workers' councils reported on their harmonious cooperation with the local authorities, there was also considerable friction and passive resistance, as indeed was only to be expected for political and other reasons. The workers' and soldiers' council of Ansbach was responsible for demobilization measures together with the local authorities, and cooperated with them in unemployment relief and in the maintenance of order; searches were carried out in agreement with the police and sizable amounts of army property

[54] Report from Stadtamhof about activities between 15 Nov. and 15 Dec. 1918, s.d.: ibid., vol. 35.
[55] Report from Floss, s.d. (Feb. 1919): ibid., vol. 34.
[56] Report from Windischeschenbach, 24 Dec. 1918: ibid.
[57] Report from Runding, 16 Mar. 1919: ibid.
[58] Report from Rosenheim, 22 Jan. 1919: ibid., vol. 8.
[59] Josef Maier to Central Workers' Council, Hartkirchen, 28 Feb. 1919: ibid., vol. 10.

recovered; the relations were friendly.[60] A representative of the Central Council in Munich noticed that relations between the councils and the local authorities were 'fruitful and good' at Freising and Landshut; no complaints were raised from either side; after a lecture at Landshut he was approached by officials who desired representation on the local workers' council; but at Straubing there were conflicts, also in the political field, and at Nuremberg he noticed considerable dissatisfaction with Munich.[61] At Augsburg, where the workers' and soldiers' council supervised the work of the town council, the *Bezirksamt* found that the public very often addressed its wishes to the workers' and soldiers' council which then passed them on to the *Bezirksamt* for further action but did not interfere otherwise, hence the mutual relations were 'untroubled'.[62] On 2 March, however, a conference of the Swabian councils decided to appoint a committee of three to control the correspondence of the Swabian *Kreisregierung* and to give or refuse consent to any of its orders and decrees. The local Swabian government was forced to agree and to give office accommodation to the control committee, but declined to pay its costs. The Ministry of the Interior, however, refused to sanction this as contrary to government policy: all it was willing to concede was the admission of the control committee to all meetings.[63] At Hassfurt on Main a 'people's representative' was appointed by the workers' and peasants' council in the person of a local businessman and the *Bezirksamt* reluctantly admitted him; there he mainly dealt with complaints and petitions, saw many petitioners personally and thus relieved the local authority of much work; it had to admit that he was fulfilling his mission with a great deal of tact and was strengthening the influence of the *Bezirksamt* vis-à-vis the public.[64]

At Bad Tölz, however, the local council simply refused to admit the representatives of the workers' council to its meetings, while the *Bezirksamt* did the opposite.[65] At Untermenzing the local council promised to admit them but then did not invite them.[66] At Marienweiher in Franconia the workers' and peasants' council claimed expenses of 17.70 marks from the mayor who refused to pay them and

[60] Report from Ansbach, 24 Dec. 1918: ibid., vol. 12.
[61] Report by Fritz Sänger, s.d. (Mar. 1919): ibid., vol. 1.
[62] *Bezirksamt* Augsburg to *Regierung* of Schwaben and Neuburg, 3 Mar. 1919: ibid., Staatsministerium des Innern, 54208.
[63] *Regierung* of Schwaben and Neuburg to Ministry of Interior, 4 Mar. 1919, and its reply, 19 Mar.: ibid., 54194, 54190.
[64] *Bezirksamt* Hassfurt to government in Würzburg, 29 Apr. 1919: ibid., 54197.
[65] Report from Bad Tölz, 10 Jan. 1919: ibid., Arbeiter- u. Soldatenrat, vol. 8.
[66] Report from Untermenzing, 28 Nov. 1918: ibid., vol. 7.

exclaimed: 'We do not need a workers' council. Anyone could come along to govern. This is just despotism, etc.' Later the mayor promised to pay the money but still refused to recognize the workers' council and to give it any seats on the local council.[67] At Mittenwald the local authorities considered even the existence of the workers' and peasants' council damaging to the state and tried to stir up the population against it, while the council vigorously complained about the inefficiency and red tape of the officials.[68] Passive resistance and difficulties on the side of the local authorities were also denounced by the workers' and peasants' council of Garmisch. It appointed a representative to control the work of the *Bezirksamt*, but the latter refused to pay the council's expenses; the *Bezirksamtmann* declared he would receive no instructions from the Central Workers' and Peasants' Council but only from the Finance Ministry. The Garmisch council decided to clear the trees away from what had been meadows for decades, and this was done immediately as they feared difficulties from the bureaucracy—fears which proved only too justified because the Finance Ministry ordered them to abstain from any interference with the work of the authorities. Garmisch had a very active council in which the Social Democrats had the majority but which also included fifteen bourgeois representatives, appointed by the officials, hotel owners, entrepreneurs, etc. It supervised the *Bezirksamt* as well as the town council, exercised price control, saw to a fair distribution of food and founded a building society to promote the construction of small flats. It enjoyed general confidence and considerable authority.[69]

A similar conflict developed in the town of Aschaffenburg on Main when the local workers' council established a housing committee because the attempts of the municipal housing office to find accommodation for about fifty-eight homeless families had been in vain. The town council, however, considered this an interference with its executive powers and published an announcement to that effect. But the workers' council denied any intended interference, as it only wanted to check on the work of the housing office and to inform it of any empty accommodation which it might ferret out, and it insisted on its right of inspection. This right was denied by the Ministry of the Interior, according to which it was reserved to the municipal authorities which could, however, ask the workers' council for

---

[67] Reports from Marienweiher, 5 and 23 Jan. 1919: ibid., vol. 11.
[68] Reports from Mittenwald, 13 and 21 Jan. 1919: ibid., vol. 7.
[69] Two reports from Garmisch s.d. (early 1919): ibid., vols. 7, 32.

assistance; nor was the latter entitled to inspect the stores of corn in the urban mills.[70] In the Franconian village of Schwarzenstein the workers' council decided to take over the distribution of food, especially of bread coupons which had been a task of the mayor, for the mayor was also a baker and had been caught selling bread without coupons. The *Bezirksamtmann*, however, declared that he had failed not as a mayor but as a baker, and the workers' council was ordered to abstain from any interference with administrative affairs —a decision that aroused strong indignation.[71] But at Rosenheim the mayor was forced to resign and was replaced by the chairman of the local people's council, a Social Democrat, elected by a popular vote; the people's council also decided to take over the functions of the municipal authorities and to suspend their meetings.[72] The deposition of the mayor of Gundelsheim near Bamberg was declared null and void by the Ministry of the Interior; even the *Bezirksamt* attested that he had proved incapable of carrying out his official duties during the war and had not shown any understanding of the situation of the poorer part of the population.[73]

In March 1919—after the murder of Eisner—several other unpopular officials were removed by popular pressure (for example, the *Bezirksamtsmänner* of Aibling, Dachau, Pfarrkirchen and Rosenheim) and the removal of others was demanded. In the case of Pfarrkirchen the reason was the official's ruthless behaviour during the war and his rude treatment of petitioners from the lower classes. The local workmen were so embittered that they threatened to take the law into their own hands if he did not resign; but even he was re-appointed.[74] In general, however, such cases did not occur very often. It seems that the large majority of the old civil servants continued unmolested and undisturbed in their functions. Popular wrath was above all directed against those who were suspected of profiting from the black market or against whom there was concrete evidence of maladministration. The Munich authorities, however, like those in Berlin, usually took the line that even in such cases the workers' and peasants' councils were not entitled to interfere and that the outcome of an official investigation must be awaited. Nor

[70] Report from Aschaffenburg, 28 Jan. 1919, and reply of Ministry of Interior, 17 Feb.: ibid., vol. 13; Staatsministerium des Innern, 54207.

[71] Report from Schwarzenstein, 27 Dec. 1918: ibid., Arbeiter- u. Soldatenrat, vol. 11.

[72] Report of 25 Mar. 1919: ibid., Staatsministerium des Innern, 54202.

[73] *Bezirksamt* Bamberg to Ministry of the Interior, 27 Nov. 1918: ibid., 54199.

[74] The *Beamtenbeirat* to the Ministry of the Interior, 7 Mar. 1919, report from Pfarrkirchen, 4 Mar. 1919: ibid., 54190; Arbeiter- u. Soldatenrat, vol. 10.

was this attitude at variance with that of the Central Council of the workers', peasants' and soldiers' councils in Munich. When it issued new 'guiding lines for the activities of the workers' and peasants' councils' shortly after its election in March 1919 it expressly limited the functions of the local workers' councils to petitions and complaints to the local authorities; requests for the removal of officials were to be addressed to the competent authority, and any independent executive activity by the councils was prohibited 'except in an emergency'.[75]

In the days of November 1918 soldiers' councils played an active part in the downfall of the old régime and the establishment of a new order. They were given far-reaching rights and were entitled to supervise all service arrangements and welfare matters, to receive and hand on complaints and decisions, and to decide on disciplinary punishments for officers and men alike. Officers were only recognized if they were confirmed by a considerable majority of their units, while more senior officers were appointed by the Bavarian Ministry of War in agreement with the workers' and soldiers' councils. The soldiers' councils also elected a Central Soldiers' Council of fifty members, with an executive committee of eleven which functioned in the War Ministry. As one of its members boasted in February 1919, 'nothing gets through which we do not know of. But technical issues we do not handle'.[76] Corps soldiers' councils were also elected in the Bavarian army corps. Thus the First Army Corps in December elected a soldiers' council of seventeen members, the large majority of whom were NCOs; there were only two private soldiers among them, but five sergeants, four military officials, four corporals, and two officer cadets.[77] In general the demobilization of the Bavarian army proceeded so quickly that the soldiers' councils did not play a major part in political developments, except in Munich. Those who remained in the barracks were above all professional soldiers and other men who had no civilian job or family to return to.

In Munich the different barracks had their own soldiers' councils, and there was a Munich executive committee which in personnel and functions overlapped with the executive committee of the Central Soldiers' Council for Bavaria. In February 1919, however, an attempt

[75] 'Richtlinien für die Tätigkeit der Arbeiter- und Bauernräte', March 1919: ibid., Arbeiter- u. Soldatenrat, vol. 3. The same rules applied to the peasant councils. For the election of the Central Council, see below, p. 201.

[76] Kolb (ed.), *Zentralrat . . .* , no. 78, pp. 563–4 (4 Feb. 1919); *Bayerische Staatszeitung*, 12 Jan. 1919, stating that officers had to be confirmed by three-fifths of the votes of their unit, while the Bavarian representative in Berlin on 4 February gave the figure as three quarters.   [77] *Bayerische Staatszeitung*, 4 Jan. 1919.

was made to separate the two executive committees and their functions more strictly and to make the Munich executive committee responsible only for the affairs of the garrison. Within the Bavarian executive committee, sub-committees for administration, propaganda and the press, and complaints, were to be formed; but the decision on all complaints was to be left to the Bavarian executive committee. Its members sat in the different departments of the War Ministry where they were functioning as organs of control. But the speaker admitted that 'hitherto there was a certain chaos' within the executive committee and no proper division of functions: a state of affairs which must come to an end.[78]

Politically, the members of the executive committees and the representatives of the Munich units and barracks stood on the left, but they were opposed to the extremists who were so vociferous in the Munich workers' council, especially after the murder of Eisner. On 1 March 1919 the representatives of all Munich units issued a leaflet in which they strongly advocated the formation of a coalition government of Social Democrats, Independents and the Bavarian Peasant League, and denounced the disruptive activities of the extreme left: 'They decline to cooperate with Spartacists and Communists and are determined to oppose the terror of the street and of an unscrupulous clique with all the power at their disposal. . . .'[79] But the executive committee was equally opposed to the formation of a 'white guard' and the organization of volunteer units in the east of Germany ordered by Noske: 'We warn the Bavarian soldiers not to fall for this swindle. . . . Where can the black-white-red restoration of Germany come from but from the fields of our East-Albian Junkers? If revolutionary Bavarian soldiers are to march, then it must be only with the aim of removing these grandees, in alliance with the proletarian agricultural workers of East-Albia, and of expropriating the landowners. . . .'[80] These were radical words but they were not accompanied by any radical deeds: the revolutionary soldiers of Bavaria were not to march into East-Albia, nor were the Junkers expropriated. In Pomerania and elsewhere there were great strikes of the agricultural labourers, but they were suppressed with the help of the army.

[78] 'Sitzung des Vollzugsausschusses des Münchner- und Landes-Soldatenrates', 23 Feb. 1919: Bayer. Hauptstaatsarchiv, Arbeiter- u. Soldatenrat, vol. 32.
[79] Leaflet signed by representatives of 14 regiments and other units: Stadtarchiv München, Revolution 1918/19.
[80] 'Kundgebung des Vollzugsausschusses der bayer. Landessoldatenräte', *München-Augsburger Abend-Zeitung*, 31 Jan. 1919.

In Munich the murder of Eisner caused an immediate radicalization which was also noticed elsewhere in Bavaria and in some places amounted to a move towards a second revolution. There were many demands for the removal of 'reactionary' officials—tendencies which were noted by the chairman of the workers' and soldiers' council of Aschaffenburg on Main.[81] At Nuremberg and elsewhere even very moderate Social Democrats who before had never thought of the councils as a permanent organization now favoured such a development, to the surprise of their representatives on the Central Council in Berlin.[82] In this atmosphere a congress of the workers', peasants' and soldiers' councils met in Munich at the end of February, a few days after Eisner's death. It adopted a radical motion by which it declared itself as 'the provisional national council of the free people's state of Bavaria' and elected an 'action committee' of thirty-three members: three each were allocated to the Social Democrats, the Independents, the extreme left and the Central Peasant Council, and seven each to the executive committees of the workers', the peasants' and the soldiers' councils. This action committee was to work out a draft constitution in cooperation with the provisional government on which the people were to decide by way of a plebiscite. The congress was to elect a new Bavarian government which was to be responsible to the provisional national council. The Diet was to remain adjourned; against any of its decisions the provisional national council claimed a right of veto, in which case the people were to have the final decision. This motion was adopted against only thirteen votes: it would have given far-reaching constitutional powers to the councils' representatives and would have introduced a combination of parliamentary and council democracy in Bavaria.[83]

Yet another motion to declare Bavaria 'a socialist Soviet republic' was defeated by the large majority of 234 to 70; and the extreme left, led by the Communist Max Levien, refused to join the action committee and the smaller Central Council which were thus composed only of members of the Social Democrats, the Independents and the Peasant League. The representatives of these three parties cooperated closely and from their ranks produced the names of the new ministers; this list was then approved by the congress. Somewhat

[81] Report from Aschaffenburg, 18 Mar. 1919, about events in late February: Bayer. Hauptstaatsarchiv, Arbeiter- u. Soldatenrat, vol. 36.

[82] Kolb (ed.), *Zentralrat* . . . , no. 91, pp. 702, 715 (25 Feb. 1919).

[83] Friedr.-Ebert-Stiftung, Nachlass Barth, I, no. 125; Bundesarchiv Koblenz, R 43 I/2212 (28 Feb. 1919). The decisions of the congress were sharply rejected by the Bavarian deputies to the National Assembly at Weimar: Huber, *Dokumente* . . . , iii, no. 101, p. 91 (1 Mar. 1919).

surprisingly the list contained only three Independents and only one member of the Peasant League (as Minister of Food) but four moderate Social Democrats and one non-party expert; a moderate Social Democrat, Martin Segitz, was to become prime minister in place of Eisner and also to take the place of the wounded Auer as Minister of the Interior. The political complexion of the government as a whole was hardly different from that formed by Eisner four months before. The comment of the *München-Augsburger Abend-Zeitung* was: 'At last, nine days after the murder of Eisner, Bavaria again has a government furnished with all the requisites of power'.[84]

The decisions taken by the congress—especially the election of the government and the adjournment of the Diet—were too radical for the Social Democrats who convened a conference of their own at Fürth, which declared the decisions 'unacceptable'. The Social Democrats declined to accept any ministerial posts. At Nuremberg their representatives met those of the Independents and the Peasant League and they agreed that the Diet should be summoned immediately for a short session, that the two socialist parties should form the government which would be recognized by the Diet and granted far-reaching powers by it; only the members of the government were to exercise legislative and executive powers, while the action committee and the Central Council were excluded from exercising these rights; the local workers' and peasants' councils were given an advisory voice and the right of cooperation on the local level; they could also put forward complaints and legal suggestions to the government and the Diet; a representative each of the workers', the peasants' and the soldiers' councils could attend cabinet meetings in an advisory capacity.[85] The agreement still excluded the councils and their organs from the levers of power and granted them merely advisory functions.

At the council congress which was still in session the agreement was defended by an Independent spokesman, Felix Fechenbach, on the grounds that his party could not possibly form a government on its own, nor could Bavaria with such a government become a member state of the German republic. Above all, he declared, 'Munich was not Bavaria', whereupon the anarchist writer Erich Mühsam shouted: 'The Congress is Bavaria!' But Fechenbach replied:

[84] *München-Augsburger Abend-Zeitung*, 3 Mar. 1919; Mitchell, *Revolution . . .* , p. 286.

[85] *Bayerische Staatszeitung*, 9 Mar. 1919; telegram Count Zech to Auswärtiges Amt, Munich, 5 Mar.: Bundesarchiv, R 43 I/2212.

No, this congress is not Bavaria; it is a meeting of members of the workers', peasants' and soldiers' councils. . . I have the impression as if a high wall existed around Munich over which you cannot look. . . If here in Munich a government is formed according to your intentions, the Diet will assemble at Bamberg and a new government will be established there, and as soon as we have two governments the one at Bamberg will not find it difficult to isolate Munich. You will be able to govern for two weeks at most, and then the country will side with the government at Bamberg. . . . My impression is that the councils, the moment they assemble here, are possessed by a power mania which makes them blind. This blindness will have terrible consequences. . . .[86]

It was a remarkably accurate forecast of what was to happen only a few weeks later when Munich intellectuals and radicals proclaimed the Councils' Republic. The agreement reached between the left-wing parties was accepted by the congress, and a Social Democrat, Johannes Hoffmann, became prime minister; Segitz remained as Minister of the Interior; only the Ministries of Social Welfare and of Commerce and Industry were allocated to Independents. The acceptance was, it seems, largely due to the representatives of the Peasant League who threatened to withdraw from the congress if it were rejected—which would have meant passive resistance on the side of the peasantry. But Mühsam warned openly that a third revolution would occur if the agreement were accepted. The session of congress was closed on 9 March. A few days later the Diet met as arranged; it passed an act which granted the required far-reaching powers to the Hoffmann government, and was then adjourned.[87]

Once more it seemed that common sense had prevailed and that an orderly government was installed which would rule Bavaria according to democratic principles. But this solution was not accepted by the extreme left. The Central Council elected by the congress of council representatives also tried to ensure more orderly procedures for the future. Only a few days after the closure of the congress it announced a change of composition for future congresses. The number of delegates was limited to 162, half of whom were to be representatives of workers' councils, one-third of peasant councils, and one sixth of soldiers' councils. Fixed numbers were allocated to each district of Bavaria, e.g. Upper Bavaria 19 workers' and 12 peasants' delegates, Lower Bavaria 10 and 12 respectively, Swabia

[86] *Bayerische Staatszeitung*, 7 Mar. 1919.
[87] *München-Augsburger Abend-Zeitung*, 13 Mar. 1919; Mitchell, *Revolution . . .* , pp. 288-9.

10 and 9, etc.[88] The uneven distribution and confusion which had marked the congress of March were to be avoided in future. Indeed, one prominent participant thought that it had been more a congress of speeches than of councils, during which intellectuals such as Kaufmann, Löwenfeld and Mühsam had continuously made speeches and attacked each other: in these circumstances it had not been a joy to attend the congress.[89] If in Munich a dislike of the radical intellectuals became noticeable, this was much more marked in the countryside. Even earlier the poet Rainer Maria Rilke remarked to Oskar Maria Graf:

> I do not know, but a cleavage runs through this revolution. In reality it is made only by the workers and the mutinous soldiers. The people in the country remain indifferent and do not join in. . . The peasants are even outspokenly hostile to the revolution. They consider that it all is just a crazy spectacle (*unsinniges Spektakel*). . . 'That is only being staged by people,' they say, 'who do not want to work.'[90]

How justified Rilke's remarks were was to be proved by the events of April 1919, by the tragedy of the Munich Councils' Republic. Whatever goodwill the Bavarian revolution had so far enjoyed on the side of the peasantry, or rather a section of the peasantry, was forfeited during those few weeks.

The peasant councils which came into being in other parts of Germany were nowhere as vigorous as they were in Bavaria, and were nowhere backed by an official peasant organization. The *Bund der Landwirte* which represented the agrarian interest was dominated by the big landowners, hence bitterly hostile to the very idea of peasant councils, which after all might promote the cause of land reform. The socialists, on the other hand, whether moderate or radical, considered the peasants reactionary and were unwilling to concede to them an influence equal to that of the workers' and soldiers' councils. The first proclamation of the Berlin workers' and soldiers' councils of 10 November 1918 stated emphatically that the workers' and soldiers' councils were the bearers of political power and then added rather ambiguously: 'In the countryside peasant councils will be formed for the same purpose'.[91] On the twelfth the new central government issued a proclamation that peasant councils should be

[88] 'Bekanntmachung des Zentralrates', 12 Mar. 1919: *Bayerische Staatszeitung*, 13 Mar. 1919.   [89] *München-Augsburger Abend-Zeitung*, 13 Mar. 1919.
[90] Schmolze (ed.), *Revolution . . .* , p. 172, as reported by Graf.
[91] Matthias (ed.), *Regierung . . .* , i, no. 7, p. 32.

formed everywhere. But a week later the union of agricultural labourers demanded that these should be councils of peasants and agricultural labourers, and this demand was accepted by the government.[92] On these councils, both on the local and on the *Kreis* level, peasants and labourers were to have equal representation—a feature which can hardly have endeared the new institution to the peasant organizations. When the executive committee of the Berlin workers' and soldiers' councils published new guide-lines for the rural population in December this was somewhat modified. The rural electorate was divided into two groups: those employing labour on the one hand, and on the other the agricultural labourers, peasants not employing any labour outside their own family, and smallholders who had to seek additional work outside their farms. Again, each of these two groups was allocated equal representation on the local as well as the *Kreis* peasant councils.[93]

From the outset the functions of the peasant councils were conceived as strictly non-political. Above all, they were to see to the provisioning of the towns: all food not absolutely required for their own consumption was to be collected and every farm was to be allocated its delivery quotas, while all illicit trading in food was to be prevented; farming operations were not to be disturbed or delayed, and agricultural productivity was to be maintained and increased. But the maintenance of law and order and the supervision of the organs of the Prussian administration, such as the *Landräte*, were to be left to the workers' and soldiers' councils, while the peasant councils were to have purely economic functions. Clearly they were not conceived—not even by the radical left—as equal partners in an order based on the council system, but as the more or less willing helpers of the workers' and soldiers' councils: 'The peasant councils serve as organs of *economic* supervision and as advisors of the workers' and soldiers' council situated in the nearest place.'[94] It was most unlikely that on the issues of food deliveries and black marketeering the peasant councils would see eye to eye with the urban councils. The central bureaucracy equally planned to let the peasant councils participate in the fight against the black market and in the collection of surplus food, which, it was hoped, would be promoted if the

[92] ibid., no. 19, p. 113, and notes 4–5; Anlauf, *Revolution in Niedersachsen*, p. 54.
[93] 'Richtlinien für die Landbevölkerung', s.d.: Int. Inst. of Soc. History, Amsterdam, Zentralrat, B-10, I. In general, however, there was parity between landowners and agricultural labourers.
[94] 'Richtlinien für die Landbevölkerung', s.d. (italics in original); announcement by the *Landrat* of Freystadt (Silesia), 18 Nov. 1918: ibid.

poorest peasants received equal rights with the wealthy and if all
local residents above the age of twenty participated in the elections
of peasant councils.[95] In the conditions then prevailing in Germany
these hopes were not likely to materialize.

That the interests of town and country were mutually opposed
also emerged when the government revoked certain laws which
regulated the conditions of work of the agricultural labourers and
virtually tied them to their place of employment (especially the
Gesindeordnung, the provisions of which went back to far earlier
centuries). The workers' and soldiers' council of Rostock immediately
announced that henceforth the agricultural labourers and servants,
including those from Poland and Russia, were only subject to the
provisions of the law of contract and were entitled to change their
employment without the employer's permission. But the peasant
councils of Rostock, Doberan and Ribnitz (all in Mecklenburg)
immediately protested that the harvesters understood this announcement in the sense that they could leave their places of employment
contrary to the stipulations of their contracts: the workers' and
soldiers' council should inform them that they were obliged to
observe their contracts, to work properly and to preserve law and
order; they must hold the workers' and soldiers' council responsible
for any damage that had arisen.[96] From neighbouring Pomerania the
soldiers' council of Stettin expressed its concern about the difficulties
which the elections of peasant councils encountered in the countryside, as the big landowners were trying to influence them and were
carrying the day in certain places.[97] The workers' and soldiers'
council of Stolp, on the other hand, announced that six large estates
of the area had not yet harvested their potatoes; it had therefore been
decided, with the consent of all local peasant councils, to open
criminal procedures against the owners and to inform the central
potato board accordingly.[98]

In Pomerania too, the big landowners who wielded the predomi-
nant influence soon achieved their admission to the peasant councils.
That of the *Landkreis* of Greifswald then consisted of two representatives of the big landowners (*Grossgrundbesitzer*), three of the small

[95] Thus Under-Secretary of State Wurm at the *Reichskonferenz* of 25 Nov. 1918:
Matthias (ed.), *Regierung* . . . , i, no 30, p. 203. Cp. the regulations issued by him on
22 Nov. in *Mitteilungen aus dem Reichsernährungsamt*, iii, no. 63, 29 Nov. 1918.

[96] The Rostock workers' and soldiers' council to the local population, s.d., reply
of the combined peasant councils, Rostock, 26 Nov. 1918: Friedr.-Ebert-Stiftung,
Nachlass Barth, IV.   [97] *Tagesbericht* 53, 27 Dec. 1918, ibid., V.

[98] The Stolp workers' and soldiers' council to the Central Council, s.d. (Jan.
1919): Int. Inst. of Soc. History, Zentralrat, B-3, I.

landowners, five of the agricultural labourers, and three of the local officials (teacher, pastor, village mayor). The parity between employers and employees was no longer observed, and the peasant council decided to accord the two landowners not an advisory voice but full voting rights. Any differences or conflicts between employers and employees were to be decided by the chairman and to be ratified by the peasant council at its next meeting. In January 1919 the Greifswald peasant council also discussed the controversial question whether the Social Democratic chairman of the urban workers' and soldiers' council should become their *Landrat* and, on the motion of the local pastor, the majority expressed their agreement; but no vote was taken,[99] perhaps because this was decidedly outside the competence of the peasant council. Differences between the workers' and soldiers' council and the *Landrat* appeared at Crossen on the Oder because the latter claimed that the peasant councils were subordinate to his office, while the former declared that they came within its jurisdiction. An uneasy compromise was then reached by which the *Landrat* undertook to obtain the workers' and soldiers' council's agreement if he desired any steps to be taken by the peasant councils; but then he suddenly announced in the local paper that new elections to the peasant councils were to be held in February 1919. The workers' and soldiers' council in its turn insisted that the peasant councils elected in November were to continue their work until an agreement was reached with the *Landrat* and complained to the *Regierungspräsident* at Frankfurt about his unilateral procedure.[100] His decision is not reported, but in previous cases of conflict between the *Landrat* and the workers' and soldiers' council he had backed his subordinate officer. In the *Kreis* of Emden, in north-western Prussia, the *Landrat* declined to defray the expenses in cases when the workers' council summoned the peasant council to discuss important issues, on the ground that such conferences were private affairs.[101] In the Hessian *Kreis* of Homberg the *Landrat* himself took the initiative and formed peasant councils which—as the local workers' council complained—consisted almost entirely of 'political enemies of the revolution, better-off peasants and their camp-followers'.[102]

---

[99] Documents of 25 Feb. and 31 Jan. 1919: Bundesarchiv Koblenz, NS. 26, vorl. 71.

[100] The Crossen executive committee to the Central Council, 19 Feb. 1919: Int. Inst. of Soc. History, Zentralrat, B-22, III.

[101] The Emden workers' council to the Prussian Ministry of the Interior, 6 May 1919: ibid., B-12, II.

[102] The Homberg workers' and peasants' council to the Central Council, 12 Mar. 1919: ibid., B-10, I.

In its reply the Central Council in Berlin once more emphasized that in each peasant council there should be parity between land-owners (independent of the size of their holdings) and labourers including independent craftsmen and 'intellectual workers' serving in agriculture, which was also the opinion of the Ministry of Food; equally, that the functions of the peasant councils were not political but exclusively economic.[103] That there was dissatisfaction with the role allocated to the peasant councils emerged at the same time at a conference of the peasants' and labourers' councils of the province of Westphalia held at Hamm. They formed a provincial peasant council, but at the same time they declined to participate in the elections to the second national congress of the workers', peasants' and soldiers' councils because the workers' and soldiers' councils 'have so far excluded the country population from political life and have as best they could hindered the development of the peasants' and agricultural labourers' councils'.[104] It might have been possible to bridge the conflict between town and country by a programme of radical land reform, especially in the eastern provinces of Prussia; but there is no indication that the urgency of such a reform was recognized by the Central Council or by any other authority.

As it was, peasant councils came into being in many rural districts, but they never developed much of a life and their activities remained very limited. This applied even more strongly to the south-west of Germany. In Baden a state peasant council was formed in November and then claimed equal rights with the other councils, but its activities remained small.[105] In Württemberg—as one leading participant tells us—peasant councils came into being only in certain villages in which a few smallholders and workers owning a little land attempted to represent the peasantry: 'phantom creations' which were a concession to the left.[106] From the Prussian province of Hanover it is reported that nothing much was heard from the peasant councils after their foundation in November 1918.[107] From the fragmentary reports available it is almost impossible to say whether they were a viable institution. If the authorities considered them so they should have allocated to them functions other than the supervision of food

[103] The Central Council to the Homberg council, 19 Mar. 1919: ibid. The reference to the Ministry of Food was to new regulations issued on 16 Jan. 1919: ibid., Nachlass Grzesinski, no. 403.

[104] The Westphalian provincial peasants' and labourers' council to the Central Council, 24 Mar. 1919: ibid., Zentralrat, B-10, I.

[105] Remmele, *Staatsumwälzung . . .* , pp. 39–40.

[106] Keil, *Erlebnisse . . .* , ii, p. 121.

[107] Anlauf, *Revolution in Niedersachsen*, p. 54.

deliveries and the prevention of black marketeering—functions which they could not fulfil in the conditions of extreme scarcity then prevailing.

The rigid exclusion of the peasant councils from any political functions, and even from any drafting of proposals for land reform, meant in practice that they were condemned to an early death, even earlier than the workers' councils with which they did not really cooperate. In this field too it emerged clearly how different the conditions in Germany were from those obtaining in Soviet Russia. If there were land-hungry peasants in Germany—and there must have been —this did not lead to the formation of rural Soviets. In Austria, the large estates were much less prominent than they were in certain parts of Germany, and the preconditions for the development of a radical peasant movement did not exist, even less so than in Germany. It was only in Hungary, before the proclamation of the Soviet Republic, that the revolutionary government took some tentative steps to limit the size of the large estates, to provide land for peasant settlement and to carry through a land reform.[108] But the conditions there were very different from those in Germany and Austria.

[108] Böhm, *Im Kreuzfeuer zweier Revolutionen*, pp. 148–53.

8 The Extreme Left

Eight days after the dissolution of the first national congress of the German workers' and soldiers' councils, on 29 December, a national conference of the Spartacus League met in Berlin to discuss the separation from the Independent Social Democrats and the foundation of a new party of the extreme left. Hitherto the Spartacists had belonged to the Independent Party, which offered them complete freedom to propagate their views and to form within it a virtually autonomous organization. The Spartacists possessed their own *Zentrale* (central committee) and their own press; their central paper was *Die Rote Fahne*, edited by Liebknecht and Luxemburg. The day of the conference also happened to be the day after the resignation of the Independent ministers from the government of the People's Representatives, which sharply emphasized the separation of 'the government socialists' from the left-wing opposition. In spite of all these facts, the conference decided, with only three votes against, to break with the Independent party and to form an independent Communist Party, the KPD. Among the dissentient votes there was, interestingly enough, that of the party's *spiritus rector* and leading intellectual, Leo Jogiches (who, like his life-long friend Rosa Luxemburg, was of Polish-Jewish extraction) but not that of Luxemburg herself. Two years before, Jogiches had warned his friends against such a decision which he considered disastrous: 'Such a split, in the given circumstances, . . . must by necessity lead to the separation of a minute circle of the best comrades from the party and must condemn these comrades to complete impotence. Such tactics we consider dangerous, even fatal.'[1] These circumstances still existed, but after the outbreak of the revolution the mood on the extreme left tended to be vastly optimistic, expecting the almost immediate outbreak of a second, more radical revolution, a seizure of power by the workers' and soldiers' councils. That these councils had just decided by an overwhelming majority to hand over their power to a National Assembly, that the Spartacists had only had ten

[1] Hermann Weber (ed.), *Der Gründungsparteitag der KPD*, Frankfurt, 1969, pp. 9, 20, 29. In contrast with the official version published at the time this is a virtually complete protocol, found among the papers of Paul Levi, now in New York.

delegates at the national congress out of nearly five hundred, that their League consisted of little groups scattered over Germany, all this was conveniently forgotten.

The decision of the Spartacists was also influenced by strong pressure from an even more radical group, the so-called Bremen Left, which maintained close connections with the Bolsheviks and now called itself 'International Communists of Germany'. But they had only local influence, at Bremen and at Hamburg, and were quite inconsiderable as a political force on the national level. In mid-December they held their own conference in Berlin and demanded a coordination of all Communist groups whether Spartacists, Left Radicals or any other. Now, on the day following the Spartacus conference, 30 December, their delegates joined those of the Spartacus League, making a total of 127 from 56 German towns, certainly not a very impressive figure. But revolutionary enthusiasm and fervour were rife, and the decisions taken at the 'foundation congress' showed that the delegates of the 'International Communists' wielded an influence disproportionate to their small number. The appearance of Karl Radek as the representative of the victorious Bolsheviks, allegedly wearing Red Army uniform, was hailed with enthusiasm;[2] and Radek, since the pre-war period, had maintained close personal relations with the Bremen Left. In this chiliastic mood—so characteristic of the atmosphere of 1918–19 in many European countries —all counsels of caution, all more realistic assessments of the situation, were swept away; the advice of the party's founders, Liebknecht and Luxemburg, was rejected on the essential issues: elections to the National Assembly and relations with the trade unions. As the history of the party in the year 1919 was to show, there was also present a vociferous semi-syndicalist, semi-anarchist element which, although weak in numbers, exercised considerable influence on the deliberations of the conference, and equally on its disastrous aftermath, the 'Spartacus Rising'.

Apart from relations with the Independent Party, the most important issue before the conference was the question whether the new Communist Party should participate in the elections to the National Assembly which were to be held three weeks later. The party leaders, through the mouth of Paul Levi, a young and brilliant lawyer from Rosa Luxemburg's circle, strongly advocated participation, although Levi at the outset admitted that his was not an easy

[2] ibid., pp. 9, 30, 44, and note 107. One of the other Bolshevik representatives was Ernst Reuter who, after 1945, was for many years the Lord Mayor of Berlin.

task and that the National Assembly 'is the banner of the counter-revolution'. His speech was punctuated by 'tumultuous interruptions'. When he pointed out that in Russia too the Bolsheviks had participated in the elections to the Constituent Assembly although they knew they would win but a small number of seats, and that they had only dissolved it by force when 'objectively the National Assembly was overtaken by the conditions then existing in Russia', a delegate shouted: 'We'll do it immediately!' The first speaker to answer Levi, Otto Rühle from Dresden, declared that until a few days ago he had been convinced that the whole issue was not worth discussing, and had only been informed of the opposite by an article by Rosa Luxemburg in *Rote Fahne*. Against her policy of 'opportunist compromise' Rühle exclaimed:

> We must continually stimulate the living politics of the street; we must not permit the movement to go to sleep again by pushing a ballot paper into the hand of the worker. . . .
>
> Comrades, let the National Assembly be moved to Schilda, then we will have here in Berlin another government, then it will be our task to try to break it up by force. And if this does not succeed then let it go to Schilda. Then we establish here in Berlin a new government. We still have two weeks. . . Our organs we create either after the National Assembly, or, if we do not succeed in disrupting it, simultaneously with the National Assembly. Now we will enter the fight in all its forms. . . .

In the end Rühle's motion against participation was accepted by 62 to 23 votes.[3] It seems that the representatives of the 'International Communists' did not participate in this vote; thus there was apparently a 4:1 majority against participation in the election, and this in spite of Rosa Luxemburg's personal intervention in the debate.[4]

With regard to relations between Communists and Independents, Liebknecht accused 'the large majority' of the latter of treason against the revolution because they allegedly favoured the meeting of the National Assembly and opposed the council system—a treason allegedly perfected at the national congress of the workers' and soldiers' councils. In reality, the exact opposite was true: at the congress the Independents had put forward motions confirming the powers of the workers' and soldiers' councils and of the Central Council elected by the congress; but these motions were rejected by

[3] ibid., pp. 88–90, 93, 96–8, 135, 137. Schilda means a silly small town the inhabitants of which are noted for their pranks.

[4] Her opinion indeed was that the party should not admit any members who were opposed to participation.

the large majority of the congress and the Independents then adopted very short-sighted tactics of boycott and abstention.[5] But they did not boycott the elections to the National Assembly as the Communists decided to do; perhaps this was the rationale behind Liebknecht's irrational remarks. Equally irrational was his statement that the Independent Party was 'today already dead', and that, if the Communists remained within its organization, this would mean 'a solidarization with the counter-revolution, a renouncement of the honour of socialism'. There was no discussion, and no vote was taken on whether the Communists should sever all links with the party which was developing into the mass party of the revolutionary working class. Clearly, there were no dissentients.[6] But there was considerable discussion of two motions which aimed at declaring membership in a trade union incompatible with that in the new party and at obliging all party members to leave the trade unions to which they belonged. The unions were to be replaced by works' councils, and these 'were to continue in the most determined manner the work of fighting against the trade unions'. It was only with difficulty that the party leaders managed to prevent these motions being put to the vote and had them referred to an 'economic committee' where they were effectively buried.[7] But the party's attitude towards the unions—which was not clearly defined at the conference—was to waver time and again during the following years. It was never decided whether the correct line was to try and conquer them from within or to destroy them.

Another important issue appeared towards the end of the conference. In Berlin there existed a strong and influential revolutionary organization: the Revolutionary Shop Stewards who practically dominated the large engineering factories and the Executive Committee of the workers' and soldiers' councils. A seven-man deputation, led by the deputy Georg Ledebour and Richard Müller, appeared at the conference to open negotiations about 'joint action' —which in practice meant that the Revolutionary Shop Stewards would leave the Independent Party and join the Communists. The deputation declared that such joint action was imperative, otherwise 'the revolutionary efforts would suffer greatly'. But they also put forward a list of demands the first of which was that the Communists must revoke their decision not to participate in the elections

[5] See above, pp. 134–5.
[6] ibid., pp. 58, 61, 66.
[7] ibid., pp. 159, 164–5, 167. These motions clearly represented the Syndicalist views held on the extreme left.

and give up their anti-parliamentary attitude. They further demanded parity on all committees, including the central leadership of the new party and a promise that in Berlin no 'actions' would be started without a prior agreement between Communists and Shop Stewards. As Müller explained, they were opposed to the constant demonstrations and to the *Putschist* tactics of the Communists: an argument countered by Liebknecht with the remark that Müller seemed to echo the opinions of *Vorwärts*, the paper of the Social Democrats. In practice there was no hope that such far-reaching demands would be accepted by the conference, and Liebknecht was right when he declared that the demands, especially those regarding 'actions' and street tactics mirrored 'an enormous distrust' of Communist tactics and propaganda methods:[8] as the following days were to prove, that distrust was only too justified. But the breaking-off of the negotiations meant that the new party lost a chance to acquire, at least in Berlin, a really strong working-class following. Without the Shop Stewards, the party had some local influence, for example at Bremen or Brunswick, but very little influence in Berlin or in the centres of heavy industry, such as the Ruhr or central Germany. Its members grossly overestimated their own strength. They mistook their own ardour for that of the 'revolutionary masses'.

The conference ended on 1 January 1919. On the fourth the Prussian government, from which the Independent ministers had resigned a few days after the resignation of the three Independent members from the Reich government, dismissed the Berlin chief of police, Emil Eichhorn, another member of the Independent Party. Legally they were entitled to do so as the chiefs of police of large towns were appointed and dismissed by the Prussian government. Eichhorn, however, refused to hand over his office and referred to the decision of the Executive Committee of the Berlin workers' and soldiers' councils which had confirmed him in his new office on 11 November.[9] The Revolutionary Shop Stewards and the Independent Social Democrats of Berlin decided to back Eichhorn and were joined by the Communists. On 5 January the three organizations issued an appeal to the Berlin workers to show by mass demonstrations that the revolutionary spirit of the November days was not dead, that they would not let themselves be deprived of the last remnants of the revolutionary achievements: their freedom, their future, the fate of the revolution were at stake! Vast masses appeared in the *Siegesallee*

[8] ibid., pp. 270–4. For the Revolutionary Shop Stewards, see above pp. 14–5.
[9] See above, p. 38.

near the Brandenburg Gate, stood and listened to the fiery oratory of Liebknecht and Ledebour, and then marched through the Linden towards the police headquarters. They demonstrated for hours, and then went home. On the same day small armed detachments occupied the buildings of the leading newspapers of Berlin, above all of *Vorwärts*, the Social Democratic paper, which in the opinion of the revolutionaries had been stolen from them during the war. It is not known who gave the order for the seizure of the buildings, but it seems at least possible that the initiative came from *agents provocateurs*. In the evening the leaders of the left-wing organizations met and appointed a Revolutionary Committee with three chairmen, Ledebour, Liebknecht and Scholze, representing the Independents, the Communists and the Revolutionary Shop Stewards respectively. They decided to resist the deposition of Eichhorn and to overthrow the government.[10]

The headquarters of the Revolutionary Committee were established in the former royal stables in the centre of Berlin, to which the People's Naval Division had withdrawn when they evacuated the palace at Christmas. But not even this 'red' unit supported the uprising against the Ebert government. No plans had been made for this venture, and its leaders were apparently taken by surprise. As Ledebour declared in court a few months later, the occupation of the newspapers created a *fait accompli* which could not be reversed; it was impossible to get the occupiers out again. The leaders were faced with the alternatives of retreat or going ahead[11]—on an issue which was important for Berlin but irrelevant to Germany as a whole. On the morning of 6 January emissaries were dispatched to various military barracks and to the War Ministry, which was to be occupied. The other ministries and the Chancery were left alone—strange tactics if the aim was to overthrow the government. But, as a witness described it, 'the royal stables were in such a state of chaos that no one could find his way about'. A leader was found for the three hundred armed men who were to occupy the War Ministry. There they were received by a lieutenant to whom one of the civilians showed a typed piece of paper:

> The Ebert–Scheidemann government has made itself impossible. It has been deposed by the undersigned Revolutionary Committee, the representative of the revolutionary socialist workers and

[10] Eichhorn, *Über die Januar-Ereignisse*, pp. 68–71; *Der Ledebour-Prozess*, pp. 44–5, 51–4, 62–4.
[11] *Der Ledebour-Prozess*, p. 64.

soldiers (Independent Social Democratic Party and Communist Party).

The undersigned Revolutionary Committee has provisionally taken over the affairs of government. . . .

The lieutenant demurred: the paper was only typed and not signed. The negotiator agreed to take it back to the royal stables and get it signed. If this were done the War Ministry would be handed over. At the stables Liebknecht and Scholze duly signed, but Ledebour was not to be found; thus Liebknecht signed on behalf of Ledebour who was 'absent at the moment'. At the Ledebour trial the lieutenant was heard as a witness and denied that this was 'a ruse of war'; he had been 'absolutely serious that, if the government was overthrown, nothing would stand in the way of an occupation. . . '.[12]

At Depot no. 3 of the *Republikanische Soldatenwehr* the negotiators were even less successful. The leader of the depot noticed that the paper was signed but not stamped. He informed his men that he had not received any orders from his headquarters, to which alone he was responsible; he doubted whether the paper was authentic as it was only duplicated and not stamped. Thereupon the majority of the men sharply protested against the emissaries, and strong indignation arose; they had to beat a hasty retreat.[13] Thus the good old ways of the bureaucracy defeated the revolutionaries who had forgotten stamp and signatures. But the whole episode shows how uncertain things were in Berlin after the break-up of the coalition government, how willing at least some people were to accept a new government— provided its orders were properly signed and stamped. This does not mean, however, that such a government could have retained power for any length of time, for it had virtually no military force at its disposal: none of the units stationed in Berlin supported the Revolutionary Committee; none had taken part in the occupation of the newspaper buildings.

Indeed, since Christmas, volunteer units and Free Corps had been formed, and these found an energetic head in Gustav Noske, now a member of the government and responsible for military affairs. In Berlin itself there were several units loyal to the government, such as the *Regiment Reichstag* and the *Maikäfer* (Guards unit) which had Social Democratic leaders. These units were busy wresting the news-

---

[12] ibid., pp. 299, 332–3; the photostatic reproduction of the paper announcing the deposition of the government, p. 55. After its signature the leader took it home; it was found later.

[13] ibid., p. 343. It seems certain that similar attempts were made at other depots and barracks, but they were equally unsuccessful.

paper buildings from the occupiers. Outside Berlin, much larger forces were assembled, above all the *Garde-Kavallerie-Schützen-Division*, commanded by the old officers and distinctly black-white-red in their political sympathies. At the beginning of January all preparations were made for their march into Berlin. From their point of view the occupation of the newspapers and the setting up of the Revolutionary Committee provided the opportunity they were waiting for. The Central Council elected by the congress of workers' and soldiers' councils attempted to negotiate with the occupiers, but the garrison of *Vorwärts* rejected any evacuation. As the Central Council consisted entirely of moderate Social Democrats, it strongly supported the Ebert government in its attempts to restore order in Berlin 'where a small minority is trying to impose a government of brutal force against the general will of the people, especially that of Berlin, and against the declared opinion of the workers' and soldiers' councils of the whole of Germany'. The criminal activities of armed bands, the Central Council declared, had made it necessary to grant extraordinary powers to the government so that law and order could finally be restored in Berlin.[14] The government accused the Spartacists of fighting for power and suppressing the voice of the people. Noske was appointed commander-in-chief. As he proclaimed: 'A worker thus stands at the head of the power of the socialist republic.'[15] Within a few days the newspaper and other occupied buildings were shelled into surrender and the revolt was crushed; the *Vorwärts* building was reoccupied on 11 January. The government's victory was complete.

Already on the tenth, Ledebour and the leading Communist Ernst Meyer had been arrested by government troops. On the fifteenth Rosa Luxemburg and Liebknecht were discovered at their hiding place, taken to the Eden hotel, the headquarters of the *Garde-Kavallerie-Schützen-Division*, and murdered 'while trying to escape'. The same was the fate of many others arrested in January and the following months. As a proclamation of the division announced, it would not leave the capital 'until order has finally been restored'.[16] Order was restored in Berlin at great cost, and this order brought with it a recovery of strength by the old military leaders, by the officers who commanded the volunteer units. The republican units which had been instrumental in the restoration of order were soon

---

[14] Kolb (ed.), *Zentralrat . . .* , no. 31, p. 222.
[15] Facsimile reproductions in *Illustrierte Geschichte der Deutschen Revolution*, pp. 276–7.   [16] Facsimile, ibid., p. 281.

pushed aside and then dissolved as 'unreliable'. The Free Corps were more reliable, with their black-white-red flags and their officers loyal to the *ancien régime*. Ironically enough, not only Rosa Luxemburg, but also Radek had strongly opposed the attempted seizure of power which they considered entirely premature—a hopeless undertaking that would enable the government 'to deal a blow to the Berlin movement which may weaken the whole movement for months'; the Communists should act as a brake; they were the only force which could prevent a catastrophe.[17]

Outside Berlin, the events of 5–6 January hardly produced an echo, except at Bremen where a Soviet republic was proclaimed on 10 January and a 'council of people's commissars' took power for three days: another chance for the volunteer units to intervene with military force and to restore order.[18] In several other towns—Brunswick, Wolfenbüttel, Dortmund, Düsseldorf—newspaper buildings were occupied by armed detachments, but evacuated again after a short time without bloodshed. No uprising broke out, in spite of all the fiery declamations at the Communist conference; but government forces used the opportunity to arrest leading Communists. The so-called Spartacus Rising remained an isolated affair which cost the young party its most eminent leaders. During the following months the government was able to consolidate its position. The elections to the National Assembly on 19 January showed up the weakness of the extreme left and led to the formation of a coalition government of the Social Democrats with the Democrats and the Catholic Centre. The provisional *Reichswehr* became a military force of growing strength, well able to cope with any internal disorders and asserting the government's will in central Germany and elsewhere.[19] The balance of forces had shifted decisively since the days of Christmas 1918 when the government seemed to be at the mercy of a small unit of red sailors, and was seriously considering leaving Berlin.

Only in Bavaria was there no sign of a reversal of the revolutionary trend. On the contrary, as we have seen, the murder of the prime minister, Eisner, in February brought about a reinforcement of the trend towards the left. The rebirth of the army in the north strengthened a fear of Prussian militarism and a dislike of Prussia which was never far from the surface. Wide circles, not only of the working class, believed that the council system would bring them salvation

---

[17] Radek to the Central Committee of the K.P.D., 9 Jan. 1919: quoted ibid., p. 282.

[18] See above, p. 149.   [19] See above, pp. 150–1, 155, 163.

from all the evils of the time—a mirage with a strong emotional appeal, a revolutionary mystique, which was powerful not only in Bavaria.[20] This tendency was strongly reinforced when the Hungarian Soviet Republic was proclaimed on 21 March, when it seemed that a similar move in Bavaria would induce Austria to join Hungary and Bavaria. Even Social Democratic circles were attracted by this idea, in contrast with the official policy of the party. On 3 April a Social Democratic meeting at Augsburg demanded from the government the proclamation of a Councils' Republic, and two days later a Social-Democratic conference for southern Bavaria accepted by 200 to 13 votes a motion in the same sense. In Munich the government negotiated with the left-wing parties, including the Communists, about the proclamation. But the latter had the good sense to reply that conditions in Germany were not ripe for such a move, least of all in Bavaria, and they rejected a Councils' Republic artificially produced around a conference table.[21] Telegrams from several local councils, however, arrived expressing support for the proclamation of such a republic.[22]

On 7 April the Bavarian Councils' Republic was officially proclaimed in Munich—without the Social Democrats and without the Communists. The new government was largely Independent Social Democrat in composition, with a few members of the Peasant League and a few anarchists. But, as Fechenbach had predicted in March, the Hoffmann government transferred its seat to Bamberg and refused to resign. The strong working-class organizations of northern Bavaria were opposed to the new Munich venture. The workers' and soldiers' council of Nuremberg voted by 138 to 70 against it. The Peasant League was divided. Gandorfer, the chairman of the Peasant Council, expressed its support provided there was no socialization in agriculture without the consent of the Peasant Council, and none of small enterprises and of trade, while the deputies of the Peasant League sided with the Hoffmann government. The large majority of the peasant population were hostile to Munich and its intellectuals.[23] The leading lights of the new order in Munich were Dr Gustav Landauer, an anarchist writer, best known for his biography of Shakespeare, Dr Erich Mühsam, another anarchist writer, and

[20] R. Müller, *Bürgerkrieg* . . . , p. 194. Dittmann, in his unpublished memoirs—D 17, p. 16—makes the same point (Int. Inst. of Soc. History).

[21] ibid., p. 192; *Illustrierte Geschichte der Deutschen Revolution*, pp. 390-1.

[22] Bayer. Hauptstaatsarchiv, Arbeiter- u. Soldatenrat, vol. 30: telegrams from Ansbach, Deggendorf, Fürth, Weissenburg.

[23] Telegram from Nuremberg, ibid.; Mattes, *Bayer. Bauernräte*, p. 189; *Bayerische Staatszeitung*, 10 Apr. 1919.

Ernst Toller, a young writer and poet, then twenty-five years old. None of them was a Bavarian; none had any practical political experience.

At first the attitüde of the Social Democrats was equivocal. Those in Munich favoured the Councils' Republic; Schneppenhorst, the minister responsible for military affairs, strongly pressed for its proclamation.[24] Even the Prime Minister, Hoffmann, seems to have wavered. According to a report to the Berlin Foreign Office, others 'induced him at the last moment to establish a counter-government at Bamberg. . . Without this decision the towns of Northern Bavaria would have followed Munich, and the Bavarian Councils' Republic would have been viable for a considerable time. Today the attempt to isolate Munich and to rally the country around Bamberg can be considered as barely having succeeded. . . '.[25] Even in the strongly Catholic Regensburg a mass meeting of thousands voted against one dissentient voice in favour of the Councils' Republic; similar reports came from several small towns in the Upper Palatinate.[26] After the murder of Eisner, a report from Munich emphasized, the idea had gained ground that the socialist parties must unite; even the moderates considered this a legacy of Eisner that must be fulfilled; the leaders had to adhere to it if they wanted to preserve their influence and avoid bloodshed, hence some of them openly advocated the council system. Thus the views of the different socialist parties began to approximate.[27] All this makes the proclamation of 7 April understandable in the political climate of the time: it does not excuse the amateurism and adventurism of those responsible.

As it was the venture only lasted six days. On 13 April a counter-*Putsch* took place in Munich against the Central Council, the leading organ of the new republic, and in favour of the Hoffmann government at Bamberg. But it was defeated by left-wing troops. On the same day a meeting of workers' and soldiers' councils declared the government deposed, appointed Dr Eugen Leviné the chairman of a new Executive Committee of four and transferred all legislative and executive powers to an Action Committee of fifteen: these were the governing organs of the 'Second Councils' Republic', and they were dominated by the Communists. Leviné, who was born in

[24] *Die Münchener Tragödie*, Berlin, 1919, pp. 58–9; *Illustrierte Geschichte der Deutschen Revolution*, p. 391.

[25] Geh. Legationsrat Riezler to Auswärtiges Amt, Bamberg, 26 Apr. 1919: Bundesarchiv Koblenz, R 43 I/2212.

[26] Report from Regensburg, 8 Apr. 1919: Bayer. Hauptstaatsarchiv, Arbeiter- u. Soldatenrat, vol. 30.

[27] Report of 23 Apr. 1919: ibid., Geh. Staatsarchiv, MA. 99902.

Russia but educated in Germany, had been sent to Munich some five weeks before by Paul Levi (the leader of the German Communists after the murder of Liebknecht and Luxemburg) to assume the leadership of the local Communist organization. During this short time he strove to reorganize the party and to terminate its co-operation with other left-wing groups, above all to base the party's work on factory cells led by works' councils (*Betriebsräte*). Under his guidance the works' councils played a decisive part in the government of the second Councils' Republic. They met almost daily and formed a kind of parliamentary assembly. The works' councils were also entrusted with complete control of the management of factories and enterprises. A Red Army was founded to defend the new order and the workers of Munich were armed. All illicit food stores were to be confiscated; any delivery of coal required a permit issued by the Executive Committee. Food indeed was the weakest point of the new régime, for the Hoffmann government imposed a blockade on the area controlled by Munich, and the Bavarian peasants were more than reluctant to deliver anything. If Leviné had declared on 12 April that the Councils' Republic could not possibly maintain itself for any length of time, this was now more true than ever.[28]

Within Munich itself, however, the mood of the working class was not hostile to the Councils' Republic, and Bavarian particularism was reinforcing this mood:

> Time and again one could hear in the discussions in the streets that Bavaria was called upon to promote the world revolution, that the whole world was now looking towards Bavaria, etc. The speakers were often quite reasonable people. Time and again it was also emphasized that Bavaria would have nothing to do with the Reich government, the hostility to which has been nourished for a long time. . . .
>
> It would be a fateful error if it were assumed that in Munich the same clear division between Spartacists and other socialists exists as for example in Berlin. For the present policy of the Communists constantly aims at uniting the *whole working class* against capitalism and in favour of world revolution. . . .[29]

Meanwhile the Hoffmann government, in leaflets dropped on Munich from the air, promised food and coal as well as the preservation of the council system. In late April even Gandorfer declared he

[28] *Die Münchener Tragödie*, pp. 13–14; Mitchell, *Revolution in Bavaria*, pp. 308, 317–19, 322–3; Huber, *Dokumente* . . . , iii, nos. 111–12, p. 99; article in *Münchner Rote Fahne*, 12 Apr. 1919, quoted in *Illustr. Geschichte der Deutschen Revolution*, p. 392.

[29] Report of 23 Apr. 1919: Bayer. Hauptstaatsarchiv, Geh. Staatsarchiv, MA. 99902.

could no longer cooperate with the Munich régime because it did not accept the conditions put forward by the Central Peasant Council, and its office in Munich was closed. At the same time Riezler reported from Bamberg that the crisis was pushing the peasants and the middle classes to the right; 'with the collapse of the Gandorfer firm, the whole bubble of a revolutionary peasantry bursts: the country is and remains a peasant country and, with the support of the unemployed, it can be governed without, but not against the peasantry. . . '. From the outset only small groups of the peasantry in Upper and Lower Bavaria had supported the council régime; now even this cooperation came to an end.[30]

On 27 April a new crisis developed in Munich. The works' councils which had elected the Action Committee only two weeks before passed a vote of no-confidence so that it was forced to resign. The Communist leaders left, and Independent Social Democrats like Toller took over from them. The new Action Committee attempted to negotiate with the Hoffmann government, but the negotiations broke down when the government demanded that all leaders be handed over.[31] When its initial attempts to muster military forces in Bavaria failed, government troops and Free Corps from the whole of Germany were mobilized and concentrated against Munich, among them one Bavarian Free Corps commanded by Colonel von Epp. Against this vastly superior force the badly led and equipped Red Army had no chance, and after severe fighting Munich was reconquered with heavy casualties. On both sides hostages and prisoners were shot without trial. Government troops also murdered Dr Landauer and fifty-three Russian prisoners-of-war who had nothing to do with the fighting. On 1 May the government troops entered Munich and the Councils' Republic was at an end. The white terror began.

The leaders of the Councils' Republic, especially men like Landauer and Toller, were utopians who wanted, as Toller put it, to create a new world. To a lesser extent this utopianism was shared by the leading Communists, Levien and Leviné. That it also penetrated to the working class emerges even from the dry language of official reports. They based all their hopes on the council system which would enable the people to participate directly in the government, as Eisner too had hoped. All this had very little to do with Bolshevism,

---

[30] Riezler to Auswärtiges Amt, 26 Apr. 1919: Bundesarchiv Koblenz, R 43 I/2212; in general Mattes, *Bayer. Bauernräte*, pp. 191–2.
[31] *Die Münchener Tragödie*, pp. 15–16; Mitchell, *Revolution . . .* , pp. 326–7.

and the links between Munich and Moscow—precariously maintained via Budapest—were more than tenuous. The Munich Councils' Republic can hardly be called a Soviet republic although this has often been done. No Bolshevik emissaries were active in Munich in 1919. But by the defeat of the Councils' Republic the whole council system was severely discredited; so was the Hoffmann government which returned to Munich. Three months later the Executive Committee of the Bavarian workers' councils reported to Berlin:

> With us circumstances are such that every *Bezirksamtmann* and every senior official governs as he pleases and pays no attention whatever to the government of the Bavarian Free State. Since 1 May, when the whole reactionary population was armed, the government has largely lost its authority, especially in the countryside where the peasants and the *gendarmerie* treat the *Bezirksamtmänner* as they please. . . .[32]

During the same month the Bavarian government abolished by decree the right of the workers' councils to participate in meetings of the organs of local government, on the ground that some of their members had meanwhile been elected to these bodies.[33] During the summer the majority of the peasant councils ceased to function, and by the beginning of 1920 the whole movement reached its end, without any formal act of dissolution. What had begun as a spontaneous widespread experiment in popular self-government succumbed to a new political climate.

The Austrian Communist Party was founded eight weeks before the German party, on 3 November 1918, but it was considerably weaker. Its influence was virtually limited to Vienna and some industrial towns of Lower Austria, such as Ternitz and Wiener Neustadt, while the German Communists had comparatively strong groups in the north-west, in Saxony and Brunswick, and in the south. In Austria the Social Democratic Party throughout retained control and preserved the loyalty of its followers, in spite of all Communist efforts to undermine it. While in later years the German Communists became a mass party and in some industrial areas stronger than the Social Democrats, this never happened in Austria. It was not due to the *Putschist* tactics adopted by the Communists, which were very much the same in both countries, nor to the economic situation,

[32] The *Vollzugsrat* of the Bavarian workers' councils to the Central Council, 18 Aug. 1919: Int. Inst. of Soc. History, Zentralrat, B-12, VI.

[33] ibid.: decree 7 Aug. 1919.

which if anything was worse in Austria than it was in Germany. But it had something to do with the fact that the Austrian Social Democrats stood considerably to the left of the German party; there was no Austrian Noske, and no white terror under the auspices of a government led by Social Democrats. It was these facts which above all caused so many German workers to move to the left, first to the Independent Social Democrats, and later to the Communists. In Austria too, there was deep disappointment with the outcome of the revolution, but this did not benefit the extreme left.

During the war years young Austrian intellectuals who were opposed to the war formed a Karl Marx Club to fight the pro-war policy of the Social Democrats—like the Spartacus group of Rosa Luxemburg and her circle. Friedrich Adler's murder of the prime minister Count Stürgkh in 1916 gave a new impetus to the Austrian left and brought Adler the sympathies of wide sections of the workers. Prisoners-of-war, returned from Russia after the outbreak of the revolution, increased the strength of the left. When Adler was released from prison the nascent Communists offered him the leadership, which he declined. As we have seen, the formation of the Viennese *Volkswehr* enabled the Communists to set up a 'Red Guard' which became one of the *Volkswehr* battalions, and to gain influence also in some other *Volkswehr* units which contained many returned prisoners-of-war. The official proclamation of the republic on 12 November provided these red units with the opportunity of showing their colours and stirring up unrest, but they led to Social Democratic counter-measures which were in the long run successful.[34] That the weight of counter-propaganda and of the measures taken in Vienna was felt by the Communists immediately is proved by a curious cry for help which they addressed to the new Bavarian Prime Minister, Eisner, claiming that 'the bourgeois-capitalist-democratic government of German Austria aimed at destroying them root and branch ... by force and without mercy'. They did not want to gain anything in German Austria that was not being realized then in Germany, hence they appealed to their 'more fortunate comrades' to help with their forces, and to help soon! They knew themselves to be innocent of the events of 12 November, but had to endure 'a wild political incitement and persecution from all sides'.[35] There was no indication how Eisner was supposed to render help to the Austrian Communists.

[34] Botz, 'Beiträge zur Geschichte . . .', Vienna Ph.D. thesis 1966, pp. 54–9. For the 12 November events, see above, pp. 85–6.

[35] Arbeitskomitte (*sic*) der kommunistischen Partei Deutschösterreichs to Eisner, Vienna, 20 Nov. 1918: Bayer. Hauptstaatsarchiv, Geh. Staatsarchiv, MA. I. 983.

During the winter of 1918–19 the Communists carried on a lively propaganda, especially among the unemployed and within the *Volkswehr* units, putting forward demands which the government was unable to fulfil, but without achieving any notable success. This propaganda was directed above all against the Social Democratic leaders whom they attacked in the most violent manner:

> The rabble leading the organized working masses, who in the war saved their own skins, filled their own pockets and bellies and readily served as the hunting pack of the monarchist government, now are the workers' representatives in the highest offices of state of the democratic republic. . . . They are enthroned on chairs, broad-bottomed and determined to form—together with all great exploiters and war profiteers, with bishops and the high nobility— a new historical convent (*sic*), a welfare committee for all great robbers and thieves, behind the walls of which all superior swindlers can take refuge with immunity. . . .[36]

Considering that Otto Bauer and Julius Deutsch, now Ministers in the coalition government, had both fought in the war, this violent propaganda was not likely to win over many Social Democrats. In February 1919 First Lieutenant Kisch, who vehemently attacked the Social Democratic Party in a soldiers' meeting, was shouted down by the soldiers with 'We do not want any Spartacism!' and was unable to continue.[37]

In Vienna the Communists founded a 'revolutionary soldiers' committee' which was addressed by another leader of the Red Guard, Leo Rothziegel. He exclaimed that more dangerous than the recognized enemy, the capitalists, were the false friends, the helots of capitalism, the Scheidemanns, whatever name they bore—

> those social traitors who have led the proud organization of German Social Democracy . . . into the camp of imperialism, who have remained there to the last, and who are today committing endless atrocities against their own class to save the bourgeoisie. . . . We are supposed to join this Scheidemann Germany. When capitalism has been overthrown here it will be unnecessary to consider this, then we will join the nation which is socialist, for we very much prefer socialist Russia to capitalist Germany. (Thunderous applause.) . . .[38]

According to Viennese police reports of the winter of 1919, the

[36] *Soziale Revolution*, 22 Jan. 1919, quoted by Julius Braunthal, *Kommunisten und Sozialdemokraten*, Vienna, 1920, p. 20; report of Polizeidirektion Wien, 25 Jan. 1919: Landesregierungsarchiv Tirol, Präsidialakten 1919, XII. 76. c.1.

[37] Vienna police report, 24 Feb. 1919: Verwaltungsarchiv Wien, Staatsamt des Innern, 22/NÖ, box 5066.

[38] Report about meeting on 16 Mar. 1919: *Der Rote Soldat*, no. 9, 20 Mar. 1919.

Spartacist risings in Berlin and Bremen found a considerable echo in Vienna and caused much excitement. The majority were pleased by the victory of the government forces; but among the working class there were numerous sympathizers with Spartacus and many remarked that in Vienna too force would have to be used if the election results did not go in favour of the proletariat. The German elections of 19 January disappointed many, partly because they hoped for a defeat of the bourgeois parties, partly because of the defeat of the Independent Social Democrats. According to the same reports, the moderate Social Democratic leaders were steadily losing influence among the masses; the demonstrations of the unemployed met with much sympathy.[39]

Neither unemployment and economic misery, nor the Spartacist risings—which were quickly defeated—acted as a strong stimulus to the Austrian Communists; that stimulus was provided by the proclamation of the Hungarian Soviet Republic in March 1919, followed soon after by similar events in Bavaria. For a short time it seemed that Austria would have Communist neighbours in the east as well as the west, especially when the Hungarian Red Army advanced victoriously in Slovakia and almost reached Bratislava. In March and April there were endless rumours that a Soviet Republic would be proclaimed at Wiener Neustadt; elsewhere, too, great excitement was observed among the Communists who hoped that with the aid of the *Volkswehr* they would soon establish the dictatorship of the proletariat, even without the use of force.[40] From Budapest, emissaries and large sums of money were sent to Vienna to promote the cause, and the Béla Kun government declared its readiness to supply Vienna with food after a successful revolt.[41] At the end of March two of its emissaries spoke in Vienna and demanded the arming of the working class; as soon as Austria joined Hungary the Austrian workers—but not the bourgeoisie—would receive ample food from Hungary. Another Hungarian significantly criticized the Austrian Communists for their tardiness: for them, he claimed, the proclamation of the Soviet Republic was much easier than for the Hungarians because they would be supported by the *Volks-*

[39] Police reports of 14 and 22 Jan., 5 Feb. and 12 Mar. 1919: Botz, 'Beiträge zur Geschichte . . .', iii, Quellen, pp. 11, 12, 14–15, 21.
[40] Report by Landesgendarmeriekommando for Styria, 24 Mar. 1919: Steiermärk. Landesarchiv, Akten der k.k. Statthalterei, E.91, 1918.
[41] Telegrams by Baron Cnobloch, the Austrian ambassador, Budapest, 28–29 March, 4, 13, 15 Apr. 1919: Haus-, Hof- u. Staatsarchiv, Nachlass Otto Bauer, Karton 262, IX.

wehr.[42] Similar promises were made by a Hungarian in a meeting at Graz who painted the conditions in Budapest in the rosiest colours: no one was allowed to earn more than 3,000 crowns a month, the proletarians had moved into the palaces of the rich, social differences had disappeared, manual and intellectual workers were all comrades, all restaurant prices were the same, whether in the first hotel or the last pot-house, and there was no more unemployment because the unemployed entered the Red Army to defend their ideal state; only one energetic effort would be necessary, 'and splendidly, like the rising sun, the new, healthy workers' state will arise'. According to an earlier police report Communist agitation at Graz was growing in intensity and meeting with much more success than at the end of 1918.[43]

In the Wiener Neustadt area too the Communists held many well-attended meetings; their demands for joining Soviet Hungary found much sympathy, even among moderate socialists, while those who spoke against them were often shouted down. There too, Hungarian Communists painted the sky in the rosiest colours: soon the Red Armies of Russia and Hungary would unite, at Belgrade the proletarians had seized power, and the Bulgars, Rumanians and Croats too would join the Hungarian Soviet Republic within the next few days; the Hungarian proletarians had given up half their rations for Austria which would be sent as soon as the Soviet Republic was proclaimed there. But in this case the speaker's assertions were contradicted point by point by local Social Democrats who expressed their sympathies with Hungary but emphasized how dependent Austria was upon the food deliveries of the Entente countries which were holding Austria captive, while Hungary would not be able to send such quantities of food.[44] In Vienna too the Social Democrats were holding numerous meetings to prevent riots and to enlighten the population, but bad food conditions were helping the Communists. According to the same report, Deutsch, the Defence Minister, considered 'the situation critical but not hopeless', and the Social Democrats were doing their best to act as a brake.[45] A British traveller reported from Vienna in April more sceptically:

[42] Vienna police reports, 30 and 31 Mar. 1919: Verwaltungsarchiv Wien, Staatsamt des Innern, 22/NÖ, box 5066.

[43] Police reports of 14 Jan. and 19 Apr. 1919: Steiermärk. Landesarchiv, Akten der k.k. Statthalterei, E. 91, 1918 (iv).

[44] Helmer, *50 Jahre erlebte Geschichte*, p. 85; police report of 25 Apr. 1919: Verwaltungsarchiv Wien, Staatsamt des Innern, 22/NÖ, box 5066.

[45] Party meeting, 27 Mar. 1919: ibid., Verhandlungsschriften der 'Grossdeutschen Vereinigung'.

The population as a whole is extraordinarily docile and quiet, and is most unlikely to break out into Bolshevism, but the danger is that unless they are promptly reorganized and fed they will not have the energy or the wish to combat Bolshevist penetration (why should they fight a régime under which they will be no worse off than the present one?); besides the people of Vienna have no backbone, and are prepared to follow any leader. . . .[46]

In Vienna matters came to a head on 17 April when the Communists organized a mass demonstration in front of the parliament house and the crowds broke into it and set it on fire. On the thirteenth the Austrian ambassador in Budapest had wired to Vienna warning his government against a Communist *Putsch* prepared for the sixteenth of which he had heard from the direct entourage of Béla Kun. On the seventeenth the Communist leaders met to decide on their course of action, a meeting to which Adler went to convince them that the proclamation of a Soviet Republic would only harm the working class. When a vote was taken those in favour of immediate proclamation remained in a minority. The Hungarians had to inform Budapest: 'The cucumber season is bad.' On the following day the Viennese factory trusties refused to call a general strike.[47] The government remained calm and declined to give way to the demand of the chief of police that a state of siege be proclaimed because the police had been fired on in the vicinity of parliament and there had been considerable damage to property. In Renner's opinion the pre-conditions for the state of siege did not exist so that such a measure was unnecessary.[48] Order was restored by *Volkswehr* units without great difficulty. But the police reported on that day utterances by several workers that previously the Social Democratic state secretaries had walked about in shabby clothes and torn shoes, but now they gave orders to shoot the people, exactly like the former authorities; many considered the help given to war invalids and returned prisoners insufficient and put the blame on the government which relied on the police and thus provoked violence.[49]

At Wiener Neustadt a Communist speaker sharply attacked the Social Democrats on account of the events of 17 April and the Workers' Defence Force because it had prevented invalids and un-

[46] Notes by Capt. de Vars Hazard, s.d.: PRO, FO 371, vol. 3508, no. 66064.

[47] Wire by Baron Cnobloch, 13 Apr. 1919: Haus-, Hof- u. Staatsarchiv, Nachlass Bauer, Karton 262, IX; Botz, 'Beiträge zur Geschichte . . .', pp. 92–3.

[48] Verwaltungsarchiv Wien, Kabinettsratsprotokolle, no. 63, point 5, 18 Apr. 1919, 'streng vertraulicher Anhang'.

[49] Police report of 24 Apr. 1919: Botz, 'Beiträge . . .', iii, pp. 30–1. The remarkable thing about the *Volkswehr* action was that two companies of the 'Red Guard' participated in restoring order.

employed from taking possession of the Schönbrunn Palace by appearing armed with machine guns. But he was opposed by a left-wing socialist who argued that it was stupid and criminal to talk about a Soviet government; that the speaker was a political child and belonged to a Jewish clan which appeared in the open when there was a chance of nicking something; the socialist had been in touch with the Hungarians at Sopron about the question of provisioning Wiener Neustadt, but the Hungarians themselves had not enough to eat.[50] Anti-semitism was a curious weapon for a socialist, but the police too emphasized that many prominent Communists—Dr Friedländer and his wife, later famous under the name of Ruth Fischer, as well as the Hungarian emissaries—were Jewish. In the middle of May the Communists of Ternitz, where they had a majority in some of the works' councils, demanded the proclamation of the Soviet Republic, and this was put before a large meeting of the workers' councils of the Neunkirchen district. But before any decision was taken a Communist delegation, including two of the works' councillors, went to Hungary to find out what conditions were like. After a week they reported back to the district workers' councils at Neunkirchen: they related what they had seen in Budapest and quoted a request of the Hungarian Communists to wait because they needed soldiers and arms more urgently than anything else. There was icy silence, and then an uproar during which the two reporters were accused as 'traitors'. The Social Democrats present suggested a vote, and the Communist motion was rejected by a large majority. No Soviet Republic was proclaimed although the Communists shouted that the vote had been falsified.[51]

The districts of Wiener Neustadt and Neunkirchen-Ternitz (to the south of Vienna and close to the Hungarian frontier) were the only ones where the Communists had strong local influence. Membership of the party was growing and reached a figure in the neighbourhood of 40,000 in late May 1919.[52] This was partly due to the increasing number of unemployed, partly to the large amounts of money which continued to flow from Hungary. When an Austrian pilot was arrested on the suspicion of treason, 100,000 crowns was found, a sum he had received from a leading Communist in Sopron, Karl Toman, to bring into Austria. When interviewed by the police

[50] Police report, 29 Apr. 1919: Verwaltungsarchiv Wien, Staatsamt des Innern, 22/NÖ, box 5066.
[51] Helmer, *50 Jahre erlebte Geschichte*, pp. 85–7.
[52] Gerhard Botz, 'Die kommunistischen Putschversuche in Wien 1918/19' *Österreich in Geschichte und Literatur*, xiv 1, 1970, p. 16.

Toman declared he had been given the money in Budapest to start a Communist daily paper in Vienna. When the police searched the flats of prominent Communists, two receipts were found hidden among the ashes of a stove, one signed by Toman for the sum of 250,000 crowns, and another signed by two Red sailors for 20,000 crowns.[53] Even after the overthrow of the Councils' Republic in Munich on 1 May, Vienna continued to be of vital importance to the Béla Kun régime if Hungary was not to remain isolated, and if the Hungarian campaign against the Czechs was to prosper.

Communist activity grew in the course of May for another reason. The Allied powers pressed for a reduction in the strength of the *Volkswehr*; under strong Italian pressure the Austrian government agreed to the discharge of about 30,000 men by the end of June. In Vienna the Communists strongly opposed any reduction and in the plenary meeting of the soldiers' councils moved to ignore the order 'passed at the instigation of the capitalist exploiters'. But the motion was rejected by 174 to 71 votes, and a moderate proposal submitted by Deutsch, to effect a reduction of 25 per cent, was accepted.[54] A few days later a Communist demonstration to protest against the reduction attracted about 4,000 people; Toman exclaimed that the demonstration showed the *Volkswehr* men standing at ease: if this proved insufficient they would press their demands by other means. The police reported that rumours connecting the demonstration with the proclamation of a Soviet Republic were generally believed and almost caused a panic.[55]

In early June Otto Bauer, the Foreign Secretary, expressed his political worries to Chancellor Renner who was negotiating with the Allies at St Germain: the war between Hungary and Czechoslovakia would have the gravest consequences for Austria because it increased on the Hungarian side the interest in the proclamation of a Soviet Republic in Austria so as to cut the transport of Entente troops and supplies into Bohemia.

> The outlook for them is not unfavourable. The Communists here have skilfully exploited the reduction of the *Volkswehr* ordered by the Entente; the fear of dismissal drives the *Volkswehr* men on to the side of the Communists. Thus the Communist movement is once more in the ascendancy. . . In addition, there is the change

[53] Police report of 30 May 1919: Verwaltungsarchiv Wien, Staatsamt des Innern, 22/NÖ, box 5066.

[54] Deutsch, *Aus Österreichs Revolution*, p. 101.

[55] Police report of 5 June 1919: Verwaltungsarchiv Wien, Staatsamt des Innern, 22/NÖ, box 5066.

in the leadership of the Communist Party; Friedländer and Strasser have been removed as too weak, and leadership has been assumed by a directory of three headed by Toman. For all these reasons I believe that the Communists are preparing a *Putsch* which perhaps might be supported by a Hungarian attack against Wiener Neustadt. . . .

Bauer's worries were shared by the leader of the British Military Mission in Vienna, Colonel Sir Thomas Cuninghame, who enquired what the Social Democrats would do if a Soviet dictatorship became inevitable. Curiously enough, he advised Bauer to take part in the venture, 'otherwise there would be the same "luny-bin" as in Budapest'. When Bauer remonstrated that this would be against his convictions, Cuninghame replied that it would be his task 'to divert the tendency of such a dictatorship from the social to the national, above all to the gaining of German Bohemia'.[56] This was strange advice—and contrary to official British policy; but perhaps Cuninghame reckoned with the conquest of Czech Bohemia by the Hungarians who had already conquered most of Slovakia, and with a westward spread of the world-revolutionary movement.

Bauer's information on the change of the Communist leadership was only partially correct. The central committee of the Austrian Communist Party had indeed been dissolved 'on account of the weak attitude of its petty-bourgeois elements, incapable of leading the last frontal attack against the bourgeoisie', and had been replaced by a directory consisting of Toman, Koritschoner, Melcher and Dr Wertheim. But the new *spiritus rector* of the party was Dr Ernst (Ernö) Bettelheim, sent from Budapest in mid-May with plenary powers to reorganize the party and to proclaim the Soviet Republic. The Hungarian Communists, deeply disappointed with the meagre results hitherto obtained, were determined to put matters right in Austria, and this meant the replacement of the Friedländers by more determined leaders and the preparation of another *Putsch*. Bettelheim established his office in the barracks of Battalion 41, where the 'revolutionary soldiers' committee' was also functioning. Communist influence among the *Volkswehr* clearly was of decisive importance for such an undertaking. According to police informants, the decision to remove the Friedländers was due to the personal intervention of Lenin, but equally to certain anti-semitic tendencies among the Viennese Communists as well as to dissatisfaction with the

[56] Bauer to Renner, 8 June 1919: Haus-, Hof- u. Staatsarchiv, Nachlass Otto Bauer, Karton 261.

financial mismanagement of the former leaders; hence Bettelheim had been appointed Austrian 'party dictator'.[57]

By 11 June the police were also able to report that 'within the next few days, in any case by 14 or 15 June 1919, the Viennese Communists would attempt a *Putsch* with the help of the emissaries of the Hungarian Soviet government sent to Vienna'. Apart from other sources, a Hungarian citizen had given information on this plan; according to him, the Hungarian government was aware that a Communist régime could not last on account of economic conditions, but they intended to occupy the Viennese banks, if only for a short time, to acquire the means for a continuation of the war in Hungary.[58] How Bettelheim himself saw the situation can be seen from a curious document apparently found on him when he was arrested later:

> The force of the proletarian revolution showed itself, as if called forth by a miracle, in Vienna and in the countryside to such an extent that one could expect the proclamation of the Soviet Republic on 15 June. Discussion followed upon discussion, meeting upon meeting. The whole of German Austria trembled when faced by the fighting ardour of the proletariat. The government lost its head, the police were perplexed. It seemed as if Vienna would give in to the inevitable. One single assault was necessary to transfer all power into the hands of the proletariat. . . .

Also, according to Bettelheim, 'everybody knew that the Hungarian revolution could only be saved by the Austrian one, that the revolution advancing to the east (*sic*) and the south could only take its route through Vienna'.[59] Everybody also apparently knew the date of the planned revolution.

On 13 June one member of the new directory, Koritschoner, appeared unexpectedly at Ternitz, demanded the summoning of the local workers' council and the immediate proclamation of the Soviet dictatorship, so as to inspire Vienna to action. The workers' council sat the whole night, but Koritschoner was unable to persuade them, unless Wiener Neustadt and Neunkirchen decided likewise. The next morning, therefore, Koritschoner went to Neunkirchen, where the same thing happened. At Wiener Neustadt the workers' councils declared that they made their own policy and did not follow the

[57] Botz, 'Beiträge zur Geschichte . . .', pp. 101–2; police reports of 25 May and 3 June 1919: Verwaltungsarchiv Wien, Staatsamt des Innern, 22/gen. box 4860; Pol. Dir. Wien Berichte 1919.

[58] Police report, 11 June 1919: ibid., Staatsamt des Innern, 22/NÖ, box 5067.

[59] Bettelheim's justification was published in *Der Kampf*, xii 27, pp. 645 ff., 4 Oct. 1919; copy in Polizeiarchiv Wien, Nachlass Schober, Polit. Informationen 1919.

Communist slogans. On the fifteenth the local socialist paper, *Gleichheit*, was rung up from Sopron to find out whether the Soviet Republic had already been proclaimed, as the Sopron paper was going to press and intended to announce the great event. When informed to the contrary they enquired, startled: 'But why not yet?' On the fourteenth a Communist meeting at Stockerau was informed by a Viennese speaker that tomorrow was the day when they must come to the aid of the Viennese who would proclaim the Soviet dictatorship. But not even the local Communist trusties had prior information of these plans.[60]

In Vienna, meanwhile, strong opposition to Bettelheim's scheme developed among the Communists, and members of the different factions went to visit factories and barracks to make propaganda for their views. The workers' council of Vienna published a strong declaration against the intended *Putsch*. The Executive Committee of the soldiers' councils also took precautionary measures and confined all battalions to barracks from 5 pm on 14 June. The soldiers' council of Battalion 41 declared themselves willing to obey the order 'so as to preserve the proletarian united front of the soldiers', while some Communists appealed to them to demonstrate, arms in hand, for a Soviet dictatorship.[61] It is uncertain what the intentions of the Communist leaders were at this stage. In any case, on the evening of 14 June they assembled in full strength at party headquarters, either to draw up final plans or to iron out the differences which had arisen within their ranks. There the police, who expected the worst, arrested them—altogether 122 people, among them several Hungarians—and took them to police headquarters. On the following morning the Minister of the Interior ordered that the arrested twenty members of the Viennese workers' councils should be released immediately, and the others after their identity was established. The several thousand demonstrators who assembled in front of the town hall on that morning did not know about his decision; they first went to parliament to obtain the release of those arrested, and then tried to reach police headquarters. The police blocked all approaches; the crowd tried to break through, and were ordered to desist, but continued to attack the cordon. The police, claiming they had been fired on, fired back; seven people were killed, and many more wounded. As on 17 April the *Volkswehr* was ordered out to preserve

---

[60] Stenographisches Protokoll der Kreiskonferenz des Wiener Arbeiterrates, 17 June 1919, pp. 10–11, 52: Parteiarchiv der SPÖ, Vienna (information given to Adler by members of the workers' councils).

[61] Deutsch, *Aus Österreichs Revolution*, p. 105; Gulick, *Austria* . . . , i, p. 80.

order. There were no further clashes, and even Battalion 41 remained in barracks. The *Putsch* was over.[62]

On the following day Elfriede Friedländer appeared in the Battalion's barracks and accused the men of betraying the Communist cause; the opportunity had passed, now nothing more could be done and they were responsible for the failure. Many men contradicted her, while others applauded. The two sides clashed sharply and the situation had to be saved by some more moderate soldiers. In the opinion of Bettelheim too, treason and 'corrupt demagogues' caused the failure, and among the traitors were party leaders as well as members of the 'revolutionary soldiers' committee', who had prevented the Battalion from attacking the police.[63] Karl Radek, however, sharply condemned Bettelheim's action, his appointment of a party directory, his indiscriminate spending of money, the whole new conception by which the proletariat was to be liberated, not by itself but by its leaders.[64] Three months before L. B. Namier noted on a Foreign Office document: 'As far as I can gather from the Austrian press, in Vienna the "Communists" are just a joke, and their different attempts have always a strong touch of opera bouffe.'[65] On this point Namier and Radek were in agreement.

With the worsening of the military situation in Hungary the danger to Austria receded, and Hungarian interference reached its end. On 1 August Béla Kun resigned; on the next day he, Jenö Landler and Ernö Pór arrived in Vienna as exiles, followed soon by József Pogány, Mátyás Rákosi and many others. All were interned in Austria for the time being.[66] Bettelheim was arrested in a sanatorium a few days later. A white régime succeeded the red dictatorship in Hungary. In Germany too, the extreme left was decisively defeated. All dreams of world revolution receded.

As far as the Austrian Communists were concerned, the defeat of their *Putsch* did not cause the adoption of more moderate tactics. At

---

[62] Police reports of 15 and 17 June 1919: Verwaltungsarchiv Wien, Pol. Dir. Wien Berichte 1919. Botz, 'Beiträge zur Geschichte . . .', p. 115.

[63] Botz, iii, Quellen, pp. 51–2; Bettelheim in *Der Kampf*, xii 27, 4 Oct. 1919, pp. 647–8.

[64] Karl Radek, 'Die Lehren eines Putschversuchs', *Die Kommunistische Internationale*, 1920, vol. ii, no. 9; reprinted by Paul Levi, *Unser Weg wider den Putschismus*, Berlin, 1921, 2nd ed., pp. 58–64.

[65] Marginal note, 15 Mar. 1919, on PRO, FO 371, Austria-Hungary, vol. 3541, no. 39907.

[66] Police report, 3 Aug. 1919: Verwaltungsarchiv Wien, Pol. Dir. Wien Berichte 1919. Eventually most of those interned in Austria were sent to Soviet Russia, as the government resisted all requests for extradition to Hungary: for a discussion in the cabinet on the issue of political asylum, see below, pp. 302–3.

the beginning of July delegates from the whole of Austria met for a two-day conference. There Elfriede Friedländer and Gilbert Melcher sharply attacked Bettelheim and his *Putschism*—as Melcher had already done before 15 June; he was now repeatedly interrupted and called a counter-revolutionary. When the new central committee was elected both critics lost their seats (as did Dr Friedländer) while Toman and Koritschoner—both members of the directory appointed by Bettelheim—retained theirs. The conference expressed its confidence in the directory and its policy and, even more significantly, decided to proclaim the Soviet Republic on 21 July. In the opinion of Bettelheim, the majority of those present opted for 'the quickest and most energetic pursuit of revolutionary activity. Those present at the conference went away in the conviction that the Soviet dictatorship would be proclaimed on 21 July. . . New radical leaders were elected, in the belief that they would accomplish even more radical work. . . '. The police considered the outcome a victory of the manual over the intellectual workers whose only representative on the new central committee was Koritschoner; they also expected a radicalization of party tactics.[67]

Directives 'for the creation of a well-disciplined party organization' adopted at the conference rejected 'in principle any common action, any compromise with the counter-revolutionary Social Patriots, the servants and lackeys of the bourgeoisie'. If, as in Germany, the left wing—Adler and Bauer—should split off from the Social Democrats, the Austrian Communist Party must immediately start to fight it most energetically.

> Any pact, any attempt to formulate a common programme, any cooperation with it would mean a departure from the social revolution and the idea of a ruthless dictatorship of the proletariat and thus inevitably lead the party into the morass of a pseudo-revolutionary policy of illusions. . . .

On the other hand, the directives warned against all actions and enterprises 'which at most can bring about passing successes' and which would lead to a later capitulation, 'in so far as they would damage the final goal'. If, however, the government signed the peace treaty with the Entente powers, the Austrian Communist Party would demand the overthrow of the government and the take-over

[67] Police reports of 9 and 12 July 1919: Haus-, Hof- u. Staatsarchiv, Nachlass Bauer, Karton 262, and Verwaltungsarchiv Wien, Staatsamt des Innern, 22/gen., box 4860; *Der Kampf*, xii 27, 4 Oct. 1919, p. 648; Botz, 'Beiträge zur Geschichte . . .', p. 134.

of political power by the proletariat.[68] There was no criticism of the *Putsch* tactics of 15 June, not even any criticism of Bettelheim and his arbitrary intervention. At a further party conference at the end of August, Toman declared that the party must now stand at ease, but hope should not be given up: an allusion to the collapse of the Hungarian Soviet régime. The conference was very badly attended; three comrades appeared from outside Vienna and declared they would only come back to Vienna if the party worked satisfactorily. The secretary of the Communist youth organization was attacked on account of his passivity. According to the police, the whole conference was 'stormy' and produced no result.[69] Indeed, inside the party there was strong opposition from the extreme left, an opposition which accused the leadership of opportunism and of failing to use the 'favourable situation' which had allegedly existed on 17 April and 15 June. The opposition groups, so the Third International was informed, had united and appointed a provisional central committee to carry out the policy and decisions of the International.[70]

If in Vienna the result of the June defeat was mutual recrimination and an open factional struggle, outside Vienna and the Wiener Neustadt area the Communists throughout remained very weak. Their bitter attacks on the Social Democratic leaders at Graz and at Linz only served to alienate the workers. At Linz the Communists accused the Social Democrats of using the same methods against the workers as the bourgeois had done 'only to preserve their golden chairs. The gratitude of the exploiters will be assured to them'.[71] At Graz the same policy resulted in a decision of the Workers' Auxiliary Corps to expel all Communists. At Graz, too, all known Communists were arrested after local unrest in the spring of 1919 and the party offices closed by the police, which caused 'a complete disorganization of the Communist Party'. At the end of the year the police reported that while the Social Democrats were steadily losing influence, this did not benefit the Communists; their followers were mainly youngsters most of whom were anti-semitic.[72] In Upper Austria,

[68] Copy of the *Direktiven* in Parteiarchiv der SPÖ, Akten des Reichsvollzugsausschusses der Arbeiterräte Deutschösterreichs.

[69] Police report, 3 Sept. 1919: Verwaltungsarchiv Wien, Pol. Dir. Wien Berichte 1919.

[70] Circular of the Communist *Kreisleitung* of Floridsdorf of 24 Aug. 1919, found on a Communist courier sent to Moscow: ibid., Staatsamt des Innern, 22/gen., box 4860.

[71] Oberösterreichisches Landesarchiv, k.k. Statthalterei—Präsidium, no. 274.

[72] *Tagespost*, Graz, 28 Apr. 1919; police reports of 17 May and 6 Dec. 1919: Steiermärk. Landesarchiv, Akten der k.k. Statthalterei—Präsidium, E.91, 1918.

several Communist meetings scheduled for the summer of 1919 had to be cancelled because of poor attendance, and another was taken over by Social Democrats because among about two thousand participants there were only a dozen Communists.[73]

It is, of course, an open question whether the Communists would have been more successful if they had adopted less wild and *Putschist* tactics. But, in Austrian terms, their violent attacks on the Social Democrats, even on their left wing, were entirely irresponsible, and so were the attempts to proclaim a Soviet Republic. On 16 June 1919 —a day after the Communist failure in Vienna—the most eminent left-wing leader, Otto Bauer, explained to Béla Kun why he considered it impossible to establish the dictatorship of the proletariat:

> German Austria is not a state but a loose bundle of provinces which have been left after the dissolution of the old empire. The provinces are totally different from Vienna, they hate Vienna and daily toy with the idea of separation from the capital on which rests the power of the proletariat and which deprives them of food. The power of the working class in the provinces which have few towns is far too small to overcome these centrifugal tendencies. . . . In these circumstances the coherence of the German Austrian lands is much too loose to be able to withstand a serious upheaval. The proclamation of the Soviet dictatorship would thus probably lead to the immediate secession of the mainly rural and therefore clerical-agrarian provinces from Vienna. In Upper Austria Salzburg, Tyrol, Carinthia, central Styria, the workers would be overcome by armed peasants; these lands would repudiate Vienna; the power of the proletarian government would be limited to Vienna, the Wiener Neustadt industrial area and Upper Styria; the provisioning of these districts would be absolutely impossible, and under the pressure of famine the dictatorship would collapse within a very brief time. . . .
>
> Our military situation vis-à-vis the Entente is entirely different from Hungary. The Entente could not allow its routes to Czechoslovakia and Poland via Vienna to be blocked because it would mean the collapse of its whole power-political system. Vienna is far more important to it than Budapest. At the same time it would be far easier for it to defeat us than Hungary. It would not give us time to form a Red Army but occupy us first. Militarily this would be very easy. The Italians have occupied Carinthia and Tyrol. They could thus move some brigades to Vienna within a few days. The Czechs are stationed an hour from Vienna by fast train, and a glance at the railway network shows that for them an operation against Vienna would be a far easier task than any operation in

[73] Police reports of 25 June and 22 Aug. 1919: Oberösterreich. Landesarchiv, k.k. Statthalterei—Präsidium, no. 274.

Slovakia. For the whole action not more than three divisions would be required; the Italians and Czechs together could easily muster that many. . . .

In these circumstances I believe that it is our task to avoid an adventure which would soon end in the defeat and complete disarmament of the working class. I believe on the contrary that it is our task to wait, to preserve the working class, its fighting capability and its fighting means, until the prospects appear more favourable for an energetic move forward. . . .[74]

In Bauer's opinion, such further developments could only occur in the larger European countries, either in Germany if that country refused to sign the Treaty of Versailles, or in the Entente countries if they got involved in another war with Germany; but until then those in the small countries could do nothing but remain ready and avoid defeats so that they would be prepared for any eventuality.

It was a very understandable and responsible attitude. Unfortunately, it was not shared by the Communists. The difference cannot be explained in terms of different social origin. The Jewish intellectuals who were so prominent on the left wing of the Social Democrats and among the Communist leaders usually were of middle-class origin and had academic degrees. And perhaps the Austrian police were justified when they assumed that a more working-class leadership would mean a shift to the left, and not a more moderate course for the Communist Party. In any case, neither in Germany nor in Austria did the catastrophes of the year 1919 lead to the adoption of a more realistic course.

In only one country in central Europe—and indeed only one country outside Russia—did the Communists succeed in gaining power in 1919 and in retaining it for more than a few days: that was Hungary. If Austria was less developed than Germany, Hungary was far more backward than Austria. Above all, the agrarian problem was largely unsolved; vast estates were farmed by peasants who lived in semi-servile conditions, and the nobility enjoyed greater privileges than in any other European country. Industrial development was far behind that of the more western parts of the Habsburg monarchy. At the end of October 1918 a revolutionary government was formed under the liberal Count Mihály Károlyi, who had been a strong opponent of the government during the war.[75] His government was a coalition

[74] Extracts from a lengthy letter of Bauer to Béla Kun, 16 June 1919: Haus-, Hof- u. Staatsarchiv, Nachlass Bauer, Karton 262, IX.
[75] See above, pp. 52–3.

of two small liberal parties (neither of which had a strong following) with the Social Democrats, who had a mass following but only among the industrial workers. The government was weak—weaker even than the contemporary governments in Germany and Austria. It was unable to cope with the economic difficulties of an exhausted country, with the grievances and demands of the population, and with the problems of administration which was in a state of near-chaos. In these circumstances the super-radical propaganda of the nascent Communist Party, mainly led by prisoners-of-war returned from Russia, found a ready echo among the urban masses. As the government was unable to start badly needed social reforms and to solve the land question, the masses increasingly turned against it. The government was equally unable to obtain from the Allies any concession on the issue of the frontiers of Hungary, for Hungary's neighbours to the north, east and south—Czechoslovakia, Rumania and Yugoslavia—were determined to exploit the victory to the full and to annex large territories of the former kingdom inhabited by a mixed population. Any success abroad might have strengthened the Károlyi government, but that it was denied.

In Hungary too, workers' and soldiers' councils were formed after the outbreak of the revolution, and their power co-existed with that of the government. When that of the latter decreased that of the councils increased correspondingly. When the government was slow to grant the councils' demands they took the law into their own hands. In late February 1919 agricultural labourers, impatient of waiting for the promised land reform, took over certain estates which had been royal property. In March 'directorates' took over the administration of some counties; in others the district officials were driven out or forcibly replaced. In the towns demonstration followed upon demonstration, with ever-growing demands. The moderate Social Democratic leaders lost their influence within the party, which became decidedly more left-wing. On 13 March the Budapest police recognized the authority of the soldiers' council; even in Budapest government authority declined sharply. Some three weeks before a crowd instigated by the Communists had wrecked the offices of a well-known newspaper. On the next day the same tactics were to be applied to the Social Democratic paper; in front of its offices shooting broke out, in the course of which seven policemen were killed and eighty people wounded. Then the government took action; about seventy leading Communists were arrested during the last days of February and the Communist papers banned. But they soon reappeared, and no attempt was made to enforce the ban. The imprisonment of the arrested leaders too was less than rigorous, and they carried on their political activities with the help of the prison authorities. The Communists quickly recovered from the setback and renewed their violent agitation against the government.[76]

It was in this situation, when the government was fast losing control, that the Allies put forward far-reaching demands which could only have the effect of completely undermining its position. On 20 March Colonel Vyx of the French Military Mission, accompanied by Allied officers, handed to President Károlyi a note from the Council of Four which demanded a withdrawal of the Hungarian forces facing the Rumanian army in the east. This would have given the Rumanians several thousand square miles and several important towns in addition to what they already held. This ultimatum was to be accepted by 21 March and the withdrawal to begin on the following day. The government felt unable to accept the ultimatum and resigned. The only possibility now was for the Social Democrats to take over the government, but this they could only do if the Communists ceased to attack them. The Social Democrats met and decided to seek the cooperation of the Communists, and one of them was dispatched to the prison where the Communist leaders were held. The emissary suggested that the two parties should unite, and it was decided to form a 'completely united' Hungarian Socialist Party. The Communists, whose fortunes had been so suddenly reversed, were able to impose their terms on the negotiators. It was agreed that unification 'takes place on the basis that both parties participate in the direction of the party and the power of government. The party is taking over power in the name of the proletariat. . . . The envisaged elections to the National Assembly are therefore naturally and finally abandoned. . . '. The Budapest workers' council consented to the unification of the parties, proclaimed the dictatorship of the proletariat and entrusted the Revolutionary Directorate with executive powers. The Hungarian Soviet Republic was proclaimed amidst general jubilation.[77]

In the new government of People's Commissars there were fourteen Communists and seventeen Social Democrats, apart from

[76] Böhm, *Im Kreuzfeuer . . .* , pp. 197–8, 202–3; F. T. Zsuppán, 'The Early Activities of the Hungarian Communist Party, 1918–19', *The Slavonic and East European Review*, xliii, no. 101, 1965, pp. 328–33; Istvan Deak, 'Budapest and the Hungarian Revolutions of 1918–1919', ibid., xlvi, no. 106, 1968, pp. 134–5; R. L. Tőkés, *Béla Kun and the Hungarian Soviet Republic*, New York and London, 1967, pp. 122, 128–9.

[77] Böhm, *Im Kreuzfeuer . . .* , pp. 266–7, 271, 277–8; Zsuppán, 'Early Activities . . .', pp. 333–4; Deak, 'Budapest . . .', p. 135.

two non-party members. Only the Communist leader Béla Kun occupied a leading post, that of foreign affairs, while all others were held by Social Democrats. But they were 'assisted' by Communist deputy commissars who often wielded considerable power; and many leading Social Democrats now sided with the Communists on important issues and some of them openly joined the rising party. Thus, although the Social Democrats retained their influence among the organized workers and in the Budapest workers' council, they did not possess a majority in the government, and in practice the tug of war between the members of the officially united party continued unabated. Moreover, it was clear from the beginning that the Hungarian Soviet Republic could only survive if outside help reached it; as the neighbouring states remained resolutely hostile, this could only come from Soviet Russia. The Communist leaders firmly believed that the Red Army was approaching from the north and would save Hungary.[78] But no Russian help materialized—except precarious communications by aeroplane and radio. Foreign affairs were entrusted to Béla Kun, so as to bring about close cooperation with Russia, but in the end all his appeals were in vain; so were those directed 'To All!' in the hope of obtaining help from the international proletariat.

The radicalized masses expected measures from the new government to fulfil their social demands, and threatened to carry out 'socialization' independent of any government action. Almost immediately the Deputy People's Commissar Mátyás Rákosi ordered all shops, except those selling food and the chemists, to close and to sell their wares only with the consent of the Commissariat; those contravening the decree were to be tried by a revolutionary tribunal and sentenced to death. The decree had to be revoked on the following day, but the damage was done, and shops remained closed. The eight-hour day was introduced and piece-work abolished. The workers were divided into certain wage categories according to length of service, and the wage differences between them and white-collar workers and officials abolished. These well-meant innovations created chaotic conditions in the factories and brought about a decline of production. The same was true of the hasty measures of socialization which comprised everything, from industrial and commercial enterprises of any kind, to hotels, houses, shops, educational establishments, cinemas, down to personal jewellery and small savings.

---

[78] Tökés, *Béla Kun* . . . , p. 137; Böhm, *Im Kreuzfeuer* . . . , p. 483; Deak, 'Budapest . . .', p. 136; Zsuppán, 'Early Activities . . .', p. 334.

Government emissaries would enter houses and take inventories of all contents, warning the housewives not to touch anything because it was now national property. The banks too were nationalized and all deposits confiscated. No one was allowed to withdraw more than ten per cent from his account to a maximum amount of 2,000 crowns per month; but these limits did not apply to the payment of wages and the buying of raw materials. The large estates, which the land-hungry rural population was busy sharing out as the peasants did in Russia, were not to be divided up, but were to be managed by state appointees on cooperative lines. In practice the new managers were often the former owners and little changed for the peasants and labourers who worked on the estates; their land-hunger remained unsatisfied.[79]

Dissatisfaction was aroused by other measures of the new régime. The country population was enraged by fierce anti-religious propaganda carried on by unauthorized agitators, and by their threats that smaller farms too would be nationalized. The government issued a new currency which the peasants refused to accept in exchange for their food, so that little food reached the towns. Food was then requisitioned by military force. Priests were persecuted, churches closed and crucifixes burnt by local zealots. All this caused severe discontent which in the end led to open rebellion. The workers too became dissatisfied on account of worsening living conditions, arbitrary bureaucratic interventions, usually by totally unqualified people, woefully inadequate allowances paid to dependents of red soldiers, falling production, and the general spread of anarchy in the country. At the beginning of June the railwaymen went on strike; communications were paralysed. At the end of May an official report from western Hungary drew a disastrous picture:

> The peasantry everywhere is counter-revolutionary, the working class is entirely passive and feels uncommitted to the dictatorship of the proletariat. The military do not obey orders. There is not a single day on which reports of counter-revolutionary activities are not received. . . In the county of Mosonmagyaróvár many villages have revolted and have only been overcome in veritable battles. . . Where they are unable to rise openly the peasantry suffers our rule full of grim fury. It would be possible to deal with them quickly if only the workers were sufficiently revolutionary; but they are not ready for any sacrifices. At Székesfehérvár 1,800

[79] Böhm, *Im Kreuzfeuer* . . . , pp. 302–4, 308–9; Tökés, *Béla Kun* . . . , pp. 156–7 and n. 44; Deak, 'Budapest . . .', p. 136; Catherine Károlyi, *A Life Together*, London, 1966, p. 201.

workers were mobilized, but only 600 could be retained in the barracks. . . .[80]

The government tried to rule the towns and villages through Commissars sent out with plenary powers in the administrative and judicial spheres. This was euphemistically called the dictatorship of the proletariat, but was in practice arbitrary government, often exercised by irresponsible men; many of them had no experience of administrative matters, no knowledge of the working class; many followed their private interests or ambitions; many were Jews. But even more than the activities of the Commissars the red terror antagonized the people. In Budapest and elsewhere hundreds of hostages were arrested, usually members of the middle classes. Terrorist detachments came into being, the most notorious of which called itself *Lenin fiúk* ('Lenin Boys') and was commanded by a certain Cherny who had learnt his sinister trade in Moscow. The 'Lenin boys' requisitioned houses, arrested wealthy capitalists and aristocrats, and later released them for large sums. Others they summarily shot. They were quick to discover 'counter-revolutionary plots' but slow to defend Hungary at the front. On 21 April the government institutionalized the terror by creating a special Commission to maintain order and discipline and to combat the counter-revolution. Its head was Tibor Szamuely, a close friend of Cherny's and like him trained in Moscow. Through his energy attempted revolts were crushed; many real or alleged counter-revolutionaries were killed or summarily executed at his orders. Even striking railwaymen were condemned to death. The peasants learned to hate the government, which treated them in this way; even red units, sent to assist Szamuely, when attacked by his bodyguard indignantly demanded that he be replaced. The government had to order Szamuely to annul the death sentences passed on strikers, but it was unable to stop the terrorist activities. Anti-semitism grew all the stronger as a result of the red terror.[81] It later became a potent weapon in the hands of the real counter-revolution.

The fate of Hungary, however, was not decided by the red terror and not even by the ineptitude of the government, important though

[80] Böhm, *Im Kreuzfeuer* . . . , pp. 404–5, 450; Deak, 'Budapest . . .', pp. 137–8; Tökés, *Béla Kun* . . . , p. 193; Anon., *Entstehung und Zusammenbruch der ungarischen Rätediktatur*, Vienna, 1919, pp. 18–19.

[81] Böhm, *Im Kreuzfeuer* . . . , pp. 33–4, 423–4, 437–9, 492; Tökés, *Béla Kun* . . . , pp. 159, 193; Deak, 'Budapest . . .', p. 138; F. T. Zsuppán, 'The Hungarian Soviet Republic and the British Military Representatives', *Slavonic and East European Review*, xlvii, no. 108, 1969, p. 202.

these factors were, but by developments at the front. Since the government had rejected the Vyx ultimatum Hungary was again technically at war, and the Rumanian and Czechoslovak forces were not slow to advance further into the country. In April the military situation deteriorated rapidly. At first the government attempted to recruit a Red Army from volunteers, mainly organized workers, but this was a dismal failure. On the front to the east of the Tisza the Hungarian units retreated hastily and many of them panicked. Workers' and soldiers' councils often intervened in the operations, gave military orders and made confusion worse. The Czechs too were advancing rapidly in Slovakia and finally linked up with the Rumanians, thus preventing any Russian aid from reaching Hungary. On 19 April the government decided to mobilize the working class and issued a proclamation 'The Revolution is in Danger'. In Budapest twenty-five workers' battalions were organized to preserve law and order. An energetic Social Democrat, Vilmos Böhm, was appointed commander-in-chief. On the twenty-sixth he addressed the government and warned it of his dire need of reliable soldiers and tangible help instead of the totally unreliable volunteers. The retreat continued across the Tisza, and it seemed as if disaster would soon overtake not only the army but the entire régime.[82]

The situation was saved partly by the determination of Böhm, partly by his outstanding chief of staff, General Aurél Stromfeld, partly by the fact that the Rumanians did not cross the Tisza and advance to Budapest. An army of 50,000 was mobilized and equipped within an astonishingly short time, largely through the efforts of the Budapest trade unions and workers' councils. It was decided to take the offensive, not against the Rumanians, nor against the Yugoslav-French forces in the south, but against the Czechs in the north, the weakest link in the circle surrounding Hungary. The offensive was surprisingly successful in the second half of May and large parts of Slovakia were 'liberated'. The link between Czechs and Rumanians was broken, Košice and many other towns were taken, the Hungarian Red Army was approaching the northern frontier of the former kingdom, and then the Rumanians were thrown back across the Tisza. It was only in part working-class enthusiasm which made this success possible; it was above all nationalism. There were many peasant regiments whose soldiers fought to regain the land they had lost. 'Every small town or village conquered from the enemy increased

[82] Böhm, *Im Kreuzfeuer* . . . , pp. 300, 338–9, 342–3; Zsuppán, 'Hungarian Soviet Republic . . .', pp. 206–8.

the nationalist mood among the soldiers from the agrarian or the industrial working class as well as among the officers. This nationalism lent new energy to the army and inspired it to new victories', as its former commander-in-chief wrote later.[83] Nationalism proved the unifying force beyond all social and political differences, and independent of all Communist ideology.

Yet the victory did not last. Böhm believed that it was the collapse in the interior which vitiated all military successes. And it is true that dissatisfaction first affected the workers' battalions recruited in Budapest factories. On account of the worsening situation at home soldiers left the front and returned to Budapest. Commanding officers no longer dared to give the order to attack because many units simply did not carry it out. Another reason was a government decision to stop the offensive in Slovakia in a vain attempt to appease the Allies,[84] a decision which alienated many nationalist officers. Above all, however, revolutionary and nationalist enthusiasm was sufficient to sustain a short victorious offensive, but quite insufficient to maintain, for any length of time, the army of a small country, short of all vital supplies and surrounded by hostile forces. No Russian aid arrived because the Russian Red Army had to retreat in the Ukraine, and this was the essential factor, even as far as the Communists were concerned. In late July another offensive was started across the Tisza against the Rumanians, and this was a complete failure. After a few days it came to a halt, and then turned into retreat which became a rout. The Red Army began to dissolve. The leading People's Commissars went to the front and found that the army was disintegrating. Kun reported in Budapest that the military situation was hopeless. Although some members of the government were in favour of resistance to the bitter end, there was nothing that the government could do, for dissatisfaction in the rear was by now as strong as dissolution at the front.[85]

On 1 August the government and the directorate of the united Socialist Party met in common session. They unanimously decided to resign and to hand over to a new government appointed by the trade unions. In his final speech Kun declared:

No one will succeed in governing this country. The proletariat, which was discontented under our rule, which was shouting in the factories loudly and in spite of all propaganda: 'Down with the

[83] Böhm, *Im Kreuzfeuer* . . . , pp. 360, 367, 449–50; Tökés, *Béla Kun* . . . , pp. 163, 206.
[84] Böhm, *Im Kreuzfeuer* . . . , pp. 450, 460–3; Tökés, *Béla Kun* . . . , p. 200.
[85] Böhm, *Im Kreuzfeuer* . . . , pp. 512–13, 519, 521.

Dictatorship!', this proletariat will be much more discontented with all other governments. . . .

The Budapest workers' council then elected a new government, with the trade union leader Gyula Peidl as prime minister, a moderate Social Democrat who had retired from political life on 21 March. The new government issued a proclamation that the Government of People's Commissars had resigned after an ultimatum issued by the Entente powers and that the new government was constituted in accordance with their wishes. But the new government only lasted a very short time and was replaced by a right-wing government. After the red terror there came the white terror. When the Rumanians once more crossed the Tisza to occupy Budapest there was no resistance; nor was there any when the Peidl government was overthrown by a right-wing *coup*, carried out by a handful of conspirators.[86]

During the four months that the Communists ruled in Hungary it became abundantly clear that their own forces were entirely insufficient to govern the small country. Their survival depended on external factors, on Russian aid, on the spread of world revolution—hence their desperate efforts to overthrow the Austrian government. But if Vienna had fallen, their difficulties would not have been solved but would have grown, as they did not have enough food for their own needs. In Hungary the Communists could only maintain themselves in power because they succeeded in winning over the bulk of the Social Democrats to the establishment of the 'dictatorship of the proletariat', and the Social Democrats possessed throughout strong influence in the trade unions, among the workers' councils, and in the united Socialist Party. They were much weaker than the Austrian Social Democrats, but much stronger than the Russian Mensheviks. Even so the experiment of Communist rule was a dismal failure: it quickly succeeded in alienating not only the middle classes and the peasantry, but also the working class in whose name it was claiming to rule. The result was a weakening of all left-wing forces in Hungary, the coming into power of a régime of white terror, and the survival of a totally antiquated social and political structure until the end of the Second World War.

[86] Böhm, *Im Kreuzfeuer* . . . , pp. 521–3; Deak, 'Budapest . . .', p. 137.

9 The Extreme Right

The German Right was stunned by the events of November 1918 and did nothing to oppose them. Where non-socialist ministers entered the new governments—as happened immediately in some states—they were liberals or Catholics who were not opposed to the new order but supported it, however reluctantly. The same applied to the Reich government when it became a coalition government after the elections to the National Assembly. It was as if the Right was politically dead, unable to muster any forces in support of the monarchy and against the democratic order. In the elections to the National Assembly, however, a right-wing party participated in the form of the German Nationalist People's Party. It polled 10 per cent of the votes and obtained 44 seats out of a total of 421: a creditable performance only two months after the outbreak of the revolution. Although the party had changed its name and even included in it the word 'people's'—as most other parties did as evidence of their democratic nature—it had not undergone a change of heart; throughout the years of the Weimar Republic it was to remain the protagonist of everything that was reactionary and backward-looking to the days of glory. Yet it accepted the parliamentary forms of opposition and was not pledged to the violent overthrow of the new order. Most of its leaders and supporters did not belong to the 'extreme right', but were right-wing conservatives, monarchists, anti-democrats, authoritarians, etc. who were more at home in the nineteenth than in the twentieth century.

They were also anti-semites, and the party never admitted any Jewish members. Later one of the party leaders, Count Westarp, wrote in his memoirs:

> From my experience the cry of 'Jew' would come from the audience at almost all political meetings when criticism was expressed of political circumstances. Besides, I was often able to notice that a sleepy meeting would wake up and the house applaud as soon as I started on the subject of the Jews. Not infrequently I personally felt a more important and more timely theme for discussion would have been the liberation of Germany or the fight against the

republican system. But for the success of the meeting the Jewish
question could not be omitted. . . .[1]

Political anti-semitism in Germany went back well into the nineteenth century and had become a factor of considerable importance
on the political right—partly in an attempt to wean the workers from
socialism. In the 1890s as many as 16 anti-semitic deputies had been
elected to the Reichstag; the Pan-German League founded at that
time was strongly anti-semitic and had a large membership, especially
among teachers, officials and white-collar workers. Anti-semitism
usually went hand in hand with an aggressive nationalism and
imperialism, with a feeling of 'racial' superiority of the Germans over
other nations and races, especially the Poles and other Slavs. Now
this feeling of superiority was rudely shattered, Germany was defeated, her empire vanished, Poland was reborn and claiming large
territories which most Germans considered German. What was
easier than to make the Jews responsible for the catastrophic defeat,
for the revolution which sprang from it, and for the complete change
in the fortunes of the German nation?

To this the fact must be added that for the first time in Germany
Jews were now in leading political positions: not only among the
Spartacists and other extremist groups, but also among the workers'
and soldiers' councils and elsewhere. Two members of the new
central government—Haase and Landsberg—were Jewish, and so
was the new prime minister of Bavaria, Eisner, and the prime
minister of Prussia, Hirsch. In the eyes of all anti-semites, the Jews
were profiting from the November revolution: it was only a short
step to identify them with the 'November criminals'. Before the end
of 1918 Berlin was flooded with leaflets which encouraged the
population to pogroms, and with others which cried out: 'Kill
Liebknecht!' Another claimed that the seat of the Executive Committee of the workers' and soldiers' councils was the synagogue in the
house of deputies, and its private address in the Jewish quarter
behind the *Alexanderplatz*, 'for short: Jewish Switzerland'. On 11
December 1918 *Vorwärts* reported that Jews and Christians who
looked somewhat Jewish had been attacked publicly.[2] In the election
campaign of January 1919 posters proclaimed: 'The German Democratic Party is the party of Jewry' and 'Germanism—not Judaism!

---

[1] Unpublished Westarp MS. quoted by L. Hertzman, *DNVP—Right-wing
opposition in the Weimar Republic*, Lincoln, Nebraska, 1963, p. 129.
[2] Eichhorn, *Über die Januar-Ereignisse*, p. 14; Hermann Müller, *Die November-
Revolution*, p. 109.

Not religion but race!'[3] Another large poster denounced Spartacus:

> The fatherland stands close to the abyss. Save it! It is not threatened from without, but from within: by the Spartacus group. Kill its leaders! Kill Liebkneckt! Then you will get peace, work and bread!
>
> The front-line soldiers.[4]

In this atmosphere, which became even more violent on account of the Spartacus Rising and the political murders which accompanied it, a newly-founded organization assumed primary importance in the spread of anti-semitism. In mid-February 1919 the leaders of the Pan-German League met at Bamberg and decided to form a comprehensive anti-semitic association to take up the struggle against the Jews on a larger scale, which would at the same time attract the many existing small *völkisch* and anti-semitic groups. The foundation committee consisted of four leading Pan-Germans, among them their chairman, Heinrich Claß, and a retired General, Konstantin von Gebsattel, who was his close friend. The first paragraph of the statutes of the new *Deutscher Schutz- und Trutz-Bund* said:

> The League aims at the moral rebirth of the German nation through the awakening and furthering of its healthy special traits. It considers the oppressive and disintegrating influence of Jewry as the main cause of the collapse, and the elimination of this influence as the pre-condition of political and economic reconstruction and the saving of German culture. . . .

Gebsattel became the League's leader, and a former officer, Alfred Roth, its general manager. Roth was equally active in the Hammer League, an old *völkisch* organization which already before the war had issued large amounts of anti-semitic literature. Now the two leagues used the same central office at Hamburg, and members of the Hammer League automatically qualified for membership in the other; the first few thousand membership numbers were reserved for members of the Hammer League. In practical terms the two leagues soon merged under Roth's guidance. Money was provided by Claß who donated 100,000 marks as well as Roth's salary of 15,000 marks a year for two years.[5]

The Pan-German League had always been strongly anti-semitic,

---

[3] Hertzman, *DNVP . . .*, p. 126.

[4] Facsimile in *Illustrierte Geschichte der Deutschen Revolution*, p. 241.

[5] Uwe Lohalm, *Völkischer Radikalismus—Die Geschichte des Deutschvölkischen Schutz- und Trutzbundes 1919-1923*, Hamburg, 1970, pp. 15, 19–23, 81, 100.

but the propaganda of the new organization enabled it to open the battle against the republic on a broader front and to discredit its representatives as the tools of a general anti-German Jewish conspiracy. The slogans of the Jewish conspiracy and the Jewish stab-in-the-back, which had allegedly brought down the German empire and the German army, were widely believed because so many Germans were unwilling to accept defeat. If the army was undefeated—and even Ebert proclaimed this when welcoming the returning divisions—its honour was saved. Its leaders were free from any blame which could be put on Jews and Bolsheviks. The terms of the Treaty of Versailles seemed to confirm the thesis of an anti-German world conspiracy and added many recruits to the *völkisch* camp. In the conditions of 1919 the membership of the *Schutz- und Trutz-Bund* thus grew quickly. In August, apart from the head office at Hamburg, there were offices at Berlin, Frankfurt, Nuremberg and Stuttgart, with paid employees in each. In early October the League amalgamated with yet another old *völkisch* organization, the *Deutschvölkischer Bund*, and hence became the *Deutschvölkischer Schutz- und Trutz-Bund* until its dissolution by the authorities in 1922. By the end of 1919 it had become the strongest anti-semitic organization in Germany, with 85 local groups and another 71 in the process of formation. It had more than 25,000 members, and up to 1,200 new members were registered every week at its headquarters. By August 1920 the figure had almost quadrupled and stood at over 95,000; in October it passed the 100,000 mark.[6] Its membership was mainly drawn from the middle and lower middle classes, and among its leaders civil servants, teachers, former officers and members of the professions were particularly prominent.[7] It was a respectable, middle-class organization with its membership spread over the whole of Germany. It symbolized the fact that the German middle classes never became reconciled to the existence of a democratic republic.

Particularly susceptible to anti-semitic propaganda were the soldiers of the new volunteer units and Free Corps which were founded on the orders of the government to fight Bolshevism. Many of the soldiers were professional officers and NCOs of the imperial army whose very existence was destroyed by the collapse and revolution. Their pride was in the black-white-red colours under which they had fought for four years. In the Free Corps they were able once more to parade them through the streets of large industrial towns and to regain their lost self-esteem in bloody street-fighting against ill-

6 ibid., pp. 84–5, 88–9, 176–7.   7 See the tables ibid., pp. 108–9.

armed and ill-led 'reds'. In July 1919 soldiers of the Ehrhardt Brigade, which had taken part in the storming of Munich, hoisted the imperial war colours on the palace of Berlin which only six months before had been defended by red sailors. On the first anniversary of the revolution its soldiers deposited wreaths with black-white-red ribbons at the statue of Bismarck in front of the Reichstag building. The Brigade song proudly proclaimed:

> Swastika on the steel helmet,
> Black, white and red our ribbon,
> The Brigade of Ehrhardt,
> That is our name.

The men despised Noske, the new Defence Minister, who wanted to express his thanks to them after their return from Munich but did so in a 'loose-fitting jacket and badly cut trousers'.[8] They despised equally the whole republican government and the new black-red-gold colours.

The Ehrhardt Brigade was not the only Free Corps which showed the swastika, nor the only one in which anti-semitic propaganda was prominent. A soldier of the Lützow Free Corps remembered that he had followed lecture courses on politics and anti-semitism arranged by the unit. From these he drew the conclusion 'that German working men were deliberately being deceived by so-called labour leaders (Jews), to forestall a union of all people of German blood'.[9] Another soldier was won over to the *Deutschvölkischer Schutz- und Trutz-Bund* by his corporal. When the two were discharged the last man of their battery had been enlightened about the Jewish question.[10] The *völkisch* ideology was easily combined with the radical and anti-democratic nationalism which permeated the Free Corps. Already in January 1919 two very moderate Social Democrats had expressed their deep misgivings about the volunteer units in a meeting of the Central Council in Berlin. 'I must say,' one of them stated, 'it makes my flesh creep. There are officers among them far removed from any socialist ideas, who are simply glad to be able to use their swords once more. I must say I shudder at what may come. . . .' And the other, a later Social Democratic Reichstag deputy, attributed the responsibility to the political mistakes of the Independents, 'but the largest responsibility is that of our comrades who sit in the government. . . .

---

[8] Friedrich Freksa, *Kapitän Ehrhardt*, Berlin, 1924, pp. 91, 129, 130, 149, 161, 202.
[9] Theodore Abel, *How Hitler came into Power*, New York, 1938, p. 50.
[10] Otto Schroeder, 'Meine Kampferlebnisse', 15 Feb. 1937: Bundesarchiv Koblenz, NS 26, vorl. 528.

History will record the fact that the German Socialists have only been able to retain power with the help of such men'.[11] This discussion took place a few days before the march of the Free Corps into Berlin and the murder of Liebknecht and Luxemburg, which proved that the apprehensions were only too justified.

At the end of April 1919, when government troops occupied the Ruhr district, the Free Corps Lichtschlag used the opportunity to arrest all members of local workers' councils who belonged to the Independent Social Democrats, although those arrested at Gevelsberg, Schwelm, etc. 'in their views and deeds tend more towards the right than to the extreme left. They are idealists who absolutely condemn civil war, robbery and looting and have expressed this repeatedly by word and deed. . . In the *Kreise* of Hagen and Schwelm there is no basis for wild strikes, the workers throughout are willing and industrious. . . '. The Central Council was asked to intervene with the Minister of Defence to obtain the release of those arrested so that they would be able to fulfil their functions in the interest of the common weal. Therefore the Central Council wrote to Noske that daily it received complaint after complaint about the mistakes of the military authorities which made the workers more and more irritated:

> The Central Council has considered it its duty to mediate towards all sides and is prepared to continue to fulfil this duty. But it does not intend to conceal the fact that, according to its conviction, we in Germany have slowly reached a dead end from which we cannot escape if we do not employ suitable means to quieten the workers and to give up the use of military power as far as it is at all possible. . . .[12]

It was a far stronger condemnation of Noske's policy and of the revival of the army's power than could have been made by parties further to the left. Ten months later the Kapp *Putsch* was to show to what extent the Free Corps and *Reichswehr* units were prepared to move against the republican government and to overthrow it.

In the whole of Germany anti-semitism and openly right-wing tendencies were increasing but they were nowhere stronger than in Bavaria, especially after the defeat of the Councils' Republic. Even before, the existence of the Eisner government and the very fact of the revolution caused an anti-semitic reaction on the extreme right.

[11] Kolb (ed.), *Zentralrat . . .* , no. 41, pp. 287, 289: meeting of 9 Jan. 1919.
[12] The chairman of the Voerde workers' council to the Central Council, 6 May, the Central Council to Noske, 9 May 1919: Bundesarchiv Koblenz, R 43 I/2706.

In December 1918 a *völkisch* writer, Dietrich Eckart, published the first issue of an anti-semitic journal, *Auf gut deutsch*, which henceforth preached the struggle against World Jewry, against democracy and Jewish capitalism. Also in December, a Bavarian paper, *Der Bayerische Wald*, indicted the new government in Berlin as well as those of the states as dominated by Jews:

> Among the people's representatives and the other leading men in Berlin we find the names of Cohn, Bernstein, Haase, Oppen-heimer, Rosenfeld, Herzfeld, Simon, Landsberg, etc. Among the radical Independents and Spartacists Liebknecht, Levi and Rosa Luxemburg play the leading role. The foreign policy of the member states is conducted in Bavaria by Eisner, in Württemberg by Heymann, in Saxony by Lipinski, in German Austria by Bauer. . . .
>
> Who are the true victors over Germany? The French, the English, the Americans? No! No one rules so absolutely in the German 'Free States' as Jewry. The granting of equal rights in 1848 has been replaced in 1871 by the predominance, and in 1918 by the sole rule of the Jewish people in Germany.[13]

At the end of December reactionary circles in Munich tried to organize a *Bürgerwehr*, a citizens' defence corps, as a counterweight to the local red units and with the aim of restoring the monarchy. Money was provided by the well-known *völkisch* publisher, Julius Friedrich Lehmann. The prime mover behind the scenes was another *völkisch* writer, Rudolf von Sebottendorf, the local Master of a secret, quasi-masonic Order, the *Germanen-Orden*, which had its headquarters in the fashionable Hotel 'Vier Jahreszeiten', the meeting-place of the Munich anti-semites, Pan-Germans and *Völkische*. Sebottendorf was also closely associated with a local *völkisch* paper, the *Münchener Beobachter*, in which he virulently attacked Eisner. The Minister of the Interior, Auer, at first supported the formation of the *Bürgerwehr*; but a government decision forced him to withdraw his support and the venture collapsed.[14]

During the early months of 1919 Eckart continued to fulminate against the Jews in the columns of *Auf gut deutsch*. The events of the time—the Spartacus Rising, the proclamation of the Hungarian Soviet Republic, the more radical course in Bavaria after the murder of Eisner—proved to him the existence of a Jewish World Conspiracy. Democracy too was an invention of the Jewish spirit, the Social

[13] *Der Bayerische Wald*, Furth i/Wald, no. 145, 3 Dec. 1918.
[14] Ludwig Oesterreich, editor of *Deutscher Sport*, to Eisner, 4 Jan. 1919: Bayer. Hauptstaatsarchiv, Geh. Staatsarchiv, MA. I. 985. In general Schade, *Kurt Eisner . . .*, pp. 79–80; Mitchell, *Revolution in Bavaria*, pp. 200–4.

Democratic Party was founded by Jews to uproot the Germans, and Communism was the means by which the Jews intended to subjugate the world. In a Baltic German refugee, Alfred Rosenberg, who arrived in Munich in November 1918, Eckart found a permanent and willing collaborator, well versed from Russia in anti-semitic propaganda. In this there appeared a particularly radical, anti-capitalist note, directed against Jewish bankers and 'loan capital'. In April 1919, one day before the proclamation of the Munich Councils' Republic, Eckart distributed from moving cars a leaflet 'To all working people!':

> Such 'Rothschilds' exist among us in numbers: the Mendelssohns, the Bleichröders, the Friedländers, the Warburgs, to name only some of the most important. . . But in spite of this our 'saviours of the people' time and again attack the landowners as the worst, even as the only exploiters, while they never mention, not even in the most gentle fashion, the true blood-suckers! They divert us on purpose to the much lesser evil so that we should not see the principal evil, the all-devouring loan capital; and thus they have tricked us from the days of Marx and Lassalle to those of Levien, Landauer and Mühsam! Are your eyes now being opened?[15]

In May Eckart published Gottfried Feder's 'Manifesto for the Breaking of the Shackles of Interest'. It was the anti-capitalist, pseudo-socialist line which made Eckart, Feder and Rosenberg a few months later such valuable allies of a virtually unknown anti-semitic and *völkisch* agitator, Adolf Hitler.

Among the welter of *völkisch* and extreme right-wing groups which sprang up in Munich in 1919 there also was a 'German Workers' Party' which was founded at the beginning of January. Its distinction was that its founder members actually were industrial workers, and not writers and other intellectuals. It began with a 'political workers' circle' started by Anton Drexler, a craftsman in the central railway repair shop of Munich. He invited some of his colleagues, whom he thought of a like mind, to his house, where the circle was formed in December 1918. Well in line with the secrecy surrounding many *völkisch* enterprises it was laid down that the circle was not to have more than seven members. At the beginning of 1919 preliminary work had progressed so far that Drexler thought of founding a 'German Socialist Workers' Party', but one of those present objected to the word socialist. Thus the German Workers' Party was born on

[15] Margarete Plewnia, *Auf dem Weg zu Hitler—Der 'völkische' Publizist Dietrich Eckart*, Bremen, 1970, pp. 29–30, 35, 37, 49. On p. 50 the facsimile of the leaflet of 6 Apr. 1919.

5 January in the presence of about twenty to thirty railway workers. Drexler's views were not different from those of Eckart and other *Völkische*. He blamed the Jews for the collapse of Germany and the outbreak of the revolution: they and the Freemasons aimed at destroying 'all that was Germanic'. These views Drexler propagated among his workmates when they came to collect or exchange tools in his workshop, and some of them were persuaded to attend his circle.[16]

The new party's meetings held in the course of January were not addressed by Drexler, but by a journalist, Karl Harrer. His main point was that Germany would have been bound to win the war if all had remained united, for the military situation throughout was in her favour; but thousands of Bolshevik propaganda leaflets had been distributed in the army and succeeded 'in sowing the poison of revolution'. No German had an interest in this, but

> the big Jewish capitalists had prepared the ground in never-ceasing work through decades and had won over the workers to their interests by sweet words and hollow phrases. Their numerous agents who were active as party leaders (especially of Social Democracy) worked with full pressure for the revolution.

At the end of the meeting those present agreed: 'The Jews and their helpers are responsible for the loss of the war'. But those attending the meetings were few, and the party did not engage in any outside propaganda by leaflets or public meetings. In the spring of 1919 it usually met in the rooms of the Thule Society which in its turn was closely connected with the Germanic Order.[17] Later party meetings were addressed by Dietrich Eckart and Gottfried Feder.

All *völkisch* groups in Munich, and anti-semitism in general, received a great impetus from the events of April 1919, the proclamation of the Councils' Republic with its prominent Jewish leadership and the reconquest by government troops. Foreign Jews were generally held responsible for the excesses of the Councils' Republic. Bavarian officers who took part in the conquest, such as Colonel von Epp, became popular heroes, especially among the students.[18] That many Bavarians had also participated in the work of the Councils'

[16] Information given by Michael Lotter, one of the founder members, in 1935 and 1941: Bundesarchiv Koblenz, NS 26, vorl. 78.

[17] Reports about party meetings on 16, 22 and 30 Jan. 1919: ibid., NS 26, vorl. 76.

[18] Thus Generalkommando Oven to Reichswehrgruppenkommando, 18 May 1919: Bayer. Hauptstaatsarchiv, Geh. Staatsarchiv, MA. 99902.

Republic was conveniently overlooked. In June 1919 the chief of
police of Munich reported: 'There is growing excitement against the
foreign and the native Jews because they are accused of having promoted the Bolshevik trend by promoting disintegration and giving
financial support. . . '. In August the army reported from Augsburg
that the local anti-semitic association already had 1,200 members,
'mainly from better circles', that anti-semitic propaganda was
flourishing, and that riots and looting had occurred in several towns
on account of this Jew-baiting, which must be sharply watched.[19] In
October a Munich police report noted the exploitation of discontent about food prices for purposes of anti-semitic propaganda.
The reporter considered it possible that pogroms might occur. In
November there was a big 'national' demonstration in the Odeon
Square against the 'Berlin Jewish Government', attended also by
many soldiers. After it ended Jews were physically attacked, chiefly
by students.[20] In November, too, the Bavarian Minister of the
Interior issued a circular to all local governments instructing the
police to pay more attention to the ever-growing anti-semitic
propaganda and to keep an eye on the anti-semitic press; masses of
leaflets were being distributed against the Jews, and it was essential
to ascertain their producers and distributors.[21] At that time the
Deutschvölkischer Schutz- und Trutz-Bund alone had 1,500 members in
Munich.[22]

By the autumn of 1919 a new orator of the *völkisch* cause had made
his appearance in Munich and was beginning to address meetings of
the German Workers' Party. The first such meeting of which we have
a record was addressed by 'Herr Hitler' on the subject of the Treaty
of Brest Litovsk 'in a masterly fashion'; the meeting was attended by
very many students, officers and soldiers, but by only twenty to thirty
workers. Hitler mainly talked on the subject of Versailles: 'since the
creation of the world no nation has had to declare its willingness to
sign such a treaty of shame. . . '. The man responsible for its acceptance must go and should not even remain as a teacher at Butten-
hausen; from the audience someone shouted: 'The same fate as
Eisner's awaits him'. The chairman, Harrer, put the blame on Jews,
Freemasons and Social Democrats who brought about the present
situation, and asked those present to join the German Workers'

[19] Reports of 7 June and 27 Aug. 1919: ibid., Staatsministerium des Innern,
66280.
[20] Lohalm, *Völkischer Radikalismus . . .* , p. 291.
[21] Circular of Ministry of the Interior, 27 Nov. 1919: Staatsarchiv für Oberbayern, RA. Fasz. 3788, no. 57814.   [22] Lohalm, p. 291.

Party, 'the first and only party free of Jews because its statutes prevent the admission of any Jews'.[23] Hitler had been discovered as a 'born orator' by the Bavarian army, which used him to address returned prisoners-of-war and sent him as a liaison agent into the new German Workers' Party, where his fiery oratory soon assured him a leading position. At Munich as well as at Nuremberg groups of yet another *völkisch* organization were founded in the autumn of 1919: the 'German-Socialist Party'. The founding meeting at Nuremberg, in November, took place in the restaurant *Germanenhalle*; those present, 'working men of all trades', considered that the main causes of all miseries were 'our faulty agrarian legislation, our asocial Roman law, our faulty money system, and the political equality of those alien to our race and people', and were convinced 'that true socialism can only flourish on a *völkisch* basis'. The group soon had 300 members, that at Munich 400.[24] In contrast with the *Deutschvölkischer Schutz- und Trutz-Bund* the German Workers' Party and the German-Socialist Party were able to attract members from the lower classes by putting forward radical social demands, by their insistence on a 'German' socialism, and partly too by imitating the propaganda methods of the left-wing parties.

Everywhere in Germany in 1919 the political development was sharply to the right; the forces which in November 1918 briefly vanished from the scene—the bureaucracy, the officer corps, the conservatives and nationalists—were recovering from the shock and regaining their strength. But nowhere did the pendulum swing as far to the right as in Bavaria; there the extreme right and the manifold *völkisch* parties and groups were flourishing, and the *Einwohnerwehren* (defence units) were a real power in the land, as they were in no other part of Germany. Soon they were to dominate the political scene. It is true that Bavaria still had a Social Democratic government, but this wielded no real power and suffered from growing unpopularity. In March 1920—after the Kapp *Putsch*—it was replaced by a right-wing government. When the Diet was re-elected in June 1920 the right-wing parties gained an absolute majority with 85 out of 158 seats; while the Social Democrats lost 60 per cent of their votes and only gained 26 seats—losses which were only very partly made good

[23] Ernst Deuerlein, 'Hitlers Eintritt in die Politik', *Vierteljahrshefte für Zeitgeschichte*, vii, 1959, no. 14, pp. 206–7 (meeting of 13 Nov. 1919). Harrer's claim was entirely unjustified.

[24] Handwritten notes in Bundesarchiv Koblenz, Nachlass Streicher, AL. 9; Bericht über den Parteitag der 'Deutschsozialistischen Partei' Erste Tagung, ibid., NS 26, vorl. 109.

by the gains of the Independents.[25] It was in this political climate that the German Workers' Party became a mass party.

In Austria anti-semitism had been stronger than in Germany even before 1914, and Vienna had a considerably more influential Jewish community than Berlin; it played a leading part in the intellectual, cultural and economic life of the city. Vienna too attracted many eastern Jews as Galicia and the Bukovina were parts of the Habsburg Monarchy. When Galicia became Polish in 1918 and the Bukovina Rumanian, many eastern Jews migrated to Vienna, which they preferred to the uncertainties and the strong nationalism which faced them in eastern Europe. This influx fanned anti-semitic feelings in Vienna which in any case were never far from the surface. They were particularly strong among the students of Vienna University where in the late nineteenth century Georg Ritter von Schönerer had found his most enthusiastic followers, especially among the student corporations which were Pan-German and anti-semitic, accepting only 'Aryan' Germans as members. Their anti-semitism was partly caused by fear of Jewish competition as the percentage of Jewish students tended to be very high. According to a right-wing Catholic Tyrolese newspaper, during the war years Catholics only outnumbered Jews by about 20 per cent in the faculties of law and philosophy, and in the faculty of medicine there were more than two Jewish students to every Catholic one. The paper alleged that these figures contained 'a terrible threat': the increasing Jewishness of the university could lead to Jewish domination of the whole state.[26] Soon the student corporations and other 'Aryans' were to attempt to exclude Jewish students by force from the university, and veritable battles developed between the two sides.

A few days after the outbreak of the revolution the same paper objected to the proclamation of the National Assembly which emphasized that henceforth Austria included only citizens of *one* race: they had forgotten the Jews who in some parts of Austria were 'very numerous and very powerful. They are also much too strongly represented in the state offices of the new German Austria so that precautions ought to be taken against the Jewish influence which has been one of the principal causes of the ruin of the old state. . . '. The

[25] See the detailed figures in Huber, *Dokumente . . .* , iii, p. 610.

[26] *Neue Tiroler Stimmen*, Innsbruck, 22 Jan. 1919. The figures given were: faculty of medicine 3,347 Jews, 1,588 Catholics; faculty of law 3,062 Jews, 3,791 Catholics; faculty of philosophy 2,781 Jews, 3,372 Catholics; all apply to the winter terms of the war years: no source is given.

Tyrol must defend itself from the outset against any suppression of its special character and its special interests.[27] By January the paper had become much more outspoken and found in anti-semitism an effective electoral weapon against Social Democracy:

> Not one vote to the alien red party which intends to barter away our liberties to the Viennese Jews and Berlin Bolsheviks, so that we Tyrolese will be nothing more than slaves who work themselves to the bone, pay taxes and starve for the benefit of alien exploiters. . . .

In one electoral meeting, according to the paper, a Catholic clergyman 'in sharp words branded the inadmissible procedure of the Viennese Jew government (*Judenregierung*) in the matter of Catholic marriage'. The meeting unanimously protested against the proposals of the Ministry of Justice for divorce, and in particular against the appointment of a Jew 'in this purely Christian matter' which it considered 'a brazen and malevolent provocation of the Christian people'.[28] Here in a nutshell were the elements that were to poison the relations between Vienna and the provinces during the years to come: red, atheist Vienna, dominated by Jews, determined to destroy provincial liberties and Christian institutions. Given the rural and strongly Catholic character not only of the Tyrol but equally of Styria, Carinthia and Salzburg, these were only too effective weapons in the hands of unscrupulous Christian Social and other politicians, some of whom were prominent clergymen.

In November 1918 a Christian Social deputy of the Carinthian Diet, the clergyman Konrad Walcher of St Veit, exclaimed among interruptions from the Social Democrats, that it would be possible to reach an understanding with those of Carinthia if they did not always receive instructions from the *Arbeiter-Zeitung* of Vienna: they should rather read the Catholic *Tagblatt* than the Jewish *Arbeiter-Zeitung*, for it was better to live under the crooked crozier than under the 'rule of the crooked noses'; he was eagerly perusing the columns of *Arbeiter-Zeitung* in which the Jew was openly stating his point of view and was advocating the silencing of the representatives of the peasants and the burghers.[29] In December the chief of police of Graz was of the opinion that the Social Democrats committed the tactical mistake of stressing their tolerance towards Jews too much:

[27] ibid., 13 Nov. 1918.
[28] ibid., 9 and 21 Jan. 1919 (meeting of 19 Jan.).
[29] Meeting of the provisional Diet, 22 Nov. 1918: Kärntner Landesarchiv, Umsturzzeit, Lt. IV/6.

Among the people there is an outspoken dislike, not to say hatred, of the Jews. All who have been on active service cannot see any Jews without getting livid because they lorded it behind the front and in the hospitals, but were not to be seen at the front, except perhaps some Jewish officers. In the hinterland the Jews were the first to introduce food smuggling, illicit trade and with them high prices. The others have only learnt from the Jews how to do it. . . .[30]

In an election meeting of January 1919 at Graz, an officer described 'in an inspiring speech' the Jewish-socialist sedition at the front and in the hinterland 'that has caused the collapse of the army'. He informed his audience that the 'German Aryan ex-servicemen' of Austria had formed an association and demanded a strongly disciplined army in place of the *Volkswehr* which consisted of dubious elements; they were protesting 'against the preference shown to alien elements which were pushing ahead excessively'. He was supported by a local lawyer, Dr von Kaisersfeld, who argued that the Jewish influence in political and economic affairs had caused the disastrous end of the war.[31] In another election meeting, at Hall on Inn, a mining engineer, Hans Reinl, attacked the *Innsbrucker Nachrichten* because they printed no anti-semitic articles but many Jewish advertisements. Only the Christian Social and conservative papers were still opposed to the Jews, 'the gravest danger to the German people', so that he would henceforth vote Christian Social, and no longer German Liberal.[32]

It does not seem, however, that the speaker found it difficult to place his violent anti-semitic articles in the local press; for in December a prominent Christian Social paper published four long articles on 'The Racial-Political Causes of the Collapse', usually on its front page. In them he attacked Trotsky '(correctly: Bronnstein)' who had allegedly committed more murders 'during the first year of his glorious reign' than Ivan the Terrible during his whole life: were the Pan-Germans and the military to be held responsible for this too, or Ballin, Rathenau and similar advisers? 'The real victor in this war everywhere was Jewry.' Everywhere the Jews had known how to exploit economic and political developments and how to gain power through war profits and exorbitant prices, by making use of the general dissatisfaction, and at the same time posing as advocates of

[30] Polizeidirektion Graz to Präsidium der Landesregierung, 15 Dec. 1918: Steiermärk. Landesarchiv, Akten der k.k. Statthalterei—Präsidium, E. 91, 1918 (iv).

[31] *Tagespost*, Graz, 11 Jan. 1919.

[32] *Neue Tiroler Stimmen*, 13 Feb. 1919 (meeting of 7 Feb.).

the lower races. 'In this case too they are flesh of their flesh and blood of their blood.' Whoever refused to believe it should look at the pictures of the men of the revolution in the illustrated papers:

Perhaps then the idea will occur to him that all these fellows with their thick lips, fanatical eyes, bent legs, untidy beards and grizzled hair—from the repulsive mulatto face of Liebknecht to the primitive mongol type of Ebert—should much rather decorate the anthropological department of a waxworks than the meetings of the government of the German Reich. Or he should walk through the proletarian quarters of the large cities and study the faces of the passers-by. To a very large extent it is mongol blood or the inheritance of pre-historical primeval races that he will encounter there under the mask of European clothes. Huns and Tatars have left their traces in our homeland, and there still smoulders, like the spark under the ashes, the powerless hatred of palaeolithic dwarf peoples against the Germanic conqueror. . . .

These lower races were now trying to rise, at the behest of the Jewish pied piper; he 'leads them to the attack against everything that may be comprehended under the symbol of the cross, . . . hordes of slaves, a hundred times deceived, which he will push down without mercy as soon as they have let him taste, if only for a short time, the joys of being the ruler. . . '.[33] These racialist phantasies were written at the end of 1918—many years before *Mein Kampf*—but they represent the same picture of a relentless struggle between superior and inferior races, a struggle exploited and led all over the world by Jews aiming at establishing their own rule over it. It was the ideology of the Austrian racialists and Pan-Germans, only with a strong Christian component.

In May 1919 the Tyrolese Peasant League held a large meeting at Innsbruck under the slogan 'Away from Vienna!' The principal speech was given by a prominent Christian Social politician and local lawyer, Dr Richard Steidle, who exclaimed that the old Vienna had committed many sins against the *Länder*, but the new Social Democratic Vienna surpassed the worst expectations:

Above all, the handing over of all influence in economy and government to Jewry, alien to our people and race, has pushed us into an abyss from which only foreign aid will be able to save us. . . . People of the Tyrol, preserve the rights of your homeland!

[33] The four articles, signed 'Ing. H.R.', appeared in *Neue Tiroler Stimmen*, 9, 10, 30 Dec. 1918 and 2 Jan. 1919. Hans Reinl, the likely author, was a local *Bergrat* and academically-trained engineer: see *Haller Lokalanzeiger*, Hall, 13 Apr. 1957. Neither Liebknecht nor Ebert was Jewish, nor was Liebknecht ever a member of the German government.

Peasant, burgher and worker, those who are Tyrolese, do not allow yourselves to be commanded by foreigners and to be pushed into misery. Especially you, peasants, help to restore order in your own country and hold out your hands to your brothers in the other Alpine lands to fight Viennese Asiatic rule. As long as this is not broken things cannot and will not improve. Only a thorough reckoning with the spirit of Jewry and its helpers can save the German Alpine lands. . . .[34]

When a Tyrolese Anti-Semitic League was founded in November the principal speakers were three prominent local politicians, among them Dr Steidle and Dr Straffner. The meeting demanded that all those should be declared Jews by nationality who had even one Jewish great-grandfather or great-grandmother; Jews should not be allowed to buy any property, to own newspapers or become journalists, teachers or professors; books written by Jews should not be used in schools and universities; the number of Jewish students should be regulated by a *numerus clausus*, and so should be that of Jewish officials, lawyers and doctors; no Jews should be admitted to the army, or as traders in timber and cattle. Another demand, voiced soon after, was that all Jews who had no right of domicile in the Tyrol or had only acquired it since 1914 were to be expelled, 'irrespective of any threat of the Jewish ephemeral government in Vienna which will be removed shortly by the wrath of the deceived people'.[35]

Anti-semitism and anti-Viennese feeling were stronger in the Tyrol than elsewhere in the provinces, but similar reports came from other areas. In May 1919 a correspondent wrote to Adler from Klagenfurt about the widespread anti-semitic incitement and 'Away from Vienna' movement in which the Peasant League was joined by Christian Socials and German Democrats.[36] The same tendency was reported by a delegate from Salzburg in July; the representatives of the bourgeois parties always argued 'the Jews, the Viennese Jews!' and the slogan 'Away from Vienna' had even been taken up by the local Communists. Indeed, the Salzburg Christian Social Party demanded—on the basis of national self-determination—that the Jews be recognized as a separate non-German nationality and that non-Germans be excluded from all public offices and representative

[34] Reports about meeting of 25 May in *Tagespost*, Graz, 27 and 29 May 1919.
[35] Tiroler Antisemitenbund to the government, 18 Nov. 1919; Forderungen des Tiroler Antisemitenbundes, 30 Nov. 1919; Entschliessung of 22 Feb. 1920: Landesregierungsarchiv Tirol, Präsidialakten 1919, XII 77, XII 76 e, 1921 XII 76 e.
[36] Alois Steiner to Adler, 22 May 1919: Arbeiterkammer Wien, Adler-Archiv.

bodies.[37] The police headquarters of Graz reported that the workers were perplexed and resentful because of the pushing behaviour of the Jews and their rise to leading posts; '. . . a noticeable anti-Semitic wave is permeating the working class which is likely to benefit the Christian Social Party'. The anti-semitic Proletarian League at Graz had many followers and was conducting active propaganda, which was countered by the Social Democrats.[38]

There was another, smaller party which was even more strongly anti-semitic than the Christian Socials: the Pan-Germans (*Grossdeutsche*) or German Liberals (*Deutschfreiheitliche*), to which many of Schönerer's old followers belonged. In February 1919 one of their deputies declared that he was strictly anti-semitic, hence opposed to the admission of any Jews to the party, and this was then agreed by the deputies present. In October the same deputy claimed that the anti-semitic movement induced many to leave the Social Democrats, but such people were repelled by any monarchist propaganda, hence the subject of the monarchy must be avoided at anti-semitic meetings. Another deputy complained that the Viennese press was entirely in Jewish hands and was in favour of a Danubian federation. He had long tried to create an 'Aryan' paper, with 'Aryan' personnel and a 'national' policy, but even then it might happen that 30 per cent of the capital was provided by Jews. In December he was able to report a success: the foundation of the *Deutsche Bodenbank*, a 'purely Aryan' bank with a capital of 10 million crowns and a management which consisted entirely of 'national' men. But the Jewish press had its attractions for the deputies: although they were 'in principle' opposed to writing for it, it was 'in practice often difficult to avoid it if they did not want to be excluded from any public notice', as the chairman regretfully put it. In spite of his hesitations it was then agreed to forbid the members any cooperation with Jewish papers.[39]

In Vienna soon after the revolution the police reported that anti-semitic tendencies were increasing, especially among the middle classes. One reason given was the terror emanating from the 'Red Guard', which allegedly was largely Jewish—a factor that might cause anti-Jewish pogroms. Another reason mentioned was the considerable influx of refugees from Galicia; this caused much excite-

[37] ibid., Stenographisches Protokoll der II. Reichskonferenz der Arbeiterräte Deutschösterreichs, 3. Sitzung, 2 July 1919, p. 4; *Salzburger Chronik*, 7 Dec. 1919.

[38] Polizeidirektion Graz to Landesregierung, 4 Nov. 1919: Steiermärk. Landesarchiv, Akten der k.k. Statthalterei—Präsidium, E. 91, 1918 (iv).

[39] Verwaltungsarchiv Wien, Verhandlungsschriften der 'Grossdeutschen Vereinigung', 26 Feb., 17 Sept., 9 Oct., 10 Dec. 1919, 8 June 1920.

ment among the Viennese and a demand that the frontiers be closed as the refugees were now foreigners and would increase the food difficulties in Vienna.[40] In December the 'Association of German Aryan Ex-Servicemen' held a public meeting which was attended by about 800 people. The meeting passed quietly until in the discussion a Social Democrat sharply criticized the officer corps; on account of tumultuous interruptions he was unable to continue. After him several speakers violently attacked Jewish preponderance in the leading positions and demanded that the police and *gendarmerie* be increased strongly so as to prevent any excesses by the *Volkswehr*. The principal speakers were professors who talked about the causes and the outcome of the war and encouraged those present to take a more active part in politics as 'German Aryans'.[41]

In June the *Reichspost* announced the formation of a new 'Anti-Semitic League' 'to free our people from Jewish rule'.[42] In June, too, the newly founded 'German Austrian People's Party' held a meeting attended by about six hundred people. It was addressed by its founder, the journalist Anton Orel, on the subject of 'The old Austria and the new Jewish Republic; the Bankruptcy of the red Jews'. He declared that the present government—in contrast with the former one—stood entirely under the influence of alien elements which lacked any German feelings; the 'red Jews' had only one interest: to destroy the old Austria, for only in that way could they achieve their aim of ruling over the people; the Russian pogroms should be a warning to the Austrian Jews not to try the patience of the people too hard; the measures taken by the Jews in Hungary under Béla Kun would bring about a terrible vengeance.[43] In August there was a similar meeting organized by the 'German National Socialist Workers' Party' which was attended by many employees of the railways in Bohemia and Moravia who had been forced to leave Czechoslovakia. The chairman, Dr Walter Riehl, compared their lot with that of 'the Galician Jews inhabiting palaces in Vienna', while the government did nothing for the German railwaymen and postmen from Bohemia; his speech was punctuated by anti-semitic invectives

---

[40] Police reports of 13 and 28 Nov., 4 Dec. 1918: Polizeiarchiv Wien, Staats- u. sicherheitspol. Agenden 1918, box 9.

[41] Police report, 26 Dec. 1918: Kriegsarchiv Wien, Staatsamt für Heerwesen 1918, Fasz. 9.

[42] *Reichspost*, 29 June 1919. The existence of this paper disproved the Pan-German claim that the entire Viennese press was in Jewish hands, for it had a strong anti-semitic bias, and enjoyed a wide circulation.

[43] Police report, 29 June 1919: Verwaltungsarchiv Wien, Staatsamt des Innern, 22/gen., box 4860.

shouted by the audience. These were repeated during a demonstration after the meeting which first went to the *Ballhausplatz* to submit a petition; it was then once more addressed by Riehl who emphasized that it was not directed against the Jews resident in Vienna, but only against those coming in from Poland.[44] Coming from that quarter this was a considerably more moderate line than that of Orel and many other right-wing extremists, at variance too with the line adopted by the Bavarian National Socialists when they took over that name from Austria.

It was the topic of the eastern Jews who had come to Vienna since 1914 which was taken up by the extreme right in the autumn of 1919, a topic certain to find a popular echo in the conditions of extreme shortage of food and living accommodation. In September the 'German People's Council' organized a mass meeting in the town hall of Vienna to demand the immediate expulsion of all eastern Jews. According to the police about five thousand people were present, according to the press ten to fifteen thousand. The deputy Dr Ursin developed the Pan-German and anti-semitic programme, demanded the dissolution of the Jewish-financed banks and their replacement by a *völkisch* bank, the expropriation of Jewish property, and a change in the law about the acquisition of citizenship. The former deputy Dr Jerzabek exclaimed that in the state of New Palestine which was wrongly called German Austria the Jews ruled absolutely over the 'Aryan' people. Dr Riehl declared that the Pan-Germans had no intention of entering the government as the present system would collapse within a few weeks. Several thousand people who could not get into the hall were addressed outside by other speakers who equally sharply attacked the Jews.[45] Ten days later the 'Anti-Semitic League' organized a similar meeting in the same place which was attended by about two thousand five hundred people, while another three thousand stood outside; but press reports put the figure as high as fifteen thousand. The secretary of the German Postmen's Association, Pogatschnig, protested against the pressure allegedly exercised by the Jews on the 'Aryan' population which had become 'completely unbearable': if the government did not find ways and means to terminate this state of affairs, the people would have to help themselves. The Christian Social deputy Volkert blamed the Jews for causing the outbreak of the war and for growing

[44] Police report, 20 Aug. 1919: ibid., Pol. Dir. Wien, Berichte 1919. Riehl was the *Obmann* of the National Socialists, the *Gauleiter* was K. Schulz.
[45] Police report, 25 Sept. 1919, ibid.; *Tagespost*, Graz, evening ed., 26 Sept. 1919.

wealthy and fat while the people were starving; '. . . we live in a republic but the House of Judah is sitting on the throne'. Anton Orel demanded that not only the eastern Jews but all Jews must be removed 'to stave off the threatened destruction of Vienna at the last moment'; the next speaker too pleaded for the removal of the western as well as the eastern Jews. A resolution was adopted urging the government to carry out the expulsion of the eastern Jews within a fortnight.[46] The subject of the western Jews was not mentioned, probably because the leaders disagreed on this issue.

In a comprehensive report drawn up in November the Vienna police pointed out that anti-semitism was becoming more and more noticeable: 'The exasperation with the eastern Jews who either engage in food-smuggling and overcharging or do nothing whatever grows daily, as does the hatred of the Jewish Communists. . . '.[47] In December the National Socialists held a party conference which was attended by delegates from the various districts of Lower Austria, from Linz and Upper Austria, Leoben, Graz, Salzburg, Villach and Innsbruck, as well as by representatives of several 'German' trade unions. Simultaneously there was a meeting of representatives of the National Socialist parties of 'Greater Germany', attended by the leaders of the party from Czechoslovakia (notably Rudolf Jung and Hans Knirsch), Polish Silesia and Germany. But, interestingly enough, the latter were not those of the Munich German Workers' Party, but the engineer Alfred Brunner from Düsseldorf, the founder of the 'German-Socialist Party', and an unnamed representative from Bavaria. All these groups and parties were small, but that in Bohemia was considerably stronger than any other; it was founded as the German Workers' Party in 1904 and was the first to adopt the name of 'National Socialist'. Hence it was allocated four votes in the 'all-German' meeting, the Austrians two, the German-Socialists and the Upper Silesian group one each. The main reports at both meetings were given by Dr Riehl, including one on the 'United Front of all National Socialists'; others were contributed by Jung, Knirsch, and Dr Schilling from Bohemia.[48] It was the first inter-state meeting of the National Socialists, and as such of some importance. But the Austrian groups were all small. That at Innsbruck at the end of 1919 had 48 members, of whom '25 gentlemen and 4 ladies' attended the

[46] Police report, 5 Oct. 1919: Verwaltungsarchiv, Pol. Dir. Wien, Berichte 1919; *Tagespost*, Graz, evening ed., 6 Oct. 1919.
[47] Police Directorate, 17 Nov. 1919: Verwaltungsarchiv, Staatsamt des Innern, 22/gen., box 4860.
[48] *Deutsche Arbeiter-Presse—Nationalsozialistisches Wochenblatt*, no. 49, 6 Dec. 1919.

annual meeting, where the party chairman, an engineer named Arnelt, reported on the party conference in Vienna. Another speaker emphasized that the new party rejected the class struggle and considered private property justified, but was not opposed to the nationalization of large enterprises; it intended to be 'as it were a party in between the Liberals, Christian Socials and Social Democrats'—a somewhat surprising statement considering its extremist propaganda.[49] Among the leaders of the party the academic element was strong: at the conference in Vienna there had been at least five delegates with a 'Dr', one with a 'Prof.', and another four with an 'Ing.' in front of their names, indicating some higher education, at a university or a technical college.

In general, the *völkisch* camp suffered from a surfeit of small groups and rival leaders. Apart from those mentioned, there also existed a 'Union of Radical Socialists' and an 'Anti-Semitic Proletarian League', and their programmes were often indistinguishable. In Vienna 'the three large national parties'—the Pan-Germans, the German Nationalists and the German People's League—united at the end of 1919 and, as a deputy reported, even the National Socialists were 'not in principle opposed to a unification'. But as another deputy remarked: 'It really is a work of art to bring about unification and to give it some punch'; the conflict of interests was too strong, and the danger of division existed everywhere.[50] There was growing up, however, a much larger organization of the extreme right, not in the towns but in the countryside, and therefore much less conspicuous: the *Heimwehren*.

The first *Heimwehren* were formed in November 1918, in the first instance to prevent looting and forcible requisitioning by the returning troops or prisoners-of-war; and they were issued with arms by authority of the government.[51] In Styria and Carinthia they were organized by army officers to oppose the advance of the Yugoslavs. In the Tyrol the principal organizer was the Christian Social leader Dr Steidle, a leading anti-semite, who was successful in procuring weapons for his units. In Upper Styria another lawyer, Dr Walter Pfrimer, founded armed units in the autumn of 1918. In the area of Graz and central Styria former officers were active in the organization. In February 1919 a complaint was posted to Graz from Knittelfeld that

[49] Police report, 3 Jan. 1920: Landesregierungsarchiv Tirol, Präsidialakten 1920, XII 77.
[50] Verwaltungsarchiv Wien, Verhandlungsschriften der 'Grossdeutschen Vereinigung', meeting of 16 Dec. 1919: report by Dr Ursin.   [51] See above, p. 25.

weapons were being sent into the villages on sleighs on the instruction of a major of the *Volkswehr*; the local workers demanded that this be stopped and the *Heimwehren* be dissolved. The local authority admitted the facts but declared that the *Heimwehren* were entirely non-political, serving in the interest of the common weal and 'only for the defence of the rural population against the ever growing bands of robbers and other vagrants'. Ample funds were available; according to a report of the military police, one account at Graz contained about three million crowns for the purchase of arms.[52] As one of the local leaders admitted later, the units in Styria were furnished with about 17,000 rifles, 286 machine guns and 12 pieces of artillery, partly from *Volkswehr* depots; even aeroplanes were acquired.[53] In June 1919 the leader for Lower Styria claimed that he had always pursued 'purely *völkisch* aims', such as 'the defence and regaining of German land and the maintenance of law and order'; those who had learnt so little from the collapse that they indulged in drinking bouts and affairs with females deriding any moral code must be induced to leave, otherwise the organization would suffer severe damage.[54] Clearly, the Styrian *Heimwehr* was neither 'entirely non-political', nor beneficial to all as had been claimed.

In June 1920 the British diplomatic representative reported from Vienna:

> There is no doubt that peasants who have all along had arms are now being organized into regular formations in the Tyrol and Styria to resist any attack from armed workmen or perhaps to attack them. In short, the scene seems to be set rather for a civil war than for a new coalition government. . . .

Deutsch, the Secretary of State for War, had urged him 'very seriously' that the Allies should see to the disarmament of both sides.[55] Otto Bauer too, in a discussion with right-wing deputies, remarked on the fact that the arming of the *Heimwehren* called forth armaments on the side of the workers.[56] But the *Heimwehren* were far more numerous and far better supplied with weapons than any

---

[52] Reports from Knittelfeld, 14 Feb. and 15 Mar., and by Graz military police, 22 July 1919: Steiermärk. Landesarchiv, Akten der k.k. Statthalterei—Präsidium, E. 91, 1919 and 1918 (ii).

[53] Anton Rintelen, *Erinnerungen an Österreichs Weg*, Munich, 1941, pp. 126–7, 130.

[54] Order of Untersteirisches Bauernkommando, 14 June 1919: Steiermärk. Landesarchiv, k.k. Statthalterei, E. 91, 1918 (ii).

[55] F.O. Lindley to FO, 11 June 1919: PRO, FO 371, File 5445, vol. 3538, no. 203366.

[56] Verwaltungsarchiv Wien, Verhandlungsschriften der 'Grossdeutschen Vereinigung', 17 June 1920.

workers' units, such as existed at Graz and elsewhere. If it came to a civil war the outcome was hardly in doubt.

Apart from Styria, the *Heimwehren* were particularly well organized and armed in the Tyrol where the working-class movement was weak, and they cooperated much more closely with similar organizations across the border in Bavaria. In both countries, too, there were much older riflemen's associations on which the *Heimwehren* could be based. Large quantities of weapons were sent into the villages, and former Austrian and Bavarian officers served as military advisors. The leadership at Innsbruck was in the hands of Dr Steidle and Dr Schmidt who represented the two leading bourgeois parties, the Christian Socials and the Pan-Germans.[57] The organization could develop without encountering any obstacle as the Tyrolese government was very much to the right and certainly not disposed to make any difficulties. In the autumn of 1920, however, the Tyrolese *Heimwehren* planned to hold a large-scale Shooting Festival (*Landesschiessen*) at Innsbruck which was to be attended also by many units of Bavarian riflemen. This met with the opposition of the Viennese government which feared Allied intervention and counter-measures by the organized workers who considered the enterprise a provocation. Even the chief of police of Vienna, Schober, held that it was 'entirely ill-timed' and that at least the Tyrolese government should be advised to prevent the entry of armed Bavarian riflemen. The Tyrolese *Landeshauptmann*, Schraffl, thought that the situation could only be saved if the Austrian government could persuade the Bavarian government to prohibit their entry. Meanwhile the railwaymen went on strike on the Tyrolese lines to achieve this aim, and they received arms from the Social Democrats so that they would be able to defend themselves. Armed workers' detachments also occupied the gas and electricity works. The engine-drivers removed vital parts so that the engines could not be used by strike-breakers. No trains were running. But the Tyrolese government refused to prohibit the Festival, as the Viennese government desired, and the principal assembly took place in the presence of the leading members of the government, including the *Landeshauptmann* in his capacity of Chief Riflemen's Master of the Tyrol: a clear defiance of the wishes of the central government.[58] This government no longer included any

[57] Stenographisches Protokoll der Tagung des Reichsarbeiterrates, 31.5.–2.6.1920, p. 282, Parteiarchiv der SPÖ, Vienna.

[58] Verwaltungsarchiv Wien, Ministerratsprotokolle, no. 4, 19 Nov. 1920; *Landeshauptmann* Schraffl to Minister of the Interior, 2 Dec. 1920: Landesregierungsarchiv Tirol, Präsidialakten 1922, II 11 g.

Social Democrats; the leading members of the government, in Vienna as well as at Innsbruck, belonged to the Christian Social Party, as did Dr Steidle, the Tyrolese *Heimwehr* leader.

As the Social Democrats claimed, the aim of the Bavarian officers and others cooperating with the *Heimwehren* was the restoration of the Wittelsbach dynasty and the separation of Bavaria from Germany,[59] which might then be joined by Salzburg and the Tyrol. And indeed there were close connections between the Bavarian *Orgesch* (Organisation Escherich) and a similar organization in Austria, the *Orka* (Organisation Kanzler), which was strong in the Alpine provinces. Its founding meeting in Vienna, held at about the same time, was attended by about four hundred men, mainly officers, ex-servicemen and students. Apart from several officers the meeting was addressed by Dr Riehl who welcomed the new organization 'which would fight against the red International and the terror emanating from it'.[60] It was from these well-armed and well-led military organizations that the principal threat to the republican order emanated, not from the small groups of *Völkische* and National Socialists. But, as Dr Riehl's appearance shows, the two camps were linked by political and personal bonds, and the ideology of the *Heimwehren* was at least partly *völkisch* and anti-semitic. Already by the end of 1920 the situation was fast approaching one of incipient civil war in which 'red' Vienna and other towns would be like small islands surrounded by a hostile sea. In the end, however, the civil war only broke out in 1934—with results that were only too predictable.

[59] Thus a poster of 17 Nov. 1920: ibid.
[60] Police report, 8 Dec. 1920: Polizeiarchiv Wien, Polizeiberichte 1919–1921 (meeting of 7 Dec.). Rudolf Kanzler himself was a Bavarian, not an Austrian.

10 The National Issue

For Germany as well as for Austria, military defeat and the collapse of the old empires brought with them far-reaching territorial demands by the victors and by newly-constituted national states such as Poland and Czechoslovakia. As far as Germany was concerned the cession of Alsace-Lorraine to France was almost inevitable, and indeed this demand had been included in the Fourteen Points of President Wilson, and accepted by Germany. Much more controversial was another of Wilson's Points which demanded the creation of an independent Polish State 'which should include the territories inhabited by indisputably Polish populations, which should be assured a free and secure access to the sea. . . '. For in the Prussian provinces of West Prussia, Posen and Upper Silesia there were large areas with a mixed German-Polish population which naturally were claimed by both sides. And 'free and secure access to the sea' for Poland would mean the inclusion of the region at the mouth of the Vistula where the important city and harbour of Danzig was purely German. Germany, moreover, depended heavily on supplies of corn from the eastern provinces and of coal from Upper Silesia, while this coal was equally vital to the new Polish state. As the German official responsible for coal supply and distribution pointed out in November 1918, Berlin would be without gas if supplies from Upper Silesia were cut off and this would cause 'a terrible catastrophe'. In a later cabinet meeting Noske emphasized that without the Upper Silesian coal the major part of the German food industry would be at a standstill, especially as coal production in the rest of Germany was less than half the peace-time output; wherever the Polish Legionaries established themselves transports of food to Germany ceased; if this happened famine would occur within less than four weeks; in his opinion catastrophe could only be prevented by the formation of a new army.[1]

During November workers' and soldiers' councils came into being

[1] Matthias (ed.), *Regierung . . .* , i, no. 20, p. 118; ii, no. 93, p. 185: cabinet meetings of 21 Nov. 1918 and 3 Jan. 1919.

in the towns of the eastern provinces as they did throughout Germany. In many of these local councils Germans and Poles at first co-operated peacefully as no one knew where the frontiers would ultimately be drawn; in other areas there was friction from the outset. From Posen (Poznań) it was reported at the end of November that the workers' and soldiers' council as well as the executive council for the whole province consisted of Germans and Poles in equal numbers; most of the Germans were politically democrats, not Social Democrats, while the Poles were allegedly democratic and adherents of a Greater Poland, but opposed to a separation of Poznania from Germany before the conclusion of peace. The workers' and soldiers' council complained that the officers commanding the returning front-line units and those of the *Heimatschutz Ost*—volunteer units to defend the eastern provinces—refused to recognize the executive authority of the council. A few days later an even more significant complaint was raised: *Heimatschutz* units were causing much disquiet among the population; in towns which were absolutely peaceful, where Germans and Poles were cooperating under conditions of parity, fully armed units suddenly marched in with no clear purpose, which was bound to cause friction.[2] The chairman of the workers' and soldiers' council of Thorn (Toruń) did not believe in any Polish danger as both sides were cooperating well and the Poles were repre-sented on the executive council. But in December large formations were sent there to defend the frontier by order of Seventeenth Army Corps at Danzig, and some of their officers proceeded to dissolve local workers' and soldiers' councils, while that of Thorn repudiated this order and wanted to carry out any necessary defence measures without outside help.[3] At Culmsee (Chełmża), farther down the Vistula, the workers' and soldiers' council which took over the public utilities consisted mostly of Poles,[4] a fact that might explain the strong action taken by German officers.

At Graudenz (Grudziądz), however, strong friction appeared from the outset. The workers' and soldiers' council complained about the 'Greater Polish agitation'; this resulted in the formation of purely Polish soldiers' councils, even in very small places, which all claimed to exercise power and negotiated independently with Berlin; they

[2] Reports from Posen, s.d. (late November) and 7 Dec. 1918: Friedr.-Ebert Stiftung, Nachlass Barth, I, no. 116; V, 'Tagesbericht' 38.

[3] Reports from Thorn, 28 Nov., s.d. and 24 Dec. 1918: ibid., V, 'Tagesbericht' 30; I, no. 123.

[4] Report of 23 Nov. 1918: ibid., V, Zweigstelle 6 der Informationsstelle der Reichsregierung.

also prevented a unified leadership of the defence units as these soldiers' councils interfered with the orders given by the regional government. Another source of complaint was a decree from Berlin which admitted Polish as a second official language: this was bound to strengthen the Polish movement and caused many Poles to refuse to talk German, and so brought about considerable administrative difficulties.[5] In early December a German unit marched into Witkowo near Gniezno, removed the workers' council and the *Landrat* from their offices, pulled down the red flags and hoisted the black-white-red colours, declaring they had orders to protect the Germans.[6] In Upper Silesia, where Haase was sent in November as a representative of the Reich government, the Germans were opposed to admitting Poles to the workers' councils because this would facilitate the Polish agitation, the strength of which was allegedly underestimated by the Social Democrats and the workers' councils. But Haase was in favour of admitting Polish representatives in order to prevent the formation of purely Polish councils as had recently happened in one *Kreis*. In his opinion, the workers' councils should not engage in national propaganda, whether pro-German or pro-Polish, which should be left to other organizations and to the press.[7]

In general, Haase was in favour of using peaceful means because any military measures would lead to catastrophe; while Landsberg declared that the government could not renounce the use of troops if peaceful means did not bring about a settlement. The only question, he said, was whether troops were available; hence the government had to consult the High Command on whether it could send units to Upper Silesia. The official responsible for the distribution of coal considered that the dispatch of troops would have a calming effect; but a member of the Executive Committee of the Berlin workers' and soldiers' councils quite rightly countered his argument by stating that this would cause a Polish rising. Haase doubted whether the troops would not soon disperse even if they were available. The foundation of the *Heimatschutz Ost* reminded him of the old *Ostmarkenverein*, which had been formed in the late nineteenth century to strengthen the German position in eastern Europe: it would antagonize the Poles. Ebert was of the opinion that troops must be sent to secure the economy, otherwise Berlin would not be able to survive.[8] A few days

[5] Reports from Graudenz, 30 Nov. and 7 Dec. 1918: ibid., V, 'Tagesbericht' 32, 'Sonderbericht über die politische und militärische Lage'.

[6] Telegram from Gniezno, 9 Dec. 1918: ibid., I, no. 120.

[7] Matthias (ed.), *Regierung* . . . , i, nos. 23–4, pp. 131, 134 (22 Nov. 1918).

[8] ibid., i, no. 20, pp. 118, 122: Cabinet meeting of 21 Nov. 1918.

later the Under-Secretary of State in the Ministry of Food also considered that the *Heimatschutz Ost* was one of the causes of anti-German feeling in Poland. He warned against the carrying of political conflicts into the Polish provinces and advised a compromise; Poland had surplus food which could be sent to Germany if the population did not stop deliveries for political reasons; there was no positive evidence that the Poles did not want to deliver food, although this might happen; hitherto the Poles of Poznania had been friendly and accommodating and, in any case, nothing could be achieved by force of arms.[9]

There was thus a clear division of opinion within the government. Later Landsberg claimed that the three moderate Social Democrats had threatened to resign if no military measures were taken to protect the frontiers, while Haase had opposed such action. In the end a compromise had been reached that all defensive measures should be entrusted to local units, including soldiers of Polish nationality. But the Poles had deceived the Germans and were now claiming purely German districts, such as Danzig, Marienburg and Thorn. In his opinion everything must be done to counter this aggression which was threatening Germany's existence.[10] At Gniezno, in any case, Polish officers and clergymen won over local units to the Polish side and the Germans were disarmed. Units of the 4th Division then retook Gniezno, but again the local troops were persuaded by the clergy to change sides. At Bydgoszcz (Bromberg) the soldiers' council had first negotiated with the Poles, but it now believed that the situation could only be saved by the dispatch of troops; 6,000 men would be sufficient to end the Polish threat, as the government emissary sent there reported. But the military expert present declared that Germany had not yet any well-disciplined units available; while the Poles were welded together by the national idea which was their strongest element, the Germans had nothing like it with which to oppose them.[11]

At the beginning of 1919 the Reich government—now without the Independents—decided to appeal for volunteers on a much larger scale 'to prevent Polish imperialism from seizing further territories in the east'. They should make it impossible for 'foreigners to penetrate

[9] Staatssekretär Wurm at the Reichskonferenz of 25 Nov. 1918: ibid., no. 30, p. 203.
[10] ibid., ii, no. 78, pp. 117–18: Cabinet meeting of 28 Dec. 1918. But there is no documentary evidence of the threat of resignation: ibid., note 37.
[11] Regierungsassessor Krahmer and Major Freiherr von Willisen at the Cabinet meeting of 2 Jan. 1919: ibid., ii, no. 91, pp. 178–9.

into Germany as if it were a derelict house and to occupy it. . . .
Every revolution, the French like the Russian, has created volunteer
armies from nothing under the flag of its new ideals. Follow the call
of the German revolution. . . '.[12] Leinert, the chairman of the Central
Council, supported the appeal, but believed that it must not give the
impression that the government wanted to create a military force to
fight the Independents and Spartacists:

> It must state that we will become the prey of alien peoples if the
> population does not pull itself together, that the Poles are putting
> us to shame with their enormous national pride. . . We must not
> allow ourselves to be shattered by a nation that stands as low as
> the Poles and to be deprived of the great achievements created by
> the workers which culminate in the victory of the revolution. These
> achievements must be protected if we do not want to be lost
> irretrievably, if we do not want to starve. . . Now it looks as if
> the Poles will simply cut off East and West Prussia entirely, and
> we do nothing. This puts our people to such shame that it must
> not continue. The army must be created quickly. . . .

Noske agreed that catastrophe could only be prevented by the
creation of a new army.[13] This clearly was the second motive for the
creation of the volunteer units and Free Corps; the first was the one
criticized by Leinert, the danger threatening the government from
the left.

There is little doubt that the anti-Polish appeal fell on fruitful soil,
and not only on the political right, as Leinert's remarks showed.
During the same month the chairman of the General Soldiers'
Council of Seventh Army Corps at Münster exclaimed:

> The matter at issue is the securing of the frontiers of our country.
> We must not look with folded arms at the events in the east. We
> must see to it that the Poles do not penetrate any farther into the
> country! (Interruption: With such burglars we cannot nego-
> tiate!) . . . They want to take away the industrial areas of Upper
> Silesia. We must not suffer them to rob us of the last industrial
> areas! . . .

—a curious point, considering the proximity of Münster to the Ruhr
area. Another member of the soldiers' council also opposed any
negotiations with 'such people': 'they are just imperialists who intend
to occupy purely German lands. . . '.[14] This was only two months

---

[12] Appeal of 7 Jan. 1919: facsimile in Volkmar Kellermann, *Schwarzer Adler—
Weisser Adler*, Cologne, 1970, p. 37.

[13] Matthias (ed.), *Regierung . . .* , ii, no. 93, pp. 185–7 (meeting of 3 Jan. 1919).

[14] Schulte, *Münstersche Chronik zu Spartakismus und Separatismus Anfang 1919*, p. 140
(meeting of 17 Jan. 1919).

after the workers' and soldiers' councils of Poznania had declared that they were 'well able to take over defence duties at the frontiers and in the interior of the province in close cooperation with the native German, the Polish and the Jewish soldiers and the general population'.[15] In the interval national passion had dissipated all counsels of prudence on both sides. In August 1919 the first Polish rising occurred in Upper Silesia and was suppressed by German forces. But the matter did not end there. Bitter struggles between German and Polish forces took place during the following years, in which several German Free Corps took a very prominent part, secretly aided by the new army. The acceptance of the Treaty of Versailles by Germany was preceded by an elaborate scheme on the side of senior German officers to reconquer Poznania and the other former German provinces, with or without the consent of the government.[16] Throughout the years of the Weimar Republic relations between Germany and Poland remained acrimonious and Germany was never reconciled to the loss of her former eastern provinces, in particular of the Polish Corridor along the Vistula.

While Germany was engaged in only one major frontier struggle, that with Poland, Austria had to face hostile neighbours in the north, south and east, partly former members of the Habsburg Monarchy, partly old enemies. Indeed, of the six states now surrounding Austria only two—Germany and Switzerland—had no territorial conflict with her, while bitter struggles ensued with the other four—Italy, Yugoslavia, Hungary and Czechoslovakia—either because they claimed territories which were wholly or partly German-speaking or because German minorities within their frontiers wanted to be united with Austria. After the collapse of the monarchy its Slav subjects naturally claimed the right of national self-determination; but they were not prepared to extend the same right to the German-speaking population, which would have meant the loss of substantial lands and important natural resources, especially for Czechoslovakia. In many cases it was impossible to draw a clear frontier-line between Germans and non-Germans. In the South Tyrol, where a clear language frontier existed between Germans and Italians, Italy was entirely unwilling to give up her claim to the Brenner frontier, which had been promised to her by the Allies in April 1915. In the end, however,

---

[15] *Freiheit*, 21 Nov. 1918, quoted by Matthias, *Regierung* . . . , i, p. 120 n. 16.
[16] For details see, F. L. Carsten, *Reichswehr und Politik*, Cologne, 1964, pp. 45–50 (English edition, Oxford, 1966, pp. 38–43).

two plebiscites were held in disputed areas, Carinthia and the Burgenland, which took into account the wishes of the local population, and more stable frontiers emerged after years of conflict. Between the victorious Allies and Austria there was another national issue: whether Austria—now entirely German-speaking—would be allowed to unite with Germany, as most Austrians hoped, whether the old dream of 1848 would come true now that the Habsburgs, Hohenzollerns and Wittelsbachs had all disappeared from the scene. It is difficult to say which of these issues was the most important from the Austrian point of view. They all aroused strong emotions, none perhaps more so than the question of the South Tyrol which has remained alive to the present day. It also influenced relations between Vienna and Innsbruck.[17]

At the end of October 1918 the Tyrolese National Council demanded to be represented at all negotiations touching the fate of the Tyrol: for, on account of its geographical position and political conditions, the Tyrol was more immediately threatened by dismemberment or the forcible separation of certain districts than any other part of German Austria.[18] When it became clear that the Italian government was determined to annex the German South Tyrol and to obtain the Brenner frontier, conservative and clerical circles at Innsbruck hoped to be able to prevent this by setting up a Tyrolese Republic independent of Vienna, as a buffer state between Italy and Germany; emissaries were sent to Berne to negotiate with the Allies to this effect. In December Sir Horace Rumbold reported to Balfour from Berne:

> The Italians, not content with annexing Italian Tyrol proper (Ala-Trent) have now occupied the southern part of German Tyrol. . . . In short, the principle of self-determination has gone by the board. If the occupation is confirmed by the Peace Conference, then German North Tyrol . . . will have no option but to join Bavaria, for which there is no desire among the Tyrolese. On the other hand if German South Tyrol is rescued from permanent Italien occupation, the whole German-speaking portion of the Tyrol, namely, North and South German Tyrol, will form a buffer state between Germany and Italy, and the German Italian frontiers will not be conterminous. The Bishop [of Feldkirch] . . . says that there is no wish in German Tyrol for incorporation either in the German-Austrian Republic or in Germany. . . .

At Innsbruck Professor Michael Mayr, an important member of the

[17] For the background see, Karl R. Stadler, *The Birth of the Austrian Republic 1918–1921*, Leyden, 1966, pp. 93–109.
[18] *Neue Tiroler Stimmen*, 28 Oct. 1918.

government responsible for food and foreign affairs, gave an interview to *Le Temps* which showed almost identical views.[19] From Salzburg a professor of theology wrote to Mayr that their aim must be to remove the Italians from the German parts of Tyrol; in his opinion this would not only be difficult, but most likely impossible, if the Tyrol was part of Austria or of Bavaria, hence it should become independent:

> The Tyrolese have never felt 'Austrian' in a general sense, nor 'Viennese' either. The Tyrol has always made the heaviest sacrifices for Austria; the thanks of Austria (the dynasty not entirely excepted) have always been meagre.
>
> In addition the great weight of Vienna would always outbalance us to a greater or lesser extent. The worst of all misfortunes would be to be governed by the Viennese Jews. But even if a partly acceptable government should be formed in Vienna the situation for the Tyrol would by no means be always satisfactory. Even then it would be ruled in the interests of Vienna, and a large city, and the Tyrol would have to put up with it. No! For my person I should like to shout to the Tyrolese eagle: fly alone! . . . Finally, we do not really fit in anywhere—we are of our own kind. I have always felt this outside the Tyrol. . . .[20]

The Clericals in particular supported the scheme of Tyrolese independence, but they were vigorously opposed by the Social Democrats, who favoured 'a united free German Reich'. When the Tyrolese Diet was elected in February 1919 the two parties in favour of the *Anschluss*—Social Democrats and German Nationalists—together obtained 58,000 votes against 83,000 cast for the clerical and peasant parties. But an acute observer of the Austrian scene in the Foreign Office, Lewis Namier, was not convinced that all the 83,000 were in favour of independence:

> It is a characteristic fact that the Clerical leaders are much more emphatically in favour of separation in private conversations than in public, which would seem to indicate that they do not feel sure of the support of their own followers.
>
> A majority in favour of an independent Tyrolese Republic might, however, be obtained if by those means the German districts south of the Brenner could be saved from annexation by Italy; and I fully agree with Mr Randall as to the advantages of such a Tyrolese Republic. . . .[21]

[19] PRO, FO 371, File 123, vol. 3507, fos. 52–4.

[20] Dr Melchior Abfalter to Mayr, 7 Dec. 1918: Landesregierungsarchiv Tirol, Nachlass Michael Mayr, V/6.

[21] S. Abram to Bauer, 8 Feb. 1919: Haus-, Hof- u. Staatsarchiv, Nachlass Bauer, Karton 262, VII; Namier's note on election results of 16 Feb. 1919: PRO, FO 371, File 123, vol. 3508, no. 38034.

At a meeting of representatives of the Austrian commercial and industrial chambers held during the same month the speaker from Innsbruck emphasized that an attempt must be made to save the South Tyrol whatever the price might be. If that could only be achieved by the Tyrol declaring itself independent, this would have to be done, even if it were contrary to its economic interests which pointed more towards union with Germany.[22] At the beginning of May, before the start of the negotiations at St Germain, the Tyrolese Diet voted in favour of the proclamation of an 'independent, democratic and neutral Free State of Tyrol', if only in this way the unity of the German and Ladin-speaking districts could be preserved; but if—contrary to the principles proclaimed by President Wilson—the South Tyrol should be separated, then the rest of the Tyrol would have no other choice but to join Germany so as to preserve its economic viability.[23]

Otto Bauer, the Austrian Foreign Minister, attempted to win over the Italian government to a scheme by which the German South Tyrol would remain part of Austria, but would be neutralized, without any fortresses or garrisons; if war broke out Italy as well as Germany could demand that Swiss troops should occupy the country; if Italy agreed, Austria would be willing to fulfil all her other wishes, in particular to put at her disposal all Austrian investments in the Balkans. But the Italian negotiator informed Bauer that resistance in Italy to such a compromise was very strong, in particular on the side of the general staff.[24] Renner, negotiating at St Germain on behalf of Austria, was convinced that the Tyrolese government, to save the country's unity, was willing to accept Italian sovereignty for the north. Even the Tyrolese representative at St Germain had to admit that Renner in his negotiations with the Italians strongly espoused the cause of the South Tyrol. In the representative's eyes the 'last and only chance still to achieve something' was that Bauer should resign and be replaced by Renner who had won some recognition at St Germain: this chance 'must be used'.[25] But it was all in vain. In July Prince Borghese, the Italian

[22] Note of 19 Feb. 1919: Haus-, Hof- u. Staatsarchiv, Fasz. 5a, Präsidialakten 1919, Anschlussfrage.

[23] *Landeshauptmann* Shraffl to the government, 5 May 1919: Landesregierungs-archiv Tirol, Präsidialakten 1920, II 11 g.

[24] Bauer to Dr Aemilian Schoepfer, 21 Feb. 1919: Haus-, Hof- u. Staatsarchiv, Nachlass Bauer, Karton 262, VII.

[25] Renner to Bauer, 26 May 1919, quoted by Viktor Reimann, *Zu Gross für Österreich*, Vienna, 1968, p. 311; Geisler to Mayr, 21 July 1919: Landesregierungs-archiv Tirol, Nachlass Mayr, V/6.

plenipotentiary, informed Bauer that his government was not willing to enter a discussion which might question the complete sovereignty of the Kingdom of Italy over the Alto Adige. Prince Borghese added orally that public opinion in Italy was extremely dissatisfied about the small concessions made to Italy at the Peace Conference, hence his government could not possibly give up an area that had been allocated to it a long time ago by all its allies. No change in the decision of the Italian government was to be hoped for.[26]

There was nothing that the Austrian government could do but bow to the inevitable: Otto Bauer resigned at the end of July. In October the Tyrolese Diet once more protested to the British government and pointed to the likely consequences of the annexation:

> It is impossible that peace and concord can ever reign between us and Italy so long as our brothers on the other side of the Brenner are suffering under a foreign yoke. A yoke which is becoming from day to day harder and more insupportable. Italy is doing her utmost to destroy the German spirit in South Tyrol. Under all kinds of excuses our German teachers and officials are being replaced by the Italians. These oppressed inhabitants are not suffered to express their wishes and opinions. . . .

The protest was forwarded to Lord Curzon, the Foreign Secretary, by Lord Robert Cecil with the comment: 'Of all the outrageous things that were done at Paris there is nothing worse than the treatment of the Southern Tyrol: indeed, I doubt whether anything more shameless was done at Vienna! . . .' In reply Curzon wrote: 'Personally I am in close sympathy both with the writer of this letter and yourself, and, if an opportunity were to occur of rectifying the mistake which I think has been made, I would gladly take it. But for the present I do not see how it is to be done'.[27] Thus the South Tyrolese were left to the tender mercies of the Italian government and its italianizing policy, which was to gain new momentum when Mussolini became prime minister a few years later.

If Austrian opposition to the Italian policy of annexation was entirely unsuccessful, it achieved considerable success, curiously enough, against the similar policy of another Allied government, that of Serbia which became Yugoslavia. During the war the large majority of the communes of Carinthia—237 out of a total of 263—protested against Yugoslav plans of annexation, while 26 communes

---

[26] Bauer to Tiroler Landesrat, 8 July 1919: Haus-, Hof- u. Staatsarchiv, Nachlass Bauer, Karton 262, VII.

[27] Schraffl to Lord Cecil, 22 Oct., Lord Cecil to Lord Curzon, 1 Nov., Curzon to Cecil, 17 Nov. 1919: PRO, FO 371, File 123, vol. 3511, no. 149238.

declined to do so. Indeed, many communes with a strong Slovene majority had passed resolutions of protest signed by all members of the local committee.[28] While the Austrian government in October 1918 was in favour of the Drau river as the future frontier with Yugoslavia, protests against this line came from *völkisch* circles which denied the central government the right to interfere in a matter concerning only Carinthia. At the time of the collapse, the Provisional Diet of Carinthia also emphasized that for a thousand years Carinthia had formed one economic area—with German and German-Slovene mixed parts—that it had clear natural frontiers and was a cultural entity the arbitrary partition of which would cause severe damage.[29] At first Slovene units occupied parts of southern Styria which had a Slovene rural population but some German towns, such as Marburg and Radkersburg, without posing a direct threat to Carinthia. In the Provisional Diet the Pan-German deputies protested against the misuse of church services by the Slovene clergy in districts with a mixed population for purposes of political propaganda and incitement; those continuing to do so should be deprived and if need be arrested. But the Diet took no action on the proposal.[30] It still favoured negotiations with the Yugoslavs so as to avoid any clashes.

By the beginning of December, however, the situation deteriorated. Small Yugoslav units penetrated into Carinthia from the south, crossed the Drau and threatened the towns of Klagenfurt and Villach. In view of their actions the Provisional Diet decided to oppose such penetrations by force and to entrust all necessary measures to the local military command. The peasants of the Lavant valley rose spontaneously, formed military units and drove out the occupying forces; representatives of all political parties promised support against the Yugoslavs.[31] The commanding officer, Colonel Hülgerth, was in favour of taking the offensive in the Gail valley near Villach. Yet the Social Democrats and some *Volkswehr* units, while supporting any defensive action, were opposed to an attack on the

[28] *Freie Stimmen*, 2 July 1918: Kärntner Landesarchiv, Umsturzzeit, Lt. I/3.

[29] Resolution taken at Villach by the Association 'Deutsche Einheit' on 17 Oct.; proposal by Dr Arthur Lemisch at the meeting of the political parties to form a Provisional Diet on 26 Oct. 1918: ibid., Präsidialakten, Fasz. IV, no. 23; Umsturzzeit, Lt. III/5.

[30] Meeting of 18 Nov. 1918: ibid., Umsturzzeit, Lt. IV/4; in general see Bauer, *Österreich. Revolution*, p. 134; Stadler, *Birth of Austrian Republic . . .* , pp. 110–11.

[31] Carinthian Wehrausschuss to Staatsamt für Heerwesen, 4 Dec.; urgent motion of deputy Dr Dörflinger and others, 5 Dec.; report of Lt. Mayrhofer on action in Lavant valley, s.d.; meeting of Carinthian Landesauschuss, 7 Jan. 1919: Kärntner Landesarchiv, Umsturzzeit, Lt. III/7, Lt. IV/9, Landesausschuss, Fasz. II, no. 8.

occupied area, though the soldiers' council of Klagenfurt declared that its units desired an offensive and had to be held back. A Pan-German deputy pointed out that the Karawanken chain was the natural frontier in the south and should be gained, and a Christian Social deputy was only willing to recognize the right of the military command to improve its lines. In spite of these political differences an offensive began on 5 January and was largely successful; an armistice was signed a week later which virtually limited the Yugoslav occupation to the area south of the Drau.[32]

This was not the end of the fighting. It flared up again in April 1919 when the Yugoslavs attacked towards Klagenfurt and at first made considerable progress. The Carinthian government mobilized the classes 1882 to 1899; this should have produced an army of 25,000 to 30,000 men, but in effect only about 11,000 appeared because the population of Upper Carinthia was largely indifferent and in areas with a mixed population many feared the Yugoslavs. In some districts only very few men obeyed the order.[33] But the Carinthian *Volkswehr* gave a good account of itself, and reinforcements were sent from Vienna and other areas, including officers and NCOs as well as artillery. At the beginning of May Colonel Hülgerth counter-attacked and again was largely successful. The President of the Italian Armistice Commission, General Segré, told Deutsch that he had no official information about the fighting, that the Austrian forces must not cross the line of demarcation along the Drau, and that the press should report as little as possible about the matter. Renner accordingly informed the Carinthian government that the troops should not cross the Drau as such an action would damage the Austrian cause; the impression of a war with Yugoslavia must be avoided at all cost.[34] General Segré wired to Ljubljana that all military operations must be stopped and assured the Yugoslavs that the Austrians would do the same. This caused strong protests in Carinthia. Colonel Hülgerth declared that the Viennese government had again made promises without consulting Carinthia and that it was absolutely impossible to break off military operations at this moment; the gains must first be consolidated, and he could not change his military plans; the time had passed when any value could be attached to Yugoslav promises and treaties. The Carinthian government wired to Vienna that the communication had caused

[32] Martin Wutte, *Kärntens Freiheitskampf*, 2nd ed., Weimar, 1943, p. 137; Bauer, *Österreich. Revolution*, p. 134.

[33] Wutte, *Freiheitskampf*, pp. 182, 254–5.

[34] Verwaltungsarchiv Wien, Kabinettsratsprotokolle, no. 66, 2 May 1919.

alarm and dismay: 'no force on earth can stop the hostilities here unless at least the area between the Drau and the southern railway is liberated. Request urgently not to make any binding promises to Segré which would not be honoured here'.[35]

The Viennese *Volkswehr* units did not cross the Drau; but the Carinthian volunteer units were not to be stopped and pursued the Yugoslavs to the southern frontier of Carinthia. General Segré protested in Vienna against this violation of the armistice for which he declared Austria responsible. The Austrian government was of the opinion that the offensive was endangering the whole state, and above all Carinthia, which would be held responsible at the peace negotiations. The Entente threatened to take counter-measures.[36] Within Carinthia, too, there was opposition to the offensive and to the military measures taken by the local government. The workers' and soldiers' council of Villach and the local *Volkswehr* were willing to support any defensive measures 'against the robber-like incursions of an imperialist enemy' but not an offensive; they also criticized the proclamation of martial law and the indiscriminate arming of the peasants—which indeed was done on a large scale, even in districts not at all threatened by the Yugoslavs.[37] At the end of May the Yugoslavs counter-attacked with full force, the Austrians had to retreat, and in early June Klagenfurt and other towns were occupied for the time being. But even before that time the Entente powers had decided to hold a plebiscite in the basin of Klagenfurt. Until this was held, in October 1920, the government and Diet of Carinthia had to meet at St Veit on the Glan, outside the area of Yugoslav occupation. General Segré and the Italians did not favour the far-reaching Yugoslav plans, nor the tendencies in Carinthia to separate from Vienna, which he actively opposed.[38] In Vienna it was clearly felt that Italian support was essential if the Yugoslav claims were to be resisted with any chance of success, while the Carinthian nationalists were opposed to any compromise. The two points of view could hardly be reconciled.

[35] The Carinthian Landesbefehlshaber to the Carinthian government, 4 May; the Carinthian government to Foreign Ministry, 4 May 1919: Kärntner Landesarchiv, Präsidialakten, Fasz. Va, no. 24; Wutte, *Freiheitskampf*, p. 230.

[36] The Carinthian Landesbefehlshaber to the Carinthian government, 6 May; telephone message by Dr Angerer from Vienna, 7 May 1919: Kärntner Landesarchiv, Präsidialakten, Fasz. Va, no. 24.

[37] The Villach workers' and soldiers' council to the government, 4 May 1919: ibid., Fasz. V; Carinthian report in: 'Protokoll der Tagung des Reichsarbeiterrates, 31. Mai—2. Juni 1920 in Wien', p. 200, Parteiarchiv der SPÖ, Vienna.

[38] Landesausschuss meeting of 30 June 1919: Kärntner Landesarchiv, Landesausschuss, Fasz. II, no. 8; Stadler, *Birth of Austrian Republic*, p. 115.

In southern Styria there was the same clash of opinion. In July the *Bezirkshauptmann* of Leibnitz reported that all along the frontier of Yugoslav occupation, younger activist elements, led by officers of the reserve, were recruiting men for an attack against the Yugoslavs and an advance towards Marburg (Maribor); the majority of the population, however, was opposed to the scheme and, according to his long experience of the district, only a minute number of volunteers could be reckoned with. All those with whom he had discussed the enterprise expressed the wish that the plan for an offensive should be dropped and the government informed accordingly; even if Marburg were taken it could not be held and the whole district would experience the same fate which had overtaken Carinthia; he considered it his duty to warn most emphatically against any offensive action; no cooperation of the frontier areas could be expected in such a case.[39] What emerges from these and similar reports from Carinthia is that large sections of the people were willing to defend their home towns and villages but not to go over to the offensive: there was very little national enthusiasm and a widespread belief that the final decision would in any case be taken by the Entente. After four years of war there was little inclination to continue fighting.[40]

When the plebiscite was finally held in October 1920—mainly in the districts to the south of the Drau, which had a Slovene majority—59 per cent voted in favour of Austria and 41 per cent for Yugoslavia. This meant that about 10,000 of those who spoke Slovene had nevertheless voted to remain Austrian: a remarkable result at a time of fierce national passions and bitter conflict.[41] The right of self-determination was put to the test—the only Austrian territory where this was done—with the result that historical and economic factors triumphed over nationalism and Carinthia remained undivided.

The result of a plebiscite held more than a year later in parts of the so-called Burgenland—the western counties of Hungary—was exactly the opposite; for the area was eventually divided and its capital, Sopron, handed over to Hungary, so separating it from the surrounding countryside. This area had always been Hungarian but was largely inhabited by a German-speaking peasant population.

---

[39] Reports of *Bezirkshauptmann* of Leibnitz, 6 and 16 July 1919: Steiermärk. Landesarchiv, Akten der k.k. Statthalterei—Präsidium, E. 91, 1918 (ii).

[40] For Carinthia, see above, p. 282; Wutte, *Freiheitskampf*, pp. 254-5.

[41] Stadler, *Birth of Austrian Republic*, p. 126; Wutte, *Freiheitskampf*, p. 471 (the figure of 40.06 per cent voting for Yugoslavia is an error: the correct one is 40.96 per cent).

After the collapse a spontaneous movement to join Austria developed, and for a long time this caused severe difficulties in relations between Vienna and Budapest. As early as 13 November 1918 the Austrian Minister of Food told the cabinet that he considered negotiations with Hungary about food deliveries hopeless on account of this movement which was causing a conflict with Hungary; but he intended to negotiate separately with Western Hungary to obtain food from there. A few days later the Hungarian ambassador threatened that Hungary would stop all food deliveries to Austria if the Austrians marched into the Burgenland. Deputations of the local peasants came to Vienna to petition for unity with Austria. The Austrian State Council claimed that the counties of Pressburg (Bratislava), Ödenburg (Sopron), Wieselburg and Eisenburg belonged to Austria geographically, economically and nationally, and were indispensable for the provisioning of Vienna; hence Austria must insist at the Peace Conference that they become part of Austria. The same demand was put forward by a German People's Council formed in Western Hungary, while the Hungarian government threatened to arrest any purchasers of food sent there from Austria.[42]

A police report from Wiener Neustadt claimed that in Ödenburg (Sopron) and its area the workers were pro-Austrian and held a large public meeting on 22 December to demonstrate their wishes; the lower middle classes desired to remain under Hungary but with a German-speaking administration; the clergy, teachers, officials and merchants were anti-German and strongly pro-Hungarian. The Hungarian government called together German leaders from the four counties which voted in favour of cultural autonomy; in the district of Eisenstadt there was considerable excitement on account of the Croat population in many of the villages which desired an occupation by the Yugoslavs. Meanwhile arms were smuggled into the area from Austria, and Austrian officers tried to force the pace by crossing the frontier and attempting to disarm the *gendarmerie*— actions which again endangered food deliveries from Hungary, and caused grave worries in Vienna.[43] The Entente powers were in favour of assigning the territory to Austria—except Pressburg (Bratislava) which was occupied by the Czechs—but this met with fierce opposition from Hungary, not least from the Béla Kun

[42] Verwaltungsarchiv Wien, Kabinettstratsprotokolle, meetings of 13 and 18 Nov. 1918; Beschlüsse des deutschösterreichischen Staatsrates, meetings of 18 and 22 Nov. 1918; Stadler, *Birth of Austrian Republic*, p. 129.

[43] Reports of 8 and 28 Dec. 1918: ibid., Staatsamt des Innern, 22/gen., box 4860.

government. Yet in September 1919 the Burgenland was assigned to Austria, against the protests of the new Hungarian government. Renner, however, declared that the cession created 'an unchangeable and indisputable fact' which had been sanctioned by the 'highest Areopagus of the world'.[44] Austria, which had to bury so many of its national dreams, was determined to hold on to this one gain, sharply criticizing the 'unfriendly attitude of the Hungarian government'; Renner's attitude was supported by the whole cabinet. But there was very little that Austria could do.

The Hungarians equally ignored repeated Allied demands for an immediate cession of the disputed territory. When Lieutenant-Colonel Cuninghame visited the Burgenland early in 1920 he found from his conversations and personal observations 'that the people (*Volk*) desire attachment to Austria, but that the officials (*Beamtenschaft*) including, particularly, the priests, are vehemently opposed to it'. Things had changed since the summer of 1919—the days of Béla Kun—when the Magyar officials were 'not so adverse to the idea of junction with Austria'; but on the Austrian side too 'a large part of the Christian Socialist Party is now anxious to keep on good terms with the present régime in Hungary, and would sacrifice the chances of securing territorial extension for this purpose', in contrast with the Social Democrats 'to whom the present régime in Hungary is antipathetic. . . '. In the view of another British military observer, even the opinion of the peasantry had changed for political reasons: 'Villages which during the Bolshevism (*sic*) were clamouring to become Austria are now totally opposed to the annexation as they confess they see a greater future for Hungary than for Austria. . . '.[45] There were clashes between armed 'volunteer' detachments and the *gendarmerie* of both sides; the Allies advised Austria to renounce Ödenburg (Sopron) for the remainder of the Burgenland. But in the end it was agreed to hold a plebiscite in Sopron and eight nearby communes, and this was done in December 1921. In Sopron itself the Hungarians won almost 73 per cent of the vote, in the surrounding countryside the Austrians were victorious with 54.5 per cent. The result was a partition by which the Burgenland was deprived of its natural capital, which made no sense in economic terms. At the

---

[44] Renner's instruction for Baron Cnobloch, 5 Oct. 1919: Haus-, Hof- u. Staatsarchiv, Nachlass Bauer, Karton 262, IX. In general see: Stadler, *Birth of Austrian Republic*, pp. 134–6.

[45] Reports by Lt.-Col. Sir Thomas Cuninghame and Capt. D. B. Aitken of 9 Feb. and 1 Mar. 1920: PRO, FO 371, vol. 3519, no. 178589, vol. 3520, no. 183646.

beginning of 1922 Sopron was handed over to Hungary; all Austrian protests were entirely ineffective.[46]

The Burgenland was the only territory which Austria gained from any of its neighbours, and it was not a very important gain. But there was a far more important territory which the Austrian Republic claimed on the same ground—that its German-speaking inhabitants wanted to join Austria: the German districts of Bohemia and Moravia. This claim, however, met with the determined opposition of the new Czechoslovak government which, on historical and economic grounds, would not brook any change in the historical frontiers of the country and was unwilling even to discuss the issue. Indeed, Bohemia and Moravia always had a mixed Czech and German population, and Germans lived intermixed with Czechs in many places so that it would have been almost impossible to draw a frontier separating one nationality from the other. The main areas of German population were in the north of Bohemia, on the frontiers not of Austria but of Germany, and their combination with Austria, in whatever form, would have presented virtually insurmountable difficulties of communications and frontiers—unless Austria became part of Germany. In this sense the two issues of German Bohemia and the *Anschluss* were very closely linked. But there were smaller German-speaking areas in southern Bohemia and Moravia, and they could have been absorbed in Upper and Lower Austria without any difficulty if the Czechs had been willing to cede them. This, of course, would have been no solution for the remaining three million Germans in the Czechoslovak Republic who were not given an opportunity to express their wishes. They had lived under Habsburg rulers for four centuries, and there can be little doubt about their national and political preferences.

From the outset the German Austrians claimed the right of national self-determination according to the principles of President Wilson. In their opinion this included the entire territory inhabited by Germans, and especially the German areas of Bohemia, which were to be incorporated in one state. The Provisional National Assembly formed by the German deputies on 21 October 1918 declared its opposition to any annexation of lands inhabited by 'German peasants, workers and burghers' by other nations and singled out the 'Sudeten lands' in its claim of 'territorial power over the entire area of German settlement'.[47] A prominent Bohemian German nationalist

[46] Stadler, *Birth of Austrian Republic*, pp. 138–41; Zöllner, *Geschichte Österreichs*, pp. 496–7.
[47] Bauer, *Österreich. Revolution*, p. 77; Gulick, *Austria . . .*, i, p. 53.

politician, Dr Lodgman von Auen, was appointed representative of the German Austrian state in Prague—an appointment that could hardly be welcome there. In early November the provisional Austrian government tried to negotiate with the Czechoslovak government about the arrangements for 'the political and economic conditions in German Bohemia and the Sudetenland'. On the next day it decided to take 'adequate measures' to prevent any further occupation of the Sudeten lands by Czech troops.[48] How this was to be done was not said, for Austria had no means to protect northern Bohemia unless it called on German help (this was a few days before the German collapse). But a proposal to do so was expressly rejected. In southern Bohemia too, Czech forces were advancing towards the Upper Austrian frontier without meeting any resistance. The German Bohemian district commissioner was arrested and taken to Prague, but the occupation of Krumau (Krumlov) was postponed after negotiations with the German national committee there. At Kaplitz (Kaplice) nearby, local *Volkswehr* units were determined to oppose the Czech advance, so that a clash was feared as the *Volkswehr* was well organized and supplied with sufficient arms.[49]

In this climate any negotiations between Vienna and Prague about deliveries of food and coal were bound to run into severe difficulties. On 11 November the Austrian Under-Secretary of State for Trade reported, after negotiations in Prague, that the Czechoslovak government declined to enter any agreement and was exploiting the Austrian food situation so as to obtain from Austria some utterance which could be used as a *votum* of the local population in favour of the Czechoslovak state at the Peace Conference. On the next day Chancellor Renner announced that the German districts of southern Bohemia and Moravia had decided to join Upper and Lower Austria, and on the twenty-second an Austrian State Law proclaimed that not only these, but also German Bohemia and the Sudetenland were parts of German Austria. This would have added something like 3,300,000 people to its population, about 5 per cent of whom were Czech-speaking.[50] There was never much hope that the Allies would be disposed to listen to such far-reaching claims. About the same time Otto Bauer addressed an urgent appeal to

[48] Verwaltungsarchiv Wien, Beschlüsse des deutschösterreichischen Staatsrates, 31 Oct., 5 and 6 Nov. 1918.
[49] The provisional Land government of South Bohemia to the Staatsrat, 8 Nov. 1918: Kriegsarchiv Wien, Staatsamt für Heerwesen 1918, Fasz. 6.
[50] Verwaltungsarchiv Wien, Beschlüsse des deutschösterreichischen Staatsrates, 9 Nov. 1918; Kabinettstratsprotokolle, 11 Nov. 1918; Stadler, *Birth of Austrian Republic*, pp. 83–4, 149.

Arthur Henderson, not only for food and coal—as no deliveries were reaching Austria from Bohemia and Hungary—but also against the intentions of Czechoslovakia to annex German Bohemia with its three and a half million Germans:

> These Germans do not want to join the Czechoslovak state. Their forcible incorporation in the Czechoslovak state would therefore be a crying violation of the right of national self-determination. But in addition to that this *irredenta* of 3,500,000, who are confronted by about 8 million Czechs, would for all future times form a constant threat to European peace. The German nation would never renounce its justified claim to reunion with its brothers, thus the relationship between the Czech state and Germany would be the same as that between Serbia and Austria which drew the world into the war. . . .[51]

At the beginning of 1919 Bauer repeated to a British representative that Austria 'cannot allow three and a half million Germans to be snatched from it. If the Peace Conference supports the Czech claim there will be no peace for many years, as German Bohemia under Czech rule will be a source of weakness to Bohemia and a constant cause of nationalist agitation in German Austria. . . '. In Bauer's opinion this was 'the greatest political problem' for the Austrian government: in other words, he put it above the issues of the South Tyrol and of the *Anschluss*. According to the British military representative in Vienna, the Socialists and the German Nationalists pressed for the retention of German Bohemia, while the Christian Socials were 'more accommodating and have reconciled themselves already to the notion of losing the Bohemian Germans. . . '.[52] As we shall see, they were also much less keen on the *Anschluss* with Germany.

Before the end of 1918 the government of German Bohemia was forced to leave its seat at Reichenberg (Liberec) which was then occupied by Czech troops. According to the Social Democratic leader from German Bohemia, the workers were 'holding out firmly, but the middle classes were full of fear. The mood must be improved'.[53] His view was partly confirmed when representatives of the Austrian chambers of commerce and industry met early in 1919 to discuss the question of the *Anschluss* and the problems arising from it. The representative from Eger (Cheb), close to Bavaria, pointed out that

[51] Letter of 20 Nov. 1918: Haus-, Hof- u. Staatsarchiv, Nachlass Bauer, Karton 261.

[52] PRO, FO 371, vol. 3529, nos. 5444, 27254 (reports of 4 Jan. and ? Feb. 1919).

[53] Report by Seliger, 20 Dec. 1918: Parteiarchiv der SPÖ, Sitzungsprotokolle des Parteivorstandes 1913–1925.

there was considerable opposition to joining Germany as many enterprises feared for their viability on account of German competition, but the china industry was in favour, as were industrial circles 'by and large, . . . but if one talked with the individuals concerned, they would constantly raise doubts. . . '. This rather mixed tendency also existed elsewhere. The representative from Reichenberg reported that the machine tool industry had certain fears—as did the iron industry of Eger—because of raw materials, but that the much more important textile industry was expressly in favour of *Anschluss* without any reservations. In general, at least in industrial circles, the mood was in favour of joining Germany directly, not as a part of German Austria.[54] That the Allies would agree to such a strengthening of the German industrial potential was even more unlikely than their consent to a union of German Bohemia with Austria.

Already in November the Austrian government decided to try and prevent a further occupation of German Bohemian lands by Czech troops, not by military resistance, but by the formation of *Volkswehr* units in the immediately threatened areas. It was hoped that by their mere presence these would deter small Czech units from advancing; force was only to be shown, but not to be used; if the Czechs came in superior strength the *Volkswehr* was to retreat so as to avoid useless bloodshed.[55] These orders were sent to the commanding officers not only of Upper and Lower Austria, but also of northern Bohemia—proof partly of the goodwill, but above all of the military impotence of the Austrian side; no one could seriously expect such measures to stop the Czech advance. Some days later the Austrian State Council went further and empowered the local government of German South Moravia to recruit troops strong enough to liberate the areas occupied by the Czechs and to prevent any incursion by them in future. They were to be assisted by a thousand men of the Viennese *Volkswehr* and a machine gun unit; the Viennese *Volkswehr* command was instructed to do everything necessary to support the actions in South Moravia.[56] This motion was put forward by a Pan-German state councillor and mirrored the more aggressive attitude of his party, which only reluctantly supported the foreign policy of the Austrian government.

[54] Haus-, Hof- u. Staatsarchiv, Präsidialakten 1919, Anschlussfrage, Fasz. 5a (meeting 19 Feb. 1919).
[55] Order of 18 Nov. 1918: Kriegsarchiv, Staatsamt für Heerwesen 1918, Fasz. 1.
[56] Decision with two separate motions by Staatsrat Teufel of 26 Nov. 1918: Verwaltungsarchiv, Beschlüsse des deutschösterreichischen Staatsrates.

Difficulties, however, developed immediately with the *Volkswehr* units selected for the march to Znaim (Znojmo). One battalion was dissatisfied with the conditions the *Volkswehr* command was willing to grant and in particular demanded that any next-of-kin of a man killed in action should be paid a monthly pension of 300 crowns, plus another 150 for any under-age child he might leave, that the town of Znaim should pay 20 crowns per day to every soldier, and also be responsible for feeding the battalion. After negotiations with the soldiers' council of the battalion the conditions were partly met and the unit departed. Of another battalion numbering 180 men which left some days later, no less than 130 were sent back as 'unreliable'. When the first battalion reached Znaim the soldiers pronounced themselves opposed to any fight with Czech forces, and their attitude quickly influenced the local *Volkswehr*, or at least sections of it which were 'less interested in the defence of their homeland than in material benefits'. In general they began to think that a battle outside Znaim was hopeless because the Viennese *Volkswehr* would not back them against the Czechs within the gates. The order to avoid the shedding of blood condemned the units to remain on the defensive and left all the initiative to the Czechs.[57] The Viennese *Volkswehr* command in its turn suggested the evacuation of southern Bohemia and Moravia as far as the historical frontier of Bohemia, for the German population was showing no enthusiasm whatever for a defence against the Czechs, the *Volkswehr* units sent there had to avoid any battle with regular Czech units, and the future of the disputed area would in any case be decided by the Peace Conference. The colonel in charge of the Znaim district was equally pessimistic.[58] A machine gun company sent to Gänserndorf (to the north-east of Vienna) found the local population so hostile and the total lack of preparation for their reception so infuriating that they declared they would return to Vienna; all efforts by the officers and the soldiers' council to change their mind were in vain. The local peasants simply declared they would prefer the Czechs to come because that would mean lower taxes and no war debts. Thus the soldiers naturally asked themselves for whom they should sacrifice themselves; in their opinion, the Czech units were troops of the Entente which according to the

[57] Soldiers' Council of 2nd Battalion Regiment No. 1 to *Volkswehr* Command Vienna, 28 Nov., report of Capt. Ludwig, 7 Dec., the commanding officer of Kreis Südmähren to Oberbefehlshaber, 6 Dec. 1918: Kriegsarchiv, Volkswehrkommando Wien 1918, Fasz. 8 and 9 ; Staatsamt für Heerwesen 1918, Fasz. 8.

[58] Reports of Colonel Straub of 4 Dec. and the Viennese *Volkswehr* command of ? Dec. 1919: Kriegsarchiv, Volkswehrkommando Provinz 1918, Fasz. 1.

armistice conditions they were not obliged to fight. And the men of another machine gun unit sent to the frontier took exactly the same view.[59]

Clearly, there was even less national enthusiasm in Lower Austria and its adjoining districts than in Carinthia and southern Styria. The reason is fairly obvious. In the latter areas the Austrians were defending themselves against Yugoslav incursions, which threatened even purely German districts; but the Czechs were not attacking Lower Austria or threatening Vienna—in that case the *Volkswehr* would have fought. Southern Bohemia was a different matter, and the fact that German was spoken on both sides of the frontier seems to have counted for little. It is true that Viennese police reports several times mentioned that people were very 'embittered' about the Czechs and Hungarians because they refused to send food and coal to Vienna, but that was another matter. Even the police added that little attention was shown to political news, such as Czech claims to German Bohemia and separatist tendencies in the Tyrol.[60] In any case, the attentions of the Viennese were too much occupied by the severe food and coal shortages and by local events to give much time to national or other general political issues. But, when the Czechoslovak army was defeated in June 1919 by the Hungarians, this aroused widespread interest and, among the working class, a certain pride in the achievements of the Red Army of a Soviet government.[61]

The mood of general indifference and lack of national enthusiasm even affected German Bohemia and the Sudetenland, in spite of all national propaganda. In November 1918 the National Committee of Tachau (Tachov) in western Bohemia reported to the Land government of German Bohemia that the large majority of the urban and rural population was influenced by worries about food and the supply of necessities, the unrest in German Bohemia, the unfavourable armistice conditions, and the economic links of the area with Czech Bohemia: lacking 'a proper national consciousness', they believed that the German Bohemians had no alternative but to join the Czechoslovak state, and a large section of the population even desired this because they would fare better in it.[62] In December Renner

[59] Reports of Viennese *Volkswehr* command, Kreis B, 19 Jan., and of Landesbefehlshaber Wien of 17 Jan. and 28 Feb. 1919: Kriegsarchiv, Landesbefehlshaber Wien 1919, Fasz. 20; Staatsamt für Heerwesen 1919, Abt. 5, Fasz. 198.

[60] Police reports, 20 Nov. 1918, 12 Mar. 1919: Polizeiarchiv Wien, Staats- u. sicherheitspol. Agenden 1918, box 9; Botz, 'Beiträge . . .' iii, Quellen, p. 21.

[61] Police report, 11 June 1919: ibid., p. 40.

[62] Bezirksnationalausschuss Tachau to Landesregierung, 8 Nov. 1918: quoted

informed Bauer after conversations with leading Bohemian Social
Democrats that, in their opinion, 99 per cent of the Germans would
vote for joining Czechoslovakia if the Czechs offered them national
autonomy; similar voices were reaching him from German Bohemia,
and he feared that their policy of national separation would suffer
shipwreck.[63] An officer who travelled in German Bohemia shortly
before the Czechs marched in, complained about the indifference
of the people. 'The general opinion was that what mattered was to
get something to eat—who cares where from.'[64] An Austrian Social
Democrat received 'from the best source' a report that the industrialists of German Bohemia were openly pleased with the incorporation
in Czechoslovakia; they regarded profits with more respect than the
Volk and adhered to the motto: *'ubi bene ibi patria'*.[65]

In fact there was nothing left for the Austrian government but to
bow to the inevitable and to accept the conditions of St Germain.
In June 1919 Otter Bauer once more solemnly protested in the
Austrian National Assembly:

> The separation of German Bohemia and the Sudetenland from
> German Austria has been justified by their geographical position.
> But this argument certainly does not apply to those German areas
> of Bohemia and Moravia which directly adjoin Upper and Lower
> Austria and form a contiguous German-language territory with
> Upper and Lower Austria and the Alpine lands: the Böhmer-
> waldgau and the *Kreis* of Znaim. That these two districts should
> go to Czechoslovakia cannot be justified with geographical, nor
> with ethnographical, nor with economic arguments; there is only
> one argument that can justify this demand: the historical one, the
> argument of the historical frontiers. But historical frontiers are
> only considered immovable where this works in favour of the
> Czechoslovaks and against us.
>
> The peace proposals of the Associated Powers do not respect our
> historical frontiers, the frontiers of the German lands. They give
> Znaim to the Czechoslovaks because it belongs historically to
> Moravia, but they also give them Feldsberg and Hohenau although
> historically they belong to Lower Austria. . . .

Bauer went on to emphasize the economic loss which Vienna in
particular would suffer if it were separated from the districts which

by Hanns Haas, 'Österreich-Ungarn als Friedensproblem', Salzburg Ph.D. thesis,
1968, MS., p. 149.
    [63] Letter of 12 Dec. 1918: Haus-, Hof- u. Staatsarchiv, Nachlass Bauer, Karton
262, X.
    [64] Paul Molisch, *Die sudetendeutsche Freiheitsbewegung 1918/19*, Vienna, 1932,
pp. 118–19.
    [65] Unsigned letter of 5 May 1919: Arbeiterkammer Wien, Briefe an Friedrich
Adler, 1918/1919.

had always supplied it with milk, vegetables and other food. 'If the frontiers are drawn according to the maxim that each neighbour can take whatever is valuable in our area then the rest cannot become a viable state. . . '.[66] Indeed Bauer was convinced that the economic conditions of St Germain were even harsher than the territorial clauses. A peace imposing such conditions upon Austria would not be a peace, and could not possibly last.

There was another national hope which many Austrians entertained in 1918 and which had to be buried in 1919 because of the Allies' verdict: the *Anschluss*. A united and democratic Germany had been the dream of 1848, and after 1866 many liberals and Pan-Germans refused to accept a permanent separation from Bismarck's Germany. The party which called itself 'German-liberal', 'German-national' or 'Pan-German'—although now a right-wing party—was the heir to this tradition, and often accused the other parties of lack of enthusiasm for the cause. But the Social Democrats, too, were by tradition and conviction in favour of joining Germany, especially a Germany without the Hohenzollerns and governed by their political friends. The founders of the two parties—August Bebel and Victor Adler—had been in favour of the *Anschluss* long before 1918. In October, before the collapse, Bauer had moved at an internal party meeting that the German Austrians should join the German Reich if an agreement with the other nationalities proved impossible. The editorials of the *Arbeiter-Zeitung* during that month constantly made propaganda for a union with Germany.[67] As Bauer explained to Arthur Henderson in November,

> German Austria always was part of the German Empire, and the connection was only broken by the feud of the Habsburg and Hohenzollern dynasties. As the two ruling houses have now been deprived of their power, the true reason for separation has disappeared. . . .

Moreover, the union of the two countries would not strengthen Prussianism but the democratic influences of southern Germany.[68]

[66] Speech of 7 June 1919: *Unser Friede!* Flugblätter für Deutschösterreichs Recht, no. 33, Vienna, 1919, pp. 9–10, 16, 20. For a similar protest by the Upper Austrian Diet, see Oberösterreich. Landesarchiv, Landtagsakten nos. 28 and 65 (23 June and 12 Aug. 1919). Feldsberg and Hohenau are villages to the north-east of Vienna near the March river.

[67] Parteiarchiv der SPÖ, Sitzungsprotokolle des Parteivorstandes 1913–1925 (meeting of 11 Oct. 1918); Deutsch, *Ein weiter Weg*, pp. 74–5; Gulick, *Austria . . .*, i, p. 53.

[68] Bauer to Henderson, 20 Nov. 1918: Haus-, Hof- u. Staatsarchiv, Nachlass Bauer, Karton 261.

In Austria, the principal dissentient voice was that of the largest party, the Christian Socials, who disliked German Protestantism and, after November 1918, disliked even more strongly the German Socialists then entrenched in power. In December an eminent party leader, the later Chancellor Dr Ignaz Seipel, wrote to a German friend:

> There is not yet any certainty whither God wants us German Austrians to go, and that is the cardinal point. The old Austria is by no means dead. The 'Danubian Federation' will certainly come and rejuvenate it. . . .

All the talk about the *Anschluss* had already caused the loss of German Bohemia to the Czechs and would bring the loss of the South Tyrol, for the world would not suffer Germany to reach across the Brenner.

> But the following is completely decisive. We will only join Germany if it becomes a truly free state. We have nothing to seek in the Germany of today in which there is the terror of the soldiers' councils, in which a socialist dictatorship exists, in which a Kurt Eisner can rule, etc. . . .
>
> As long as order is not guaranteed in your country, union would mean a great danger. You must not overlook that with us the National Assembly has not been pushed aside for one moment, that in it all parties cooperate, while you have no Reichstag and therefore no legal government. . . .

Thus the Christian Social Party had to demand that Germany must transform itself into a free state before the Austrians could join it.[69] When the power of the soldiers' councils had been dismantled and the German National Assembly been elected the attitude of the party remained cool, to say the least, even when the Catholic Centre Party entered the German government. Any union with Germany would have meant giving up all hope of a Habsburg restoration—a hope privately entertained by many party leaders.

The attitude of the new German government was also cool. When the Austrian 'comrades' requested coal and food from Germany and expressed their wish for union, the Germans decided not to mention the latter question in their reply 'on account of the international situation'. Later in November the Austrian ambassador, the historian Dr Hartmann, appeared uninvited at the conference of the German states and communicated the wish of his government to be accepted as a member state. However, the Under-Secretary of State at the Foreign Office, Dr Solf, warned that such a step would not be

[69] Letter of 17 Dec. 1918, sent to Bauer by Hartmann on 14 Jan. 1919: ibid., Karton 262.

approved by the Entente and might endanger the early conclusion
of peace. Ebert at first seemed to accept Hartmann's plea; but then
he began to waver, and finally agreed with Solf's negative attitude—
as he had done on previous occasions.[70]

In spite of all difficulties, Bauer steadfastly pursued his course of
promoting the *Anschluss*, in close collaboration with Hartmann in
Berlin. At the beginning of 1919 he informed Hartmann that the
whole issue had become the subject of rather heated discussions and
that it was no overstatement to say that a large majority in the
bourgeois parties was opposed to it. In view of this it was impossible
to consider the *Anschluss* a *fait accompli* and not to discuss other
possibilities. Thus the Austrians should declare their readiness to
negotiate about a Danubian Federation, negotiations which they
would conduct loyally; only if they failed—as they were bound to do
—would they revert to the *Anschluss* which would then become
inevitable. If the coming elections produced a clerical majority, that
would be the most serious blow to the idea of *Anschluss*. Some days
later Bauer repeated that the government was forced to negotiate
about the Danubian Federation if the Entente so desired, otherwise
all efforts to save German Bohemia and South Tyrol would become
hopeless, but this did not mean giving up the *Anschluss* plan. The
Austrian envoy in The Hague was instructed to emphasize that
Austria had no industries, the exports of which could pay for the coal
and corn she had to import; thus Austria could not remain alone but
had to join either a Danubian Federation or Germany; but the
former was impossible because it was rejected by the Poles and
Yugoslavs, and it was hardly conceivable that the Czechs would
want to federate with their two historical enemies, the Austrians and
the Hungarians; if the Czechs thought of it as an anti-German
bulwark, the Austrians could not be expected to join an anti-
German combination.[71] When the representatives of the Austrian
chambers of commerce and industry met in February 1919, most of
them pronounced in favour of the *Anschluss*, in spite of the economic
difficulties this would cause, and against the plan of a Danubian
Federation. Among the population of Vienna, too, the idea was
gaining ground in the early weeks of 1919.[72]

[70] Matthias (ed.), *Regierung* . . . , i, no. 11, p. 45; Ritter (ed.), *Deutsche Revolution* . . . , pp. 370, 371–2 (memoirs of Col. von Haeften).
[71] Bauer to Hartmann, 3 and 13 Jan. 1919; instruction for Dr Medinger in The Hague, 25 Jan. 1919: Haus-, Hof- u. Staatsarchiv, Nachlass Bauer, Karton 261.
[72] ibid., Präsidialakten 1919, Anschlussfrage, Fasz. 5a (meeting of 19 Feb. 1919 with representatives of Carinthia, Styria, Tyrol, Upper Austria, Vorarlberg, and

At the end of February Bauer travelled to Berlin to conduct secret negotiations about the *Anschluss*, but he returned some days later severely disappointed; the economic experts he met there were extremely reluctant, the question of converting crowns into marks was a major obstacle, and there was no enthusiasm whatever in Berlin for Austria. A leading Christian Social minister informed a British representative that the 'journey was a complete failure because Germans [were] unwilling to complicate existing difficulties by union with German-Austria'. The informant suggested a confidential hint by a British representative that it would become easier to feed Austria if the agitation for the *Anschluss* were dropped.[73] In fact the attitude of the Allies remained adamant, even without any prompting from the Christian Social side. In June Bauer wrote to Chancellor Renner, who was then negotiating at St Germain, that any retreat in the *Anschluss* matter would be 'the biggest mistake', for even in bourgeois circles, which hitherto had been very cool, the idea had gained considerable ground.[74] But in the end Bauer had to admit defeat on the three issues on which he had fought a losing battle: German Bohemia, the *Anschluss* and the South Tyrol. The result was his resignation from the office of Foreign Minister. He had earned the reluctant admiration even of the Pan-Germans who considered him the only minister who possessed energy; no one dared to oppose him, and even Renner was silent when Bauer talked.[75] Austrian foreign policy had to adapt itself to the realities of Allied power, and by October neither the Social Democrats nor the Christian Socials any longer talked about the *Anschluss*—an attitude sharply criticized by the Pan-German deputies.[76] There was little else that the government could do, for it depended entirely on Allied shipments of food and other measures of economic aid.[77]

The Habsburg monarchy had left the Austrian Germans without a nationality of their own. In contrast with the Swiss Germans, they felt that they were Germans and—after the disappearance of the

German Bohemia); police report of 5 Feb. 1919: Botz, 'Beiträge . . .', iii, Quellen, p. 14.

[73] Report of 9 Mar. 1919: PRO, FO 371, vol. 3529, no. 40970; Reimann, *Zu Gross für Österreich*, p. 296.

[74] Letter of 8 June 1919: Haus-, Hof- u. Staatsarchiv, Nachlass Bauer, Karton 261.

[75] Verwaltungsarchiv Wien, Verhandlungsschriften der 'Grossdeutschen Vereinigung' (meeting of 17 Sept. 1919).

[76] ibid., Dr Ursin in meeting of 9 Oct. 1919.

[77] Thus, for example, a message of the Austrian Foreign Office, drafted by B. Kautsky, to Hartmann in Berlin, 15 July 1919: Haus-, Hof- u. Staatsarchiv, Nachlass Bauer, Karton 261.

dynasties—there was nothing to separate the two branches of one national family, which also included the Germans of Bohemia and Moravia.[78] This was not Pan-Germanism, and did not express a feeling of superiority towards the non-German neighbours, but much more a conviction that the few million Austrians would be unable to stand on their own feet, especially in view of the hostility shown by the neighbouring states towards Austria. As the British diplomatic representative in Vienna put it at the end of 1919:

> It is not strange that the Social Democrats call aloud for union with Germany and that the cry is finding from day to day a deeper echo among the mass of the population. The newspapers of this morning announce that the German Government have decided to send as much flour as possible to Vienna immediately, relying on its being made good later out of supplies destined for Austria. The friend in need is not likely to lose over this transaction, and, if the Allies really intend to keep Austria and Germany apart, it is essential that they should force the New States to follow a line of action which will allow the population of this country to live. . . .[79]

It may seem strange in retrospect that the most eloquent defender of the national aspirations of the German Austrians was a Jewish intellectual of strong Marxist views. But there was little that was incongruous in this in the situation of 1918. After the death of Victor Adler, Otto Bauer was the intellectual leader of his party, and his great gifts were soon recognized by his political enemies. That his endeavours were in vain, that he failed to obtain any major concession from the Allies, can hardly be blamed on him. The result of his defeat was a growth of German nationalism—a growth that equally occurred in Germany under the conditions of defeat and economic crisis, of continuing hostilities with France and Poland.

[78] Most Austrians were *grossdeutsch*—in favour of uniting with Germany—not *alldeutsch*—in favour of uniting *all* Germans in one state: an important difference which cannot be rendered in English.

[79] F. O. Lindley to Lord Curzon, 22 Nov. 1919: PRO, FO 371, File 5445, vol. 3531, no. 155982.

11 Moving to the Right

In the course of 1919 the political pendulum, in Germany as well as in Austria, swung sharply to the right. It is true that in both countries the first half of the year saw attempts by the extreme left to seize power; it is also true that, in Germany, large sections of the working class moved from the Social Democrats to the Independents, and some to the Communists. But what really mattered in terms of political power was that the left-wing risings were decisively defeated, not by forces loyal to the Ebert government, but by the Free Corps from which the provisional *Reichswehr* was formed. In the Weimar Republic the *Reichswehr*, more than any other political force, became the arbiter in the political field; in an emergency its generals were entrusted with the exercise of political power or with reducing to obedience a refractory state government—measures expressly provided for in the Weimar Constitution. As early as March 1920 the Free Corps felt strong enough to proclaim resistance to an order which dissolved them according to the terms of the Treaty of Versailles, to march into Berlin and to overthrow the government, which had to escape to the south. In Berlin a counter-revolutionary government under Dr Wolfgang Kapp and General von Lüttwitz was installed; but the trade unions proclaimed a general strike, and this defeated the Kapp *Putsch* within a few days. Left-wing risings in the Ruhr and elsewhere which followed upon the Kapp enterprise were defeated by the same Free Corps which had just mutinied against the government. The one general who had been willing to defend the legitimate government against the mutinous Free Corps, General Reinhardt, resigned as chief of the army command and was replaced by General von Seeckt who had refused to fight 'with live ammunition between Berlin and Potsdam'.[1] Although the Kapp *Putsch* was defeated, the result in the military field was a considerable strengthening of conservative tendencies. Under General von Seeckt the *Reichswehr* truly became a 'state within the state', the true power behind the empty throne.

[1] For details see Carsten, *Reichswehr* . . . , pp. 89–90, 99–103 (English edition, pp. 78–80, 89–93).

In the political field, too, the defeat of the Kapp *Putsch* did not bring a swing to the left, as might have been expected, but the opposite. A general election was held in June 1920—the first after the election of the National Assembly seventeen months before—and resulted in a shattering defeat of the moderate parties which formed the government and a decisive victory of the political right. The two right-wing parties, the Nationalists and the People's Party, almost doubled their vote and increased their parliamentary representation from 63 to 136 seats. The three parties which had formed the 'Weimar coalition'—Social Democrats, Democrats and Centre—were reduced from 76 per cent of the poll to 43, and from 329 to 205 seats. They lost the overall majority which they had gained in 1919, never to regain it. As the result of this electoral defeat (the party polled only 6 million votes instead of 11.5 million) the Social Democrats left the government, and a moderate Catholic, Konstantin Fehrenbach, became Chancellor, presiding over a purely bourgeois government. On the extreme left the Independents gained considerably from the Social Democrats, and a small Communist Party appeared for the first time. But their combined strength only amounted to 20 per cent of the electorate and 88 seats in parliament: considerably less than that of the two right-wing parties. What the election of 1920 showed for the first time was a polarization—a polarization which benefited the right far more than the left. Exactly the same trend was to reappear during the crisis of 1923 and during the final crisis of the Weimar Republic in the 1930s. As its most noted historian put it in 1934: 'In so far as the November Revolution had aimed at establishing a democracy under the leadership of the socialist working class, it had suffered shipwreck in the summer of 1920, and that was final'.[2] The right reasserted its influence with 29 per cent of the total vote, a percentage which was to grow very considerably during the following years.

The Austrian Social Democrats resigned from the coalition government at the same time as their German comrades—as a result not of a general election but of internal conflict. The coalition was then replaced by a 'proportional cabinet' of all parties which was to conduct affairs until the general elections of October 1920. These had the same result as in Germany: a victory of the right-wing parties, especially the Christian Socials, and a defeat of the Social Democrats,

---

[2] Rosenberg, *Geschichte der Deutschen Republik*, p. 116. For the figures of 1919 and 1920, see Huber, *Dokumente . . .* , iii, p. 606.

although much less severe than in Germany. The Christian Socials increased their vote from 36 to 42 per cent of the total and henceforth alone formed the government; the Social Democrats dropped from 41 to 36 per cent, while the third party, the Pan-Germans, only suffered a slight loss.[3] The weight of the countryside, which was Catholic and conservative, asserted itself against Vienna. In contrast with Germany, where the Social Democrats several times re-entered the government during the 1920s, this did not occur in Austria, where they remained permanently in opposition and considerably further to the left than the German party. Nor could they compensate for the loss of power at the centre by their domination of the government in some large states, as the German Social Democrats did in Prussia and in Saxony. It was only Vienna that remained a red bastion, the central position of the Austrian Socialists, until that too was destroyed in 1934. There the Social Democrats could show how well they could run a large city and practise progressive social policies; but the party was only to regain political power on a larger scale after the Second World War.

Even before the coalition government broke up in 1920 it experienced severe strains. In May the British High Commissioner wrote from Vienna:

> I have the honour to report that relations between the Christian Socialist and the Social Democratic Parties . . . have become so strained that it seems unlikely that the Government will last much longer in its present form. I have more than once called attention to the fundamental differences separating a party of peasants with an ingrained distrust of Vienna and strong anti-Semitic leanings and a party of town socialists, many of whose most prominent leaders are Jews. . . .[4]

In the autumn of 1919 Otto Bauer stressed in several letters to Karl Kautsky the great difficulties facing the coalition government. In his opinion the economic situation was such that the country could only be saved by 'the most radical and heroic means', but no coalition with a bourgeois party would ever be willing to adopt such means; nor would a purely socialist government be able to force any radical infringements of property rights on to the peasantry, and the *Länder* would probably reply by seceding from Vienna. As such a radical

[3] Detailed figures on the elections in Gulick, *Austria* . . . , i, p. 690, Bauer, *Österreich. Revolution*, p. 225, and Jacques Hannak, *Karl Renner und seine Zeit*, Vienna, 1965, pp. 372, 409, with some differences.

[4] F. O. Lindley to Lord Curzon, 22 May 1920: PRO, FO 371, File 5445, vol. 3538, no. 199727.

reformation could be carried through neither with the peasants nor against them, the country would sink further and further into the morass and inflation would get worse; the danger remained that economic misery would bring either Bolshevism or counter-revolution, or one after the other. Some months later he repeated that this was the real danger; the Social Democrats were unable to leave the government because they could not entrust a bourgeois government with the formation of the new army—which had to be done within three months after the conclusion of the peace treaty—and because a bourgeois government would bring about a severe conflict with the workers and the *Volkswehr*; thus the party was forced to remain in the government and to carry the responsibility for the inevitable misery; nothing could be done about this, but they must carry on 'in the hope of thus at least saving the democracy that has been gained'. At the beginning of 1920 Bauer once more emphasized that the difficulties within the government were constantly increasing: 'the Christian Socials sabotage everything and the *Länder* simply refuse to obey the central government in anything.'[5] The tone of these letters was profoundly pessimistic, as Bauer saw no way out of the situation and expected that a general election would bring the party severe losses.

In August 1919 there was an acrimonious discussion within the cabinet about the granting of political asylum to Béla Kun and the other Hungarian Communists after the collapse of the Soviet Republic. The Secretary of State for Agriculture, Josef Stöckler, dissented from the policy of the majority because the granting of asylum had made a very bad impression among the people, diminished the authority of the government and contributed to a worsening of its relations with the *Länder*. If the providing of quarters for the Hungarian Communists meant that they were to be protected, no one would understand it, for this would amount to a declaration of solidarity with their aims. The Hungarian Soviet government had posed a threat to the existing order in Austria, but the primary task of the government was the preservation of order, while the granting of asylum would bring about severe disorders. The Minister of the Interior, Eldersch, pointed out that as early as June the government had been approached with regard to the safety of the Hungarian People's Commissars in case of an upheaval in Hungary and agreed to grant them asylum, except to Tibor Szamuely; the opinion of

[5] Bauer to Kautsky, 2 Sept., 25 Nov. 1919, 26 Jan. 1920: Int. Inst. of Social History, Nachlass Kautsky, D II 463–534.

Stöckler amounted to a refusal of this grant; the right of asylum existed independent of the political opinions of the beneficiaries. Chancellor Renner declared that in the past Austrian conservative governments had granted asylum to Lenin and other Russian revolutionaries as well as to the Poles who from Galicia engaged in revolutionary propaganda. Bauer added that he believed implicitly that the Austrian population could not understand the granting of political asylum to people of different opinions, for Austria had no democratic traditions, but in England and Switzerland every anarchist and revolutionary was given asylum; as little as he could conceive of democratic government without the general and equal franchise, as little was he willing to concede a democratic character to a government or remain a member of one which refused the granting of political asylum. This attitude was supported by Seitz, the chairman of the State Council. Even a Christian Social member of the government, Johann Zerdik, came out in favour of the right of asylum, in spite of the mood prevailing among the population; and Stöckler modified his point of view in so far as he considered it unnecessary to adapt all government actions to the changing moods of the people. Bauer, in summing up, made a clear distinction between Kun and Szamuely: the latter had been a sadist and a murderer; the revolutionary tribunals in Hungary passed inhuman verdicts, but the same applied to the courts-martial of the war period; both had been measures of despotic and terrorist régimes and there was little to choose between those of Kun and Tisza, the former Hungarian prime minister who was murdered in 1918. It was then decided to grant the Hungarians the right of asylum, except in cases where a court found that a crime had been committed and the Hungarian government demanded extradition.[6] A government declaration explained these points to the population.

It proved far more difficult, indeed impossible, to reach agreement on another controversial issue, that of the new army. The Peace of St Germain limited Austria to an army of professional soldiers of a maximum strength of 30,000 with limited arms—exactly as the *Reichswehr* was limited to 100,000 long-serving soldiers without heavy weapons. In Austria, however, this did not create the severe problem of reduction which it created in Germany, for the *Volkswehr* by August 1919 had a strength of only about 35,000 men. But there were 12,000 professional officers; according to Deutsch, it was absolutely

---

[6] Verwaltungsarchiv Wien, Kabinettsratsprotokolle, no. 96, 8 Aug. 1919; draft with many corrections, 'confidential', not in protocol.

inconceivable that the Entente powers would allow Austria to take over a large proportion of officers into the new army, or to form larger units consisting entirely of officers; the only loophole in the treaty was to declare all officers fulfilling administrative functions to be officials and thus civilians (a loophole used extensively in Germany too). To his party comrades Deutsch emphasized that it was vital to get into the new army 'none but reliable Social Democrats', but the difficulty was that of recruiting good workers; he was opposed to accepting officers as other ranks in the new army. From the Social Democratic point of view the position was favourable only in Lower Austria and Salzburg, and bad everywhere else.[7]

Originally Deutsch had favoured the introduction of a militia system 'as evidence of their rejection of the old militarism' as the *Volkswehr* was not conceived as a permanent institution. A militia system 'on the basis of the Swiss model' was also favoured by the Tyrol and other Alpine provinces which desired to reduce the *Volkswehr* and to exclude 'foreign elements' from the army; a militia could be recruited from the province in question and would enable the *Länder* to take over matters of security.[8] When a militia was made impossible by the Treaty of St Germain, the Tyrolese authorities still adhered to the idea of a decentralized army: in the army of 30,000 each *Land* was to be allocated a fixed contingent according to its needs; in the first instance natives of the *Land* in question were to be recruited; each *Land* was to have a commanding officer who was to be subordinate to the *Land* government in all questions not reserved to the commander-in-chief; the *Land* government was to be consulted on all questions of personnel; officers were only to be commissioned with its consent; the soldiers' councils were to be replaced by trusties whose functions were to be limited to economic questions and the receiving and handing on of soldiers' complaints and requests, but were not to include issues relating to officers and personnel and the power of command; politics were to be eliminated from the army.[9] This far-reaching programme strongly reflected the dislike of the *Volkswehr*, of the soldiers' councils and the centralizing tendencies

[7] ibid., no. 96, 8 Aug. 1919; Parteiarchiv der SPÖ, Sitzungsprotokolle des Parteivorstandes 1913–1925 (meeting of 7 Sept. 1919). Deutsch's remarks are not given in full, but only summarized.

[8] Verwaltungsarchiv Wien, Protokolle über die Sitzungen des Vollzugsausschusses der Soldatenräte der Volkswehr Wiens, p. 46 (meeting of 27 Jan. 1919); Landesarchiv Salzburg, Präsidialakten 1919, 1–9 (conference of Alpine provinces of 12–13 May 1919).

[9] The Tyrolese Landesrat to the Upper Austrian Diet, 23 Aug. 1919: Oberösterreich. Landesarchiv, Landtagsakten, no. 66, Beilage 3.

emanating from Vienna, which was felt in the provinces. But in Vienna too the same tendencies appeared among the non-socialist parties. In September the Pan-German deputies complained that nothing could be found out about the new Army Law which was being drafted by Deutsch together with his closest collaborators; the *Volkswehr* must not form the basis of the new army, otherwise it would reappear in another form; the soldiers' councils beyond the battalion level must disappear; the *Länder* must exercise pressure 'so that this question can be settled in our sense', and a permanent control must be exercised.[10]

In October the Pan-German deputies discussed the programme of the coalition government and complained that the Christian Social ministers would be powerless to counteract the tendencies in the army fostered by Deutsch, especially in the educational sphere where even lectures on Marx and the council system were envisaged. According to Deutsch the soldiers' councils had two tasks: to keep the republican spirit alive and to represent the soldiers' interests, but in Pan-German opinion they should only have the latter function; the Social Democrats would incorporate the *Volkswehr* in the new army, and thus nothing would be changed. Another Pan-German deputy stated that the soldiers of the new army must lose their political rights, otherwise it would again become a party army of the Social Democrats. This was supported by a third deputy who mentioned that the Carinthian army committee had already decided to ban all politics from the army and to deprive soldiers of the franchise; it was impossible to possess it and to remain unpolitical; this was not an issue of party politics, but a question of the life and death of the nation. In December the Pan-German deputies once more discussed army reform: the *Land* government should have the decisive voice, not the soldiers' councils; the Christian Socials should be mobilized against the Social Democrats; the demand must be put forward that only natives of the *Land* in question should be accepted as soldiers, which would eliminate many recruits from the *Volkswehr*.[11] It is remarkable how closely these demands corresponded to the Tyrolese programme put forward some months before, although this came from the Christian Social side. In February 1920, shortly before the Army Law was passed by the National Assembly, the Pan-German deputies strongly criticized the draft because it abolished the office of

[10] Verwaltungsarchiv Wien, Verhandlungsschriften der 'Grossdeutschen Vereinigung' (meeting of 19 Sept. 1919).
[11] ibid., meetings of 22 Oct., 13 Dec. 1919.

military commander-in-chief and made the Secretary of State—in
other words Deutsch—commander-in-chief; if politics were not removed from the army it would be dominated by the Social Democrats; an army in which the soldiers had the right to vote could not
be non-political, and it was dishonest of the Christian Socials to
maintain the contrary; the system of soldiers' councils was being
perpetuated on four levels, with a National Executive Committee at
the head; it was the duty of the Pan-Germans to win over the
Christian Socials and to support them because they were opposed to
Deutsch.[12]

Meanwhile the Social Democrats too were making strenuous
efforts to retain their influence, 'at least partly', in the new army. In
practice this meant seeing that in Vienna, Graz and other industrial
towns as many *Volkswehr* men as possible transferred to the new
army, recruiting reliable Social Democrats for it, and preventing the
recruiting of too many professional officers and NCOs of the old
army, even with inferior ranks.[13] The Social Democrats equally
endeavoured to maintain the system of soldiers' councils, and in this
they were successful. At the end of February 1920 their Christian
Social coalition partners accepted it under the name of *Vertrauensmänner* (trusties).[14] According to Paragraph 31 of the Army Law of
18 March, trusties, elected separately by the officers and the other
ranks, were to be reponsible for preserving the interests and the
contractual rights of the soldiers and were to be consulted on issues of
recruitment, food and billeting, the raising of complaints and their
settlement, questions of leave, discipline and dismissals; but the
trusties were not entitled to issue orders or requests to those of a lower
echelon or to interfere with the power of command of the officers. In
this respect the army was to be very different from the Viennese
Volkswehr, in which the soldiers' councils had exercised much greater
powers, but different too from the German *Reichswehr* in which the
trusties were in practice degraded to 'kitchen committees' by
General von Seeckt. Another difference was that the Austrian soldiers,
in contrast with the German ones, were entitled to vote in general
and local elections, and even to become parliamentary candidates.
But there was to be no party political activity within the army, only a

[12] ibid., meeting of 12 Feb. 1920.

[13] ibid., Protokolle von Sitzungen der Soldatenräte des Kreises D. der Volkswehr
(meeting of 5 Sept. 1919); police report, Graz, 3 Mar. 1919, about meeting of
workers' councils on 2 Mar. with about 700 participants: Steiermärk. Landesarchiv, Akten der k.k. Statthalterei—Präsidium, E. 91, 1918 (iv).

[14] Verwaltungsarchiv, Verhandlungsschriften der 'Grossdeutschen Vereinigung' (26 Feb. 1920).

general education of the soldiers in a republican sense; soldiers were to possess the same rights and duties as any other citizen.[15]

In Deutsch's opinion, the acceptance of this law by the National Assembly was 'a revolutionary victory'. It was greatly facilitated by the Kapp *Putsch* in Germany which intimidated the Austrian Christian Socials and enabled the Social Democrats to overcome their opposition. The Army Law restored the officers' power of command, which they exercised in the *Volkswehr* only under the control of the soldiers' councils. The retention of civil rights by the men meant that the Social Democrats could organize the *Militär-verband*, a trade union, which also took over certain educational functions and was animated by socialist ideas. These factors enabled the Social Democrats to recruit qualified party members, especially younger ones, for the army—in contrast with Germany where this was practically impossible in view of the spirit and composition of the *Reichswehr*. In Austria, the other parties too tried to induce their followers to go into the army, but it seems that the Social Democrats were the most successful. The large majority of those other ranks who had been commissioned as *Volkswehr* lieutenants against strong bourgeois resistance were also taken over.[16] The Austrian example proved once more that it was not the difficulty of recruiting young Social Democrats for the army which was the decisive factor, but the spirit of the *Reichswehr* and its careful methods of selection of officers and other ranks—methods which the German Social Democrats were unable to change. On the other hand, the Austrian Christian Socials and conservatives remained highly critical not only of Deutsch, but of the Army Law and the new army in general. Dr Rintelen, the *Heimwehr* leader and governor of Styria, did not mince words in a conversation with a British diplomatic representative:

> In his opinion the result will be the creation of a purely Social Democratic army, of little military value, and extremely obnoxious to Christian Socialist opinion. Sooner than have such an army he said that the Christian Socialist Party would prefer to have no army at all in Austria. . . .[17]

In particular the question of the *Volkswehr* lieutenants aroused strong resistance. When the Ministry of War commissioned four

[15] *Wehrgesetz*, 18 Mar. 1920, §§ 25–7, 31: *Staatsgesetzblatt für die Republik Öster-reich*, 1920, pp. 236–7. For Germany, see Carsten, *Reichswehr . . .*, pp. 40, 126.

[16] Deutsch, *Aus Österreichs Revolution*, pp. 140, 143; Bauer, *Österreich. Revolution*, pp. 215–17; K. Haas, 'Studien zur Wehrpolitik . . .', MS, pp. 112–18. For the *Volkswehr* lieutenants, see above, p. 83.

[17] R. F. O. Bridgeman to Lord Curzon, 30 Apr. 1920: PRO, FO 371, File 5445, vol. 3537, no. 196013.

lieutenants of the battalion at Villach at the beginning of 1920, the
government of Carinthia not only protested sharply because it had
not been consulted, but refused to recognize the appointments as
valid—a protest it repeated after some weeks when no reply had been
received. The same attitude was taken by the Tyrolese government
when four NCOs were commissioned there; if the Ministry of War
persisted in its policy of promotion those concerned must leave the
Tyrol.[18] The commanding officer of the Tyrol, Colonel Eccher,
informed the local *Volkswehr* units that he would consider those men
who did not give notice candidates for the new army from whom he
must demand discipline and devotion to duty. He hoped that a new
chapter was starting in the service of the *Volkswehr*; the companies
destined for the new army would be thoroughly trained every morning and afternoon and would be used for guard duties only if absolutely necessary; all unmarried soldiers would have to live in
barracks.[19] He and other officers of the old army were determined to
eradicate the *Volkswehr* spirit as quickly as possible, which was
comparatively easy in the Tyrol and Carinthia, but more difficult in
Vienna.

A new crisis broke out, this time affecting the fate of the coalition
government, when Deutsch in May 1920 published, without prior
discussion in the cabinet, detailed regulations for the trusties (soldiers'
councils) which, in contrast with the Army Law, put the obnoxious
words 'soldiers' councils' in brackets behind the word 'trusties'. The
regulations established the procedure of their election in great detail
and laid down their numbers and rights at the different levels of the
army, from detachment to Ministry of War; in the execution of their
tasks the trusties were not to be impeded nor to be held to account:
they were only responsible to their electors; they could only be transferred with the consent of the trusties attached to the Minister of
War (the Central Soldiers' Council).[20] This decree was sharply
attacked in the press and elsewhere. In the Tyrol, Dr Steidle in
particular criticized the creation of the Central Soldiers' Council at the
Ministry of War, which had not been envisaged in the Army Law, as
well as the far-reaching rights and immunities of the soldiers' councils
which would make it impossible to discipline them; 'the army will

[18] The Carinthian government to Ministry of War, 24 Jan., 4 Mar., 19 Apr. 1920;
the Tyrolese government to the same, 6 Apr. 1920: Landesregierungsarchiv Tirol,
Präsidialakten 1920, I 6 a, II 10 b.
[19] Col. Eccher to Ministry of War, 12 Mar. 1920: Kriegsarchiv Wien, Staatsamt
für Heerwesen, Abt. 5a, 1920, Fasz. 708.
[20] 'Verordnungsblatt des Österreichischen Staatsamtes für Heereswesen', 1920,
no. 26, 29 May 1920, pp. 132–5.

constitute a permanent severe threat to the country, its institutions and public life'. The Tyrolese *Landeshauptmann*, in repeating these points, demanded that the decree be revoked immediately and that the *Land* governments be consulted before any new instructions were issued. Copies of his protest were sent to all *Land* governments 'so as to achieve a uniform attitude'.[21] A few days later the Pan-German deputies in the National Assembly moved urgently that the decree was contrary to the provisions of the Army Law. A Social Democratic deputy replied heatedly and thus provoked not only the Pan-Germans but even more so the Christian Socials. In their name the deputy Kunschak argued that the Social Democrats should say openly whether the Christian Socials as their partners in the coalition must make their decisions according to Social Democratic orders: 'then the coalition has ceased to exist from that moment'.

It turned out that both parties which had long been sharply divided were equally pleased with the idea of terminating it, especially in view of the coming elections. The left wing of the Social Democrats wanted to fight them as an opposition party, to prevent masses of workers from abstaining. But the Pan-Germans were strongly against a coalition with the Christian Socials, whom they accused of 'underhand tactics'—benefiting from being members of the government but posing as 'the strongest opposition party' in front of the electors.[22] According to the British High Commissioner, the Christian Social leaders too would have preferred to go into opposition to fight the elections:

> Messrs Kunschak and Seipl (*sic*), the leaders in question, believe that, if they withdraw from the government now, they will be able in the next few months to form a solid 'bourgeois' block which will . . . secure the downfall of the Social Democrats. . . .[23]

When the matter was discussed in the cabinet the Christian Social spokesman declared that the cabinet could no longer function satisfactorily because Deutsch's decree violated the law and he had usurped a right which could only be exercised by the cabinet. Deutsch, however, had felt empowered to issue the decree by a remark of the chairman at a previous meeting when Deutsch

[21] Dr Steidle to Tyrolese government, the Tyrolese *Landeshauptmann* to Ministry of War, both 5 June 1920: Landesregierungsarchiv Tirol, Präsidialakten 1920, II 10 b.

[22] Jedlicka, *Heer im Schatten* . . . , pp. 29–30; Verwaltungsarchiv Wien, Verhandlungsschriften der 'Grossdeutschen Vereinigung' (meeting of 12 June 1920).

[23] F. O. Lindley to Lord Curzon, 22 May 1920: PRO, FO 371, File 5445, vol. 3538, no. 199727.

submitted detailed regulations about the army's equipment, that such 'minor matters' should be dealt with by the ministers independently, a remark that had not been queried. But the Christian Socials retorted that from this no one could possibly draw the conclusion that he was entitled to issue decrees in 'highly political affairs' without consulting the cabinet. They insisted on resigning, and their resignations were accepted.[24] The Pan-Germans debated whether they should enter a coalition with the Christian Social Party; several deputies were in favour of a bourgeois coalition as in Bavaria; the 'disguised Bolshevism' must end and the Social Democrats be removed from the government. One Pan-German deputy exclaimed cheerfully: 'Out with the Jewish gang!' The Pan-Germans did meet the Christian Socials and tried to impress upon them that there might be civil war and to make them consider what means of power they would have at their disposal. But Dr Seipel considered the situation less dangerous and thought that the Social Democrats were merely threatening. Kunschak declared that the Christian Socials might accept Renner, but not Deutsch, their *bête noire*. Both parties were in favour of a 'neutral' government, but the Social Democrats declined to participate, and the other two parties refused to form it without the Social Democrats or to form a purely bourgeois government. When Deutsch's controversial decree came up for discussion among the party leaders, the Social Democrats refused its revocation, and equally refused to enter a government without Deutsch.[25] To them this was clearly an issue of vital importance, and finally their tactics prevailed, at least for the moment.

In the end the government crisis was solved in a typically Austrian way. An all-party government was formed to conduct official business until after the elections, on the basis of their proportional strength in the National Assembly. The two large parties demanded that the Pan-Germans must re-enter the government, in which they were allocated the Ministry of Justice. No party was to be responsible for any Minister from another party. Renner, who had been responsible for guiding Austria through the turmoil of revolution and to the conclusion of the peace treaty, ceased to be the Chancellor. The new cabinet only had a chairman: the Innsbruck historian Michael Mayr, a leading Christian Social politician, and his party also took over the Ministry of the Interior. But for the next three months Deutsch

[24] Verwaltungsarchiv Wien, Kabinettsratsprotokolle (meetings of 11, 16 and 25 June 1920).

[25] ibid., Verhandlungsschriften der 'Grossdeutschen Vereinigung', meetings of 16, 17, 18 and 23 June 1920.

remained Secretary of State for War, and Renner for Foreign Affairs. After the general election of October the Social Democrats finally left the government.[26]

Many soldiers of the *Volkswehr* were taken over into the new army, and many joined the trade union founded by the Social Democrats which only slowly lost its influence. Under Deutsch's Christian Social successors the soldiers' councils were gradually deprived of their power although they continued to exist at all levels. In 1923 the name was finally changed to 'trusties' because the bourgeois parties strongly objected to that of soldiers' councils.[27] In practice it turned out that the soldiers' councils and the soldiers' union were of real importance only as long as there was a Social Democrat at the head of the War Ministry and of the army. Under non-socialist Ministers they were condemned to political impotence, but they were still able to prevent the Austrian *Bundesheer* from becoming—like the *Reichswehr*—a state within the state and a menace to the state. In contrast with the *Reichswehr* which followed its own political course, the Austrian army simply obeyed the orders of the government, even when ordered to shoot Social Democrats as it did in 1934. There is no reason to suppose that it would have refused to carry out government orders if the Social Democrats had remained in the government.

While the coalition government lasted it was becoming steadily more unpopular, unable to cope with the ever-present food crisis and the economic distress. In November 1919 the Viennese police reported:

The present constitution and the Social Democratic Party are held responsible for all misery and all difficulties. The members of the middle classes, who at first followed the call of Social Democracy not unwillingly because they hoped for an improvement of the situation, are disappointed because, as *they* say, nothing whatever is being done by the government in which Social Democracy has the strongest influence, to alleviate the distress of the people. The government, although it has been in power for a whole year, has not done anything to promote economic improvement. Even the desperate condition of the currency is blamed on the Austrian Republic, and it is alleged that it is only the result of the distrust of foreign countries in a government which lacks the energy to guarantee economic reconstruction. . . .

Moods such as these predominate outside the factories and affect

[26] ibid., Kabinettsratsprotokolle (meetings of 7 July and 25 Oct. 1920); Verhandlungsschriften der 'Grossdeutschen Vereinigung' (meeting of 23 June 1920).
[27] K. Haas, 'Studien zur Wehrpolitik . . .', MS. pp. 125–6, 132–4, 148.

two thirds of the Viennese population. They begin to remember the great merits which Lueger and the Christian Socials gained in the service of Vienna. . . .

There is a general cry for a strong government which would do everything to take into account the needs of the people and further the interests of the *whole* working population of this country. . . .

Only a few days later the police repeated that the population was 'deeply depressed and extremely irritable. The mood is embittered against the government and it is being reproached with neglecting to take in time the precautions necessary to stave off the direst distress. . . '.[28] From Graz too the *gendarmerie* reported that increases in food and tobacco prices caused great excitement in the town and 'vastly increased the embitterment against the government'; the non-organized sections of the working class which had voted for the Social Democrats in February 1919 'are today strongly opposed to this party and to the present government. . . '. This was best illustrated by the fact that the subscriptions to the *Arbeiterwille* of the Social Democrats had fallen from 20,000 to 5,000.[29]

If the population of Vienna and other towns became more and more critical of the government, this applied equally to the small towns and villages of which most of Austria consisted. They were opposed to Vienna on religious as well as on political grounds. Indeed, 'opposed' is a severe understatement and does not describe the mood of hatred which slowly spread in the provinces—hatred of 'red' Vienna, its strong workers' movement, its over-large and allegedly parasitic population which consumed too much food, its Jews, and its government on which both 'reds' and Jews were represented. This mood was particularly strong in the villages where the peasants were being armed and the *Heimwehren* came into being. The peasants sabotaged the food collections for the towns; when military units were sent into the villages to requisition food relations became worse. Occasionally small groups of soldiers or shop-stewards went into the villages near Vienna to obtain food, which aroused the fury of the peasants, especially as such food could be sold again for exorbitant prices. The measures of social welfare inaugurated by the new government were hardly less popular. After all, the peasants did not

[28] Police reports of 17 and 20 Nov. 1919: Verwaltungsarchiv Wien, Staatsamt des Innern, 22/gen., box 4860; 22/NÖ, box 5067.
[29] Landesgendarmeriekommando of Styria to the Styrian government, 6 Dec. 1919: Steiermärk. Landesarchiv, Akten der k.k. Statthalterei—Präsidium, E. 91, 1918 (iv).

work only eight hours, and to them the unemployed who received government benefits were idlers who were unwilling to work. The peasants objected equally to the continuation of measures of war economy, to forced delivery quotas interfering with their rights of private property, and allegedly preserved by an alliance of Jewish war profiteers with the new 'Jewish' government. In the villages of the Lower Austrian district of Krems there was, as early as November 1918, a movement to stop food deliveries to Vienna—until its 'Red Guard' had been disarmed.[30]

Similar difficulties with regard to food deliveries developed in the other *Länder* of Austria. In the Styrian district of Deutschlandsberg, peasants who resisted the requisitioning of cattle by the *gendarmerie* were arrested in January 1919 and their cattle driven away by force. Four Styrian districts delivered virtually no cattle, in spite of all government efforts to convince the peasants that the towns must be fed; the official buyers did not dare to enter the villages; in Graz it was impossible to meet the small meat ration of 6 ounces per head. Hence the Styrian government considered that sharper measures had to be used. But resistance to the requisitioning of cattle continued throughout the province; in one district the peasants used violence, disarmed the requisitioning units and severely maltreated an officer who tried to intervene. In one village hundreds of armed peasants forced the requisitioning *gendarmerie* to withdraw hastily; elsewhere they assembled at a given signal to prevent the driving away of requisitioned cattle. In another village the government representative was almost killed and several *gendarmes* wounded. At Pöllau, in February 1919, the peasants stormed and looted a shop; later they demanded that their leader, who had been arrested, be set free, otherwise they would set fire to the market. One *Bezirkshauptmann* reported in March that the situation in his district was 'getting more dangerous every day. . . '.[31]

In the same month the Tyrolese government announced that several districts had not fulfilled their cattle deliveries; thereupon other districts, which hitherto had fulfilled their quotas, declared they would stop deliveries if the sluggish districts were not forced to do their duty. Thus the government decided to enforce the obligation to

---

[30] Report by Ministry of War, Abt. 5, 18 Nov. 1918: Kriegsarchiv Wien, Staatsamt für Heerwesen 1918, Fasz. 4; in general Bauer, *Österr. Revolution*, pp. 123–4; J. Braunthal, *The Tragedy of Austria*, London, 1948, p. 72.

[31] Protocols of the meetings of the Styrian Diet, 24 Jan. and 13 Mar. 1919; reports of 8 and 15 Mar. 1919: Steiermärk. Landesarchiv, Akten der k.k. Statthalterei—Präsidium, E. 91, 1919–1920.

deliver, if need be by troops. But this was not very successful. The peasants of the Pitztal demanded a price of six crowns per kilo of live weight and, when this was not paid, threatened to drive their cattle home; in one village they besieged the *gendarmerie*. The district of Lienz did not deliver a single kilo of meat but traded their cattle to the Italians. The district of Landeck on Inn, instead of the quota of 105,450 kilos, delivered 14,000 and had arrears of 73,000 kilos, so that in Innsbruck and other towns it was impossible to meet the meat ration.[32] In the spring of 1920 a Social Democratic leader from Leoben threatened that if the peasants did not deliver meat at the official low prices the workers would go and get it; a few thousand men could be quickly assembled and would set fire to the villages: then the peasants would be willing to deliver.[33]

In March 1919 a very worried Ministry of the Interior announced that the peasants in several parts of Austria resisted requisitioning by force and attacked the government agents entrusted with this duty; the authorities of the state were occupied with the task of preventing anarchist or communist attempts to use violence; but it would be impossible in the long run to counter the use of violence by two sides. The unlawful refusals to deliver would lead to forcible requisitioning by industrial workers and the *Volkswehr*, 'which might undermine the whole structure of the state and with which it would be very difficult to cope'. If such developments occurred, food deliveries by the Entente countries might also be affected, and the consequences could be disastrous.[34] In February 1920 a veritable peasant rising occurred in the Lower Austrian village of Ruprechtschofen when farms were visited by search commissions to discover hidden stores of corn. The NCOs of the *Volkswehr* unit at Melk who were employed for this purpose stayed the night at the local inn; there they were sought out in the morning by some thirty peasants who hurled invectives and attacked them. When two *gendarmes* from St Leonhard appeared on the scene they were unable to stop the riot, as the number of the attackers had meanwhile increased to 150 or 200. Three NCOs and the local government secretary who tried to intervene escaped to the first floor where they hid for several hours. The peasants shouted: 'We are living in the republic, we do not know any laws and are free

[32] Landesregierungsarchiv Tirol, Präsidialakten 1919, XII.76.c.2 (decision of 26 Mar. 1919); *Innsbrucker Nachrichten*, 6 May 1919.

[33] Police report, 23 May 1920: Steiermärk. Landesarchiv, Akten der k.k. Statthalterei—Präsidium, E.91, 1918 (iv).

[34] Circular to all *Land* governments, 10 Mar. 1919: Verwaltungsarchiv Wien, Staatsamt des Innern, 22/gen., box 4860.

men', and others wanted to search for the hidden men whom they intended to hang. By midday reinforcements arrived so that the NCOs were àble to return to their unit. Two peasants were arrested and taken to St Leonhard, where hundreds demonstrated and demanded that they be set free. In fact both were released at the beginning of April, and the forcible requisitioning of corn in the area was discontinued.[35] To that extent peasant resistance was successful.

In September 1919 the Upper Austrian Diet expressed its disapproval of 'irresponsible elements who restrain the peasants from delivering food and incite them to pursue demands which cannot be fulfilled'; the authorities should break any resistance to the carrying out of the law with all severity and without regard to person, party or social position. Fifteen months later the *Landeshauptmann* once more sharply condemned the activities of those who tried to obtain the freeing of the cattle trade by threatening to stop deliveries. In the Diet there was general applause at this declaration which again demonstrated how powerless the authorities were when faced by a recalcitrant peasantry.[36] Another factor with which the government was powerless to deal was the progressive devaluation of the crown. As early as December 1918 the Viennese police reported that only well-to-do people were able to buy clothes and shoes for their families in addition to food. At the time of the collapse the crown was still worth 40 Swiss centimes (about 10 American cents), but by the beginning of 1919 its value was only 6 American cents, and a year later less than a tenth of that sum. As the police put it: 'money has become almost valueless'.[37] It was well-nigh impossible to induce the peasants to accept this money at official prices in exchange for their valuable produce, while it fetched far more in the black market.

If the relations between the government and the peasantry were largely dominated by economic issues, the same did not apply to its relations with the governments of the Austrian *Länder*, which were dominated by political conflicts. Of the seven *Länder* which made up the Austrian Republic, the Social Democrats had a small majority only in Lower Austria (and after its separation from Vienna only in

---

[35] ibid., Staatsamt des Innern, 22/NÖ, box 5068 (reports of 27 and 29 Feb. 1920); Kriegsarchiv, Staatsamt für Heerwesen, Abt. 5a, 1920, Fasz. 706 (report of Major H. Ratzenberger, 27 Feb. 1920).

[36] Oberösterreich. Landesarchiv, Landtagsakten no. 28 (meetings of 11 Sept. 1919 and 14 Dec. 1920).

[37] Police reports of 12 Dec. 1918 and 17 Nov. 1919: Polizeiarchiv Wien, Staats- u. sicherheitspol. Agenden 1918, box 9; Verwaltungsarchiv Wien, Staatsamt des Innern, 22/gen., box 4860; Braunthal, *Tragedy of Austria*, p. 43.

Vienna). In the other six *Länder* they gained hardly more than one quarter of the seats in the local Diets in the elections held during the early months of 1919. In the Tyrolese elections of June they lost heavily compared with those of February 1919 and only obtained 11 seats out of 56, while the Christian Social Party gained an absolute majority with 38. In Vorarlberg the Social Democrats obtained 5 seats out of 30, in Upper Austria 22 out of 72.[38] Thus the composition of the central government, in which the Social Democrats held key posts until the autumn of 1920, became more and more obnoxious to the *Länder* governments: hence too the embittered conflicts between them and the Ministry of War about the control of the army, the commissions granted to some NCOs and the role of the soldiers' councils which have been mentioned above. These conflicts were particularly sharp between Vienna and Innsbruck, but they existed also with the other *Land* governments.

Conflict began as soon as the Austrian Republic came into being. On 6 November 1918 the government of Salzburg objected to any democratization of local government (the *Bezirkshauptmannschaften*) which might be planned in Vienna. If it was argued that this was the wish of the population, this did not apply to the Alpine lands: there the people had confidence in the appointed officials, for they guarded its interests in administrative matters better than any laymen who might be elected for political reasons but not on account of their qualifications. Another very weighty reason to object to any 'democratization', the Salzburg government pointed out, was that it would create the same undesirable relationships within the *Länder* that already existed between them and the central government. The Tyrolese government went further in its comment. It supported the arguments put forward by Salzburg and added that any democratization was bound to lead directly to a paralyzing of the whole administration and would increase 'the existing disorder and disintegration in our public affairs'; it would thus meet with 'the most energetic resistance of the local population'.[39] In fact the *Bezirkshauptmannschaften* were not 'democratized', but were made subordinate to the *Land* government in question, thus considerably increasing its powers.[40] The *Bezirkshauptmann* retained his position virtually un-

---

[38] *Protokoll der Verhandlungen des Parteitages der sozialdemokratischen Arbeiterpartei Deutschösterreichs*, 31 Oct.–3 Nov. 1919, Vienna, 1920, p. 57; *Innsbrucker Nachrichten*, 18 and 20 June 1919.

[39] The Salzburg government to the Ministry of the Interior, 6 Nov., the Tyrolese government on 21 Nov. 1918: Landesregierungsarchiv Tirol, Präsidialakten 1918, I.6.a.

[40] Verwaltungsarchiv Wien, Kabinettsratsprotokolle, 23 Nov. 1918.

changed, exactly as the *Landrat* in Prussia; in both countries the revolution failed to achieve the 'democratization' of this highly important office. Therefore the Social Democrats continued to criticize the *Bezirkshauptleute*, 'who today still feel like the dictators of the old Austria and still believe that they can disregard the demands of the people for self-government'. But the Pan-Germans considered them the only institution that 'is still functioning'.[41]

At the beginning of December 1918 the Secretary of State for Food complained in the cabinet about the *Land* governments which were exceeding their competences with regard to food shipments; he asked for remedies to be adopted, otherwise it would be impossible to maintain a central food administration. His plea was supported by two other State Secretaries who also accused the *Land* governments of arbitrary actions in their fields; both were Christian Socials, not Social Democrats. New complaints about the passive, and in many cases disobedient attitude of the *Land* governments towards the Viennese central Ministries were raised only two weeks later.[42] At the beginning of 1919 the Under-Secretary of State for Trade spoke at length about the 'pernicious regionalism' of the *Länder* which even during the war caused passive resistance to Vienna in the administration; through the revolution this turned into complete disintegration; the danger now was that these arbitrary actions, often caused by passing emergencies, became a permanent state of affairs and would make impossible any central direction of the administration; political considerations, which might be summed up in the slogan 'Away from Vienna!', were an additional factor; its basis was the hazy notion of a danger allegedly threatening from Vienna; a city of two millions was felt to be something intolerable, a parasitic weight on the population of the rest of the state; there were also certain political differences in the attitude of the population; the *Länder* did not want their political attitude to be dictated by the capital, and the great mass of the rural population feared that unrest in Vienna could lead to a political development similar to that in Berlin which had done great damage (this was a few days after the fight for the palace in Berlin which ended in a government defeat). The Secretary of State for Agriculture agreed with most of the points made by the speaker; the dislike of Vienna was caused partly by the *Volkswehr* which constituted a potential danger to the population, and partly by the

[41] Arbeiterkammer Wien, Protokoll der II. Reichskonferenz der Arbeiterräte Deutschösterreichs, 4. Sitzung, p. 6 (3 July 1919); Verwaltungsarchiv, Verhandlungsschriften der 'Grossdeutschen Vereinigung' (meeting of 22 Oct. 1919).

[42] Verwaltungsarchiv, Kabinettsratsprotokolle, 2 and 14 Dec. 1918.

continuing existence of the various central offices.[43] In this case too, the speakers were not Social Democrats. The Christian Social Ministers in Vienna were unable to overcome the hostile attitude of their own party friends.

Centrifugal tendencies equally appeared when representatives of the *Länder* met the central government to discuss the future constitution at the beginning of February. According to the Carinthian representative, the *Länder* adopted 'a sharply negative point of view against Vienna. Words were heard such as: "We do not need a walking school for the handicapped; we do not need tutelage or dictatorship, and we want to decide for ourselves what hitherto has been done by the State Council. . . . We will reach an agreement between the *Länder* without Vienna; in other words, we reserve full powers to ourselves." ' According to this report, Vorarlberg—which at that time aimed at uniting with Switzerland—was particularly vocal. The representatives of Salzburg and the Tyrol declared that they would decide within a few days whether they would unite with Germany on their own and cut all links with Vienna; those of Carinthia—threatened by the Yugoslavs—did not reject cooperation with Vienna but emphasized the special character of their country, which must be preserved.[44] When the *Landeshauptleute* of the Austrian *Länder* met in April, those of Salzburg, Tyrol and Upper Austria stood out for complete autonomy of the *Länder*; the influence of the Viennese government was steadily declining in the provinces.[45] During the spring of 1919 the central government was preoccupied with the Communist danger in Vienna and the interferences of the Béla Kun government. The more Vienna seemed to veer towards the left, the greater the gulf became which separated it from the provinces.

In May delegates from the Alpine lands met at Salzburg. The Deputy *Landeshauptmann* of Salzburg, Dr Rehrl, accused Vienna of taking no notice of the wishes and proposals of the *Länder* and of issuing decrees without consulting them; this tutelage by Vienna, which showed itself in the smallest matters, was causing continuous friction because the central government did not respect the rights of the *Länder*. According to Rehrl, Chancellor Renner aimed at introducing in Austria the English county system, but this would violate the legislative rights of the *Länder* which were to be made illusory by

[43] ibid., 3 Jan. 1919.
[44] Kärntner Landesarchiv, Umsturzzeit, Lt.V/17 (report of 6 Feb. 1919).
[45] ibid., Landesausschuss, Fasz. II, no. 8 (9 Apr. 1919).

administrative measures. Legislation in economic matters should be delegated to the *Länder* which must form the basis of the Austrian state if the *Anschluss* did not succeed; but even if it did succeed they must remain the foundation; the *Länder* should also remain responsible for security matters. Another speaker criticized the policy pursued by the central government which only called forth separatist tendencies in the *Länder*.[46] Another meeting of the *Länder* representatives, held at Innsbruck in June, discussed the question of how they could protect themselves against a Soviet government: this would be difficult for Upper Austria where there were few arms and a frontier that could not be protected, easier for Styria, and easiest for the Tyrol which had weapons galore. The *gendarmerie* was to be strengthened, and arms were to be distributed to reliable groups.[47] The Pan-Germans considered that the *Länder* must take precautions so as not to become the victims of a Soviet government; in Vienna there existed a dual government; the responsibility for this state of affairs lay with the government's weakness and its inability to obtain credit.[48] The term dual government probably referred to the *Volkswehr* and the strong power wielded by the soldiers' councils. The government of Salzburg did take precautions against the danger of internal unrest by requesting help from Bavaria. It feared apparently that in such an eventuality the *Volkswehr* would not be reliable, or rather that it could only count on 'two companies with capable officers as a last, reliable reserve'. In Bavaria the request met with official approval, for it was considered 'important to have in the south a bastion of trustworthy, German Austrian forces against the dangers threatening the government'.[49] During the following months the cooperation between the reactionary forces of Bavaria and those of Salzburg and the Tyrol became much closer.[50]

From Klagenfurt a correspondent wrote to Adler in May 1919 that there was strong anti-semitism as well as a movement 'Away from Vienna!' which was supported by the Peasant League, the Christian Socials and the German Democrats. Another Carinthian Social Democrat complained about the strength of local particularism

[46] 'Protokoll über die Konferenz der alpenländischen Delegierten in Salzburg', 12 May 1919: Landesarchiv Salzburg, Präsidialakten 1919, 1–9.

[47] Verwaltungsarchiv Wien, Verhandlungsschriften der 'Grossdeutschen Vereinigung' (meeting of 25 June 1919). I have not found any protocol of this meeting.

[48] ibid., meeting of 2 July 1919.

[49] Dr Ewinger, State Commissar for South Bavaria, to Prime Minister Hoffmann, 29 June 1919: Bayer. Hauptstaatsarchiv, Geh. Staatsarchiv, MA. 100412.

[50] See above, pp. 269–70.

and separatism. He maintained that it was above all the merit of the
workers' councils to have made it clear to the local gentry 'that they
could not create an independent Carinthia, a Carinthian Republic,
an "Away from Vienna", or an Alpine Republic without the
workers. . . '.[51] That there was more to this than mere rumour is
confirmed by a curious approach made in June by the Italian
General Segré to the government of Carinthia: he expressed his
astonishment 'that in Carinthia tendencies were noticeable to
separate from Vienna, which made an unfavourable impression on
the Italians'.[52] The head of the British Military Mission, on the other
hand, when reporting on certain reforms in the local *Volkswehr*,
which he described as 'a partisan gang, set up for political purposes
by the Socialist Party', commented:

> The changes are slow but are evident. In consequence of the
> negligent or really harmful attitude of the Viennese authorities,
> the Carinthian government is ignoring the latter, carrying out the
> modifications on its own responsibility and is not informing
> Vienna of the steps it is taking so as to avoid the inevitable inter-
> ference of the Viennese Socialists. . . .[53]

The British general was clearly well primed by the Carinthian
officers with whom he associated and whose hostile views on the
Volkswehr and the soldiers' councils he forwarded to London.

What it looked like in a rural area of Lower Austria in the summer
of 1919, another correspondent told Adler:

> The reactionaries have worked hard, and there is a white terror.
> Our party officers could take the German Nationalists as their
> example of how one has to work in the country politically and
> organizationally. Although in the Waidhofen district even in the
> villages half the population is proletarian (real wage earners), not
> a soul dares any longer to profess himself a Social Democrat. . . .
> An intellectual here can only bestir himself if he is as rich as the
> Sheikh. But real proletarians cannot dare to do so. . . .

He feared a terrible awakening.[54] In July the government of Styria
informed Vienna that Styria would separate from Vienna if the

---

[51] Alois Steiner to Adler, 22 May 1919: Arbeiterkammer Wien, Adlerarchiv;
Protokoll der II. Reichskonferenz der Arbeiterräte Deutschösterreichs, 1. Sitzung,
p. 54 (30 June 1919), ibid.

[52] Kärntner Landesarchiv, Landesausschuss, Fasz. II, no. 8 (30 June 1919).

[53] Brig. Gen. Delmer Radcliffe to the Chief of the Imperial General Staff, 18
Sept. 1919: PRO, FO 371, File 123, vol. 3510, no. 135177. For his attitude to the
Volkswehr, see above p. 100.

[54] Emil Schisko to Adler, s.d.: Arbeiterkammer Wien, Adlerarchiv. Waidhofen
is situated on the Ybbs, a tributary of the Danube.

Communists brought about a change of government there; the wavering attitude of the central government vis-à-vis the Communist menace caused the conviction to spread among the population that in that case the fate of Styria should not remain linked with that of Vienna.[55]

When the Social Democrats assembled for their party congress in the autumn of 1919 Karl Seitz attacked the separatism of the *Länder* because it prevented the use of water power for hydro-electric purposes:

> The separatism of the *Länder* was already attracting unfavourable notice during the war. Each single *Land* makes itself independent and watches jealously so as not to let anything go outside, to use all natural resources within the *Land*. This nonsense has found protagonists in all *Länder* and they have protested against the use of the water. It is the same thing when some *Länder* close their frontiers to their ores, others to their food. . . . This is one of the saddest developments: if it continues it will inevitably lead to the disintegration of the state. . . .

A leading Tyrolese Social Democrat accused his party comrades in the government, especially Chancellor Renner, of being too soft-hearted towards the bourgeois; at Innsbruck the Social Democrats had been willing to oppose sharply the separatism of the Christian Socials; but then the latter showed them a telegram or another communication from the Chancellor which proved that the comrades in the government were less determined than those of Innsbruck. He attributed the separatism of the *Länder* to the fact that they were not viable, with the sole exception of Upper Austria. The Tyrol and Salzburg depended on German tourists who brought money into the country, and Carinthia too was a tourist country; only in Styria it was somewhat different on account of the iron and coal deposits.[56] But the influence of the Social Democrats was declining and they alone were unable to counter the strong tendencies towards *Land* autonomy which made themselves felt in every sphere, political, economic and military. The British military representative attributed this above all to fear:

> The attitude of the provinces is dictated not only by the fear of isolation, but also by the fear of the political upset sure to be

[55] The Styrian Landes-Ausschuss to the Austrian State Chancery, 3 July 1919: Verwaltungsarchiv Wien, Staatsamt des Innern, 22/gen., box 4860.

[56] *Protokoll der Verhandlungen des Parteitages* . . . , 31 Oct.–3 Nov. 1919, pp. 153, 162.

created in Vienna by any continuation of such desperate circumstances. . . .[57]

Apart from the widespread fear of Bolshevism, mentioned also by
the police, there were several other factors involved. Historically,
there was the fact that 'German Austria' had never been one state,
but only linked, before 1918, by a common bond of loyalty to the
ruling house which had accumulated these lands in the course of
centuries. With the disappearance of the Habsburgs there was very
little that these lands had in common, even less than the German
states which Bismarck had united. There was the common Catholic-
ism, but with the Social Democrats ruling in Vienna this became a
divisive rather than a unifying factor. The industrial revolution and
the working-class movement that sprang from it caused deep fissures
in Austrian society which, outside Vienna and a few other towns,
remained rural and traditional, highly critical of Vienna, its culture,
its quick development in many fields, its cosmopolitanism, its Jews
and its socialists. This antipathy was fanned and exploited by the
Church and the Christian Social Party. Or to put it differently: after
only a very short interval did the natural weight of the provinces and
their largely rural population assert itself, as did the strong Catholic-
ism of the Tyrol and other areas. Although Germany was divided
religiously and also contained many rural areas, the Hohenzollerns
forged a greater unity than the Habsburgs. The Prussian state
created by the ruling house was more uniform and more centralized
than the Austrian territories, and surprisingly enough it survived
even the revolution of 1918 with its institutions intact. Although
there were separatist tendencies in Bavaria and elsewhere they were
easily suppressed. But the really unifying force in 1919 was the army:
it crushed any left-wing extremism which in the case of Bavaria
might have developed into separatism. In this respect too, the
creation of the Hohenzollern kings proved more durable than that
of the Habsburgs. The Austrian army disintegrated and had to be
replaced by the *Volkswehr*. The Prussian army survived even the
defeat of 1918, and the officer corps of the *Reichswehr* was the direct
successor to that of the Prussian army. In this respect the history of
Austria and of Germany differed fundamentally in the years
after 1918.

[57] Report by Lt.-Col. Cuninghame, 17 Oct. 1919: PRO, FO 371, File 5445, vol.
3531, no. 144566.

12 A Revolution Defeated

Was there a revolution in Germany and Austria in October-November 1918, or merely a military collapse, a successful mutiny of the defeated armies and navies? This thesis has often been put forward, sometimes together with another: that the reforms of October 1918 and the formation of the government of Prince Max of Baden transformed Germany into a constitutional monarchy in which the decisive political powers were wielded by parliament, and no longer by the emperor. If the result of the revolution was the achievement of parliamentary democracy, this had been so to say anticipated by the constitutional reforms, hence the revolution was 'unnecessary'. As so often in the course of German history, a successful 'revolution from above' had pre-empted the revolution from below. This thesis, put forward above all by Arthur Rosenberg,[1] takes no account of the spontaneous mass movement which, starting from Kiel and Wilhelmshaven, within a few days engulfed a whole country and everywhere led to the assumption of political power by revolutionary organs, the workers' and soldiers' councils. These councils had not been planned nor were they organized by any political party or group, although workers' councils came into being in both Germany and Austria during the great strikes of January 1918 and the idea of the councils was clearly borrowed from Russia. Almost simultaneously they sprang up everywhere, in every state and every town, and they did not start with workers', but with soldiers' councils elected by the military units at home and at the front, in barracks and on board battleships. It is this vast and impressive movement, carried out with almost military discipline, that gives the lie to the allegation that there was no revolution but only a collapse. What started as a naval mutiny within a few days overthrew a mighty empire which seemed to have been built for eternity.

Nor was it the last imperial Chancellor, Prince Max of Baden, who appointed his successor as he attempted to do on 9 November: the new government of 'the People's Representatives' was formed in negotiations between the two socialist parties and confirmed in office

[1] *The Birth of the German Republic, 1871–1918*, London, 1931, pp. 247–9, 254, 273.

by the organ of the revolution, the workers' and soldiers' councils of Berlin, in a plenary meeting of 10 November. Their Executive Committee equally appointed the new government of Prussia and even the chief of police of Berlin. Similar events took place in Munich and the capitals of the other German states. Everywhere the local workers' and soldiers' councils took measures immediately after their formation to maintain law and order, to carry through the demobilization of the armed forces and to guarantee food supplies. As they had no means of doing this themselves they used the existing administrative authorities, over which they established political control. None of the authorities resisted this 'take-over' or disputed the revolutionary authority of the workers' and soldiers' councils; although a few leading civil servants resigned the large majority obeyed the new masters. If there had been resistance or opposition the workers' and soldiers' councils might have been tempted to a much more radical interference with the existing machinery of government, or to carrying out large-scale replacements of recalcitrant reactionary officials. The spontaneous mass movement also forced the hands of the political leaders: it condemned to impotence, at least for the moment, the leaders of the bourgeois parties, and it compelled the reluctant Social Democrats to put themselves at its head. It was immaterial whether Ebert hated 'the revolution like sin':[2] he had to become its leader—or to leave the leadership in rival hands. He did not become the Reich Chancellor, but the chairman of the Council of People's Representatives, and he owed his dignity to the workers' and soldiers' councils.

The case of Austria is more difficult; there the workers' and soldiers' councils did not take over political power, the new government was a coalition government of the three political parties, and it was appointed by a provisional National Assembly composed of the German deputies of the former *Reichsrat*. The Christian Social leader Dr Seipel was quite justified when he pointed out to a German colleague in December 1918:

> The party coalition has remained in force until this moment, no major unrest has disturbed the bourgeois order. . . . You must not overlook the fact that with us the National Assembly in which all parties cooperate has not been pushed aside for one moment, while you have no Reichstag and therefore no legal government. . . .[3]

[2] See Groener's letter of 5 Feb. 1936: Bundesarchiv-Militärarchiv, Nachlass Groener, box 8, no. 37.
[3] Seipel to ?, 17 Dec. 1918: Haus-, Hof- u. Staatsarchiv, Nachlass Otto Bauer, Karton 262, enclosed in letter from L. M. Hartmann to Bauer, Berlin, 14 Jan. 1919.

It is true, of course, that in Germany all this was to change within a few weeks: a National Assembly was elected in January 1919 and a coalition government with bourgeois parties was formed soon after. But during November and December 1918 Germany was considerably more revolutionary than Austria, while during the spring of 1919 the opposite became true. Yet in Austria too a revolution had occurred. The German deputies of the *Reichsrat* had not authority to appoint a provisional government, the emperor was forced to renounce the exercise of his constitutional powers, and the Habsburg state disappeared for good. It was replaced by something entirely new: a state of the German-speaking provinces which also claimed authority over German-speaking Bohemia and Moravia. This in itself was a revolutionary act as these provinces had never formed a state, had never been more closely united than they were with the non-German-speaking provinces. 'German Austria' was the product of a constitutional and political revolution, although great efforts were made from the outset to disguise this fact. Revolutionary, too, was the *Volkswehr* which immediately replaced the disintegrating Imperial and Royal Army. But workers' and soldiers' councils played a far less important part than they did in Germany, at least during the first few weeks of the revolution; later they became of major importance, especially in the *Volkswehr*.

In both countries, the strength of the extreme left, the Communists, was insignificant, and there never was any serious danger of a Bolshevist development. In both countries, the working class was only a minority of the population, concentrated in certain large towns, but the Communists did not even succeed in winning over a sizable proportion of the working class. Their *Putschist* tactics only deepened the split within the working-class movement, drove the moderate Social Democrats to the right and strengthened the conservatives and the political right in general. The fear of Bolshevism became a very potent political weapon. Huge posters proclaimed all over Germany: 'Anarchy is the helper of reaction and famine', and pictured 'the Danger of Bolshevism' in the form of Death holding a blood-dripping dagger in his teeth. The most intelligent leaders of the Communists—people like Leo Jogiches or Rosa Luxemburg—were fully aware of the fact that the Communists must first win over the masses before there was any hope of establishing the 'dictatorship of the proletariat', that battles joined prematurely would only lead to catastrophe. They were driven into these battles by the revolutionary enthusiasm of their followers or—in the case of Austria—even more so by the promptings from Budapest. In 1918–1919 there is virtually no evidence of any direct intervention from Moscow in the same sense; even Karl Radek did his best to prevent an attempt at a seizure of power in January 1919. But the super-radicalism and utopianism of Spartacist propaganda provided the extreme right with its first chance after November 1918.

The elections of January-February 1919 proved that the majority of the population did not want any socialist experiments and seemed satisfied with the political and constitutional changes which had been introduced. A 'second revolution' would not find large popular support, except in certain industrial areas. As the armistice was concluded simultaneously with the political revolution, the slogan of 'peace' could no longer be used by the extreme left, as it was in Russia after February 1917; nor were the peasants willing to join a revolutionary movement. Even the slogan of 'socialization' of the industries 'ripe' for this measure did not arouse much popular enthusiasm. If the aim of the revolution was not socialism, in whatever form, but the protection of private property, this did not necessarily imply that it would remain limited to the political and constitutional field. It aimed at 'democratization'—democratization in the political, administrative, military and economic spheres. But even in this it was only very partially successful. It did gain the introduction of the parliamentary system and of the equal and direct franchise, in Germany as well as in Austria, and this was perhaps the most significant gain. The adoption of the parliamentary system had been the most important political aim of the working-class movement in the pre-war period, the aim of generations of Social Democrats ever since the days of Lassalle and Bebel. It is hardly surprising that Ebert wanted to leave the decision on the question of monarchy or republic to a National Assembly. Nor is it surprising that the first national congress of the German workers' and soldiers' councils in December 1918 decided that a National Assembly was to meet as soon as possible. This was the true tradition of Social Democracy, and even the Independent Social Democrats only aimed at postponing its meeting. This, however, implied that if the elections resulted in a bourgeois majority, Germany and Austria would become bourgeois democracies.

Yet 'democratization' was not achieved in other fields. The power of the Prussian *Landrat* and of the Austrian *Bezirkshauptmann* remained unchanged and was not replaced by that of an elected authority. Everywhere in Germany and Austria the officials of the old régime were encouraged to stay in office and to carry out their duties as before. The attempts of local workers' and soldiers' councils to have particularly obnoxious officials removed came to nothing because they were backed by their superiors in the bureaucratic apparatus which survived virtually intact. Even those who openly demonstrated their contempt of the new order or their monarchist sympathies were kept in office; so was Under-Secretary of State Dr Solf, who refused to shake hands with his superior Minister because the latter had allegedly taken Russian money. What is more important, people like Solf very quickly acquired a far-reaching influence on the policy and decisions of the new government.[4] The whole judicial machinery, too, remained intact, as the judges were considered irremovable—to the detriment of later political jurisdiction. As early as January 1919 the philosopher Ernst Troeltsch wrote:

> The civil service (*Beamtenschaft*) has continued virtually without any changes of personnel. The officials, even the most conservative, have accepted the facts and stay in office, but govern, talk and conduct themselves entirely in the old style. . . .[5]

In Germany and Austria, the civil service also included the judiciary, as well as the teaching personnel of the universities and schools. It is true that the local and regional administration was for a time supervised ('controlled') by the workers' and soldiers' councils; but after a few months this supervision lapsed, and the whole state apparatus re-emerged in full strength, with a new consciousness of its power and influence.[6]

In Germany the same applied even more markedly in the military sphere. The government of the People's Representatives was convinced that it needed the cooperation of the officer corps to bring back the armies from west and east and to carry through their demobilization. This enabled the High Command to put forward political demands immediately. Later, cooperation with it became even more essential in the eyes of the government in view of the dangers emanating from the Poles in the east and from the Spartacists at home. Officers with democratic views and units organized by Social Democrats or Democrats were considered 'unreliable' and pushed aside. Officers who proudly proclaimed that they were monarchists and loyal to the fugitive emperor were believed to be

[4] See above, pp. 45, 132, 296.
[5] Ernst Troeltsch, *Spektator-Briefe*, 1924, p. 37, quoted by Reinhard Rürup, *Probleme der Revolution in Deutschland 1918/19*, Wiesbaden, 1968, p. 57, n. 49.
[6] ibid., p. 36.

'reliable' and worthy of leading the new army. Groener aimed at keeping intact the old officer corps with its anti-democratic spirit and its antiquated social composition and code of honour, and he was entirely successful in doing so.[7] While certain changes of personnel were later made in the Prussian bureaucracy, the army knew how to defend itself against any outside interference. But in Austria the *Volkswehr* proved that it was possible to recruit an army permeated by a spirit of loyalty, not to the Habsburgs, but to the new republican order. More than that: the Viennese *Volkswehr* proved that it was possible to combine the institution of the soldiers' councils with a republican army. But the *Volkswehr* did not last and was soon replaced by a more conservative and traditional army.

Once the immediate shock of the revolution was absorbed, the social forces which had dominated the former empires, the bureaucracy, the officer corps, the bankers and industrialists, the leaders of the more conservative parties and of the churches, strenuously tried to regain the ground which they had lost and to reoccupy the leading positions to which they felt entitled. They quickly found out that this could also be done in a parliamentary democracy, that social change —even if it could not be postponed for ever—could at least be postponed for a long time. Otto Bauer was absolutely right when he wrote in 1919:

> Democracy in the state is not yet realized with the transfer of the highest legislative power to a parliament elected by a general and equal franchise. Democracy also demands that the local administration in *Land*, district and commune should be transferred to democratic and representative institutions. . . .[8]

He could have added that democracy further demands the breaking of the influence of the old ruling orders and of their virtual monopoly of the positions of power. It seems that neither the German nor the Austrian Social Democrats understood the importance of this change. They may not have been strong enough to carry it out, but they were apparently not aware of the issue, or perhaps they trusted that political democracy would eventually also lead to social change. As far as the German Social Democrats were concerned, they were far too preoccupied with the danger threatening them from the left to be able to assess the situation realistically. To them, the danger from the right seemed to be non-existent, or at least far less serious

---

[7] Groener, *Lebenserinnerungen*, pp. 467–8.

[8] Otto Bauer, *Der Weg zum Sozialismus*, 2nd ed., Vienna, 1919, p. 12. The importance of this issue was also realized by many local workers' and soldiers' councils.

than that from the left. The same cannot be said of the Austrian Social Democrats, but they had no means of overcoming the opposition of the Christian Social Party, of the Church and of the governments of the *Länder*, which started at the time of the revolution.

The opposition of the entrenched forces of the bureaucracy, the officer corps, the churches, the middle classes and their parties did not show itself as quickly in Germany as it did in Austria, but it developed nevertheless. It could have been overcome under very favourable circumstances—for example, if the war had continued and everything had had to be subordinated to its prosecution, or if Germany had refused to sign the Treaty of Versailles. In any case, a continuation of the revolutionary impetus of November would have been essential, but this soon petered out, and only survived locally in the form of a left-wing *Putsch* or the establishment of a Councils' Republic by left-wing extremists. Instead of inspiring the working class to further revolutionary deeds, these attempts only succeeded in alienating its more moderate sections and in provoking a reaction of the political right. They diminished, rather than increased the chances of a further revolutionary development. They also served to discredit the whole idea of the councils which were wrongly identified with left-wing extremism and 'Bolshevism'. In February 1919 the well-known pacifist Friedrich Wilhelm Foerster wrote to Eisner how much he regretted 'that the idea of the councils has been so badly compromised by the Russian "examples" '; above all, he thought, the council system must no longer be opposed to the National Assembly. And during the same month a member of the Central Council in Berlin remarked that it had to be taken into account 'that the workers' and soldiers' councils have aroused hatred in wide circles by several mistakes which cannot be denied. . . .'[9] The only German left-wing party which was in favour of preserving the councils, the Independent Social Democrats, was badly split on this issue. Its left wing more or less identified the council system with the dictatorship of the proletariat and was busy developing schemes of 'pure' councils; while its right wing gradually approximated to the position of the Social Democrats who believed that, with the meeting of the National Assembly and the election of local representative assemblies, the councils had fulfilled their functions and might be dispensed with.

Indeed, from the outset the German Social Democratic leaders, in

[9] Foerster to Eisner, 11 Feb. 1919: Int. Inst. of Social History, Amsterdam, Kleine Korrespondenz; Kolb (ed.), *Zentralrat . . .*, no. 92, p. 721 (26 Feb. 1919).

Berlin and in the provinces, took their stand against the workers' and soldiers' councils. Although the large majority of them were firmly controlled by members of their own party, the party leaders associated them with 'disorder' and 'chaos' which must be avoided at all cost. How could the armies be brought back safely if disorder spread in Germany? How could the food supplies be guaranteed and the railways continue to run if strikes spread in the country? How could the officials be expected to carry on with their work if this was being 'interfered with' by local councils? How could democratic freedoms be established if they curtailed the freedom of the press? How could the independence of the judiciary be guaranteed if some local councils intervened in the process of the law? These considerations made Ebert, Scheidemann and Landsberg bitterly hostile to the councils as such and induced them to side with the bureaucracy which, naturally enough, deeply resented any interference with its age-old methods of administration—and that by revolutionary organs composed of 'red' socialists. It was not equally natural that the leading Social Democrats sided so absolutely against a movement that was not hostile to them and might have given them valuable support. But they feared a Bolshevik development and saw in the council movement a confirmation of this fear. Hence they were once again driven back to rely on the old powers which they considered a factor of stability—without which they would not be able to hold out successfully against the forces of disorder and disintegration.[10] In doing so they considerably deepened the split which rent the German working-class movement. The breach, which had been caused by differing attitudes towards the war and the granting of war credits, became a breach over the policy to be pursued towards the National Assembly and the councils, which were seen as alternatives, as forms of government diametrically opposed to each other.

For all these reasons the revolutionary impetus was soon replaced by internecine conflict which was to remain characteristic of the German working-class movement until its defeat by Hitler. It has often been argued that it was the split between Social Democrats and Independents—and later between Social Democrats and Communists—that brought about this disaster. But the Austrian example shows that a united working-class movement (the Communists being unimportant) was equally defeated. As the revolution of 1918 failed to destroy the strength of the forces opposed to it they quickly revived. As the left wing did not succeed in propelling the revolution

[10] Matthias, *Regierung der Volksbeauftragten*, i, p. cxxix.

on to a more radical course, the old social forces were able to stage a comeback. This seems to be the fundamental difference between the French Revolution of 1789 and the revolution of 1918. In France, Paris and the *sans-culottes* time and again provided a new impetus which forced the revolutionary movement on to a more radical path and thus destroyed not only the *ancien régime*, but with it the former ruling classes and its institutions, the nobility, the bureaucracy, the army and the Church. A century and a quarter later this did not happen in central Europe. There were important political and constitutional changes, but the social system remained. The working class alone was too weak to enforce the 'democratization' of society. In Germany, even the nobility retained its large estates and its privileged position in the service of the state. The institutions created by the Hohenzollern kings—above all the army and the bureaucracy —survived and gained new strength. Eighteen months after the outbreak of the revolution the Social Democrats were pushed out of the government which passed into the hands of the moderate and conservative parties. Germany remained a parliamentary democracy, but only for another ten years.

In Austria, the working class was much weaker than in Germany and surrounded by even more hostile forces. Hence the Social Democrats put all their hopes in the *Anschluss*, an *Anschluss* that would bring them the support of the much stronger German socialist movement. At the end of 1918 the Party Executive issued a proclamation to the electors:

> For us there remains only one way: the *Anschluss* with Germany. . . .
> Now a new Germany has arisen: the Hohenzollerns have been chased away; the German people have freed themselves from the rule of Prussianism; in the great German socialist people's republic the German working class in fierce struggles is fighting to achieve socialism! This Germany displeases our ruling classes. . . . But we desire to join red Germany! The German-Austrian Republic must join the great all-German Republic as a separate federal state! The *Anschluss* with Germany now means joining socialism![11]

These were the hopes of 1918; they were soon buried. The Austrian Social Democrats—even more than their German comrades—were driven on to the defensive. This was emphasized when Otto Bauer, two years later, addressed the party congress of the Austrian Social Democrats:

[11] Proclamation of 29 Dec. 1918: *Protokoll der Verhandlungen des Parteitages der sozialdemokrarischen Arbeiterpartei Deutschösterreichs*, 31 Oct.–3 Nov. 1919, Vienna, 1920, p. 41.

We stand by the principle of the bourgeois republic. The bourgeois republic does not mean the emancipation of the proletariat, but it provides, to quote a phrase of Marx, the most favourable ground for the struggle for the emancipation of the proletariat. Thus we will in the first instance have to defend this bourgeois republic against reactionaries, against monarchist attempts. . . . We all know, further, that from Bavaria and from Hungary attempts are being supported to form here the reactionary *Heimwehren*, to arm and to organize them, to prepare an army for the counter-revolution. . . .

It was therefore necessary to continue 'a policy of caution, of taking the facts into account'. Bauer still hoped that this period might soon reach its end, that a new period was beginning when the working class would be able to fight its enemies 'with freer hands', that it would regain its freedom of movement.[12] These hopes too were to be disappointed. In Germany, although the great crisis of 1923 did offer new opportunities to the socialists they were not used. The next great crisis, that of the 1930s, saw the working class once more on the defensive and brought about its disastrous defeat; and the same occurred in Austria.

After all that has been said it may seem unnecessary to point out how fundamentally different from the events described above was the course of the Russian revolution, which proceeded from a moderate to a more radical phase, culminated in the Bolshevik seizure of power and ended in a party dictatorship. One fundamental difference, which Otto Bauer emphasized as early as 1 November 1918, was that in Russia the peasants were an active revolutionary class which aimed at the expropriation of the large estates; but in central Europe the peasants nowhere joined the revolutionary movement *en masse*. Another important difference was that in Russia the war continued for another year after the beginning of the revolution so that the longing of the masses for peace benefited the one party which promised an immediate end to hostilities. In central Europe the revolution and the end of the war coincided; hence the extreme left was deprived of what was the most effective weapon in the Bolshevik armoury. In Russia thanks to these circumstances, the Bolsheviks were able to gain control of some of the most important urban Soviets before their seizure of power; but in central Europe the Councils remained firmly under the influence of the Social Democrats or—in certain cases—the Independents. It was

[12] *Protokoll der Verhandlungen des Parteitages der sozialdemokratischen Arbeiterpartei Deutschösterreichs*, 5–7 Nov. 1920, Vienna, 1920, pp. 144–6.

only in Munich and in Hungary that the Councils, for a short period, came under Communist influence, but this was terminated by the victory of the counter-revolution. Yet even in Russia the vast majority of the Soviets, those in the villages and small towns, were not controlled by the Bolsheviks; and when the Constituent Assembly finally met at the end of 1917 it turned out that the large majority of the deputies belonged to the revolutionary peasant party, the Socialist Revolutionaries. The Bolshevik reply to this challenge was the forcible dissolution of the Constituent Assembly—a decisive step on the road to party dictatorship. But dictatorship and Soviet power were incompatible, and the Soviets too were made subject to the ruling party and ceased to be an organ of revolutionary democracy. The influence of the Soviets faded away, and elections to them became a farce. They had played an important part in the Bolshevik seizure of power; but the slogan 'All power to the Soviets!' meant in practice 'All power to the Bolshevik Party!' In Germany and Austria the democratic course was never seriously in doubt.

The workers' and soldiers' councils of central Europe did not decisively influence the course of the revolution. They were too much subject to local influences and lacked any central direction. This was provided neither by the Executive Committee of the Berlin workers' and soldiers' councils, which stood to the left of most local councils, nor by the Central Council elected by the national congress of the councils in December. As things were, effective central direction could only have come from the German Social Democratic Party or the trade unions linked with it; but both were opposed to the councils and wanted them to disappear as soon as possible, although most councils were Social Democratic in their politics. The Social Democratic leaders believed that they could not manage the government of a defeated and badly suffering country without the 'experts', including the officer corps. This meant in practice depriving the soldiers' councils of their powers; the army demobilized itself, and in the volunteer units there were no soldiers' councils. With the disappearance of the soldiers' councils the workers' councils lost half their strength, especially as they did not cooperate with the peasant councils. In Austria, the reverse applied. The powerful soldiers' councils were not supported by equally strong workers' councils, not even in Vienna; and in the provinces neither acquired much influence. The German left-wing party, the Independent Social Democrats, lost whatever power it had by 'boycotting' the elections to the Central Council and by resigning from the government some days later, followed by the same tactics of abstention in Prussia and other states. In doing so they condemned themselves to political impotence, and helped to bring about the early demise of the workers' and soldiers' councils.

It is, of course, a matter of speculation what might have happened in Germany if the tactics of both socialist parties had not been so hopelessly inadequate: if Ebert had not concluded his 'alliance' with the officer corps, if the Independents had not withdrawn from all positions of influence, if their leaders had been able to assess the situation more realistically. But the historian cannot help feeling that the story—as so often in the course of German history—is one of missed opportunities; the inexperienced leaders suffered from strong feelings of inferiority. They had been excluded from political power, and when it fell into their lap they did not know how to use it. They grievously underestimated their own strength, the strength of the movement they were leading, and overestimated that of their enemies. They also felt that in a situation of national emergency, faced by the consequences of total defeat, they must lead the nation, not divide it but unite it. In this they were doubtless right, but the methods they used to achieve unity split the nation and separated the Social Democratic leaders from their own followers. The national issue might have been used, as it was in France by the Jacobins, to promote a unity of resistance, but this opportunity was not grasped either. Perhaps Otto Bauer, well versed in the intricacies of the national question, was one of the very few to see its importance, but his policy too failed completely on account of opposition at home and abroad.

Thus the causes of the failure of the revolution of 1918 are manifold, and it would be a gross over-simplification to ascribe it merely to the split in the German working-class movement, or to the super-radicalism of the Communists, or—even more simply—to the 'treason' of Ebert and Noske, as has been done by the various sides then and later. In 1918 Germany—not Austria—was a highly advanced industrial country with a very antiquated political and social structure, a legacy of Bismarck and the period of unification. The task of the revolution was to overcome this discrepancy, to reform radically the political and social structure. This was done only in the political and constitutional sphere, and even there only partly. Even in an advanced industrial country the working class alone—and a badly disunited working class—was unable to carry out the reforms which were necessary. The Weimar Republic, which was the outcome of the compromises concluded in 1918–19, suffered from faults which fatally weakened it from the outset. The responsibility for these lay above all in the circuitous course of German history: the centuries of absolute government, the failure of the revolution of 1848, the late unification, the antiquated system that Bismarck imposed upon Germany, to name but a few of the obstacles which cast their shadow over the events of 1918. Austria was behind Germany in her general and political development so that to her the same factors applied even more strongly. The clash between the centre and the provinces, between towns and countryside, affected her much more decisively; her economic difficulties were even greater; she suffered much more important territorial losses than Germany. It is surprising, if one looks at the internal situation in 1919, that civil war did not break out much sooner than it did. The fatal weaknesses of the Austrian Republic stood out much more clearly than those of the Weimar Republic. Thus democracy did not find a secure home in central Europe, and was only established on firmer foundations after the upheavals and catastrophes of another world war, this time without a revolution.

Many may disagree with the thesis that the revolution of 1918–19 was defeated. It resulted, after all, in the disappearance of the dynasties and in the establishment of parliamentary democracy in Germany and in Austria. But this democracy was never secure; it was time and again shaken by severe crises, and it only lasted just over one decade. The 'democratization' of the political structure only partially succeeded and that of the social structure failed. The workers' and soldiers' councils which could have contributed much to this 'democratization' were dissolved or simply vanished from the scene. The old social ruling groups retained their positions; the bureaucracy continued to rule, rather than parliament. 'The Kaiser went, the generals remained.' There was not much reason to speak of a 'victory' of the revolution, and even the word 'revolution' was soon no longer mentioned. The storm had passed, and society settled down in its traditional grooves.

Bibliography

A UNPUBLISHED SOURCES

Bundesarchiv Koblenz
Reichskanzlei, Reichs- und Staatskommissare, vol. i: R 43 I/1844,
    Arbeiter- und Soldatenräte, vols. i–ii: R 43 I/1940–41,
    Streiks, vol. i: R 43 I/2118,
    Bayern, vol. i: R 43 I/2212,
    Aufstandsbewegungen und ihre Unterdrückung, vol. i: R 43 I/2706.
Hauptarchiv der NSDAP: NS 26, vorl. 68, 70, 71, 76, 78, 109, 528.
Nachlass Julius Streicher, AL 8 and 9.
Nachlass Wilhelm Solf, no. 59.

Bundesarchiv-Militärarchiv Freiburg
Nachlass Kurt von Schleicher, no. 9.
Nachlass Hans von Seeckt, box 17, no. 125.
Nachlass Wilhelm Groener, box 8, no. 37; box 5, no. 16; box 22,
    no. 241.
Friedrich-Ebert-Stiftung Bonn
Nachlass Emil Barth.
Nachlass Gustav Noske, no. 62.

Geheimes Staatsarchiv Berlin-Dahlem
Akten des Justizministeriums, Rep. 84a 22473.

International Institute of Social History Amsterdam
Zentralrat der deutschen sozialistischen Republik, B-3, vol. i; B-10,
    vol. i; B-12, vols. i–vi; B-19, vol. i; B-22, vols. iii–iv; B-23, vol. i;
    B-36, vol. i.
Nachlass Albert Grzesinski, nos. 399, 400, 403, 407, 408, 422, 424,
    452, 455, 474, 475, 504.
Erinnerungen Wilhelm Dittmann.
Nachlass Friedrich Adler, correspondence 1918–1919, i–ii.
Kleine Korrespondenz (from S.P.D. archives).
Nachlass Karl Kautsky, D II 463–534.

Bayerisches Hauptstaatsarchiv München
Arbeiter- und Soldatenrat, vols. 1–38.
Sammlung Rehse.
Staatsministerium des Innern, vols. 54190, 54194, 54197, 54199,
    54200, 54202, 54203, 54205, 54207, 54208, 66280.

Bayerisches Hauptstaatsarchiv, Abteilung II, Geheimes Staatsarchiv
MA. I. 983, 984, 985, 986.
MA. 99902, 99903, 100412.

Staatsarchiv für Oberbayern München
RA. Fasz. 3788, no. 57814.

Arbeiterkammer Wien
(Karl Heinz:) 'Die Geschichte der österreichischen Arbeiterräte',
    MS.
Stenographisches Protokoll der II. Reichskonferenz der Arbeiterräte
    Deutschösterreichs am 30. Juni 1919, MS.
Adlerarchiv, Briefe an Friedrich Adler, 1918–1919.

Haus-, Hof- und Staatsarchiv Wien
Präsidialakten 1919, Deutschland Anschlussfrage, Fasz. 5a.
Deutschösterreichs Anschlussverhandlungen mit Deutschland, Währ-
    ungs und Finanzverhandlungen 1919.
Nachlass Otto Bauer, Karton 261 and 262.

Kriegsarchiv Wien
Staatsamt für Heerwesen 1918, Fasz. 1–10.
Staatsamt für Heerwesen 1919, Fasz. 196–203 (Abteilung 5),
    Org-Gruppe 2/13, Fasz. 25.
Staatsamt für Heerwesen 1920, Fasz. 703, 706, 708, 710 (Abteilung
    5a).
Volkswehrkommando Provinz 1918, Fasz. 1–11.
Oberbefehlshaber der deutschösterreichischen Wehrmacht, 1919.
Landesbefehlshaber Wien 1919, Fasz. 20–26.
Landesbefehlshaber Innsbruck 1919, Fasz. 1–4.

Parteiarchiv der S.P.Ö. Wien
Sitzungsprotokolle des Parteivorstandes 1913–1925.
Stenographisches Protokoll des Parteitages der sozialdemokratischen
    Arbeiterpartei, 31.10.–1.11.1918.
Protokolle der Sitzungen des Reichsvollzugsausschusses der Arbeiter-
    räte.
Stenographisches Protokoll der Kreiskonferenz des Wiener Arbeiter-
    rates vom 17. June 1919.
Anträge an den Wiener Kreisarbeiterrat.
Korrespondenz des Reichsvollzugsausschusses der Arbeiterräte
    Deutschösterreichs.
Protokoll der Tagung des Reichsarbeiterrates, 31. Mai–2. Juni 1920.
Protokolle der Arbeiterräte Oberösterreichs, i–ii.

Polizeiarchiv Wien (Archiv der Bundes-Polizeidirektion)
Staats- und sicherheitspolizeiliche Agenden 1918.

Staats- und sicherheitspolizeiliche Agenden 1919.
Staats- und sicherheitspolizeiliche Agenden 1920.
Präsidial-Akte, Verwaltung 1919, box 10.
Präsidial-Akte, Verwaltung 1920, box 2.
Nachlass Johann Schober, Politische Informationen 1919;
    Polizeiberichte 1919–1921;
    Folder 'Volkswehr'.

Verwaltungsarchiv Wien
Beschlüsse des deutschösterreichischen Staatsrates.
Kabinettsratsprotokolle, ab 31.10.1918, boxes 3–17.
Ministerratsprotokolle, no. 4, 19 Nov. 1920.
Staatsamt des Innern, 22/gen., box 4860, box 4861; 22/NÖ, box
    5066, box 5067, box 5068.
Polizei-Direktion Wien, Berichte 1919;
    Berichte 1920.
Verhandlungsschriften der 'Grossdeutschen Vereinigung', 1919–
    1920.
Protokolle der Sitzungen des Vollzugsausschusses der Soldatenräte
    der Volkswehr Wiens vom 6. Dezember 1918. . . .
Protokolle von Sitzungen der Soldatenräte des Kreises D der Volks-
    wehr Wiens (ab 11. Dezember 1918).
Beschlüsse des Soldatenrates des XVI. Volkswehrbataillons Wien ab
    16. Dezember 1918.
Protokolle des Soldatenrates eines Volkswehrbataillons ab 30. Juni
    1919 [Bataillon XX].
Protokolle des Soldatenrates eines Volkswehrbataillons ab 23.
    Februar 1919 [Wiener Neustadt].

Kärntner Landesarchiv Klagenfurt
Umsturzzeit, Lt. I/3, Lt. III/5, Lt. III/7, Lt. IV/2, Lt. IV/4, Lt.
    IV/5, Lt. IV/11, Lt. V/12, Lt. V/14, Lt. V/15, Lt. V/17, Lt. X/61.
Landesausschuss, Fasz. II, no. 8; Fasz. III, no. 9.
Präsidialakten, Fasz. IV, Va, VI, VII/W.

Oberösterreichisches Landesarchiv Linz
Landtagsakten no. 28, no. 65, no. 66.
Archiv der k.k. Statthalterei—Präsidium, no. 114, no. 274, no. 398,
    no. 401.
Statthaltereiakten 1919, Fasz. 9.
Stadtarchiv Freistadt, XVII A/19.

Landesarchiv Salzburg
Präsidialakten 1918, 8m-20.
Präsidialakten 1919, 1–9, IX.

Steiermärkisches Landesarchiv Graz
Akten der k.k. steiermärkischen Statthalterei—Präsidium, E. 91, 1918 (i), (ii), (iv).
Akten der k.k. steiermärkischen Statthalterei—Präsidium, E. 91, 1919–1920.
Stenographische Berichte über die Sitzungen der steiermärkischen provisorischen Landesversammlung vom 6. November 1918 bis 30. April 1919.

Landesregierungsarchiv Tirol Innsbruck
Präsidialakten 1918, I.6.c.1; I.6.a.
Präsidialakten 1919, II.13; XII.76.c.1; XII.76.c.2; XII.76.c.3; XII.77.
Präsidialakten 1920, I.6.a; II.10.b; II.11.g; XII.76.c; XII.76.e.
Präsidialakten 1921, XII.76.e.
Präsidialakten 1922, II.11.g.
Präsidialakten 1923, XII.77.
Nachlass Professor Michael Mayr, V/6.

Public Record Office London
F.O. 371. Austria-Hungary, File 123, vols. 3507–3557.

B PUBLISHED SOURCES

Allgemeiner Kongress der Arbeiter- und Soldatenräte Deutschlands vom 16. bis 21. Dezember 1918 im Abgeordnetenhause zu Berlin—Stenographische Berichte, Berlin, 1919.
II. Kongress der Arbeiter-, Bauern- und Soldatenräte Deutschlands am 8. bis 14. April 1919 im Herrenhaus zu Berlin—Stenographisches Protokoll, Berlin, 1919.
Deuerlein, Ernst (ed.), 'Hitlers Eintritt in die Politik und die Reichswehr', Vierteljahrshefte für Zeitgeschichte, vii, 1959, pp. 177–227.
Dolchstoss-Prozess in München/Okt.–Nov. 1925—Eine Ehrenrettung des deutschen Volkes—Zeugen- und Sachverständigen-Aussagen—Eine Sammlung von Dokumenten, Munich, s.a. (1925).
Hofmiller, Josef, Revolutionstagebuch 1918/19—Aus den Tagen der Münchner Revolution, Leipzig, 1938.
Huber, Ernst Rudolf (ed.), Dokumente zur Deutschen Verfassungsgeschichte, iii, Stuttgart, 1966.
Kessler, Harry Graf, Tagebücher 1918–1937, Frankfurt, 1961.
Kolb, Eberhard (ed.), Der Zentralrat der Deutschen Sozialistischen Republik 19.12.1918–8.4.1919, Quellen zur Geschichte der Rätebewegung in Deutschland 1918/19, i. Leiden, 1968.
Kuckuk, Peter (ed.), Revolution und Räterepublik in Bremen, Frankfurt, 1969.

Ledebour-Prozess—Gesamtdarstellung des Prozesses gegen Ledebour wegen Aufruhr etc. vor dem Geschworenengericht in Berlin-Mitte vom 19. Mai bis 23. Juni 1919, auf Grund des amtlichen Stenogramms bearbeitet und mit einem Vorwort versehen von Georg Ledebour, Berlin, 1919.

Matthias, Erich (ed.), Die Regierung der Volksbeauftragten 1918/19, Quellen zur Geschichte des Parlamentarismus und der politischen Parteien, vol. vi, 2 vols., Düsseldorf, 1969.

Protokoll der Verhandlungen des Parteitages der sozialdemokratischen Arbeiterpartei Deutschösterreichs—Abgehalten in Wien vom 31. Oktober bis zum 3. November 1919, Vienna, 1920.

Protokoll der Verhandlungen des Parteitages der sozialdemokratischen Arbeiterpartei Deutschösterreichs—Abgehalten in Wien vom 5. bis zum 7. November 1920, Vienna, 1920.

Ritter, Gerhard A., and Miller, Susanne (eds.), Die deutsche Revolution 1918–1919—Dokumente, Frankfurt, 1968.

Schmolze, Gerhard (ed.), Revolution und Räterepublik in München 1918/19 in Augenzeugenberichten, Düsseldorf, 1969.

Schüddekopf, Otto Ernst (ed.) Das Heer und die Republik—Quellen zur Politik der Reichswehrführung, Hanover and Frankfurt, 1955.

Schulte, Eduard (ed.), Münstersche Chronik zu Novemberrevolte und Separatismus 1918, Veröffentlichungen der Historischen Kommission des Provinzialinstituts für Westfälische Landes- und Volkskunde, vii, Münster, 1936.

Schulte, Eduard (ed.), Münstersche Chronik zu Spartakismus und Separatismus Anfang 1919, Veröffentlichungen der Historischen Kommission für Westfälische Landes- und Volkskunde, x, Münster, 1939.

Stadtarchiv München, Collection of leaflets and press cuttings of 1918–1919.

Stenographische Berichte über die Verhandlungen des steiermärkischen Landtages 1919/1920, Graz, s.a.

Stenographischer Bericht über die Verhandlungen der bayerischen Arbeiterräte am 9. und 10. Dezember 1918, Munich, s.a. (1918).

Stenographischer Bericht über die Verhandlungen des Kongresses der Arbeiter-, Bauern- und Soldatenräte vom 25. Februar bis 8. März 1919 in München, Munich, s.a. (1919).

Unabhängige Sozialdemokratische Partei Deutschlands, Protokoll über die Verhandlungen des ausserordentlichen Parteitages vom 2. bis 6. März 1919 in Berlin, Berlin, s.a. (1919).

Unabhängige Sozialdemokratische Partei Deutschlands, Protokoll über die Verhandlungen des ausserordentlichen Parteitages vom 30. November bis 6. Dezember 1919 in Leipzig, Berlin, s.a. (1920).

Weber, Hermann (ed.), Der Gründungsparteitag der KPD—Protokoll und Materialien, Frankfurt, 1969.

C MEMOIRS AND CONTEMPORARY PAMPHLETS

Anlauf, Karl, Die Revolution in Niedersachsen—Geschichtliche Darstellungen und Erlebnisse, Hanover, 1919.

Barth, Emil, Aus der Werkstatt der deutschen Revolution, Berlin, s.a. (1919).

Bauer, Otto, Der Weg zum Sozialismus, 2nd ed., Vienna, 1919.

Beneš, Eduard, My War Memoirs, London, 1928.

Blos, Wilhelm, Von der Monarchie zum Volksstaat, zur Geschichte der Revolution in Deutschland, insbesondere in Württemberg, Stuttgart, 1923.

Böhm, Wilhelm, Im Kreuzfeuer zweier Revolutionen, Munich, 1924.

Braun, Otto, Von Weimar zu Hitler, Hamburg, 1949.

Braunthal, Julius, Die Arbeiterräte in Deutschösterreich—Ihre Geschichte und ihre Politik, Vienna, 1919.

— Auf der Suche nach dem Millennium, Vienna, 1964.

— The Tragedy of Austria, London, 1948.

Breves, Wilhelm, (ed.), Bremen in der deutschen Revolution vom November 1918 bis zum März 1919, Bremen, 1919.

Deutsch, Julius, Aus Österreichs Revolution—Militärpolitische Erinnerungen, Vienna, 1921.

— Ein weiter Weg—Lebenserinnerungen, Zürich-Leipzig-Vienna, 1960.

Eichhorn, Emil, Über die Januar-Ereignisse—Meine Tätigkeit im Berliner Polizeipräsidium und mein Anteil an den Januar-Ereignissen, Berlin, 1919.

Fischer, Anton, Die Revolutions-Kommandanturin Berlin, Berlin, s.a.

Groener, Wilhelm, Lebenserinnerungen, ed. by Friedrich Frhr. Hiller von Gaertringen, Göttingen, 1957.

Hahn, Paul, Erinnerungen aus der Revolution in Württemberg—'Der Rote Hahn, eine Revolutionserscheinung', Stuttgart, 1923.

Helmer, Oskar, 50 Jahre erlebte Geschichte, Vienna, 1957.

Károlyi, Graf Michael, Gegen eine ganze Welt—Mein Kampf um den Frieden, Munich, 1924.

Károlyi, Catherine, A Life Together, London, 1966.

Keil, Wilhelm, Erlebnisse eines Sozialdemokraten, ii, Stuttgart, 1948.

Lamp'l, Walther, Die Revolution in Gross-Hamburg, Hamburg, 1921.

Lemmer, Ernst, Manches war doch anders—Erinnerungen eines deutschen Demokraten, Frankfurt, 1968.

Levi, Paul, Unser Weg wider den Putschismus, 2nd ed., Berlin, 1921.

Lewinsohn, Ludwig, Die Revolution an der Westfront, Charlottenburg, s.a. (1919).

Müller, Richard, Was die Arbeiterräte wollen und sollen! Berlin, s.a.

Münchener Tragödie—Entstehung, Verlauf und Zusammenbruch der Räte-Republik München, Berlin, 1919.

Neumann, Paul, Hamburg unter der Regierung des Arbeiter- und Soldatenrates—Tätigkeitsbericht erstattet im Auftrage der Exekutive des Arbeiterrats Gross-Hamburg, Hamburg, 1919.

Niekisch, Ernst, Gewagtes Leben—Begegnungen und Erlebnisse, Cologne and Berlin, 1958.

Noske, Gustav, Von Kiel bis Kapp—Zur Geschichte der deutschen Revolution, Berlin, 1920.

Oehme, Walter, Damals in der Reichskanzlei—Erinnerungen aus den Jahren 1918/1919, Berlin, 1958.

Revolution in Brüssel—Bericht des Vollzugsausschusses des Zentral-Soldaten-Rates in Brüssel, Neukölln, s.a.

Rintelen, Anton, Erinnerungen an Österreichs Weg, 2nd ed., Munich, 1941.

Scheidemann, Philipp, Der Zusammenbruch, Berlin, 1921.

Severing, Carl, 1919/1920 im Wetter- und Watterwinkel, Bielefeld, 1927.

Sollmann, Wilhelm, Die Revolution in Köln, Cologne, 1918.

Stampfer, Friedrich, Der 9. November—Gedenkblätter zu seiner Wiederkehr, Berlin, 1919.

Unser Friede! Die Kundgebung der deutschösterreichischen Nationalversammlung in der Sitzung vom 7. Juni 1919—Flugblätter für Deutschösterreichs Recht, Nr. 33, Vienna, 1919.

D SECONDARY AUTHORITIES

Abel, Theodore, Why Hitler came into Power—An Answer based on the Original Life Stories of Six Hundred of his Followers, New York, 1938.

Albrecht, Willy, Landtag und Regierung in Bayern am Vorabend der Revolution von 1918, Berlin, 1968.

Ay, Karl Ludwig, Die Entstehung einer Revolution—Die Volksstimmung in Bayern während des Ersten Weltkrieges, Berlin, 1968.

Bauer, Otto, Die österreichische Revolution, Vienna, 1923.

Bernstein, Eduard, Die deutsche Revolution—Geschichte der Entstehung und ersten Arbeitsperiode der deutschen Republik, Berlin, 1921.

Botz, Gerhard, Beiträge zur Geschichte der politischen Gewalttaten in Österreich von 1918 bis 1933, Vienna Ph.D. thesis, 1966, 3 vols., MS.

— 'Die kommunistischen Putschversuche in Wien 1918/19', Österreich in Geschichte und Literatur, xiv 1, 1970, pp. 13–23.

Carsten, F. L., Reichswehr und Politik 1918–1933, Cologne, 1964.

Comfort, Richard A., Revolutionary Hamburg—Labor Politics in the early Weimar Republic, Stanford, 1966.

Deak, Istvan, 'Budapest and the Hungarian Revolutions of 1918–1919', Slavonic and East European Review, xlvi, no. 106, 1968, pp. 129–40.

Drüner, Hans, Im Schatten des Weltkrieges—Zehn Jahre Frankfurter Geschichte, Frankfurt, 1934.

Freise, Ursula, Die Tätigkeit der alliierten Kommissionen in Wien nach dem Ersten Weltkrieg, Vienna Ph.D. thesis, 1963, MS.

Freksa, Friedrich, Kapitän Ehrhardt—Abenteuer und Schicksale, Berlin, 1924.

Frölich, Paul, 10 Jahre Krieg und Bürgerkrieg, Berlin, 1924.

(Frölich, Paul), Illustrierte Geschichte der Deutschen Revolution, Berlin, 1929.

Gulick, Charles A., Austria from Habsburg to Hitler, i, Berkeley and Los Angeles, 1948.

Haas, Hanns, Österreich-Ungarn als Friedensproblem—Aspekte der Friedensregelung auf dem Gebiete der Habsburgermonarchie in den Jahren 1918–1919, Salzburg Ph.D. thesis, 1968, MS.

Haas, Karl, Studien zur Wehrpolitik der österreichischen Sozialdemokratie 1918–1926, Vienna Ph.D. thesis, 1967, MS.

Hannak, Jacques, Karl Renner und seine Zeit, Vienna, 1965.

Hertzman, Lewis, DNVP—Right-wing Opposition in the Weimar Republic 1918–1924, Lincoln, Nebraska, 1963.

Hesterberg, Ernst, Alle Macht den A.- und S.-Räten—Kampf um Schlesien, Breslau, 1932.

Jedlicka, Ludwig, Ein Heer im Schatten der Parteien—Die militärpolitische Lage Österreichs 1918–1938, Graz and Cologne, 1955.

Kolb, Eberhard, Die Arbeiterräte in der deutschen Innenpolitik 1918–1919, Düsseldorf, 1962.

Lindau, Rudolf, Revolutionäre Kämpfe 1918–1919, Berlin, 1960.

Lohalm, Uwe, Völkischer Radikalismus—Die Geschichte des Deutschvölkischen Schutz- und Trutzbundes 1919–1923, Hamburg, 1970.

Mattes, Wilhelm, Die bayerischen Bauernräte, Stuttgart and Berlin, 1921.

Mitchell, Allan, Revolution in Bavaria 1918–1919—The Eisner Regime and the Soviet Republic, Princeton, N.J., 1965.

Mühlberger, D. M., Political Developments in Iserlohn during the Weimar Republic, draft of London M.Phil. thesis.

Müller, Hermann, Die November-Revolution—Erinnerungen, 2nd ed., Berlin, 1931.

Müller, Richard, Vom Kaiserreich zur Republik, 2 vols., Vienna, 1924–25.

Müller, Richard, Der Bürgerkrieg in Deutschland—Geburtswehen der Republik, Berlin, 1925./

Oeftering, W. E., Der Umsturz 1918 in Baden, Constance, 1920.

Oertzen, Peter von, Betriebsträte in der Novemberrevolution, Düsseldorf, 1963.

Plaschka, Richard G., Cattaro-Prag—Revolte und Revolution, Graz and Cologne, 1963.

Plewnia, Margarete, Auf dem Weg zu Hitler—Der 'völkische' Publizist Dietrich Eckart, Bremen, 1970.

Prager, Eugen, Geschichte der USPD—Entstehung und Entwicklung der Unabhängigen Sozialdemokratischen Partei Deutschlands, Berlin, 1921.

Reimann, Viktor, Zu Gross für Österreich—Seipel und Bauer im Kampf um die Erste Republik, Vienna, 1968.

Remmele, Adam, Staatsumwälzung und Neuaufbau in Baden—Ein Beitrag zur politischen Geschichte Badens 1914/24, Karlsruhe, 1925.

Reventlow, Rolf, Zwischen Alliierten und Bolschewiken—Arbeiterräte in Österreich 1918–1923, Vienna, 1969.

Rosenberg, Arthur, Geschichte der Deutschen Republik, Karlsbad, 1935.

Rürup, Reinhard, Probleme der Revolution in Deutschland 1918/19, Institut für Europäische Geschichte Mainz, Vorträge No. 50, Wiesbaden, 1968.

Schade, Franz, Kurt Eisner und die bayerische Sozialdemokratie, Hanover, 1961.

Sender, Toni, The Autobiography of a German Rebel, London, 1940.

Stadler, Karl R., The Birth of the Austrian Republic 1918–1921, Leyden, 1966.

Staudinger, Anton, 'Die Ereignisse in den Ländern Deutschösterreichs im Herbst 1918', in: Ludwig Jedlicka, Ende und Anfang Österreich 1918/19, Salzburg, 1969, pp. 62–88.

Steinböck, Erwin, Die Volkswehr in Kärnten unter Berücksichtigung des Einsatzes der Freiwilligenverbände, Vienna and Graz, 1963.

Tökés, Rudolf L., Béla Kun and the Hungarian Soviet Republic, New York and London, 1967.

Tormin, Walter, Zwischen Rätediktatur und sozialer Demokratie—Die Geschichte der Rätebewegung in der deutschen Revolution 1918/19, Düsseldorf, 1954.

Weller, Karl, Die Staatsumwälzung in Württemberg 1918–1920, Stuttgart, 1930.

Winkler, Ernst, Der grosse Jänner-Streik 1918, Vienna, 1968.

Wutte, Martin, Kärntens Freiheitskampf, 2nd ed., Weimar, 1943.

Zöllner, Erich, Geschichte Österreichs, Vienna, 1961.

Zsuppán, Ferenc Tibor, 'The Early Activities of the Hungarian Communist Party, 1918–19', Slavonic and East European Review, xliii, no. 101, 1965, pp. 314–34.
— 'The Hungarian Soviet Republic and the British Military Representatives, April-June 1919', Slavonic and East European Review, xlvii, no. 108, 1969, pp. 198–218.

Index

Abfalter, Dr Melchior, 278
Adelsdorf, workers' council at, 194
Adenauer, Konrad, 35
Adler, Dr Friedrich, 22, 30, 109–10, 122, 224; murder of Count Stürgkh, 13; and workers' councils, 109–14, 116–17; and Communists, 224, 228, 235
Adler, Dr Max, 109
Adler, Dr Victor, 21, 22, 294, 298
Aibling, removal of *Bezirksamtsmann* at, 198
Allies, *see* Entente
Alsace-Lorraine, 271
Altötting, 192; peasant council at, 182; workers' council at, 192
Anarchists, 85, 211, 219
Anarchy, 325
Andrássy, Count Gyula, 49
Anklam, strikes at, 67
Ansbach, workers' and soldiers' council at, 195–6
Anschluss, 30, 187, 277–8, 287, 289–90, 294–8, 331; Christian Socials and, 295; German government and, 295–7; Social Democrats and, 294, 297–8, 331
Anti-Bolshevism, in Austria, 87, 118, 319, 321; in Germany, 17, 45, 55, 71–72, 148, 250, 254
Anti-religious measures, in Hungary, 242
Anti-semitism, 18; in army, 61; in Austria, 115, 125, 229, 231, 258–67, 301, 310, 312–13, 319; in Bavaria, 179, 252–7; in Germany, 247–57; in Hungary, 243; in Russia, 254, 264; in Tyrol, 260–2
Arco-Valley, Count Anton, 188
Arnelt, engineer, 267
Arnim, Sixt von, general, 56
Aschaffenburg, 201; workers' council at, 197–8; workers' and soldiers' council at, 201

Aschendorf, *Landrat* of, 171; workers' council at, 171
Auer, Erhard, 37, 47, 185, 188–9, 202; as Minister of Interior, 37, 47, 188, 253
Augsburg, anti-semitism in, 256; revolution in, 48; soldiers' council in, 48, 189; workers' and soldiers' council in, 196
Austrian army (*Bundesheer*), 311; Army Law (March 1920), 305–7; Christian Socials and, 304–5, 307, 309, 311; Pan-Germans and, 305–6, 309; soldiers' councils in, 306–11; Tyrolese plans for, 304–5
Austrian Empire *see* Habsburg Monarchy

Baden, nr. Vienna, *Volkswehr* at, 80, 90
Baden, state of, 41, 155; Diet of, 156–7; government of, 42, 156, 158; grand duke of, 42; peasant councils in, 208; revolution in, 41–2; *Volkswehr* in, 65, 157–8; soldiers' councils in, 42–3, 69–70; workers' councils in, 156–8; workers', peasants', people's and soldiers' councils in, 157
Bad Tölz, *Bezirksamt* of, 196; workers' council of, 196
Balfour, Arthur, Earl, 277
Ballin, Albert, 260
Baltic lands, 11, 18, 26, 77
Bamberg, 222, 249; plan of Bavarian government moving to, 203; Bavarian government at, 219–22
Barth, Emil, as a minister, 39, 59 and n. 15
Bauer, Dr Otto, 123–4, 235, 253, 268, 298, 334; and Russian revolution, 31–32, 332; as a minister, 225, 230–1, 279–80, 288–9, 297; on Soviet dictatorship, 237–8; resignation of, 280, 297; and Bohemian Germans, 289,